Internetworking With TCP/IP

Vol III:

Client-Server Programming
And Applications

BSD Socket Version

Internetworking With TCP/IP

Vol III:

Client-Server Programming And Applications

BSD Socket Version

DOUGLAS E. COMER

and

DAVID L. STEVENS

Department of Computer Sciences
Purdue University
West Lafayette, IN 47907

Prentice-Hall of India Private Limited
New Delhi - 110 001
1997

This Third Indian Reprint—Rs. 195.00
(Original U.S. Edition—Rs. 2088.00)

INTERNETWORKING WITH TCP/IP, Vol. III: Client-Server Programming and Applications (BSD Socket Version)
by Douglas E. Comer and David L. Stevens

ISBN-81-203-0928-6

The export rights of this book are vested solely with the publisher.

This Eastern Economy Edition is the authorized, complete and unabridged photo-offset reproduction of the latest American edition specially published and priced for sale only in Bangladesh, Burma, Cambodia, China, Fiji, Hong Kong, India, Indonesia, Laos, Malaysia, Nepal, Pakistan, Philippines, Singapore, South Korea, Sri Lanka, Taiwan, Thailand, and Vietnam.

Reprinted in India by special arrangement with Prentice-Hall, Inc., Englewood Cliffs, N.J., U.S.A.

Third Printing   . . .   . . .   **September, 1997**

Published by Asoke K. Ghosh, Prentice-Hall of India Private Limited, M-97, Connaught Circus, New Delhi-110001 and Printed by Tarun Offset Printers, New Delhi-110064.

To riding the wave

Contents

Foreword   xxi

Preface   xxiii

Chapter 1   Introduction And Overview   1

1.1   Use Of TCP/IP   1
1.2   Designing Applications For A Distributed Environment   2
1.3   Standard And Nonstandard Application Protocols   2
1.4   An Example Of Standard Application Protocol Use   2
1.5   An Example Connection   3
1.6   Using TELNET To Access An Alternative Service   4
1.7   Application Protocols And Software Flexibility   5
1.8   Viewing Services From The Provider's Perspective   6
1.9   The Remainder Of This Text   7
1.10   Summary   7

Chapter 2   The Client Server Model And Software Design   9

2.1   Introduction   9
2.2   Motivation   10
2.3   Terminology And Concepts   10
2.4   Summary   18

Chapter 3   Concurrent Processing In Client-Server Software   21

3.1   Introduction   21
3.2   Concurrency In Networks   21

3.3   Concurrency In Servers   23
3.4   Terminology And Concepts   24
3.5   An Example Of Concurrent Process Creation   26
3.6   Executing New Code   31
3.7   Context Switching And Protocol Software Design   31
3.8   Concurrency And Asynchronous I/O   32
3.9   Summary   32

Chapter 4   Program Interface To Protocols

35

4.1   Introduction   35
4.2   Loosely Specified Protocol Software Interface   35
4.3   Interface Functionality   36
4.4   Conceptual Interface Specification   37
4.5   System Calls   37
4.6   Two Basic Approaches To Network Communication   38
4.7   The Basic I/O Functions Available In UNIX   39
4.8   Using UNIX I/O With TCP/IP   40
4.9   Summary   40

Chapter 5   The Socket Interface

43

5.1   Introduction   43
5.2   Berkeley Sockets   43
5.3   Specifying A Protocol Interface   44
5.4   The Socket Abstraction   45
5.5   Specifying An Endpoint Address   47
5.6   A Generic Address Structure   48
5.7   Major System Calls Used With Sockets   49
5.8   Utility Routines For Integer Conversion   52
5.9   Using Socket Calls In A Program   53
5.10   Symbolic Constants For Socket Call Parameters   54
5.11   Summary   54

Chapter 6   Algorithms And Issues In Client Software Design

57

6.1   Introduction   57
6.2   Learning Algorithms Instead Of Details   57
6.3   Client Architecture   58
6.4   Identifying The Location Of A Server   58
6.5   Parsing An Address Argument   60

6.6   Looking Up A Domain Name   61
6.7   Looking Up A Well-Known Port By Name   62
6.8   Port Numbers And Network Byte Order   62
6.9   Looking Up A Protocol By Name   63
6.10   The TCP Client Algorithm   63
6.11   Allocating A Socket   64
6.12   Choosing A Local Protocol Port Number   65
6.13   A Fundamental Problem In Choosing A Local IP Address   65
6.14   Connecting A TCP Socket To A Server   66
6.15   Communicating With The Server Using TCP   66
6.16   Reading A Response From A TCP Connection   67
6.17   Closing A TCP Connection   68
6.18   Programming A UDP Client   69
6.19   Connected And Unconnected UDP Sockets   69
6.20   Using Connect With UDP   70
6.21   Communicating With A Server Using UDP   70
6.22   Closing A Socket That Uses UDP   70
6.23   Partial Close For UDP   71
6.24   A Warning About UDP Unreliability   71
6.25   Summary   71

Chapter 7   Example Client Software   75

7.1   Introduction   75
7.2   The Importance Of Small Examples   75
7.3   Hiding Details   76
7.4   An Example Procedure Library For Client Programs   76
7.5   Implementation Of ConnectTCP   77
7.6   Implementation Of ConnectUDP   78
7.7   A Procedure That Forms Connections   78
7.8   Using The Example Library   81
7.9   The DAYTIME Service   81
7.10   Implementation Of A TCP Client For DAYTIME   82
7.11   Reading From A TCP Connection   83
7.12   The TIME Service   84
7.13   Accessing The TIME Service   84
7.14   Accurate Times And Network Delays   85
7.15   A UDP Client For The TIME Service   85
7.16   The ECHO Service   87
7.17   A TCP Client For The ECHO Service   88
7.18   A UDP Client For The ECHO Service   89
7.19   Summary   91

Chapter 8   Algorithms And Issues In Server Software Design

95

8.1   *Introduction   95*
8.2   *The Conceptual Server Algorithm   95*
8.3   *Concurrent Vs. Iterative Servers   96*
8.4   *Connection-Oriented Vs. Connectionless Access   96*
8.5   *Connection-Oriented Servers   97*
8.6   *Connectionless Servers   97*
8.7   *Failure, Reliability, And Statelessness   98*
8.8   *Optimizing Stateless Servers   99*
8.9   *Four Basic Types Of Servers   101*
8.10   *Request Processing Time   102*
8.11   *Iterative Server Algorithms   102*
8.12   *An Iterative, Connection-Oriented Server Algorithm   103*
8.13   *Binding To A Well-Known Address Using INADDR_ANY   103*
8.14   *Placing The Socket In Passive Mode   104*
8.15   *Accepting Connections And Using Them   104*
8.16   *An Iterative, Connectionless Server Algorithm   104*
8.17   *Forming A Reply Address In A Connectionless Server   105*
8.18   *Concurrent Server Algorithms   106*
8.19   *Master And Slave Processes   106*
8.20   *A Concurrent, Connectionless Server Algorithm   107*
8.21   *A Concurrent, Connection-Oriented Server Algorithm   107*
8.22   *Using Separate Programs As Slaves   108*
8.23   *Apparent Concurrency Using A Single Process   109*
8.24   *When To Use Each Server Type   110*
8.25   *A Summary of Server Types   111*
8.26   *The Important Problem Of Server Deadlock   112*
8.27   *Alternative Implementations   112*
8.28   *Summary   113*

Chapter 9   Iterative, Connectionless Servers (UDP)

115

9.1   *Introduction   115*
9.2   *Creating A Passive Socket   115*
9.3   *Process Structure   118*
9.4   *An Example TIME Server   119*
9.5   *Summary   121*

Chapter 10   Iterative, Connection-Oriented Servers (TCP)   123

10.1   *Introduction*   123
10.2   *Allocating A Passive TCP Socket*   123
10.3   *A Server For The DAYTIME Service*   124
10.4   *Process Structure*   124
10.5   *An Example DAYTIME Server*   125
10.6   *Closing Connections*   128
10.7   *Connection Termination And Server Vulnerability*   128
10.8   *Summary*   129

Chapter 11   Concurrent, Connection-Oriented Servers (TCP)   131

11.1   *Introduction*   131
11.2   *Concurrent ECHO*   131
11.3   *Iterative Vs. Concurrent Implementations*   132
11.4   *Process Structure*   132
11.5   *An Example Concurrent ECHO Server*   133
11.6   *Cleaning Up Errant Processes*   137
11.7   *Summary*   138

Chapter 12   Single-Process, Concurrent Servers (TCP)   139

12.1   *Introduction*   139
12.2   *Data-driven Processing In A Server*   139
12.3   *Data-Driven Processing With A Single Process*   140
12.4   *Process Structure Of A Single-Process Server*   141
12.5   *An Example Single-Process ECHO Server*   142
12.6   *Summary*   144

Chapter 13   Multiprotocol Servers (TCP, UDP)   147

13.1   *Introduction*   147
13.2   *The Motivation For Reducing The Number Of Servers*   147
13.3   *Multiprotocol Server Design*   148
13.4   *Process Structure*   148
13.5   *An Example Multiprotocol DAYTIME Server*   149
13.6   *The Concept Of Shared Code*   153
13.7   *Concurrent Multiprotocol Servers*   153
13.8   *Summary*   153

Chapter 14   Multiservice Servers (TCP, UDP)   **155**

14.1   *Introduction   155*
14.2   *Consolidating Servers   155*
14.3   *A Connectionless, Multiservice Server Design   156*
14.4   *A Connection-Oriented, Multiservice Server Design   157*
14.5   *A Concurrent, Connection-Oriented, Multiservice Server   158*
14.6   *A Single-Process, Multiservice Server Implementation   158*
14.7   *Invoking Separate Programs From A Multiservice Server   159*
14.8   *Multiservice, Multiprotocol Designs   160*
14.9   *An Example Multiservice Server   161*
14.10   *The BSD UNIX Super Server, Inetd   168*
14.11   *Summary   168*

Chapter 15   Uniform, Efficient Management Of Server Concurrency   **171**

15.1   *Introduction   171*
15.2   *Choosing Between An Iterative And A Concurrent Design   171*
15.3   *Level Of Concurrency   172*
15.4   *Demand-Driven Concurrency   173*
15.5   *The Cost Of Concurrency   173*
15.6   *Overhead And Delay   173*
15.7   *Small Delays Can Matter   174*
15.8   *Process Preallocation   175*
15.9   *Delayed Process Allocation   179*
15.10   *The Uniform Basis For Both Techniques   180*
15.11   *Combining Techniques   181*
15.12   *Summary   181*

Chapter 16   Concurrency In Clients   **183**

16.1   *Introduction   183*
16.2   *The Advantages Of Concurrency   183*
16.3   *The Motivation For Exercising Control   184*
16.4   *Concurrent Contact With Multiple Servers   185*
16.5   *Implementing Concurrent Clients   185*
16.6   *Single-Process Implementations   187*
16.7   *An Example Concurrent Client That Uses ECHO   188*
16.8   *Execution Of The Concurrent Client   192*
16.9   *Concurrency In The Example Code   193*
16.10   *Summary   194*

Chapter 17   Tunneling At The Transport And Application Levels   195

17.1   Introduction   195
17.2   Multiprotocol Environments   195
17.3   Mixing Network Technologies   197
17.4   Dynamic Circuit Allocation   198
17.5   Encapsulation And Tunneling   199
17.6   Tunneling Through An IP Internet   199
17.7   Application-Level Tunneling Between Clients And Servers   200
17.8   Summary   201

Chapter 18   Application Level Gateways   203

18.1   Introduction   203
18.2   Clients And Servers In Constrained Environments   203
18.3   Using Application Gateways   205
18.4   Interoperability Through A Mail Gateway   206
18.5   Implementation Of A Mail Gateway   207
18.6   A Comparison Of Application Gateways And Tunneling   207
18.7   Application Gateways And Limited Functionality Systems   209
18.8   Application Gateways Used For Security   210
18.9   Application Gateways And The Extra Hop Problem   211
18.10 An Example Application Gateway   213
18.11 Implementation Of An Application Gateway   214
18.12 Code For The Application Gateway   216
18.13 An Example Gateway Exchange   217
18.14 Using Rfcd With UNIX's .forward   218
18.15 Summary   218

Chapter 19   External Data Representation (XDR)   221

19.1   Introduction   221
19.2   Representations For Data In Computers   221
19.3   The N-Squared Conversion Problem   222
19.4   Network Standard Byte Order   223
19.5   A De Facto Standard External Data Representation   224
19.6   XDR Data Types   225
19.7   Implicit Types   226
19.8   Software Support For Using XDR   226
19.9   XDR Library Routines   226
19.10 Building A Message One Piece At A Time   226

19.11   Conversion Routines In The XDR Library   228
19.12   XDR Streams, I/O, and TCP   230
19.13   Records, Record Boundaries, And Datagram I/O   231
19.14   Summary   231

Chapter 20   Remote Procedure Call Concept (RPC)   233

20.1   Introduction   233
20.2   Remote Procedure Call Model   233
20.3   Two Paradigms For Building Distributed Programs   234
20.4   A Conceptual Model For Conventional Procedure Calls   235
20.5   An Extension Of the Procedural Model   235
20.6   Execution Of Conventional Procedure Call And Return   236
20.7   The Procedural Model In Distributed Systems   237
20.8   Analogy Between Client-Server And RPC   238
20.9   Distributed Computation As A Program   239
20.10 Sun Microsystems' Remote Procedure Call Definition   240
20.11 Remote Programs And Procedures   240
20.12 Reducing The Number Of Arguments   241
20.13 Identifying Remote Programs And Procedures   241
20.14 Accommodating Multiple Versions Of A Remote Program   242
20.15 Mutual Exclusion For Procedures In A Remote Program   243
20.16 Communication Semantics   244
20.17 At Least Once Semantics   244
20.18 RPC Retransmission   245
20.19 Mapping A Remote Program To A Protocol Port   245
20.20 Dynamic Port Mapping   246
20.21 RPC Port Mapper Algorithm   247
20.22 Sun RPC Message Format   249
20.23 Marshaling Arguments For A Remote Procedure   250
20.24 Authentication   250
20.25 An Example Of RPC Message Representation   251
20.26 An Example Of The UNIX Authentication Field   252
20.27 Summary   253

Chapter 21   Distributed Program Generation (Rpcgen Concept)   255

21.1   Introduction   255
21.2   Using Remote Procedure Calls   256
21.3   Programming Mechanisms To Support RPC.   257
21.4   Dividing A Program Into Local And Remote Procedures   258
21.5   Adding Code For RPC   259

21.6   Stub Procedures   259
21.7   Multiple Remote Procedures And Dispatching   260
21.8   Name Of The Client-Side Stub Procedure   261
21.9   Using Rpcgen To Generate Distributed Programs   262
21.10   Rpcgen Output And Interface Procedures   262
21.11   Rpcgen Input And Output   263
21.12   Using Rpcgen To Build A Client And Server   264
21.13   Summary   264

Chapter 22   Distributed Program Generation (Rpcgen Example)   267

22.1   Introduction   267
22.2   An Example To Illustrate Rpcgen   268
22.3   Dictionary Lookup   268
22.4   Eight Steps To A Distributed Application   269
22.5   Step 1: Build A Conventional Application Program   270
22.6   Step 2: Divide The Program Into Two Parts   274
22.7   Step 3: Create An Rpcgen Specification   280
22.8   Step 4: Run Rpcgen   282
22.9   The .h File Produced By Rpcgen   282
22.10   The XDR Conversion File Produced By Rpcgen   283
22.11   The Client Code Produced By Rpcgen   284
22.12   The Server Code Produced By Rpcgen   286
22.13   Step 5: Write Stub Interface Procedures   289
22.14   Step 6: Compile And Link The Client Program   293
22.15   Step 7: Compile And Link The Server Program   297
22.16   Step 8: Start The Server And Execute The Client   299
22.17   Using The UNIX Make Utility   299
22.18   Summary   302

Chapter 23   Network File System Concepts (NFS)   305

23.1   Introduction   305
23.2   Remote File Access Vs. Transfer   305
23.3   Operations On Remote Files   306
23.4   File Access Among Heterogeneous Computers   306
23.5   Stateless Servers   307
23.6   NFS And UNIX File Semantics   307
23.7   Review Of The UNIX File System   307
23.8   Files Under NFS   321
23.9   NFS File Types   322
23.10   NFS File Modes   322

23.11   NFS File Attributes   323
23.12   NFS Client And Server   324
23.13   NFS Client Operation   325
23.14   NFS Client And UNIX   326
23.15   NFS Mounts   327
23.16   File Handle   328
23.17   Handles Replace Path Names   328
23.18   An NFS Client In UNIX   330
23.19   File Positioning With A Stateless Server   330
23.20   Operations On Directories   331
23.21   Reading A Directory Statelessly   331
23.22   Multiple Hierarchies In An NFS Server   332
23.23   The Mount Protocol   332
23.24   Summary   333

Chapter 24   Network File System Protocol (NFS, Mount)   335

24.1   Introduction   335
24.2   Using RPC To Define A Protocol   335
24.3   Defining A Protocol With Data Structures And Procedures   336
24.4   NFS Constant, Type, And Data Declarations   337
24.5   NFS Procedures   340
24.6   Semantics Of NFS Operations   341
24.7   The Mount Protocol   345
24.8   Procedures In The Mount Protocol   347
24.9   Semantics of Mount Operations   347
24.10   NFS And Mount Authentication   348
24.11   Summary   350

Chapter 25   A TELNET Client (Program Structure)   353

25.1   Introduction   353
25.2   Overview   354
25.3   A TELNET Client Algorithm   356
25.4   Terminal I/O In UNIX   357
25.5   Establishing Terminal Modes   361
25.6   Global Variable Used For Stored State   362
25.7   Restoring Terminal Modes Before Exit   363
25.8   Client Suspension And Resumption   364
25.9   Finite State Machine Specification   365
25.10   Embedding Commands In A TELNET Data Stream   366
25.11   Option Negotiation   367

25.12   Request/Offer Symmetry   367
25.13   TELNET Character Definitions   367
25.14   A Finite State Machine For Data From The Server   369
25.15   Transitions Among States   370
25.16   A Finite State Machine Implementation   372
25.17   A Compact FSM Representation   372
25.18   Keeping The Compact Representation At Run-Time   374
25.19   Implementation Of A Compact Representation   374
25.20   Building An FSM Transition Matrix   376
25.21   The Socket Output Finite State Machine   378
25.22   Definitions For The Socket Output FSM   380
25.23   The Option Subnegotiation Finite State Machine   381
25.24   Definitions For The Option Subnegotiation FSM   382
25.25   FSM Initialization   383
25.26   Arguments For The TELNET Client   383
25.27   The Heart Of The TELNET Client   385
25.28   Implementation Of The Main FSM   388
25.29   Summary   390

Chapter 26   A TELNET Client (Implementation Details)   393

26.1   Introduction   393
26.2   The FSM Action Procedures   393
26.3   Recording The Type Of An Option Request   394
26.4   Performing No Operation   395
26.5   Responding To WILL/WONT For The Echo Option   395
26.6   Responding To WILL/WONT For Unsupported Options   397
26.7   Responding To WILL/WONT For The No Go-Ahead Option   397
26.8   Generating DO/DONT For Binary Transmission   399
26.9   Responding To DO/DONT For Unsupported Options   400
26.10   Responding To DO/DONT For The Transmit Binary Option   401
26.11   Responding To DO/DONT For The Terminal Type Option   402
26.12   Option Subnegotiation   404
26.13   Sending Terminal Type Information   405
26.14   Terminating Subnegotiation   406
26.15   Sending A Character To The Server   407
26.16   Displaying Incoming Data On The User's Terminal   408
26.17   Using Curses To Control The User's Terminal   412
26.18   Writing A Block Of Data To The Server   413
26.19   Interacting With The Client Process   414
26.20   Responding To Illegal Commands   415
26.21   Scripting To A File   415
26.22   Implementation Of Scripting   416

26.23   Initialization Of Scripting   416
26.24   Collecting Characters Of The Script File Name   417
26.25   Opening A Script File   418
26.26   Terminating Scripting   420
26.27   Printing Status Information   421
26.28   Summary   422

Chapter 27   Practical Hints And Techniques For UNIX Servers   425

27.1   Introduction   425
27.2   Operating In Background   425
27.3   Programming A Server To Operate In Background   426
27.4   Open Descriptors And Inheritance   427
27.5   Programming A Server To Close Inherited Descriptors   428
27.6   Signals From The Controlling TTY   428
27.7   Programming A Server To Change Its Controlling TTY   428
27.8   Moving To A Safe And Known Directory   429
27.9   Programming A Server To Change Directories   429
27.10   The UNIX Umask   430
27.11   Programming A Server To Set Its Umask   430
27.12   Process Groups   430
27.13   Programming A Server To Set Its Process Group   431
27.14   Descriptors For Standard I/O   431
27.15   Programming A Server To Open Standard Descriptors   431
27.16   Mutual Exclusion For The Server   432
27.17   Programming A Server To Avoid Multiple Copies   432
27.18   Recording A Server's Process ID   433
27.19   Programming A Server To Record Its Process ID   433
27.20   Waiting For A Child Process To Exit   434
27.21   Programming A Server To Wait For Each Child To Exit   434
27.22   Extraneous Signals   434
27.23   Programming A Server To Ignore Extraneous Signals   435
27.24   Using A System Log Facility   435
27.25   Summary   440

Appendix 1   System Calls And Library Routines Used With Sockets   443

Appendix 2   Manipulation Of UNIX File And Socket Descriptors   473

Bibliography   477

Index   485

Foreword

It is indeed a pleasure to introduce the reader to the third volume of Dr. Douglas E. Comer's remarkable series: Internetworking with TCP/IP. This series, which began so innocently back in 1987, is now the premiere source for learning about the suite of protocols that have made vendor-independent computer-communications possible – the Internet suite of protocols.

In Volume 1, *Principles, Protocols, and Architectures*, we gained insight into the fundamental concepts which permeate the Internet suite. In Volume 2, *Design, Implementation, and Internals*, we gained an understanding as to how the Internet technological infrastructure is realized. To be sure, both of these works are essential to any understanding of internetworking, but it is this volume which I think has the potential for the greatest impact.

For it is in Volume 3, *Client-Server Programming and Applications*, which Doug has authored with David L. Stevens, that a whole new world opens for us. This is the world of designing and implementing new applications for the Internet infrastructure. As the reader will soon discover, this volume is a worthy peer to its predecessors: in a surprisingly readable style, it describes not only the ''how'' but the ''why.'' 'That is, not only will you learn how to architect and build client-server applications, but by reading this book you will also understand what trade-offs are involved with each design decision.

So, I invite you to sit back and enjoy reading the third volume in what I hope will be a never ending series for the theory, design, and realization of internetworking technology.

Marshall T. Rose
Theorist, Implementor, and Agent Provocateur
Mountain View, California

Preface

The first two volumes of *Internetworking With TCP/IP* have enjoyed incredible popularity; we have received positive comments from around the world. Many readers have requested information on the design of application software that operates in an internet environment. This third volume extends the series and answers the requests.

Broadly speaking, Volume *1* of this series examines the question, "What is a TCP/IP internet?" Volume *2* examines the question, "How does TCP/IP software work?" It presents more details and explores greater depth than the first volume.

This volume examines the question, "How do applications use TCP/IP?" It focuses on the client-server paradigm, and examines algorithms for both the client and server components of a distributed program. It shows an implementation that illustrates each design, and discusses techniques like application-level gateways and tunneling. In addition, it reviews several standard application protocols, and uses them to illustrate the algorithms and implementation techniques.

Beginning chapters introduce basic ideas. They discuss the client-server paradigm, the socket interface that application programs use to access TCP/IP protocol software, and the operating system primitives that application programs call to invoke system services or perform I/O. The chapter on operating system services describes concurrent processes and the system functions used to create them.

Chapters that follow the introductory material discuss client and server algorithms or give a detailed example of a particular algorithm. We have tried to show that the myriad of possible designs are not random. Instead, they follow a pattern that can be understood by considering the choice of concurrency and transport. For example, one chapter discusses a nonconcurrent server design that uses connection-oriented transport (i.e., TCP), while another discusses a similar design that uses connectionless transport (i.e., UDP).

While we describe how each design fits into the space of possible implementations, we do not try to develop an abstract "theory" of client-server interactions. Instead, we emphasize design principles that underlie practical implementations; each implementation technique has advantages in some circumstances, and each has been used in working software. We believe that understanding the conceptual ties among the designs will help the reader appreciate the strengths and weaknesses of each approach and will make it easier to choose among them.

The text contains example programs that show how each design operates in practice. Most of the examples implement standard TCP/IP application protocols. In each case, we tried to select an application protocol that would convey a single design idea without being too complex to understand. Thus, while few of the example programs are exciting, they each illustrate one important concept. This version of Volume *3* uses the BSD UNIX socket mechanism in all programming examples; a companion edition contains the same examples using AT&T's TLI protocol interface.

Later chapters discuss the remote procedure call concept and describe how it can be used to construct distributed programs. They relate the remote procedure call technique to the client-server model, and show how software can be used to generate client and server programs from a remote procedure call description. Chapters on the Network File System illustrate how remote procedure call can be used to define an application protocol. The chapters on TELNET show how small details dominate a production program and how complex the code can become for even a simple character-oriented protocol.

Much of the text concentrates on concurrent processing. Many of the concepts described may seem familiar to students who have written concurrent programs because they apply to all concurrent programs, not only network applications. Students who have not written concurrent programs may find the concepts difficult.

The text is suitable for a single semester introductory networking course at the senior or graduate level. Because the text concentrates on how to use an internet rather than on how it works, students need little background in networking to understand the material. No particular concept is too difficult for lower level courses as long as the instructor proceeds at a suitable pace. A basic course in operating systems concepts or experience with concurrent programming may provide the best background.

Students will not appreciate the material until they use it first hand. Thus, any course should have programming exercises that force the students to apply the ideas to practical programs. Undergraduates can learn the basics by repeating the designs on other application protocols. Graduate students should build more complex distributed programs that emphasize some of the subtle techniques (e.g., the concurrency management techniques in Chapter *15* and the interconnection techniques in Chapter *17*).

Many people deserve credit for their help. Members of the Internet Research Group at Purdue contributed technical information and suggestions. Several of the members, including Bobby Minnear, John Lin, Longsong Lin, and Honghai Shen proofread early drafts of chapters. Bobby decoded the NFS file handle format.

Jeff Schwab, Chris Kantarjiev, and Craig Partridge provided valuable comments on the draft manuscript. Charlotte Tubis carefully proofread the text. Scott Ballew identified several subtle oversights in both the text and code.

The idea for the RPC dictionary example came from Thomas Narten who assigned a more complex version to students in his networking class.

Christine Comer provided invaluable help. She spotted many typos missed by others, made suggestions, and contributed to the wording throughout the text.

Douglas E. Comer
David L. Stevens

Internetworking With TCP/IP

Vol III:

Client-Server Programming
And Applications

BSD Socket Version

1

Introduction And Overview

1.1 Use Of TCP/IP

In 1982, the TCP/IP Internet included a few hundred computers at two dozen sites concentrated primarily in North America. By the Spring of 1992, over 700,000 computer systems attached to the Internet in *39* countries spread across *7* continents, and its size was doubling every ten months. Approximately one third of the *4500* networks that comprised the Internet in 1992 were located outside the US.

In addition, most large corporations have chosen TCP/IP protocols for their private corporate internets, many of which are now as large as the connected Internet was ten years ago. TCP/IP accounts for a significant fraction of networking throughout the world. Its use is growing rapidly in Europe, India, South America, and countries on the Pacific rim.

Besides quantitative growth, the past decade has witnessed an important change in the way sites use TCP/IP. Early use focused on a few basic services like electronic mail, file transfer, and remote login. Now, more users are designing application protocols and building their own application software. In fact, over one fifth of all traffic on the connected Internet arises from private applications. New applications rely on TCP/IP to provide basic transport services. They add rich functionality that has enhanced the Internet environment and has enabled new groups of users to benefit from connectivity.

The variety of applications using TCP/IP is staggering: it includes hotel reservation systems, applications that monitor and control offshore oil platforms, warehouse inventory control systems, applications that permit geographically distributed machines to share file access and display graphics, applications that transfer images and manage printing presses, as well as teleconferencing and multimedia systems. In addition to existing uses, the National Research and Education Network (*NREN*) initiative authorized

1

by the United States Congress will provide improvements in the US national networking infrastructure, and will stimulate even more groups to develop applications.

As corporate internets mature, emphasis shifts from building internets to using them. As a result, more programmers need to know the fundamental principles and techniques used to design and implement distributed applications.

1.2 Designing Applications For A Distributed Environment

Programmers who build applications for a distributed computing environment follow a simple guideline: they try to make each distributed application behave as much as possible like the nondistributed version of the program. In essence, the goal of distributed computing is to provide an environment that hides the geographic location of computers and services and makes them appear to be local.

For example, a conventional database system stores information on the same machine as the application programs that access it. A distributed version of such a database system permits users to access data from computers other than the one on which the data resides. If the distributed database applications have been designed well, a user will not know whether the data being accessed is local or remote.

1.3 Standard And Nonstandard Application Protocols

The TCP/IP protocol suite includes many application protocols, and new application protocols appear daily. In fact, whenever a programmer devises a distributed program that uses TCP/IP to communicate, the programmer has invented a new application protocol. Of course, some application protocols have been documented in RFCs and adopted as part of the official TCP/IP protocol suite. We refer to such protocols as *standard application protocols*. Other protocols, invented by application programmers for private use, are referred to as *nonstandard application protocols*.

Most network managers choose to use standard application protocols whenever possible; one does not invent a new application protocol when an existing protocol suffices. For example, the TCP/IP suite contains standard application protocols for services like *file transfer*, *remote login*, and *electronic mail*. Thus, a programmer would use a standard protocol for such services.

1.4 An Example Of Standard Application Protocol Use

Remote login ranks among the most popular TCP/IP applications. Although a given remote login session only generates data at the speed a human can type and only receives data at the speed a human can read, remote login is the third highest source of packets on the connected Internet, exceeded only by file transfer and electronic mail. Many users rely on remote login as part of their working environment; they do not have a direct connection to the machines that they use for most computation.

The TCP/IP suite includes a standard application protocol for remote login known as *TELNET*. The TELNET protocol defines the format of data that an application program must send to a remote machine to log onto that system and the format of messages the remote machine sends back. It specifies how character data should be encoded for transmission and how one sends special messages to control the session or abort a remote operation.

For most users, the internal details of how the TELNET protocol encodes data are irrelevant; a user can invoke software that accesses a remote machine without knowing or caring about the implementation. In fact, using a remote service is usually as easy as using a local one. For example, computer systems that run TCP/IP protocols usually include a command that users invoke to run TELNET software. On Berkeley UNIX systems, the command is named *telnet*. To invoke it, a user types:

```
telnet machine
```

where the argument *machine* denotes the domain name of the machine to which remote login access is desired. Thus, to form a TELNET connection to machine *nic.ddn.mil* a user types:

```
telnet nic.ddn.mil
```

From the user's point of view, running *telnet* converts the user's terminal into a terminal that connects directly to the remote system. If the user is running in a windowing environment, the window in which the *telnet* command has been executed will be connected to the remote machine. Once the connection has been established, the *telnet* application sends each character the user types to the remote machine, and displays each character the remote machine emits on the user's screen.

After a user invokes *telnet* and connects to a remote system, the remote system displays a prompt that requests the user to type a login identifier and a password. The prompt a machine presents to a remote user is identical to the prompt it presents to users who login on local terminals. Thus, TELNET provides each remote user with the illusion of being on a directly-connected terminal.

1.5 An Example Connection

As an example, consider what happens when a user invokes *telnet* and connects to machine *nri.reston.va.us*:

```
telnet nri.reston.va.us
Trying...
Connected to nri.reston.va.us.
Escape character is '^]'.

SunOS UNIX (nri)

login:
```

The initial output message, *Trying...* appears while the *telnet* program converts the machine name to an IP address and tries to make a valid TCP connection to that address. As soon as the connection has been established, *telnet* prints the second and third lines, telling the user that the connection attempt has succeeded and identifying a special character that the user can type to escape from the *telnet* application temporarily if needed (e.g., if a failure occurs and the user needs to abort the connection). The notation ^] means that the user must hold the *CONTROL* key while striking the right bracket key.

The last few lines of output come from the remote machine. They identify the operating system as *SunOS*, and provide a standard login prompt. The cursor stops after the *login:* message, waiting for the user to type a valid login identifier. The user must have an account on the remote machine for the TELNET session to continue. After the user types a valid login identifier, the remote machine prompts for a password, and only permits access if the login identifier and password are valid.

1.6 Using TELNET To Access An Alternative Service

TCP/IP uses protocol port numbers to identify application services on a given machine. Software that implements a given service waits for requests at a predetermined (well-known) protocol port. For example, the remote login service accessed with the TELNET application protocol has been assigned port number *23*. Thus, when a user invokes the *telnet* program, the program connects to port *23* on the specified machine.

Interestingly, the TELNET protocol can be used to access services other than the standard remote login service. To do so, a user must specify the protocol port number of the desired service. The Berkeley UNIX *telnet* command uses an optional second argument to allow the user to specify an alternative protocol port. If the user does not supply a second argument, *telnet* uses port *23*. However, if the user supplies a port number, *telnet* connects to that port number. For example, if a user types:

```
telnet nri.reston.va.us 185
```

the *telnet* program will form a connection to protocol port number *185* at machine *nri.reston.va.us*. The machine is owned by the *Corporation For National Research Initiatives (CNRI)*.

Port *185* on the machine at *CNRI* does not supply remote login service. Instead, it offers a *Knowbot Information Service*. Thus, once a connection succeeds, the user receives information about the Knowbot service followed by a prompt for Knowbot commands:

```
Trying...
Connected to nri.reston.va.us.
Escape character is '^]'.
```

```
Knowbot Information Service (V1.0). Copyright CNRI 1990.
     All Rights Reserved.
Try ? or man for help.
>
```

The first three lines are the same as in the example above because they come from the *telnet* program and not the remote service. The remaining lines differ, and clearly show that the service available on port *185* is not a remote login service. The greater-than symbol on the last line serves as the prompt for Knowbot commands.

The Knowbot service searches well-known white pages directories to help a user find information about another user. For example, suppose one wanted to know the e-mail address for David Clark, a researcher at MIT. Typing *clark* in response to the Knowbot prompt retrieves 282 entries that each contain the name *Clark*. Most of the entries correspond to individuals with a first or last name of *Clark*, but some correspond to individuals with *Clark* in their affiliation (e.g., *Clark College*). Searching through the retrieved information reveals only one entry for a David Clark at MIT:

```
Name:          David D. Clark
Phone:         (617) 253-6003
E-Mail:        ddc@LCS.MIT.EDU
Source:        whois@nic.ddn.mil
Ident:         DDC1
Last updated:  (unknown)
```

1.7 Application Protocols And Software Flexibility

The example above shows how a single piece of software, in this instance the *telnet* program, can be used to access more than one service. The design of the TELNET protocol and its use to access the Knowbot service illustrate two important points. First, the goal of all protocol design is to find fundamental abstractions that can be reused in multiple applications. In practice, TELNET suffices for a wide variety of services because it provides a basic interactive communication facility. Conceptually, the protocol used to access a service remains separate from the service itself. Second, when architects specify application services, they use standard application protocols whenever possible. The Knowbot service described above can be accessed easily because it uses the standard TELNET protocol for communication. Furthermore, because most TCP/IP software includes an application program that users can invoke to run TELNET, no additional client software is needed to access the Knowbot service. Designers who invent new interactive applications can reuse software if they choose TELNET for their access protocol. The point can be summarized:

The TELNET protocol provides incredible flexibility because it only defines interactive communication and not the details of the service accessed. TELNET can be used as the communication mechanism for many interactive services besides remote login.

1.8 Viewing Services From The Provider's Perspective

The examples of application services given above show how a service appears from an individual user's point of view. The user runs a program that accesses a remote service, and expects to receive a reply with little or no delay.

From the perspective of a computer that supplies a service, the situation appears quite different. Users at multiple sites may choose to access a given service at the same time. When they do, each user expects to receive a response without delay.

To provide quick responses and handle many requests, a computer system that supplies an application service must use *concurrent processing*. That is, the provider cannot keep a new user waiting while it handles the previous user. Instead, the software must process more than one request at a time.

Because application programmers do not often write concurrent programs, concurrent processing can seem like magic. A single application program must manage multiple activities at the same time. In the case of TELNET, the program that provides remote login service must allow multiple users to login to a given machine and must manage multiple active login sessions. Communication for one login session must proceed without interference from others.

The need for concurrency complicates network software design, implementation, and maintenance. It mandates new algorithms and new programming techniques. Furthermore, because concurrency complicates debugging, programmers must be especially careful to document their designs and to follow good programming practices. Finally, programmers must choose a level of concurrency and consider whether their software will exhibit higher throughput if they increase or decrease the level of concurrency.

This text helps application programmers understand the design, construction, and optimization of network application software that uses concurrent processing. It describes the fundamental algorithms for both sequential and concurrent implementations of application protocols and provides an example of each. It considers the trade-offs and advantages of each design. Later chapters discuss the subtleties of concurrency management and review techniques that permit a programmer to optimize throughput automatically. To summarize:

Providing concurrent access to application services is important and difficult; many chapters of this text explain and discuss concurrent implementations of application protocol software.

1.9 The Remainder Of This Text

This text describes how to design and build distributed applications. Although it uses TCP/IP transport protocols to provide a concrete example, the discussion focuses on principles, algorithms, and general purpose techniques that apply to most network protocols. Early chapters introduce the client-server model and socket interface. Later chapters present specific algorithms and implementation techniques used in client and server software as well as interesting combinations of algorithms and techniques for managing concurrency.

In addition to its description of algorithms for client and server software, the text presents general techniques like tunneling, application-level gateways, and remote procedure calls. Finally, it examines a few standard application protocols like NFS and TELNET.

Most chapters contain example software that helps illustrate the principles discussed. The software should be considered part of the text. It shows clearly how all the details fit together and how the concepts appear in working programs.

1.10 Summary

Many programmers are building distributed applications that use TCP/IP as a transport mechanism. Before programmers can design and implement a distributed application, they need to understand the client-server model of computing, the operating system interface an application program uses to access protocol software, the fundamental algorithms used to implement client and server software, and alternatives to standard client-server interaction including the use of application gateways.

Most network services permit multiple users to access the service simultaneously. The technique of concurrent processing makes it possible to build an application program that can handle multiple requests at the same time. Much of this text focuses on techniques for the concurrent implementation of application protocols and on the problem of managing concurrency.

FOR FURTHER STUDY

The manuals that vendors supply with their operating systems contain information on how to invoke commands that access services like *TELNET*. Many sites augment the set of standard commands with locally-defined commands. Check with your site administrator to find out about locally-available commands.

EXERCISES

1.1 Use TELNET from your local machine to login to another machine. How much delay, if any, do you experience when the second machine connects to the same local area network? How much delay do you notice when connected to a remote machine?

1.2 Read the vendor's manual to find out whether your local version of the TELNET software permits connection to a port on the remote machine other than the standard port used for remote login.

1.3 Determine the set of TCP/IP services available on your local computer.

1.4 Use an FTP program to retrieve a file from a remote site. If the software does not provide statistics, estimate the transfer rate for a large file. Is the rate higher or lower than you expected?

1.5 Use the *finger* command to obtain information about users at a remote site.

2

The Client Server Model
And Software Design

2.1 Introduction

From the viewpoint of an application, TCP/IP, like most computer communication protocols, merely provides basic mechanisms used to transfer data. In particular, TCP/IP allows a programmer to establish communication between two application programs and to pass data back and forth. Thus, we say that TCP/IP provides *peer-to-peer* communication. The peer applications can execute on the same machine or on different machines.

Although TCP/IP specifies the details of how data passes between a pair of communicating applications, it does not dictate when or why peer applications interact, nor does it specify how programmers should organize such application programs in a distributed environment. In practice, one organizational method dominates the use of TCP/IP to such an extent that almost all applications use it. The method is known as the *client-server paradigm*. In fact, client-server interaction has become so fundamental in peer-to-peer networking systems that it forms the basis for most computer communication.

This text uses the client-server paradigm to describe all application programming. It considers the motivations behind the client-server model, describes the functions of the client and server components, and shows how to construct both client and server software.

Before considering how to construct software, it is important to define client-server concepts and terminology. The next sections define terminology that is used throughout the text.

9

2.2 Motivation

The fundamental motivation for the client-server paradigm arises from the problem of rendezvous. To understand the problem, imagine a human trying to start two programs on separate machines and have them communicate. Also remember that computers operate many orders of magnitude faster than humans. After the human initiates the first program, the program begins execution and sends a message to its peer. Within a few milliseconds, it determines that the peer does not yet exist, so it emits an error message and exits. Meanwhile, the human initiates the second program. Unfortunately, when the second program starts execution, it finds that the peer has already ceased execution. Even if the two programs retry to communicate continually, they can each execute so quickly that the probability of them sending messages to one another simultaneously is low.

The client-server model solves the rendezvous problem by asserting that in any pair of communicating applications, one side must start execution and wait (indefinitely) for the other side to contact it. The solution is important because TCP/IP does not respond to incoming communication requests on its own.

Because TCP/IP does not provide any mechanisms that automatically create running programs when a message arrives, a program must be waiting to accept communication before any requests arrive.

Thus, to ensure that computers are ready to communicate, most system administrators arrange to have communication programs start automatically whenever the operating system boots. Each program runs forever, waiting for the next request to arrive for the service it offers.

2.3 Terminology And Concepts

The client-server paradigm divides communicating applications into two broad categories, depending on whether the application waits for communication or initiates it. This section provides a concise, comprehensive definition of the two categories, and relies on later chapters to illustrate them and explain many of the subtleties.

2.3.1 Clients And Servers

The client-server paradigm uses the direction of initiation to categorize whether a program is a client or server. In general, an application that initiates peer-to-peer communication is called a *client*. End users usually invoke client software when they use a network service. Most client software consists of conventional application programs. Each time a client application executes, it contacts a server, sends a request, and awaits a response. When the response arrives, the client continues processing. Clients are often easier to build than servers, and usually require no special system privileges to operate.

By comparison, a *server* is any program† that waits for incoming communication requests from a client. The server receives a client's request, performs the necessary computation, and returns the result to the client.

2.3.2 Privilege And Complexity

Because servers often need to access data, computations, or protocol ports that the operating system protects, server software usually requires special system privileges. Because a server executes with special system privilege, care must be taken to ensure that it does not inadvertently pass privileges on to the clients that use it. For example, a file server that operates as a privileged program must contain code to check whether a given file can be accessed by a given client. The server cannot rely on the usual operating system checks because its privileged status overrides them.

Servers must contain code that handles the issues of:

* *Authentication* – verifying the identity of the client
* *Authorization* – determining whether a given client is permitted to access the service the server supplies
* *Data security* – guaranteeing that data is not unintentionally revealed or compromised
* *Privacy* – keeping information about an individual from unauthorized access
* *Protection* – guaranteeing that network applications cannot abuse system resources.

As we will see in later chapters, servers that perform intense computation or handle large volumes of data operate more efficiently if they handle requests concurrently. The combination of special privileges and concurrent operation usually makes servers more difficult to design and implement than clients. Later chapters provide many examples that illustrate the differences between clients and servers.

2.3.3 Standard Vs. Nonstandard Client Software

Chapter *1* describes two broad classes of client application programs: those that invoke standard TCP/IP services (e.g., electronic mail) and those that invoke services defined by the site (e.g., an institution's private database system). *Standard application services* consist of those services defined by TCP/IP and assigned well-known, universally recognized protocol port identifiers; we consider all others to be *locally-defined application services* or *nonstandard application services*.

The distinction between standard services and others is only important when communicating outside the local environment. Within a given environment, system administrators usually arrange to define service names in such a way that users cannot distinguish between local and standard services. Programmers who build network applica-

---

†Technically, a *server* is a program and not a piece of hardware. However, computer users frequently (mis)apply the term to the computer responsible for running a particular server program. For example, they might say, "That computer is our file server," when they mean, "That computer runs our file server program."

tions that will be used at other sites must understand the distinction, however, and must be careful to avoid depending on services that are only available locally.

Although TCP/IP defines many standard application protocols, most commercial computer vendors supply only a handful of standard application client programs with their TCP/IP software. For example, TCP/IP software usually includes a *remote terminal client* that uses the standard TELNET protocol for remote login, an *electronic mail client* that uses the standard SMTP protocol to transfer electronic mail to a remote system, and a *file transfer client* that uses the standard FTP protocol to transfer files between two machines.

Of course, many organizations build customized applications that use TCP/IP to communicate. Customized, nonstandard applications range from simple to complex, and include such diverse services as image transmission and video teleconferencing, voice transmission, remote real-time data collection, hotel and other on-line reservation systems, distributed database access, weather data distribution, and remote control of ocean-based drilling platforms.

2.3.4 Parameterization Of Clients

Some client software provides more generality than others. In particular, some client software allows the user to specify both the remote machine on which a server operates and the protocol port number at which the server is listening. For example, Chapter *1* shows how standard application client software can use the *TELNET* protocol to access services other than the conventional TELNET remote terminal service, as long as the program allows the user to specify a destination protocol port as well as a remote machine.

Conceptually, software that allows a user to specify a protocol port number has more input parameters than other software, so we use the term *fully parameterized client* to describe it. Many TELNET client implementations interpret an optional second argument as a port number. To specify only a remote machine, the user supplies the name of the remote machine:

telnet machine-name

Given only a machine name, the *telnet* program uses the well-known port for the TELNET service. To specify both a remote machine and a port on that machine, the user specifies both the machine name and the port number:

telnet machine-name port

Not all vendors provide full parameterization for their client application software. Therefore, on some systems, it may be difficult or impossible to use any port other than the official TELNET port. In fact, it may be necessary to modify the vendor's TELNET client software or to write new TELNET client software that accepts a port argument and uses that port. Of course, when building client software, full parameterization is recommended.

When designing client application software, include parameters that allow the user to fully specify the destination machine and destination protocol port number.

Full parameterization is especially useful when testing a new client or server because it allows testing to proceed independent of the existing software already in use. For example, a programmer can build a TELNET client and server pair, invoke them using nonstandard protocol ports, and proceed to test the software without disturbing standard services. Other users can continue to access the old TELNET service without interference during the testing.

2.3.5 Connectionless Vs. Connection-Oriented Servers

When programmers design client-server software, they must choose between two types of interaction: a *connectionless style* or a *connection-oriented style*. The two styles of interaction correspond directly to the two major transport protocols that the TCP/IP protocol suite supplies. If the client and server communicate using UDP, the interaction is connectionless; if they use TCP, the interaction is connection-oriented.

From the application programmer's point of view, the distinction between connectionless and connection-oriented interactions is critical because it determines the level of reliability that the underlying system provides. TCP provides all the reliability needed to communicate across an internet. It verifies that data arrives, and automatically retransmits segments that do not. It computes a checksum over the data to guarantee that it is not corrupted during transmission. It uses sequence numbers to ensure that the data arrives in order, and automatically eliminates duplicate packets. It provides flow control to ensure that the sender does not transmit data faster than the receiver can consume it. Finally, TCP informs both the client and server if the underlying network becomes inoperable for any reason.

By contrast, clients and servers that use UDP do not have any guarantees about reliable delivery. When a client sends a request, the request may be lost, duplicated, delayed, or delivered out of order. Similarly, a response the server sends back to a client may be lost, duplicated, delayed, or delivered out of order. The client and/or server application programs must take appropriate actions to detect and correct such errors.

UDP can be deceiving because it provides *best effort delivery*. UDP does not introduce errors – it merely depends on the underlying IP internet to deliver packets. IP, in turn, depends on the underlying hardware networks and intermediate gateways. From a programmer's point of view, the consequence of using UDP is that it works well if the underlying internet works well. For example, UDP works well in a local environment because reliability errors seldom occur in a local environment. Errors usually arise only when communication spans a wide area internet.

Programmers sometimes make the mistake of choosing connectionless transport (i.e., UDP), building an application that uses it, and then testing the application software only on a local area network. Because a local area network seldom or never delays packets, drops them, or delivers them out of order, the application software appears to work well. However, if the same software is used across a wide area internet, it may fail or produce incorrect results.

Beginners, as well as most experienced professionals, prefer to use the connection-oriented style of interaction. A connection-oriented protocol makes programming simpler, and relieves the programmer of the responsibility to detect and correct errors. In fact, adding reliability to a connectionless internet message protocol like UDP is a nontrivial undertaking that usually requires considerable experience with protocol design.

Usually, application programs only use UDP if: (1) the application protocol specifies that UDP must be used (presumably, the application protocol has been designed to handle reliability and delivery errors), (2) the application protocol relies on hardware broadcast or multicast, or (3) the application cannot tolerate the computational overhead or delay required for TCP virtual circuits. We can summarize:

> When designing client-server applications, beginners are strongly advised to use TCP because it provides reliable, connection-oriented communication. Programs only use UDP if the application protocol handles reliability, the application requires hardware broadcast or multicast, or the application cannot tolerate virtual circuit overhead.

2.3.6 Stateless Vs. Stateful Servers

Information that a server maintains about the status of ongoing interactions with clients is called *state information*. Servers that do not keep any state information are called *stateless servers*; others are called *stateful servers*.

The desire for efficiency motivates designers to keep state information in servers. Keeping a small amount of information in a server can reduce the size of messages that the client and server exchange, and can allow the server to respond to requests quickly. Essentially, state information allows a server to remember what the client requested previously and to compute an incremental response as each new request arrives. By contrast, the motivation for statelessness lies in protocol reliability: state information in a server can become incorrect if messages are lost, duplicated, or delivered out of order, or if the client computer crashes and reboots. If the server uses incorrect state information when computing a response, it may respond incorrectly.

2.3.7 A Stateful File Server Example

An example will help explain the distinction between stateless and stateful servers. Consider a file server that allows clients to remotely access information kept in the files on a local disk. The server operates as an application program. It waits for a client to contact it over the network. The client sends one of two request types. It either sends a request to extract data from a specified file or a request to store data in a specified file. The server performs the requested operation and replies to the client.

On one hand, if the file server is stateless, it maintains no information about the transactions. Each message from a client that requests the server to extract data from a file must specify the complete file name (the name could be quite lengthy), a position in the file from which the data should be extracted, and the number of bytes to extract. Similarly, each message that requests the server to store data in a file must specify the complete file name, a position in the file at which the data should be stored, and the data to store.

On the other hand, if the file server maintains state information for its clients, it can eliminate the need to pass file names in each message. The server maintains a table that holds state information about the file currently being accessed. Figure 2.1 shows one possible arrangement of the state information.

Handle	File Name	Current Position
1	test.program.c	0
2	tcp.book.doc	456
3	dept.budget.text	38
4	tetris.exe	128

Figure 2.1 Example table of state information for a stateful file server. To keep messages short, the server assigns a handle to each file. The handle appears in messages instead of a file name.

When a client first opens a file, the server adds an entry to its state table that contains the name of the file, a *handle* (a small integer used to identify the file), and a current position in the file (initially zero). The server then sends the handle back to the client for use in subsequent requests. Whenever the client wants to extract additional data from the file, it sends a small message that includes the handle. The server uses the handle to lookup the file name and current file position in its state table. The server increments the file position in the state table, so the next request from the client will extract new data. Thus, the client can send repeated requests to move through the entire file. When the client finishes using a file, it sends a message informing the server that the file will no longer be needed. In response, the server removes the stored state information. As long as all messages travel reliably between the client and server, a stateful design makes the interaction more efficient. The point is:

> In an ideal world, where networks deliver all messages reliably and computers never crash, having a server maintain a small amount of state information for each ongoing interaction can make messages smaller and processing simpler.

Although state information can improve efficiency, it can also be difficult or impossible to maintain correctly if the underlying network duplicates, delays, or delivers messages out of order (e.g., if the client and server use UDP to communicate). Consider what happens to our file server example if the network duplicates a *read* request. Recall that the server maintains a notion of file position in its state information. Assume that the server updates its notion of file position each time a client extracts data from a file. If the network duplicates a *read* request, the server will receive two copies. When the first copy arrives, the server extracts data from the file, updates the file position in its state information, and returns the result to the client. When the second copy arrives, the server extracts additional data, updates the file position again, and returns the new data to the client. The client may view the second response as a duplicate and discard it, or it may report an error because it received two different responses to a single request. In either case, the state information at the server can become incorrect because it disagrees with the client's notion of the true state.

When computers reboot, state information can also become incorrect. If a client crashes after performing an operation that creates additional state information, the server may never receive messages that allow it to discard the information. Eventually, the accumulated state information exhausts the server's memory. In our file server example, if a client opens *100* files and then crashes, the server will maintain *100* useless entries in its state table forever.

A stateful server may also become confused (or respond incorrectly) if a new client begins operation after a reboot using the same protocol port numbers as the previous client that was operating when the system crashed. It may seem that this problem can be overcome easily by having the server erase previous information from a client whenever a new request for interaction arrives. Remember, however, that the underlying internet may duplicate and delay messages, so any solution to the problem of new clients reusing protocol ports after a reboot must also handle the case where a client starts normally, but its first message to a server becomes duplicated and one copy is delayed.

In general, the problems of maintaining correct state can only be solved with complex protocols that accommodate the problems of unreliable delivery and computer system restart. To summarize:

> *In a real internet, where machines crash and reboot, and messages can be lost, delayed, duplicated, or delivered out of order, stateful designs lead to complex application protocols that are difficult to design, understand, and program correctly.*

2.3.8 Statelessness Is A Protocol Issue

Although we have discussed statelessness in the context of servers, the question of whether a server is stateless or stateful centers on the application protocol more than the implementation. If the application protocol specifies that the meaning of a particular message depends in some way on previous messages, it may be impossible to provide a stateless interaction.

In essence, the issue of statelessness focuses on whether the application protocol assumes the responsibility for reliable delivery. To avoid problems and make the interaction reliable, an application protocol designer must ensure that each message is completely unambiguous. That is, a message cannot depend on being delivered in order, nor can it depend on previous messages having been delivered. In essence, the protocol designer must build the interaction so the server gives the same response no matter when or how many times a request arrives. Mathematicians use the term *idempotent* to refer to a mathematical operation that always produces the same result. We use the term to refer to protocols that arrange for a server to give the same response to a given message no matter how many times it arrives.

> *In an internet where the underlying network can duplicate, delay or deliver messages out of order or where computers running client applications can crash unexpectedly, the server should be stateless. The server can only be stateless if the application protocol is designed to make operations idempotent.*

2.3.9 Servers As Clients

Programs do not always fit exactly into the definition of client or server. A server program may need to access network services that require it to act as a client. For example, suppose our file server program needs to obtain the time of day so it can stamp files with the time of access. Also suppose that the system on which it operates does not have a time-of-day clock. To obtain the time, the server acts as a client by sending a request to a time-of-day server as Figure 2.2 shows.

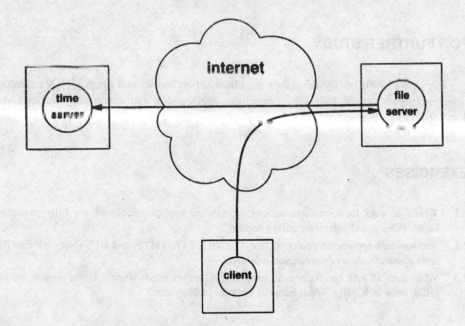

Figure 2.2 A file server program acting as a client to a time server. When the time server replies, the file server will finish its computation and return the result to the original client.

In a network environment that has many available servers, it is not unusual to find a server for one application acting as a client for another. Of course, designers must be careful to avoid circular dependencies among servers.

2.4 Summary

The client-server paradigm classifies a communicating application program as either a client or a server depending on whether it initiates communication. In addition to client and server software for standard applications, many TCP/IP users build client and server software for nonstandard applications that they define locally.

Beginners and most experienced programmers use TCP to transport messages between the client and server because it provides the reliability needed in an internet environment. Programmers only resort to UDP if TCP cannot solve the problem.

Keeping state information in the server can improve efficiency. However, if clients crash unexpectedly or the underlying transport system allows duplication, delay, or packet loss, state information can consume resources or become incorrect. Thus, most application protocol designers try to minimize state information. A stateless implementation may not be possible if the application protocol fails to make operations idempotent.

Programs cannot be divided easily into client and server categories because many programs perform both functions. A program that acts as a server for one service can act as a client to access other services.

FOR FURTHER STUDY

Stevens [1990] briefly describes the client-server model and gives UNIX examples. Other examples can be found by consulting applications that accompany various vendors' operating systems.

EXERCISES

2.1 Which of your local implementations of standard application clients are fully parameterized? Why is full parameterization needed?

2.2 Are standard application protocols like TELNET, FTP, SMTP, and NFS (Network File System) connectionless or connection-oriented?

2.3 What does TCP/IP specify should happen if no server exists when a client request arrives? (Hint: look at ICMP.) What happens on your local system?

2.4 Write down the data structures and message formats needed for a stateless file server. What happens if two or more clients access the same file? What happens if a client crashes before closing a file?

2.5 Write down the data structures and message formats needed for a stateful file server. Use the operations *open*, *read*, *write*, and *close* to access files. Arrange for *open* to return an integer used to access the file in *read* and *write* operations. How do you distinguish duplicate *open* requests from a client that sends an *open*, crashes, reboots, and sends an *open* again?

2.6 In the previous exercise, what happens in your design if two or more clients access the same file? What happens if a client crashes before closing a file?

2.7 Examine the NFS remote file access protocol carefully to identify which operations are idempotent. What errors can result if messages are lost, duplicated, or delayed?

3

Concurrent Processing In Client-Server Software

3.1 Introduction

The previous chapter defines the client-server paradigm. This chapter extends the notion of client-server interaction by discussing concurrency, a concept that provides much of the power behind client-server interactions but also makes the software difficult to design and build. The notion of concurrency also pervades later chapters, which explain in detail how servers provide concurrent access.

In addition to discussing the general concept of concurrency, this chapter also reviews the facilities that an operating system supplies to support concurrent process execution. It is important to understand the functions described in this chapter because they appear in many of the server implementations in later chapters.

3.2 Concurrency In Networks

The term *concurrency* refers to real or apparent simultaneous computing. For example, a multi-user computer system can achieve concurrency by *time-sharing*, a design that arranges to switch a single processor among multiple computations quickly enough to give the appearance of simultaneous progress; or by *multiprocessing*, a design in which multiple processors perform multiple computations simultaneously.

Concurrent processing is fundamental to distributed computing and occurs in many forms. Among machines on a single network, many pairs of application programs can communicate concurrently, sharing the network that interconnects them. For example,

21

application *A* on one machine may communicate with application *B* on another machine, while application *C* on a third machine communicates with application *D* on a fourth. Although they all share a single network, the applications appear to proceed as if they operate independently. The network hardware enforces access rules that allow each pair of communicating machines to exchange messages. The access rules prevent a given pair of applications from excluding others by consuming all the network bandwidth.

Concurrency can also occur within a given computer system. For example, multiple users on a timesharing system can each invoke a client application that communicates with an application on another machine. One user can transfer a file while another user conducts a remote login session. From a user's point of view, it appears that all client programs proceed simultaneously.

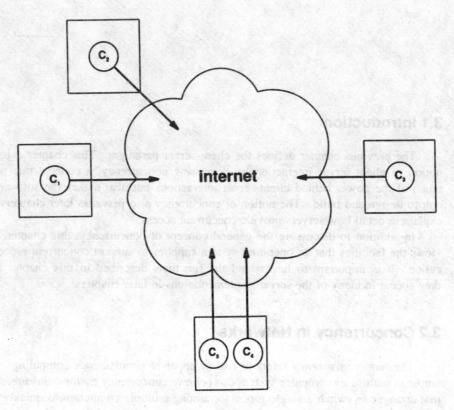

Figure 3.1 Concurrency among client programs occurs when users execute them on multiple machines simultaneously or when a multitasking operating system allows multiple copies to execute concurrently on a single computer.

In addition to concurrency among clients on a single machine, the set of all clients on a set of machines can execute concurrently. Figure 3.1 illustrates concurrency among client programs running on several machines.

Client software does not usually require any special attention or effort on the part of the programmer to make it usable concurrently. The application programmer designs and constructs each client program without regard to concurrent execution; concurrency among multiple client programs occurs automatically because the operating system allows multiple users to each invoke a client concurrently. Thus, the individual clients operate much like any conventional program. To summarize:

> *Most client software achieves concurrent operation because the underlying operating system allows users to execute client programs concurrently or because users on many machines each execute client software simultaneously. An individual client program operates like any conventional program; it does not manage concurrency explicitly.*

3.3 Concurrency In Servers

In contrast to concurrent client software, concurrency within a server requires considerable effort. As figure 3.2 shows, a single server program must handle incoming requests concurrently.

To understand why concurrency is important, consider server operations that require substantial computation or communication. For example, think of a remote login server. If it operates with no concurrency, it can handle only one remote login at a time. Once a client contacts the server, the server must ignore or refuse subsequent requests until the first user finishes. Clearly, such a design limits the utility of the server, and prevents multiple remote users from accessing a given machine at the same time.

Chapter 8 discusses algorithms and design issues for concurrent servers, showing how they operate in principle. Chapters 9 through 13 each illustrate one of the algorithms, describing the design in more detail and showing code for a working server. The remainder of this chapter concentrates on terminology and basic concepts used throughout the text.

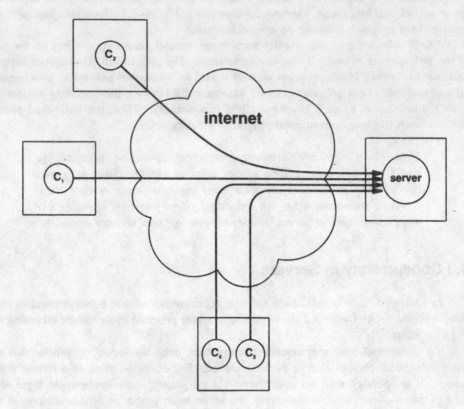

Figure 3.2 Server software must be explicitly programmed to handle con-
                current requests because multiple clients contact a server using its
                single, well-known protocol port.

3.4 Terminology And Concepts

Because few application programmers have experience with the design of concurrent programs, understanding concurrency in servers can be challenging. This section explains the basic concept of concurrent processing and shows how an operating
system supplies it. It gives examples that illustrate concurrency, and defines terminology used in later chapters.

3.4.1 The Process Concept

In concurrent processing systems, the *process* abstraction defines the fundamental unit of computation†. The most essential information associated with a process is an *instruction pointer* that specifies the address at which the process is executing. Other information associated with a process includes the identity of the user that owns it, the compiled program that it is executing, and the memory locations of the process' program text and data areas.

A process differs from a program because the process concept includes only the active execution of a computation, not the code. After the code has been loaded into a computer, the operating system allows one or more processes to execute it. In particular, a concurrent processing system allows multiple processes to execute the same piece of code "at the same time." This means that multiple processes may each be executing at some point in the code. Each process proceeds at its own rate, and each may begin or finish at an arbitrary time. Because each has a separate instruction pointer that specifies which instruction it will execute next; there is never any confusion.

Of course, on a uniprocessor architecture, the single CPU can only execute one process at any instant in time. The operating system makes the computer appear to perform more than one computation at a time by switching the CPU among all executing processes rapidly. From a human observer's point of view, many processes appear to proceed simultaneously. In fact, one process proceeds for a short time, then another process proceeds for a short time, and so on. We use the term *concurrent execution* to capture the idea. It means "apparently simultaneous execution." On a uniprocessor, the operating system handles concurrency, while on a multiprocessor, all CPUs can execute processes simultaneously.

The important concept is:

> *Application programmers build programs for a concurrent environment without knowing whether the underlying hardware consists of a uniprocessor or a multiprocessor.*

3.4.2 Programs vs. Processes

In a concurrent processing system, a conventional application program is merely a special case: it consists of a piece of code that is executed by exactly one process at a time. The notion of *process* differs from the conventional notion of *program* in other ways. For example, most application programmers think of the set of variables defined in the program as being associated with the code. However, if more than one process executes the code concurrently, it is essential that each process has its own copy of the variables. To understand why, consider the following segment of C code that prints the integers from *1* to *10*:

```
for ( i=0 ; i < 10 ; i++)
        printf("%d\n", i);
```

---

†Some systems use the terms *task*, *job*, or *thread* instead of *process*.

The iteration uses an index variable, *i*. In a conventional program, the programmer thinks of storage for variable *i* as being allocated with the code. However, if two or more processes execute the code segment concurrently, one of them may be on the sixth iteration when the other starts the first iteration. Each must have a different value for *i*. Thus, each process must have its own copy of variable *i* or confusion will result. To summarize:

> *When multiple processes execute a piece of code concurrently, each process has its own, independent copy of the variables associated with the code.*

3.4.3 Procedure Calls

In a procedure-oriented language, like Pascal or C, executed code can contain calls to subprograms (procedures or functions). Subprograms accept arguments, compute a result, and then return just after the point of the call. If multiple processes execute code concurrently, they can each be at a different point in the sequence of procedure calls. One process, *A*, can begin execution, call a procedure, and then call a second-level procedure before another process, *B*, begins. Process *B* may return from a first-level procedure call just as process *A* returns from a second-level call.

The run-time system for procedure-oriented programming languages uses a stack mechanism to handle procedure calls. The run-time system pushes a *procedure activation record* on the stack whenever it makes a procedure call. Among other things, the activation records stores information about the location in the code at which the procedure call occurs. When the procedure finishes execution, the run-time system pops the activation record from the top of the stack, and returns to the procedure from which the call occurred. Analogous to the rule for variables, concurrent programming systems provide separation between procedure calls in executing processes:

> *When multiple processes execute a piece of code concurrently, each has its own run-time stack of procedure activation records.*

3.5 An Example Of Concurrent Process Creation

3.5.1 A Sequential C Example

The following example illustrates concurrent processing in the UNIX operating system. As with most computational concepts, the programming language syntax is trivial; it occupies only a few lines of code. For example, the following code is a conventional C program that prints the integers from *1* to *5* along with their sum:

```
/* sum.c - A conventional C program that sums integers from 1 to 5  */
#include <stdio.h>
int     sum;                            /* sum is a global variable */

main() {
        int i;                          /* i is a local variable    */

        sum = 0;
        for (i=1 ; i <=5 ; i++) {       /* iterate i from 1 to 5     */
                printf("The value of i is %d\n", i);
                fflush(stdout);         /* flush the buffer          */
                sum += i;
        }
        printf("The sum is %d\n", sum);
        exit(0);                        /* terminate the program     */
}
```

When executed, the program emits six lines of output:

```
                        The value of i is 1
                        The value of i is 2
                        The value of i is 3
                        The value of i is 4
                        The value of i is 5
                        The sum is 15
```

3.5.2 A Concurrent Version

To create a new process in UNIX, a program calls the system function *fork*†. In essence, *fork* divides the running program into two (almost) identical processes, both executing at the same place in the same code. The two processes continue just as if two users had simultaneously started two copies of the application. For example, the following modified version of the above example calls *fork* to create a new process. (Note that although the introduction of concurrency changes the meaning of the program completely, the call to *fork* occupies only a single line of code.)

---

†To a programmer, the call to *fork* looks and acts like an ordinary function call in C. It is written **fork()**. At run-time, however, control passes to the operating system, which creates a new process.

```
#include <stdio.h>
int     sum;

main() {
        int i;

        sum = 0;
        fork();                          /* create a new process */
        for (i=0 ; i<=5 ; i++) {
                printf("The value of i is %d\n", i);
                fflush(stdout);
                sum += i;
        }
        printf("The sum is %d\n", sum);
        exit(0);
}
```

When a user executes the concurrent version of the program, the system begins with a single process executing the code. However, when the process reaches the call to *fork*, the system duplicates the process and allows both the original process and the newly created process to execute. Of course, each process has its own copy of the variables that the program uses. In fact, the easiest way to envision what happens is to imagine that the system makes a second copy of the entire running program. Then imagine that both copies run (just as if two users had both simultaneously executed the program). To summarize:

> *To understand the fork function, imagine that* fork *causes the operating system to make a copy of the executing program and allows both copies to run at the same time.*

On one particular uniprocessor system, the execution of our example concurrent program produces twelve lines of output:

```
                    The value of i is 1
                    The value of i is 2
                    The value of i is 3
                    The value of i is 4
                    The value of i is 5
                    The sum is 15
                    The value of i is 1
                    The value of i is 2
                    The value of i is 3
                    The value of i is 4
                    The value of i is 5
                    The sum is 15
```

On the hardware being used, the first process executed so rapidly that it was able to complete execution before the second process ran at all. Once the first process completed, the operating system switched the processor to the second process, which also ran to completion. The entire run took less than a second. The operating system overhead incurred in switching between processes and handling system calls, including the call to *fork* and the calls required to write the output, accounted for less than *20%* of the total time.

3.5.3 Timeslicing

In the example program, each process performed a trivial amount of computation as it iterated through a loop five times. Therefore, once a process gained control of the CPU, it quickly ran to completion. If we examine concurrent processes that perform substantially more computation, an interesting phenomenon occurs: the operating system allocates the available CPU power to each one for a short time before moving on to the next. We use the term *timeslicing* to describe systems that share the available CPU among several processes concurrently. For example, if a timeslicing system has only one CPU to allocate and a program divides into two processes, one of the processes will execute for a while, then the second will execute for a while, then the first will execute again, and so on. If the timeslicing system has many processes, it runs each for a short time before it runs the first one again.

A timeslicing mechanism attempts to allocate the available processing equally among all available processes. If only two processes are eligible to execute and the computer has a single processor, each receives approximately 50% of the CPU. If N processes are eligible on a computer with a single processor, each receives approximately $1/N$ of the CPU. Thus, all processes appear to proceed at an equal rate, no matter how many processes execute. With many processes executing, the rate is low; with few, the rate is high.

To see the effect of timeslicing, we need an example program in which each process executes longer than the allotted timeslice. Extending the concurrent program above to iterate 10000 times instead of 5 times produces:

```
#include <stdio.h>
int     sum;

main() {
        int i;

        sum = 0;
        fork();
        for (i=0 ; i <=10000 ; i++) {
                printf("The value of i is %d\n", i);
                fflush(stdout);
                sum += i;
        }
        printf("The total is %d\n", sum);
```

```
        exit (0);
}
```

When the resulting concurrent program is executed on the same system as before, it emits 20002 lines of output. However, instead of all output from the first process followed by all output from the second process, output from both processes is mixed together. In one run, the first process iterated 74 times before the second process executed at all. Then the second process iterated 63 times before the system switched back to the first process. On subsequent timeslices, the processes each received enough CPU service to iterate between 60 and 90 times. Of course, the two processes compete with all other processes executing on the computer, so the apparent rate of execution varies slightly depending on the mix of programs running.

3.5.4 Making Processes Diverge

So far, we have said that *fork* can be used to create a new process that executes exactly the same code as the original process. Creating a truly identical copy of a running program is neither interesting nor useful because it means that both copies perform exactly the same computation. In practice, the process created by *fork* is not absolutely identical to the original process: it differs in one small detail. *Fork* is a function that returns a value to its caller. When the function call returns, the value returned to the original process differs from the value returned to the newly created process. In the newly created process, the *fork* returns zero; in the original process, *fork* returns a small positive integer that identifies the newly created process. Technically, the value returned is called a *process identifier* or *process id*†.

Concurrent programs use the value returned by *fork* to decide how to proceed. In the most common case, the code contains a conditional statement that tests to see if the value returned is nonzero:

```
int      sum;

main() {
        int pid;

        sum = 0;
        pid = fork();
        if (pid != 0) {          /* original process       */

            printf("The original process prints this.\n");

        } else {                 /* newly created process */

            printf("The new process prints this.\n");

        }
        exit (0);
}
```

---

†Many programmers abbreviate *process id* as *pid*.

In the example code, variable *pid* records the value returned by the call to *fork*. Remember that each process has its own copy of all variables, and that *fork* will either return zero (in the newly created process) or nonzero (in the original process). Following the call to *fork*, the *if* statement checks variable *pid* to see whether the original or the newly created process is executing. The two processes each print an identifying message and exit. When the program runs, two messages appear: one from the original process and one from the newly created process. To summarize:

> *The value returned by* fork *differs in the original and newly created processes; concurrent programs use the difference to allow the new process to execute different code than the original process.*

3.6 Executing New Code

UNIX provides a mechanism that allows any process to execute an independent, separately-compiled program. The mechanism consists of a system call, *execve*†, that takes three arguments: the name of a file that contains an executable object program (i.e., a program that has been compiled), a pointer to a list of string arguments to pass to the program, and a pointer to a list of strings that comprise what UNIX calls the *environment*.

Execve replaces the code that the currently executing process runs with the code from the new program. The call does not affect any other processes. Thus, to create a new process that executes the object code from a file, a process must call *fork* and *execve*. For example, whenever the user types a command to one of the UNIX command interpreters, the command interpreter uses *fork* to create a new process for the command and *execve* to execute the code.

Execve is especially important for servers that handle diverse services. To keep the code for each service separate from the code for other services, a programmer can build, write, and compile each service as a separate program. When the server needs to handle a particular service, it can use *fork* and *execve* to create a process that runs one of the programs. Later chapters discuss the idea in more detail, and show examples of how servers use *execve*.

3.7 Context Switching And Protocol Software Design

Although the concurrent processing facilities that operating systems provide make programs more powerful and easier to understand, they do have computational cost. To make sure that all processes proceed concurrently, the operating system uses timeslicing, switching the CPU (or CPUs) among processes so fast that it appears to a human that the processes execute simultaneously.

When the operating system temporarily stops executing one process and switches to another, a *context switch* has occurred. Switching process context requires use of the CPU, and while the CPU is busy switching, none of the application processes receives

---

†Some versions of UNIX use the older name, *exec*.

any service. Thus, we view context switching as overhead needed to support concurrent processing.

To avoid unnecessary overhead, protocol software should be designed to minimize context switching. In particular, programmers must always be careful to ensure that the benefits of introducing concurrency into a server outweigh the cost of switching context among the concurrent processes. Later chapters discuss the use of concurrency in server software, present noncurrent designs as well as concurrent ones, and describe circumstances that justify the use of each.

3.8 Concurrency And Asynchronous I/O

In addition to providing support for concurrent use of the CPU, some operating systems allow a single application program to initiate and control concurrent input and output operations. In BSD UNIX, the *select* system call provides a fundamental operation around which programmers can build programs that manage concurrent I/O. In principle, *select* is easy to understand: it allows a program to ask the operating system which I/O devices are ready for use.

An an example, imagine an application program that reads characters from a TCP connection and writes them to the display screen. The program might also allow the user to type commands on the keyboard to control how the data is displayed. Because a user seldom (or never) types commands, the program cannot wait for input from the keyboard – it must continue to read and display text from the TCP connection. However, if the program attempts to read from the TCP connection and no data is available, the program will block. The user may type a command while the program is blocked waiting for input on the TCP connection. The problem is that the application cannot know whether input will arrive from the keyboard or the TCP connection first. To solve the dilemma, a UNIX program calls *select*. In doing so, it asks the operating system to let it know which source of input becomes available first. The call returns as soon as a source is ready, and the program reads from that source. For now, it is only important to understand the idea behind *select*; later chapters present the details and illustrate its use.

3.9 Summary

Concurrency is fundamental to TCP/IP applications because it allows users to access services without waiting for one another. Concurrency in clients arises easily because multiple users can execute client application software at the same time. Concurrency in servers is much more difficult to achieve because server software must be programmed explicitly to handle requests concurrently.

In UNIX, a program creates an additional process using the *fork* system call. We imagine that the call to *fork* causes the operating system to duplicate the program, causing two copies to execute instead of one. Technically, *fork* is a function call because it returns a value. The only difference between the original process and a process created by *fork* lies in the value that the call returns. In the newly created process, the call returns zero; in the original process, it returns the small, positive integer process id of the newly created process. Concurrent programs use the returned value to make new processes execute a different part of the program than the original process. A process can call *execve* at any time to have the process execute code from a separately-compiled program.

The *select* call permits a single process to manage concurrent I/O. A process uses *select* to find out which I/O device becomes ready first.

FOR FURTHER STUDY

Many texts on operating systems describe concurrent processing. Peterson and Silberschatz [1985] covers the general topic. Comer [1984] discusses the implementation of processes, message passing, and process coordination mechanisms. Leffler *et. al.* [1989] describes 4.3 BSD UNIX.

EXERCISES

3.1 Run the example programs on your local computer system. Approximately how many iterations of the output loop can a process make in a single timeslice?

3.2 Write a concurrent program that starts five processes. Arrange for each process to print a few lines of output and then halt.

3.3 Find out how systems other than UNIX create concurrent processes.

3.4 Read more about the UNIX *fork* function. What information does the newly created process share with the original process?

3.5 Write a program that uses *execve* to change the code a process executes.

3.6 Write a program that uses *select* to read from two terminals (serial lines), and displays the results on a screen with labels that identify the source.

3.7 Rewrite the program in the previous exercise so it does not use *select*. Which version is easier to understand? more efficient? easier to terminate cleanly?

4

Program Interface To Protocols

4.1 Introduction

Previous chapters describe the client-server model of interaction for communicating programs and discuss the relationship between concurrency and communication. This chapter considers general properties of the interface an application program uses to communicate in the client-server model. The following chapter illustrates these properties by giving details of a specific interface.

4.2 Loosely Specified Protocol Software Interface

In most implementations, TCP/IP protocol software resides in the computer's operating system. Thus, whenever an application program uses TCP/IP to communicate, it must interact with the operating system to request service. From a programmer's point of view, the routines the operating system supplies define the interface between the application and the protocol software, the *application interface*.

TCP/IP was designed to operate in a multi-vendor environment. To remain compatible with a wide variety of machines, TCP/IP designers carefully avoided choosing any vendor's internal data representation. In addition, the TCP/IP standards carefully avoid specifying the application interface in terms of features available only on a single vendor's operating system. Thus, the interface between TCP/IP and applications that use it has been *loosely specified*. In other words:

The TCP/IP standards do not specify the details of how application software interfaces with TCP/IP protocol software; they only suggest the required functionality, and allow system designers to choose the details.

4.2.1 Advantages And Disadvantages

Using a loose specification for the protocol interface has advantages and disadvantages. On the positive side, it provides flexibility and tolerance. It allows designers to implement TCP/IP using operating systems that range from the simplest systems available on personal computers to the sophisticated systems used on supercomputers. More important, it means designers can use either a procedural or message-passing interface style (whichever style the operating system supports).

On the negative side, a loose specification means that designers can make the interface details different for each operating system. As vendors add new interfaces that differ from existing interfaces, application programming becomes more difficult and applications become less portable across machines. Thus, while system designers favor a loose specification, application programmers desire a restricted specification because it means applications can be compiled for new machines without change.

In practice, only a few TCP/IP interfaces exist. The University of California at Berkeley defined an interface for the Berkeley UNIX operating system that has become known as the *socket interface*, or *sockets*. AT&T defined an interface for System V UNIX known by the acronym *TLI*†. A few other interfaces have been defined, but none has gained wide acceptance yet.

4.3 Interface Functionality

Although TCP/IP does not define an application program interface, the standards do suggest the functionality needed. An interface must support the following conceptual operations:

- Allocate local resources for communication
- Specify local and remote communication endpoints
- Initiate a connection (client side)
- Wait for an incoming connection (server side)
- Send or receive data
- Determine when data arrives
- Generate urgent data
- Handle incoming urgent data
- Terminate a connection gracefully
- Handle connection termination from the remote site
- Abort communication
- Handle error conditions or a connection abort
- Release local resources when communication finished

---

†TLI stands for *Transport Layer Interface*.

4.4 Conceptual Interface Specification

The TCP/IP standards do not leave implementors without any guidance. They specify a *conceptual interface* for TCP/IP that serves as an illustrative example. Because most operating systems use a procedural mechanism to transfer control from an application program into the system, the standard defines the conceptual interface as a set of procedures and functions. The standard suggests the parameters that each procedure or function requires as well as the semantics of the operation it performs. For example, the TCP standard discusses a *SEND* procedure, and lists the arguments an application needs to supply to send data on an existing TCP connection.

The point of defining conceptual operations is simple:

> *The conceptual interface defined by the TCP/IP standards does not specify data representations or programming details; it merely provides an example of one possible interface that an operating system can offer to application programs that use TCP/IP.*

Thus, the conceptual interface illustrates loosely how applications interact with TCP. Because it does not prescribe exact details, operating system designers are free to choose alternative procedure names or parameters as long as they offer equivalent functionality.

4.5 System Calls

Figure 4.1 illustrates the *system call* mechanism that most operating systems use to transfer control between an application program and the operating system procedures that supply services. To a programmer, system calls look and act like function calls.

As the figure shows, however, when an application invokes a system call, control passes from the application, through the system call interface, and into the operating system. The operating system directs the incoming call to an internal procedure that performs the requested operation. Once the internal procedure completes, control returns through the system call interface to the application, which then continues to execute. In essence, whenever an application program needs service from the operating system, the process executing the application climbs into the operating system, performs the necessary operation, and then climbs back out. As it passes through the system call interface, the process acquires privileges that allow it to read or modify data structures in the operating system. The operating system remains protected, however, because each system call branches to a procedure that the operating system designers have written.

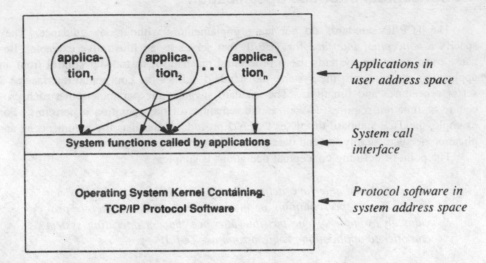

Figure 4.1 Applications interacting with TCP/IP protocol software through a
system call interface. System calls behave like other function
calls except that control transfers into the operating system.

4.6 Two Basic Approaches To Network Communication

Operating system designers must choose the exact set of procedures used to access
TCP/IP protocols when they install protocol software in an operating system. Implementations follow one of two approaches:

- The designer invents entirely new system calls that applications use to access TCP/IP.
- The designer attempts to use conventional I/O calls to access TCP/IP.

In the first approach, the designer makes a list of all conceptual operations, invents
names and parameters for each, and implements each as a system call. Because many
designers consider it unwise to create new system calls unless absolutely necessary, this
approach is seldom used. In the second approach, the designer uses conventional I/O
primitives but overloads them so they work with network protocols as well as conventional I/O devices. Of course, many designers choose a hybrid approach that uses basic
I/O functions whenever possible, but adds additional functions for those operations that
cannot be expressed conveniently.

4.7 The Basic I/O Functions Available In UNIX

To understand how conventional system calls can be extended to accommodate TCP/IP, consider the basic UNIX I/O functions. UNIX (and the many operating system variants derived from it) provides a basic set of six system functions used for input/output operations on devices or files. The table in Figure 4.2 lists the operations and their conventional meanings.

Operation	Meaning
open	Prepare a device or a file for input or output operations
close	Terminate use of a previously opened device or file
read	Obtain data from an input device or file, and place it in the application program's memory
write	Transmit data from the application program's memory to an output device or file
lseek	Move to a specific position in a file or device (this operation only applies to files or devices like disks)
ioctl†	Control a device or the software used to access it (e.g., specify the size of a buffer or change the character set mapping)

Figure 4.2 The basic I/O operations available in UNIX.

When an application program calls *open* to initiate input or output, the system returns a small integer called a *file descriptor* that the application uses in further I/O operations. The call to *open* takes three arguments: the name of a file or device to open, a set of bit flags that controls special cases such as whether to create the file if it does not exist, and an access mode that specifies read/write protections for newly created files. For example, the code segment:

```
int      desc;

desc = open("filename", O_RDWR, 0)
```

opens an existing file, *filename*, with a mode that allows both reading and writing. After obtaining the integer descriptor, *desc*, the application uses it in further I/O operations on the file. For example, the statement:

```
read(desc, buffer, 128);
```

reads *128* bytes of data from the file into array *buffer*.

---

†*ioctl* stands for Input Output ConTroL.

Finally, when an application finishes using a file, it calls *close* to deallocate the descriptor and release associated resources (e.g., internal buffers):

```
close(desc);
```

4.8 Using UNIX I/O With TCP/IP

When designers added TCP/IP protocols to UNIX, they extended the conventional UNIX I/O facilities. First, they extended the set of file descriptors and made it possible for applications to create descriptors used for network communication. Second, they extended the *read* and *write* system calls so they worked with the new network descriptors as well as with conventional file descriptors. Thus, when an application needs to send data across a TCP connection, it creates the appropriate descriptor, and then uses *write* to transfer data.

However, not all network communication fits easily into UNIX's *open-read-write-close* paradigm. An application must specify the local and remote protocol ports and the remote IP address it will use, whether it will use TCP or UDP, and whether it will initiate transfer or wait for an incoming connection (i.e., whether it wants to behave as a client or server). If it is a server, it must specify how many incoming connection requests the operating system should enqueue before rejecting them. Furthermore, if an application chooses to use UDP, it must be able to transfer UDP datagrams, not merely a stream of bytes. The designers of Berkeley UNIX added new system calls to UNIX to accommodate these special cases. The next chapter shows the details of the design.

4.9 Summary

Because TCP/IP is designed for a multi-vendor environment, the protocol standards loosely specify the interface that application programs use, allowing operating system designers freedom in choosing how to implement it. The standards do discuss a conceptual interface, but it is intended only as an illustrative example. Although the standards present the conceptual interface as a set of procedures, designers are free to choose different procedures or to use an entirely different style of interaction (e.g., message passing).

Operating systems often supply services through a mechanism known as the system call interface. When adding support for TCP/IP, designers attempt to minimize the number of new system calls by extending existing system calls where possible. However, because network communication requires operations that do not fit easily into conventional I/O procedures, most interfaces to TCP/IP require a few new system calls.

FOR FURTHER STUDY

Section 2 of the *UNIX Programmer's Manual* describes each of the socket calls in detail; section *4P* describes protocols and network device interfaces in more detail. [AT&T 1989] defines AT&T's TLI interface, an alternative to sockets used in System V UNIX.

EXERCISES

4.1 Examine a message-passing operating system. How would you extend the application program interface to accommodate network communication?

4.2 Compare the socket interface from Berkeley UNIX with AT&T's TLI. What are the major differences? How are the two similar? What reasons could designers have for choosing one design over the other?

4.3 Some hardware architectures limit the number of possible system calls to a small number (e.g., 64 or 128). How many system calls have already been assigned in your local operating system?

4.4 Think about the hardware limit on system calls discussed in the previous exercise. How can a system designer add additional system calls without changing the hardware?

4.5 Find out how recent versions of the Korn shell use */dev/tcp* to allow UNIX shell scripts to communicate with TCP. Write an example script.

5

The Socket Interface

5.1 Introduction

The previous chapter describes the interface between application programs and the TCP/IP software, and shows how most systems use the system call mechanism to transfer control to the TCP/IP software in an operating system. It also reviews the six basic I/O functions that UNIX supplies: *open*, *close*, *read*, *write*, *lseek*, and *ioctl*. This chapter describes the details of a specific set of UNIX system calls for TCP/IP and discusses how they use the UNIX I/O paradigm. It covers concepts in general, and gives the intended use of each call. Later chapters show how clients and servers use these calls, and provide examples that illustrate many of the details.

5.2 Berkeley Sockets

In the early 1980s, the Advanced Research Projects Agency (ARPA) funded a group at the University of California at Berkeley to transport TCP/IP software to the UNIX operating system and to make the resulting software available to other sites. As part of the project, the designers created an interface that applications use to communicate. They decided to use the existing UNIX system calls whenever possible and to add new system calls to support TCP/IP functions that did not fit easily into the existing set of functions. The result became known as the *socket interface†*, and the system is known as *Berkeley UNIX* or *BSD UNIX*. (TCP first appeared in release *4.1* of the Berkeley Software Distribution; the socket functions that this text describes are from release *4.3*.)

---

†The socket interface is sometimes called the *Berkeley socket interface*.

43

Because many computer vendors, especially workstation manufacturers like Sun Microsystems Incorporated, Tektronix Incorporated, and Digital Equipment Corporation, adopted Berkeley UNIX, the socket interface has become available on many machines. Consequently, the socket interface has become so widely accepted that it ranks as a *de facto* standard.

5.3 Specifying A Protocol Interface

When designers consider how to add functions to an operating system that provide application programs access to TCP/IP protocol software, they must choose names for the functions and must specify the parameters that each function accepts. In so doing, they decide the scope of services that the functions supply and the style in which applications use them. Designers must also consider whether to make the interface specific to the TCP/IP protocols or whether to plan for additional protocols. Thus, the designers must choose one of two broad approaches:

- Define functions specifically to support TCP/IP communication.
- Define functions that support network communication in general, and use parameters to make TCP/IP communication a special case.

Differences between the two approaches are easiest to understand by their impact on the names of system functions and the parameters that the functions require. For example, in the first approach, a designer might choose to have a system function named *maketcpconnection*, while in the second, a designer might choose to create a general function *makeconnection* and use a parameter to specify the TCP protocol.

Because the designers at Berkeley wanted to accommodate multiple sets of communication protocols, they used the second approach. In fact, throughout the design, they provided for generality far beyond TCP/IP. They allowed for multiple *families* of protocols, with all TCP/IP protocols represented as a single family (family *PF_INET*). They also decided to have applications specify operations using a *type of service* required instead of specifying the protocol name. Thus, instead of specifying that it wants a TCP connection, an application requests the *stream transfer* type of service using the Internet family of protocols. We can summarize:

> *The Berkeley socket interface provides generalized functions that support network communication using many possible protocols. Socket calls refer to all TCP/IP protocols as a single protocol family. The calls allow the programmer to specify the type of service required rather than the name of a specific protocol.*

The overall design of sockets and the generality they provide have been debated since their inception. Some computer scientists argue that generality is unnecessary and merely makes application programs difficult to read. Others argue that having programmers specify the type of service instead of the specific protocol makes it easier to program because it frees the programmer from understanding the details of each protocol family. Finally, some commercial vendors of TCP/IP software have argued in favor of alternative interfaces because sockets cannot be added to an operating system unless the customer has the source code, which usually requires a special license agreement and additional expense.

5.4 The Socket Abstraction

5.4.1 Socket Descriptors And File Descriptors

In UNIX, an application that needs to perform I/O calls the *open* function to create a file descriptor that it uses to access the file. As Figure 5.1 shows, the operating system implements file descriptors as an array of pointers to internal data structures. The system maintains a separate file descriptor table for each process. When a process opens a file, the system places a pointer to the internal data structures for that file in the process' file descriptor table and returns the table index to the caller. The application program only needs to remember the descriptor and to use it in subsequent calls that request operations on the file. The operating system uses the descriptor as an index into the process' descriptor table, and follows the pointer to the data structures that hold all information about the file.

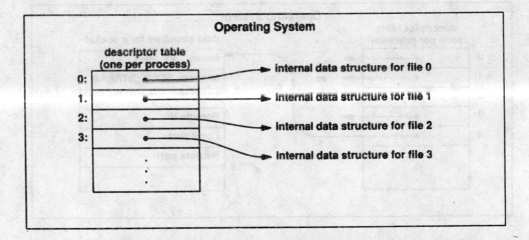

Figure 5.1 The per-process file descriptor table in UNIX. The operating system uses a process' descriptor table to store pointers to internal data structures for files that the process has opened. The process (application) uses the descriptor when referring to the file.

The socket interface adds a new abstraction for network communication, the *socket*. Like files, each active socket is identified by a small integer called its *socket descriptor*. UNIX allocates socket descriptors in the same descriptor table as file descriptors. Thus, an application cannot have both a file descriptor and a socket descriptor with the same value.

BSD UNIX contains a separate system function, *socket*, that applications call to create a socket; an application only uses *open* to create file descriptors.

The general idea underlying sockets is that a single system call is sufficient to create any socket. Once the socket has been created, an application must make additional system calls to specify the details of its exact use. The paradigm will become clear after we examine the data structures the system maintains.

5.4.2 System Data Structures For Sockets

The easiest way to understand the socket abstraction is to envision the data structures in the operating system. When an application calls *socket*, the operating system allocates a new data structure to hold the information needed for communication, and fills in a new descriptor table entry to contain a pointer to the data structure. For example, Figure 5.2 illustrates what happens to the descriptor table of Figure 5.1 after a call to *socket*†. In the example, arguments to the socket call have specified protocol family *PF_INET* and type of service *SOCK_STREAM*.

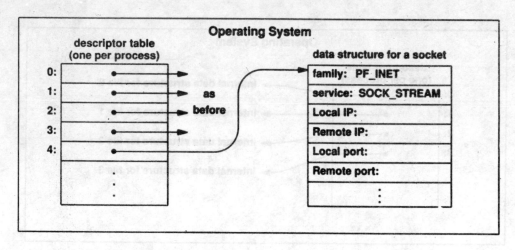

Figure 5.2 Conceptual operating system data structures after a call to *socket*. The system uses a single descriptor table for sockets and other I/O.

---

†UNIX data structures are more complex than shown in Figure 5.1; the diagram illustrates the concept, not the details.

Although the internal data structure for a socket contains many fields, the system leaves most of them unfilled when it creates the socket. As we will see, the application that created the socket must make additional system calls to fill in information in the socket data structure before the socket can be used.

5.4.3 Using Sockets

Once a socket has been created, it can be used to wait for an incoming connection or to initiate a connection. A socket used by a server to wait for an incoming connection is called a *passive socket*, while a socket used by a client to initiate a connection is called an *active socket*. The only difference between active and passive sockets lies in how applications use them; the sockets are created the same way initially.

5.5 Specifying An Endpoint Address

When a socket is created, it does not contain detailed information about how it will be used. In particular, the socket does not contain information about the protocol port numbers or IP addresses of either the local machine or the remote machine. Before an application uses a socket, it must specify one or both of these addresses.

TCP/IP protocols define a *communication endpoint* to consist of an IP address and a protocol port number. Other protocol families define their endpoint addresses in other ways. Because the socket abstraction accommodates multiple families of protocols, it does not specify how to define endpoint addresses nor does it define a particular protocol address format. Instead, it allows each protocol family to specify endpoints however it likes.

To allow protocol families the freedom to choose representations for their addresses the socket abstraction defines an *address family* for each type of address. A protocol family can use one or more address families to define address representations. The TCP/IP protocols all use a single address representation, with the address family denoted by the symbolic constant *AF_INET*.

In practice, much confusion arises between the TCP/IP protocol family, denoted *PF_INET*, and the address family it uses, denoted *AF_INET*. The chief problem is that both symbolic constants have the same numeric value (2), so programs that inadvertently use one in place of the other operate correctly. Even the Berkeley UNIX source code contains examples of misuse. Programmers should observe the distinction, however, because it helps clarify the meaning of variables and makes programs more portable.

5.6 A Generic Address Structure

Some software manipulates protocol addresses without knowing the details of how every protocol family defines its address representation. For example, it may be necessary to write a procedure that accepts an arbitrary protocol endpoint specification as an argument and chooses one of several possible actions depending on the address type. To accommodate such programs, the socket system defines a generalized format that all endpoint addresses use. The generalized format consists of a pair:

(address family, endpoint address in that family)

where the address family field contains a constant that denotes one of the preassigned address types, and the endpoint address field contains an endpoint address using the standard representation for the specified address type.

In practice, the socket software provides declarations of predefined C structures for address endpoints. Application programs use the predefined structures when they need to declare variables that store endpoint addresses or when they need to use an overlay to locate fields in a structure. The most general structure is known as a *sockaddr structure*. It contains a 2-byte address family identifier and a 14-byte array to hold an address†:

```
struct  sockaddr {              /* struct to hold an address */
        u_short  sa_family;     /* type of address           */
        char     sa_data[14];   /* value of address          */
};
```

Unfortunately, not all address families define endpoints that fit into the *sockaddr* structure. For example, BSD UNIX defines the *AF_UNIX* address family to specify what UNIX programmers think of as a named *pipe*. Endpoint addresses in the *AF_UNIX* family consist of UNIX path names that can be much longer than 14 bytes. Therefore, application programs should not use *sockaddr* in variable declarations because a variable declared to be of type *sockaddr* is not large enough to hold all possible endpoint addresses.

Confusion often arises in practice because the *sockaddr* structure accommodates addresses in the *AF_INET* family. Thus, TCP/IP software works correctly even if the programmer declares variables to be of type *sockaddr*. However, to keep programs portable and maintainable, TCP/IP code should not use the *sockaddr* structure in declarations. Instead, *sockaddr* should be used only as an overlay, and code should reference only the *sa_family* field in it.

Each protocol family that uses sockets defines the exact representation of its endpoint addresses, and the socket software provides corresponding structure declarations. Each TCP/IP endpoint address consists of a 2-byte field that identifies the address type (it must contain *AF_INET*), a 2-byte port number field, a 4-byte IP address field, and an 8-byte field that remains unused. Predefined structure *sockaddr_in* specifies the format:

---

†Berkeley plans to add a length field to the sockaddr structure to accommodate more complex protocol families that will be included in release 4.4 of their software. This text describes the structure most widely used in 1992.

```
struct  sockaddr_in {          /* struct to hold an address       */
    u_short sin_family;        /* type of address                 */
    u_short sin_port;          /* protocol port number            */
    u_long  sin_addr;          /* IP address (declared to be type */
                               /* 'struct in_addr' on some systems) */
    char    sin_zero[8];       /* unused (set to zero)            */
};
```

An application that uses TCP/IP protocols exclusively can use structure *sockaddr_in* exclusively; it never needs to use the *sockaddr* structure‡. Thus,

> *When representing a TCP/IP communication endpoint, an application program uses structure sockaddr_in, which contains both an IP address and a protocol port number. Programmers must be careful when writing programs that use a mixture of protocols because some non-TCP/IP endpoint addresses require a larger structure.*

5.7 Major System Calls Used With Sockets

Socket calls can be separated into two groups: primary calls that provide access to the underlying functionality and utility routines that help the programmer. This section describes the calls that provide the primary functionality that clients and servers need.

The details of socket system calls, their parameters, and their semantics can seem overwhelming. Much of the complexity arises because sockets have parameters that allow programs to use them in many ways. A socket can be used by a client or by a server, for stream transfer (TCP) or datagram (UDP) communication, with a specific remote endpoint address (usually needed by a client) or with an unspecified remote endpoint address (usually needed by a server).

To help understand sockets, we will begin by examining the primary socket calls and describing how a straightforward client and server use them to communicate with TCP. Later chapters each discuss one way to use sockets, and illustrate many of the details and subtleties not covered here.

5.7.1 The Socket Call

An application calls *socket* to create a new socket that can be used for network communication. The call returns a descriptor for the newly created socket. Arguments to the call specify the protocol family that the application will use (e.g., *PF_INET* for TCP/IP) and the protocol or type of service it needs (i.e., stream or datagram). For a socket that uses the Internet protocol family, the protocol or type of service argument determines whether the socket will use TCP or UDP.

---

‡Structure *sockaddr* is used to cast (i.e., change the type of) pointers or the results of system functions to make programs pass the type checking in *lint*.

5.7.2 The Connect Call

After creating a socket, a client calls *connect* to establish an active connection to a remote server. An argument to *connect* allows the client to specify the remote endpoint, which includes the remote machine's IP address and protocol port number. Once a connection has been made, a client can transfer data across it.

5.7.3 The Write Call

Both clients and servers use *write* to send data across a TCP connection. Clients usually use *write* to send requests, while servers use it to send replies. A call to *write* requires three arguments. The application passes the descriptor of a socket to which the data should be sent, the address of the data to be sent, and the length of the data. Usually, *write* copies outgoing data into buffers in the operating system kernel, and allows the application to continue execution while it transmits the data across the network. If the system buffers become full, the call to *write* may block temporarily until TCP can send data across the network and make space in the buffer for new data.

5.7.4 The Read Call

Both clients and servers use *read* to receive data from a TCP connection. Usually, after a connection has been established, the server uses *read* to receive a request that the client sends by calling *write*. After sending its request, the client uses *read* to receive a reply.

To read from a connection, an application calls *read* with three arguments. The first specifies the socket descriptor to use, the second specifies the address of a buffer, and the third specifies the length of the buffer. *Read* extracts data bytes that have arrived at that socket, and copies them to the user's buffer area. If no data has arrived, the call to *read* blocks until it does. If more data has arrived than fits into the buffer, *read* only extracts enough to fill the buffer. If less data has arrived than fits into the buffer, *read* extracts all the data and returns the number of bytes it found.

Clients and servers can also use *read* to receive messages from sockets that use UDP. As with the connection-oriented case, the caller supplies three arguments that identify a socket descriptor, the address of a buffer into which the data should be placed, and the size of the buffer. Each call to *read* extracts one incoming UDP message (i.e., one user datagram). If the buffer cannot hold the entire message, *read* fills the buffer and discards the remainder.

5.7.5 The Close Call

Once a client or server finishes using a socket, it calls *close* to deallocate it. If only one process is using the socket, *close* immediately terminates the connection and deallocates the socket. If several processes share a socket, *close* decrements a reference count and deallocates the socket when the reference count reaches zero.

5.7.6 The Bind Call

When a socket is created, it does not have any notion of endpoint addresses (neither the local nor remote addresses are assigned). An application calls *bind* to specify the local endpoint address for a socket. The call takes arguments that specify a socket descriptor and an endpoint address. For TCP/IP protocols, the endpoint address uses the *sockaddr_in* structure, which includes both an IP address and a protocol port number. Primarily, servers use *bind* to specify the well-known port at which they will await connections.

5.7.7 The Listen Call

When a socket is created, the socket is neither *active* (i.e., ready for use by a client) nor *passive* (i.e., ready for use by a server) until the application takes further action. Connection-oriented servers call *listen* to place a socket in *passive mode* and make it ready to accept incoming connections.

Most servers consist of an infinite loop that accepts the next incoming connection, handles it, and then returns to accept the next connection. Even if handling a given connection takes only a few milliseconds, it may happen that a new connection request arrives during the time the server is busy handling an existing request. To ensure that no connection request is lost, a server must pass *listen* an argument that tells the operating system to enqueue connection requests for a socket. Thus, one argument to the *listen* call specifies a socket to be placed in passive mode, while the other specifies the size of the queue to be used for that socket.

5.7.8 The Accept Call

After a server calls *socket* to create a socket, *bind* to specify a local endpoint address, and *listen* to place it in passive mode, the server calls *accept* to extract the next incoming connection request. An argument to *accept* specifies the socket from which a connection should be accepted.

Accept creates a new socket for each new connection request, and returns the descriptor of the new socket to its caller. The server uses the new socket only for the new connection; it uses the original socket to accept additional connection requests. Once it has accepted a connection, the server can transfer data on the new socket. After it finishes using the new socket, the server closes it.

5.7.9 Summary Of Socket Calls Used With TCP

The table in Figure 5.3 provides a brief summary of the system functions related to sockets.

Function Name	Meaning
socket	Create a descriptor for use in network communication
connect	Connect to a remote peer (client)
write	Send outgoing data across a connection
read	Acquire incoming data from a connection
close	Terminate communication and deallocate a descriptor
bind	Bind a local IP address and protocol port to a socket
listen	Place the socket in passive mode and set the number of incoming TCP connections the system will enqueue (server)
accept	Accept the next incoming connection (server)
recv	Receive the next incoming datagram
recvmsg	Receive the next incoming datagram (variation of recv)
recvfrom	Receive the next incoming datagram and record its source endpoint address
send	Send an outgoing datagram
sendmsg	Send an outgoing datagram (variation of send)
sendto	Send an outgoing datagram, usually to a prerecorded endpoint address
shutdown	Terminate a TCP connection in one or both directions
getpeername	After a connection arrives, obtain the remote machine's endpoint address from a socket
getsockopt	Obtain the current options for a socket
setsockopt	Change the options for a socket

Figure 5.3 A summary of the socket functions and the meaning of each.

5.8 Utility Routines For Integer Conversion

TCP/IP specifies a standard representation for binary integers used in protocol headers. The representation, known as *network byte order*, represents integers with the most significant byte first.

Although the protocol software hides most values used in headers from application programs, a programmer must be aware of the standard because some socket routines require arguments to be stored in network byte order. For example, the protocol port field of a *sockaddr_in* structure uses network byte order.

The socket routines include several functions that convert between network byte order and the local host's byte order. Programs should always call the conversion routines even if the local machine's byte order is the same as the network byte order because doing so makes the source code portable to an arbitrary architecture.

The conversion routines are divided into *short* and *long* sets to operate on 16-bit integers and 32-bit integers. Functions *htons* and *ntohs* convert a short integer from the host's native byte order to the network byte order, and vice versa. Similarly, *htonl* and *ntohl* convert long integers from the host's native byte order to network byte order and vice versa. To summarize:

> *Software that uses TCP/IP calls functions* htons, ntohs, htonl *and* ntohl *to convert binary integers between the host's native byte order and network standard byte order. Doing so makes the source code portable to any machine, regardless of its native byte order.*

5.9 Using Socket Calls In A Program

Figure 5.4 illustrates a sequence of calls made by a client and a server using TCP.

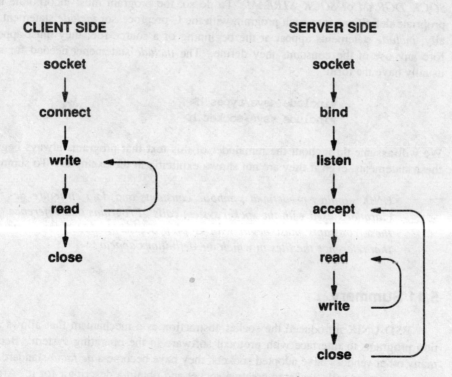

Figure 5.4 An example sequence of socket system calls made by a simple client and server using TCP. The server runs forever, waiting for new connections on the well-known port. It accepts each new connection, processes the request from the client, and then closes that connection.

The client creates a socket, calls *connect* to connect to the server, and then interacts using *write* to send requests and *read* to receive replies. When it finishes using the connection, it calls *close*. A server uses *bind* to specify the local (well-known) protocol port it will use, calls *listen* to set the length of the connection queue, and then enters a loop. Inside the loop, the server calls *accept* to wait until the next connection request arrives, uses *read* and *write* to interact with the client, and finally uses *close* to terminate the connection. The server then returns to the *accept* call, where it waits for the next connection.

5.10 Symbolic Constants For Socket Call Parameters

In addition to the system functions that implement sockets, BSD UNIX provides a set of predefined symbolic constants and data structure declarations that programs use to declare data and to specify arguments. For example, when specifying whether to use datagram service or stream service, an application program uses symbolic constants *SOCK_DGRAM* or *SOCK_STREAM*. To do so, the program must incorporate the appropriate definitions into each program with the C preprocessor *include* statement. Usually, *include* statements appear at the beginning of a source file; they must appear before any use of the constants they define. The *include* statements needed for sockets usually have the form:

```
#include <sys/types.h>
#include <sys/socket.h>
```

We will assume throughout the remainder of this text that programs always begin with these statements, even if they are not shown explicitly in the examples. To summarize:

> *UNIX supplies predefined symbolic constants and data structure declarations used with the socket system calls. Programs that reference these constants must begin with C preprocessor* include *statements that reference the files in which the definitions appear.*

5.11 Summary

BSD UNIX introduced the socket abstraction as a mechanism that allows application programs to interface with protocol software in the operating system. Because so many other vendors have adopted sockets, they have become a *de facto* standard.

A program calls *socket* to create a socket and obtain a descriptor for it. Arguments to the *socket* call specify the protocol family to be used and the type of service required. All TCP/IP protocols are part of the Internet family, specified with symbolic constant *PF_INET*. The system creates an internal data structure for the socket, fills in the protocol family, and uses the type of service argument to select a specific protocol (usually either UDP or TCP).

Additional system calls allow the application to specify a local endpoint address (*bind*), to force the socket into passive mode for use by a server (*listen*), or to force the socket into active mode for use by a client (*connect*). Servers can make further calls to obtain incoming connection requests (*accept*), and both clients and servers can send or receive information (*read* and *write*). Finally, both clients and servers can deallocate a socket once they have finished using it (*close*).

The socket structure allows each protocol family to define one or more address representations. All TCP/IP protocols use the Internet address family, *AF_INET*, which specifies that an endpoint address contains both an IP address and a protocol port number. When an application specifies a communication endpoint to a socket function, it uses predefined structure *sockaddr_in*. If a client specifies that it needs an arbitrary, unused local protocol port, the TCP/IP software will select one.

Before an application program written in C can use the predefined structures and symbolic constants associated with sockets, it must include several files that define them. In particular, we assume that all source programs begin with statements that include files *<sys/types.h>* and *<sys/socket.h>*.

FOR FURTHER STUDY

Leffler et. al. [1989] describes the Berkeley UNIX system in detail, and describes the internal data structures UNIX uses for sockets. Presotto and Ritchie [June 1990] describes an interface for TCP/IP protocols using the UNIX file system space. The *UNIX Programmer's Manual* contains specifications for the socket functions, including an exact description of arguments and return codes. The section entitled *The IPC Tutorial* is worth reading. Much of the information on socket calls can also be found in Appendix A.

EXERCISES

5.1 Look at the *include* file for sockets (usually */usr/include/sys/socket.h*). What socket types are allowed? Which socket types do not makes sense for TCP/IP protocols?

5.2 If your system has a clock with at least microsecond accuracy, measure how long it takes to execute each of the socket system calls. Why do some calls require orders of magnitude more time than others?

5.3 Read the BSD UNIX manual pages for *connect* carefully. What network traffic is generated if one calls *connect* on a socket of type *SOCK_DGRAM*?

5.4 Arrange to monitor your local network while an application executes *connect* for the first time on a socket of type *SOCK_STREAM*. How many packets do you see?

6

Algorithms And Issues In
Client Software Design

6.1 Introduction

Previous chapters consider the socket abstraction that applications use to interface with TCP/IP software, and review the system calls associated with it. This chapter discusses the basic algorithms underlying client software. It shows how applications become clients by initiating communication, how they use TCP or UDP protocols to contact a server, and how they use socket calls to interact with those protocols. The next chapter continues the discussion, and shows complete client programs that implement the ideas discussed here.

6.2 Learning Algorithms Instead Of Details

Because TCP/IP provides rich functionality that allows programs to communicate in a variety of ways, an application that uses TCP/IP must specify many details about the desired communication. For example, the application must specify whether it wishes to act as a client or a server, the endpoint address (or addresses) it will use, whether it will communicate with a connectionless or connection-oriented protocol, how it will enforce authorization and protection rules, and details such as the size of the buffers it will need.

So far, we have examined the set of operations available to an application without discussing how applications should use them. Unfortunately, knowing the low-level details of all possible system calls and their exact parameters does not provide programmers with an understanding of how to build well-designed, distributed programs. In fact, while a general understanding of the system calls used for network communication is important, few programmers remember all the details. Instead, they learn and remember the possible ways in which programs can interact across a network, and they understand the tradeoffs of each possible design. In essence, programmers know enough about the algorithms underlying distributed computing to make design decisions and to choose among alternative algorithms quickly. They then consult a programming manual to find the details needed to write a program that implements a particular algorithm on a particular system. The point is that if the programmer knows *what* a program should do, finding out *how* to do it is straightforward.

> *Although programmers need to understand the conceptual capabilities of the protocol interface, they should concentrate on learning about ways to structure communicating programs instead of memorizing the details of a particular interface.*

6.3 Client Architecture

Applications that act as clients are conceptually simpler than applications that act as servers for several reasons. First, most client software does not explicitly handle concurrent interactions with multiple servers. Second, most client software executes as a conventional application program. Unlike server software, client software does not usually require special privilege because it does not usually access privileged protocol ports. Third, most client software does not need to enforce protections. Instead, client programs can rely on the operating system to enforce protections automatically. In fact, designing and implementing client software is so straightforward that experienced application programmers can learn to write basic client applications quickly. The next sections discuss client software in general; later sections will focus on the differences between clients that use TCP and those that use UDP.

6.4 Identifying The Location Of A Server

Client software can use one of several methods to find a server's IP address and protocol port number. A client can:

- have the server's domain name or IP address specified as a constant when the program is compiled,
- require the user to identify the server when invoking the program,
- obtain information about the server from stable storage (e.g., from a file on a local disk), or
- use a separate protocol to find a server (e.g., multicast or broadcast a message to which all servers respond).

Specifying the server's address as a constant makes the client software faster and less dependent on a particular local computing environment. However, it also means that the client must be recompiled if the server is moved. More important, it means that the client cannot be used with an alternative server, even temporarily for testing. As a compromise, some clients fix a machine name instead of an IP address. Fixing the name instead of an address delays the binding until run-time. It allows a site to choose a generic name for the server and add an alias to the domain name system for that name. Using aliases permits a site manager to change the location of a server without changing client software. To move the server, the manager needs to change only the alias. For example, it is possible to add an alias for *mailhost* in the local domain and to arrange for all clients to look up the string "mailhost" instead of a specific machine. Because all clients reference the generic name instead of a specific machine, the system manager can change the location of the mail host without recompiling client software.

Storing the server's address in a file makes the client more flexible, but it means that the client program cannot execute unless the file is available. Thus, the client software cannot be transported to another machine easily.

While using a broadcast protocol to find servers works in a small, local environment, it does not scale well to large internets. Furthermore, use of a dynamic search mechanism introduces additional complexity for both clients and servers, and adds additional broadcast traffic to the network.

To avoid unnecessary complexity and dependence on the computing environment, most clients solve the problem of server specification in a simple manner: they require the user to supply an argument that identifies the server when invoking the client program. Building client software to accept the server address as an argument makes the client software general and eliminates dependency on the computing environment.

> *Allowing the user to specify a server address when invoking client software makes the client program more general and makes it possible to change server locations.*

An important point to note is that using an argument to specify the server's address results in the most flexibility. A program that accepts an address argument can be combined with other programs that extract the server address from disk, find the address using a remote nameserver, or search for it with a broadcast protocol. Thus,

> *Building client software that accepts a server address as an argument makes it easy to build extended versions of the software that use other ways to find the server address (e.g., read the address from a file on disk).*

Some services require an explicit server, while others can use any available server. For example, when a user invokes a remote login client, the user has a specific target machine in mind; logging into another machine usually does not make sense. However, if the user merely wants to find the current time of day, the user does not care which server responds. To accommodate such services, the designer can modify any of the server lookup methods discussed above so they supply a set of server names instead of a single name. Clients must also be changed so they try each server in a set until they find one that responds.

6.5 Parsing An Address Argument

Usually, a user can specify arguments on the command line when invoking a client program. In most systems, each argument passed to a client program consists of a character string. The client uses an argument's syntax to interpret its meaning. For example, most client software allows the user to supply either the domain name of the machine on which the server operates:

merlin.cs.purdue.edu

or an IP address in dotted decimal notation:

128.10.2.3

To determine whether the user has specified a name or an address, the client scans the argument to see if it contains alphabetic characters. If so, it must be a name. If it contains only digits and decimal points, the client assumes it to be a dotted decimal address and parses it accordingly.

Of course, client programs sometimes need additional information beyond the server's machine name or IP address. In particular, fully parameterized client software allows a user to specify a protocol port as well as a machine. It is possible to use an additional argument or to encode such information in a single string. For example, to specify the protocol port associated with the *smtp* service on machine with name *merlin.cs.purdue.edu*, the client could accept two arguments:

merlin.cs.purdue.edu smtp

or could combine both the machine name and protocol port into a single argument:

merlin.cs.purdue.edu:smtp

Although each client can choose the details of its argument syntax independently, having many clients with their own syntax can be confusing. From the user's point of view, consistency is always important. Thus, programmers are advised to follow whatever conventions their local system uses for client software. For example, because most existing UNIX software uses separate arguments to specify the server's machine and protocol port, new client software written for UNIX should use two arguments instead of one.

6.6 Looking Up A Domain Name

A client must specify the address of a server using structure *sockaddr_in*. Doing so means converting an address in dotted decimal notation (or a domain name in text form) into a 32-bit IP address represented in binary. Converting from dotted decimal notation to binary is trivial. Converting from a domain name, however, requires considerably more effort. The socket interface in BSD UNIX includes library routines, *inet_addr* and *gethostbyname*, that perform the conversions. *Inet_addr* takes an ASCII string that contains a dotted decimal address and returns the equivalent IP address in binary. *Gethostbyname* takes an ASCII string that contains the domain name for a machine. It returns the address of a *hostent* structure that contains, among other things, the host's IP address in binary. The *hostent* structure is declared in include file *netdb.h*:

```
struct      hostent {
char        *h_name;        /* official host name   */
char        **h_aliases;    /* other aliases        */
int         h_addrtype;     /* address type         */
int         h_length;       /* address length       */
char        **h_addr_list;  /* list of addresses    */
};
#define     h_addr  h_addr_list[0]
```

Fields that contain names and addresses must be lists because hosts that have multiple interfaces also have multiple names and addresses. For compatibility with earlier versions, the file also defines the identifier *h_addr* to refer to the first location in the host address list. Thus, a program can use *h_addr* as if it were a field of the structure.

Consider a simple example of name conversion. Suppose a client has been passed the domain name *merlin.cs.purdue.edu* in string form and needs to obtain the IP address. The client can call *gethostbyname* as in:

```
struct  hostent *hptr;
char    *examplenam = "merlin.cs.purdue.edu";

if ( hptr = gethostbyname( examplenam ) ) {
        /* IP address is now in  hptr->h_addr */
} else {
        /* error in name - handle it */
}
```

If the call is successful, *gethostbyname* returns a pointer to a valid *hostent* structure. If the name cannot be mapped into an IP address, the call returns zero. Thus, the client examines the value that *gethostbyname* returns to determine if an error occurred.

6.7 Looking Up A Well-Known Port By Name

Most client programs must look up the protocol port for the specific service they wish to invoke. For example, a client of an SMTP mail server needs to look up the well-known port assigned to SMTP. To do so, the client invokes library function *getservbyname*, which takes two arguments: a string that specifies the desired service and a string that specifies the protocol being used. It returns a pointer to a structure of type *servent*, also defined in include file *netdb.h*:

```
struct   servent {
         char *s_name;        /* official service name */
         char **s_aliases;    /* other aliases         */
         int   s_port;        /* port for this service */
         char *s_proto;       /* protocol to use       */
};
```

If a TCP client needs to look up the official protocol port number for SMTP, it calls *getservbyname*, as in the following example:

```
struct   servent *sptr;

if (sptr = getservbyname( "smtp", "tcp" )) {
        /* port number is now in sptr->s_port */
} else {
        /* error occurred - handle it */
}
```

6.8 Port Numbers And Network Byte Order

Function *getservbyname* returns the protocol port for the service in network byte order. Chapter 5 explains the concept of network byte order, and describes library routines that convert from network byte order to the byte order used on the local machine. It is sufficient to understand that *getservbyname* returns the port value in exactly the form needed for use in the *sockaddr_in* structure, but the representation may not agree with the local machine's usual representation. Thus, if a program prints out the value that *getservbyname* returns without converting to local byte order, it may appear to be incorrect.

6.9 Looking Up A Protocol By Name

The socket interface provides a mechanism that allows a client or server to map a protocol name to the integer constant assigned to that protocol. Library function *get-protobyname* performs the lookup. A call passes the protocol name in a string argument, and *getprotobyname* returns the address of a structure of type *protoent*. If *getprotobyname* cannot access the database or if the specified name does not exist, it returns zero. The database of protocol names allows a site to define aliases for each name. The *protoent* structure has a field for the official protocol name as well as a field that points to the list of aliases. The C include file *netdb.h* contains the structure declaration:

```
struct  protoent {
        char  *p_name;       /* official protocol name    */
        char **p_aliases;    /* list of aliases allowed   */
        int    p_proto;      /* official protocol number */
};
```

If a client needs to look up the official protocol number for UDP, it calls *getprotobyname*, as in the following example:

```
struct  protoent *pptr;

if (pptr = getprotobyname( "udp" )) {
        /* official protocol number is now in pptr->p_proto */
} else {
        /* error occurred - handle it */
}
```

6.10 The TCP Client Algorithm

Building client software is usually easier than building server software. Because TCP handles all reliability and flow control problems, building a client that uses TCP is the most straightforward of all network programming tasks. A TCP client follows Algorithm 6.1 to form a connection to a server and communicate with it. The sections following the algorithm discuss each of its steps in more detail.

Algorithm 6.1

1. Find the IP address and protocol port number of the server with which communication is desired.
2. Allocate a socket.
3. Specify that the connection needs an arbitrary, unused protocol port on the local machine, and allow TCP to choose one.
4. Connect the socket to the server.
5. Communicate with the server using the application-level protocol (this usually involves sending requests and awaiting replies).
6. Close the connection.

Algorithm 6.1 A connection-oriented client. The client application allocates a socket and connects it to a server. It then sends requests across the connection and receives replies back.

6.11 Allocating A Socket

Previous sections have already discussed the methods used to find the server's IP address and the *socket* function used to allocate a communication socket. Clients that use TCP must specify protocol family *PF_INET* and service *SOCK_STREAM*. A program begins with *include* statements that reference files which contain the definitions of symbolic constants used in the call and a declaration of the variable used to hold the socket descriptor. If more than one protocol in the family, specified by the first argument, offers the service requested by the second argument, the third argument to the *socket* call identifies a particular protocol. In the case of the Internet protocol family, only TCP offers the *SOCK_STREAM* service. Thus, the third argument is irrelevant; zero should be used.

```
#include <sys/types.h>
#include <sys/socket.h>

int    s;              /* socket descriptor */

s = socket(PF_INET, SOCK_STREAM, 0);
```

6.12 Choosing A Local Protocol Port Number

An application needs to specify remote and local endpoint addresses for a socket before it can be used in communication. A server operates at a well-known protocol port address, which all clients must know. However, a TCP client does not operate on a preassigned port. Instead, it must select a local protocol port to use for its endpoint address. In general, the client does not care which port it uses as long as: (1) the port does not conflict with the ports that other processes on the machine are already using and (2) the port has not been assigned to a well-known service.

Of course, when a client needs a local protocol port, it could choose an arbitrary port at random until it finds one that meets the criteria given above. However, the socket interface makes choosing a client port much simpler because it provides a way that the client can allow TCP to choose a local port automatically. The choice of a local port that meets the criteria listed above happens as a side-effect of the *connect* call.

6.13 A Fundamental Problem In Choosing A Local IP Address

When forming a connection endpoint, a client must choose a local IP address as well as a local protocol port number. For a host that attaches to one network, the choice of a local IP address is trivial. However, because gateways or multi-homed hosts have multiple IP addresses, making the choice can be difficult.

In general, the difficulty in choosing an IP address arises because the correct choice depends on routing and applications seldom have access to routing information. To understand why, imagine a computer with multiple network interfaces and, therefore, multiple IP addresses. Before an application can use TCP, it must have an endpoint address for the connection. When TCP communicates with a foreign destination, it encapsulates each TCP segment in an IP datagram and passes the datagram to the IP software. IP uses the remote destination address and its routing table to select a next-hop address and a network interface that it can use to reach the next hop.

Herein lies the problem: the IP source address in an outgoing datagram should match the IP address of the network interface over which IP routes the datagram. However, if an application chooses one of the machine's IP addresses at random, it might select an address that does not match that of the interface over which IP routes the traffic.

In practice, a client may appear to work even if the programmer chooses an incorrect address because packets may travel back to the client by a different route than they travel to the server. However, using an incorrect address violates the specification, makes network management difficult and confusing, and makes the program less reliable.

To solve the problem, the socket calls make it possible for an application to leave the local IP address field unfilled and to allow TCP/IP software to choose a local IP address automatically at the time the client connects to a server.

*Because choosing the correct local IP address requires the applica-
tion to interact with IP routing software, TCP client software usually
leaves the local endpoint address unfilled, and allows TCP/IP
software to select the correct local IP address and an unused local
protocol port number automatically.*

6.14 Connecting A TCP Socket To A Server

The *connect* system call allows a TCP client to initiate a connection. In terms of
the underlying protocol, *connect* forces the initial TCP 3-way handshake. The call to
connect does not return until a TCP connection has been established or TCP reaches a
timeout threshold and gives up. The call returns *0* if the connection attempt succeeds or
-1 if it fails. *Connect* takes three arguments:

```
retcode = connect(s, remaddr, remaddrlen)
```

where *s* is the descriptor for a socket, *remaddr* is the address of a structure of type
sockaddr_in that specifies the remote endpoint to which a connection is desired, and
remaddrlen is the length (in bytes) of the second argument.

Connect performs four tasks. First, it tests to ensure that the specified socket is
valid and that it has not already been connected. Second, it fills in the remote endpoint
address in the socket from the second argument. Third, it chooses a local endpoint address for the connection (IP address and protocol port number) if the socket does not
have one. Fourth, it initiates a TCP connection and returns a value to tell the caller
whether the connection succeeded.

6.15 Communicating With The Server Using TCP

Assuming the *connect* call succeeds in establishing a connection, the client can use
the connection to communicate with the server. Usually, the application protocol specifies a *request-response interaction* in which the client sends a sequence of *requests* and
waits for a *response* to each.

Usually, a client calls *write* to transmit each request and *read* to await a response.
For the simplest application protocols, the client sends only a single request and receives only a single response. More complicated application protocols require the client
to iterate, sending a request and waiting for a response before sending the next request.
The following code illustrates the request-response interaction by showing how a program writes a simple request over a TCP connection and reads a response:

```
/* Example code segment */

#define BLEN 120    /* buffer length to use */
char    *req = "request of some sort";
char    buf[BLEN];  /* buffer for answer    */
char    *bptr;      /* pointer to buffer    */
int     n;          /* number of bytes read */
int     buflen;     /* space left in buffer */

bptr = buf;
buflen = BLEN;

/* send request */

write(s, req, strlen(req));

/* read response (may come in many pieces) */

while ((n = read(s, bptr, buflen) > 0) {
        bptr += n;
        buflen -= n;
}
```

6.16 Reading A Response From A TCP Connection

The code in the previous example shows a client that sends a small message to a server and expects a small response (less than *120* bytes). The code contains a single call to *write*, but makes repeated calls to *read*. As long as the call to *read* returns data, the code decrements the count of space available in the buffer and moves the buffer pointer forward past the data read. Iteration is necessary on input, even if the application at the other end of the connection sends only a small amount of data because TCP is not a block-oriented protocol. Instead, TCP is stream-oriented: it guarantees to deliver the sequence of bytes that the sender writes, but it does not guarantee to deliver them in the same grouping as they were written. TCP may choose to break a block of data into pieces and transmit each piece in a separate segment (e.g., it may choose to divide the data such that each piece fills the maximum sized segment, or it may need to send a small piece if the receiver does not have sufficient buffer space for a large one). Alternatively, TCP may choose to accumulate many bytes in its output buffer before sending a segment (e.g., to fill a datagram). As a result, the receiving application may receive data in small chunks, even if the sending application passes it to TCP in a single call to *write*. Or, the receiving application may receive data in a large chunk, even if the sending application passes it to TCP in a series of calls to *write*. The idea is fundamental to programming with TCP:

Because TCP does not preserve record boundaries, any program that reads from a TCP connection must be prepared to accept data a few bytes at a time. This rule holds even if the sending application writes data in large blocks.

6.17 Closing A TCP Connection

6.17.1 The Need For Partial Close

When an application finishes using a connection completely, it can call *close* to terminate the connection gracefully and deallocate the socket. However, closing a connection is seldom simple because TCP allows two-way communication. Thus, closing a connection usually requires coordination among the client and server.

To understand the problem, consider a client and server that use the request-response interaction described above. The client software repeatedly issues requests to which the server responds. On one hand, the server cannot terminate the connection because it cannot know whether the client will send additional requests. On the other hand, while the client knows when it has no more requests to send, it may not know whether all data has arrived from the server. The latter is especially important for application protocols that transfer arbitrary amounts of data in response to a request (e.g., the response to a database query).

6.17.2 A Partial Close Operation

To resolve the connection shutdown problem, most implementations of the socket interface include an additional primitive that permits applications to shutdown a TCP connection in one direction. The *shutdown* system call takes two arguments, a socket descriptor and a direction specification, and shuts down the socket in the specified direction:

```
errcode = shutdown(s, direction);
```

The *direction* argument is an integer. If it contains *0*, no further input is allowed. If it contains *1*, no further output is allowed. Finally, if the value is *2*, the connection is shutdown in both directions.

The advantage of a partial close should now be clear: when a client finishes sending requests, it can use *shutdown* to specify that it has no further data to send without deallocating the socket. The underlying protocol reports the shutdown to the remote machine, where the server application program receives an *end-of-file* signal. Once the server detects an end-of-file, it knows no more requests will arrive. After sending its last response, the server can close the connection. To summarize:

*The partial close mechanism removes ambiguity for application proto-
cols that transmit arbitrary amounts of information in response to a
request. In such cases, the client issues a partial close after its last
request; the server then closes the connection after its last response.*

6.18 Programming A UDP Client

At first glance, programming a UDP client seems like an easy task. Algorithm 6.2
shows that the basic UDP client algorithm is similar to the client algorithm for TCP
(Algorithm 6.1).

Algorithm 6.2

1. Find the IP address and protocol port number of the server
   with which communication is desired.
2. Allocate a socket.
3. Specify that the communication needs an arbitrary, unused
   protocol port on the local machine, and allow UDP to choose
   one.
4. Specify the server to which messages must be sent.
5. Communicate with the server using the application-level protocol (this usually involves sending requests and awaiting replies).
6. Close the socket.

Algorithm 6.2 A connectionless client. The sending process creates a connected socket and uses it to send one or more requests iteratively. This algorithm ignores the issue of reliability.

The first few steps of the UDP client algorithm are much like the corresponding
steps of the TCP client algorithm. A UDP client obtains the server address and protocol
port number, and then allocates a socket for communication.

6.19 Connected And Unconnected UDP Sockets

Client applications can use UDP in one of two basic modes: *connected* and *unconnected*. In connected mode, the client uses the *connect* call to specify a remote endpoint
address (i.e., the server's IP address and protocol port number). Once it has specified
the remote endpoint, the client can send and receive messages much like a TCP client
does. In unconnected mode, the client does not connect the socket to a specific remote

endpoint. Instead, it specifies the remote destination each time it sends a message. The chief advantage of connected UDP sockets lies in their convenience for conventional client software that interacts with only one server at a time: the application only needs to specify the server once no matter how many datagrams it sends. The chief advantage of unconnected sockets lies in their flexibility; the client can wait to decide which server to contact until it has a request to send. Furthermore, the client can easily send each request to a different server.

> *UDP sockets can be* connected, *making it convenient to interact with a specific server, or they can be* unconnected, *making it necessary for the application to specify the server's address each time it sends a message.*

6.20 Using Connect With UDP

Although a client can connect a socket of type *SOCK_DGRAM*, the *connect* call does not initiate any packet exchange, nor does it test the validity of the remote endpoint address. Instead, it merely records the remote endpoint information in the socket data structure for later use. Thus, when applied to *SOCK_DGRAM* sockets, *connect* only stores an address. Even if the *connect* call succeeds, it does not mean that the remote endpoint address is valid or that the server is reachable.

6.21 Communicating With A Server Using UDP

After a UDP client calls *connect*, it can use *write* to send a message or *read* to receive a response. Unlike TCP, UDP provides message transfer. Each time the client calls *write*, UDP sends a single message to the server. The message contains all the data passed to *write*. Similarly, each call to *read* returns one complete message. Assuming the client has specified a sufficiently large buffer, the *read* call returns all the data from the next message. Therefore, a UDP client does not need to make repeated calls to *read* to obtain a single message.

6.22 Closing A Socket That Uses UDP

A UDP client calls *close* to close a socket and release the resources associated with it. Once a socket has been closed, the UDP software will reject further messages that arrive addressed to the protocol port that the socket had allocated. However, the machine on which the *close* occurs does not inform the remote endpoint that the socket is closed. Therefore, an application that uses connectionless transport must be designed so the remote side knows how long to retain a socket before closing it.

6.23 Partial Close For UDP

Shutdown can be used with a connected UDP socket to stop further transmission in a given direction. Unfortunately, unlike the partial close on a TCP connection, when applied to a UDP socket, *shutdown* does not send any messages to the other side. Instead, it merely marks the local socket as unwilling to transfer data in the direction(s) specified. Thus, if a client shuts down further output on its socket, the server will not receive any indication that the communication has ceased.

6.24 A Warning About UDP Unreliability

Our simplistic UDP client algorithm ignores a fundamental aspect of UDP: namely, that it provides unreliable datagram delivery. While a simplistic UDP client can work well on local networks that exhibit low loss, low delay, and no packet reordering, clients that follow our algorithm will not work across a complex internet. To work in an internet environment, a client must implement reliability through timeout and retransmission. It must also handle the problems of duplicate or out-of-order packets. Adding reliability can be difficult, and requires expertise in protocol design.

> *Client software that uses UDP must implement reliability with techniques like packet sequencing, acknowledgements, timeouts, and retransmission. Designing protocols that are correct, reliable, and efficient for an internet environment requires considerable expertise.*

6.25 Summary

Client programs are among the most simple network programs. The client must obtain the server's IP address and protocol port number before it can communicate; to increase flexibility, client programs often require the user to identify the server when invoking the client. The client then converts the server's address from dotted decimal notation into binary, or uses the domain name system to convert from a textual machine name into an IP address.

The TCP client algorithm is straightforward: a TCP client allocates a socket and connects it to a server. The client uses *write* to send requests to the server and *read* to receive replies. Once it finishes using a connection, either the client or server invokes *close* to terminate it.

Although a client must explicitly specify the endpoint address of the server with which it wishes to communicate, it can allow TCP/IP software to choose an unused protocol port number and to fill in the correct local IP address. Doing so avoids the problem that can arise on a gateway or multi-homed host when a client inadvertently chooses an IP address that differs from the IP address of the interface over which IP routes the traffic.

The client uses *connect* to specify a remote endpoint address for a socket. When used with TCP, *connect* initiates a 3-way handshake and ensures that communication is possible. When used with UDP, *connect* merely records the server's endpoint address for later use.

Connection shutdown can be difficult if neither the client nor the server know exactly when communication has ended. To solve the problem, the socket interface supplies the *shutdown* primitive that causes a partial close and lets the other side know that no more data will arrive. A client uses *shutdown* to close the path leading to the server; the server receives an end-of-file signal on the connection that indicates the client has finished. After the server finishes sending its last response, it uses *close* to terminate the connection.

FOR FURTHER STUDY

Many RFCs that define protocols also suggest algorithms or implementation techniques for client code. Stevens [1990] also reviews client implementation.

EXERCISES

6.1   Read about the *sendto* and *recvfrom* socket calls. Do they work with sockets using TCP or sockets using UDP?

6.2   When the domain name system resolves a machine name, it returns a set of one or more IP addresses. Why?

6.3   Build client software that uses *gethostbyname* to look up machine names at your site and print all information returned. Which official names, if any, surprised you? Do you tend to use official machine names or aliases? Describe the circumstances, if any, when aliases may not work correctly.

6.4   Measure the time required to look up a machine name (*gethostbyname*) and a service entry (*getservent*). Repeat the test for both valid and invalid names. Does a lookup for an invalid name take substantially longer than for a valid one? Explain any differences you observe.

6.5   Use a network monitor to watch the network traffic your computer generates when you look up an IP address name using *gethostbyname*. Run the experiment more than one time for each machine name you resolve. Explain the differences in network traffic between lookups.

6.6   To test whether your machine's local byte order is the same as the network byte order, write a program that uses *getservbyname* to look up the *ECHO* service for UDP and then prints the resulting protocol port value. If the local byte order and network byte order agree, the value will be 7.

6.7 Write a program that allocates a local protocol port, closes the socket, delays a few seconds, and allocates another local port. Run the program on an idle machine and on a busy timesharing system. Which port values did your program receive on each system? If they are not the same, explain.

6.8 Under what circumstances can a client program use *close* instead of *shutdown*?

6.9 Should a client use the same protocol port number each time it begins? Why or why not?

7

Example Client Software

7.1 Introduction

The previous chapter discusses the basic algorithms underlying client applications as well as specific techniques used to implement those algorithms. This chapter gives examples of complete, working client programs that illustrate the concepts in more detail. The examples use UDP as well as TCP. Most important, the chapter shows how a programmer can build a library of procedures that hide the details of socket calls and make it easier to construct client software that is portable and maintainable.

7.2 The Importance Of Small Examples

TCP/IP defines a myriad of services and the standard application protocols for accessing them. The services range in complexity from the trivial (e.g., a character generator service used only for testing protocol software) to the complex (e.g., a file transfer service that provides authentication and protection). The examples in this chapter and the next few chapters concentrate on implementations of client-server software for simple services. Later chapters review client-server applications for several of the complex services.

While it may seem that the protocols used in the examples do not offer interesting or useful services, studying them is important. First, because the services themselves require little code, the client and server software that implements them is easy to understand. More important, the small program size highlights fundamental algorithms and illustrates clearly how client and server programs use system functions. Second, studying simple services provides the reader with an intuition about the relative size of services and the number of services available. Having an intuitive understanding of small services will be especially important for the chapters that discuss the need for multiprotocol and multiservice designs.

7.3 Hiding Details

Most programmers understand the advantage of dividing large, complex programs into a set of procedures: a modular program becomes easier to understand, debug, and modify than an equivalent monolithic program. If programmers design procedures carefully, they can reuse them in other programs. Finally, choosing procedures carefully can also make a program easier to port to new computer systems.

Conceptually, procedures raise the level of the language that programmers use by hiding details. Programmers working with the low-level facilities available in most programming languages find programming tedious and prone to error. They also find themselves repeating basic segments of code in each program they write. Using procedures helps avoid repetition by providing higher-level operations. Once a particular algorithm has been encoded in a procedure, the programmer can use it in many programs without having to consider the implementation details again.

A careful use of procedures is especially important when building client and server programs. First, because network software includes declarations for items like endpoint addresses, building programs that use network services involves a myriad of tedious details not found in conventional programs. Using procedures to hide those details reduces the chance for error. Second, much of the code needed to allocate a socket, bind addresses, and form a network connection is repeated in each client; placing it in procedures allows programmers to reuse the code instead of replicating it. Third, because TCP/IP was designed to interconnect heterogeneous machines, network applications often operate on many different machine architectures. Programmers can use procedures to isolate operating system dependencies, making it easier to port code to a new machine.

7.4 An Example Procedure Library For Client Programs

To understand how procedures can make the programming task easier, consider the problem of building client programs. To establish connectivity with a server, a client must choose a protocol (like TCP or UDP), look up the server's machine name, look up and map the desired service into a protocol port number, allocate a socket, and connect it. Writing the code for each of these steps from scratch for each application wastes time. Furthermore, if programmers ever need to change any of the details, they have to modify each application. To minimize programming time, a programmer can write the code once, place it in a procedure, and simply call the procedure from each client program.

The first step of designing a procedure library is abstraction: a programmer must imagine high-level operations that would make writing programs simpler. For example, an application programmer might imagine two procedures that handle the work of allocating and connecting a socket:

$$socket = connectTCP(\textit{machine}, \textit{service});$$

and

$$socket = connectUDP(\textit{machine}, \textit{service});$$

It is important to understand that this is not a prescription for the "right" set of abstractions, it merely gives one possible way to form such a set. The important idea is:

> *The procedural abstraction allows programmers to define high-level operations, share code among applications, and reduce the chances of making mistakes with small details. Our example procedures used throughout this text merely illustrate one possible approach; programmers should feel free to choose their own abstractions.*

7.5 Implementation Of ConnectTCP

Because both of the proposed procedures, *connectTCP* and *connectUDP*, need to allocate a socket and fill in basic information, we chose to place all the low-level code in a third procedure, *connectsock*, and to implement both higher-level operations as simple calls. File *connectTCP.c* illustrates the concept:

```
/* connectTCP.c - connectTCP */


/*------------------------------------------------------------------------
 * connectTCP - connect to a specified TCP service on a specified host
 *------------------------------------------------------------------------
 */
int
connectTCP( host, service )
char    *host;          /* name of host to which connection is desired  */
char    *service;       /* service associated with the desired port     */
{
        return connectsock( host, service, "tcp");
}
```

7.6 Implementation Of ConnectUDP

File *connectUDP.c* shows how *connectsock* can be used to establish a connected
socket that uses UDP.

```
/* connectUDP.c - connectUDP */


/*------------------------------------------------------------------------
 * connectUDP - connect to a specified UDP service on a specified host
 *------------------------------------------------------------------------
 */
int
connectUDP( host, service )
char    *host;              /* name of host to which connection is desired */
char    *service;          /* service associated with the desired port     */
{
        return connectsock(host, service, "udp");
}
```

7.7 A Procedure That Forms Connections

Procedure *connectsock* contains all the code needed to allocate a socket and connect it. The caller specifies whether to create a UDP socket or a TCP socket.

```
/* connectsock.c - connectsock */

#include <sys/types.h>
#include <sys/socket.h>

#include <netinet/in.h>

#include <netdb.h>

#ifndef INADDR_NONE
#define INADDR_NONE     0xffffffff
#endif  /* INADDR_NONE */

extern int      errno;
extern char     *sys_errlist[];

u_short htons();
u_long  inet_addr();
```

```
/*------------------------------------------------------------------------
 * connectsock - allocate & connect a socket using TCP or UDP
 *------------------------------------------------------------------------
 */
int
connectsock( host, service, protocol )
char    *host;          /* name of host to which connection is desired  */
char    *service;       /* service associated with the desired port     */
char    *protocol;      /* name of protocol to use ("tcp" or "udp")     */
{
        struct hostent  *phe;   /* pointer to host information entry     */
        struct servent  *pse;   /* pointer to service information entry  */
        struct protoent *ppe;   /* pointer to protocol information entry */
        struct sockaddr_in sin; /* an Internet endpoint address          */
        int     s, type;        /* socket descriptor and socket type     */

        bzero((char *)&sin, sizeof(sin));
        sin.sin_family = AF_INET;

    /* Map service name to port number */
        if ( pse = getservbyname(service, protocol) )
                sin.sin_port = pse->s_port;
        else if ( (sin.sin_port = htons((u_short)atoi(service))) == 0 )
                errexit("can't get \"%s\" service entry\n", service);

    /* Map host name to IP address, allowing for dotted decimal */
        if ( phe = gethostbyname(host) )
                bcopy(phe->h_addr, (char *)&sin.sin_addr, phe->h_length);
        else if ( (sin.sin_addr.s_addr = inet_addr(host)) == INADDR_NONE )
                errexit("can't get \"%s\" host entry\n", host);

    /* Map protocol name to protocol number */
        if ( (ppe = getprotobyname(protocol)) == 0)
                errexit("can't get \"%s\" protocol entry\n", protocol);

    /* Use protocol to choose a socket type */
        if (strcmp(protocol, "udp") == 0)
                type = SOCK_DGRAM;
        else
                type = SOCK_STREAM;

    /* Allocate a socket */
```

```
        s = socket(PF_INET, type, ppe->p_proto);
        if (s < 0)
                errexit("can't create socket: %s\n", sys_errlist[errno]);

    /* Connect the socket */
        if (connect(s, (struct sockaddr *)&sin, sizeof(sin)) < 0)
                errexit("can't connect to %s.%s: %s\n", host, service,
                        sys_errlist[errno]);
        return s;
}
```

Although most steps are straightforward, a few details make the code seem complicated. First, the C language permits complex expressions. As a result, the expressions
in many of the condition statements contain a function call, an assignment, and a comparison, all on one line. For example, the call to *getprotobyname* appears in an expression that assigns the result to variable *ppe*, and then compares the result to *0*. If the
value returned is zero (i.e., an error occurred), the *if* statement executes a call to *errexit*.
Otherwise, the procedure continues execution. Second, the code uses two library procedures available in BSD UNIX, *bzero* and *bcopy*. Procedure *bzero* places bytes containing zero in a block of memory; it is the fastest way to zero a large structure or array.
Procedure *bcopy* copies a block of bytes from one memory location to another, regardless of the contents†. *Connectsock* uses *bzero* to fill the entire *sockaddr_in* structure
with zeroes, and then uses *bcopy* to copy the bytes of the server's IP address into field
sin_addr. Finally, *connectsock* calls procedure *connect* to connect the socket. If an error occurs, it calls *errexit*.

```
/* errexit.c - errexit */

#include <varargs.h>
#include <stdio.h>

/*------------------------------------------------------------------------
 * errexit - print an error message and exit
 *------------------------------------------------------------------------
 */
/*VARARGS1*/
int
errexit(format, va_alist)
char    *format;
va_dcl
{
        va_list args;
```

---

†Programs that copy IP addresses cannot use the UNIX library routine *strcpy* because IP addresses may
contain bytes with the value zero, which *strcpy* interprets as *end of string*.

```
        va_start(args);
        _doprnt(format, args, stderr);
        va_end(args);
        exit(1);
}
```

Errexit takes a variable number of arguments, which it passes on to *_doprnt* for output. *Errexit* follows the *printf* conventions for formatted output. The first argument specifies how the output should be formatted; remaining arguments specify values to be printed according to the given format.

7.8 Using The Example Library

Once programmers have selected abstractions and built a library of procedures, they can construct client applications. If the abstractions have been selected well, they make application programming simple and hide many of the details. To illustrate how our example library works, we will use it to construct example client applications. Because the clients each access one of the standard TCP/IP services, they also serve to illustrate several of the simpler application protocols.

7.9 The DAYTIME Service

The TCP/IP standards define an application protocol that allows a user to obtain the date and time of day in a format fit for human consumption. The service is officially named the *DAYTIME service*.

To access the DAYTIME service, the user invokes a client application. The client contacts a server to obtain the information, and then prints it. Although the standard does not specify the exact syntax, it suggests several possible formats. For example, DAYTIME could supply a date in the form:

                    weekday, month day, year time-timezone

like

                    Tuesday, February 22, 1982 17:37:43-PST

The standard specifies that DAYTIME is available for both TCP and UDP. In both cases, it operates at protocol port *13*.

The TCP version of DAYTIME uses the presence of a TCP connection to trigger output: as soon as a new connection arrives, the server forms a text string that contains the current date and time, sends the string, and then closes the connection. Thus, the client need not send any request at all. In fact, the standard specifies that the server must discard any data sent by the client.

The UDP version of DAYTIME requires the client to send a request. A request consists of an arbitrary UDP datagram. Whenever a server receives a datagram, it formats the current date and time, places the resulting string in an outgoing datagram, and sends it back to the client. Once it has sent a reply, the server discards the datagram that triggered the response.

7.10 Implementation Of A TCP Client For DAYTIME

File *TCPdaytime.c* contains code for a TCP client that accesses the DAYTIME service.

```
/* TCPdaytime.c - TCPdaytime, main */

#include <stdio.h>

extern int      errno;
extern char     *sys_errlist[];

#define LINELEN         128

/*------------------------------------------------------------------------
 * main - TCP client for DAYTIME service
 *------------------------------------------------------------------------
 */
int
main(argc, argv)
int     argc;
char    *argv[];
{
        char    *host = "localhost";    /* host to use if none supplied */
        char    *service = "daytime";   /* default service port        */

        switch (argc) {
        case 1:
                host = "localhost";
                break;
        case 3:
                service = argv[2];
                /* FALL THROUGH */
        case 2:
                host = argv[1];
                break;
        default:
```

```
                        fprintf(stderr, "usage: TCPdaytime [host [port]]\n");
                        exit(1);
                }
                TCPdaytime(host, service);
                exit(0);
        }


/*------------------------------------------------------------------
 * TCPdaytime - invoke Daytime on specified host and print results
 *------------------------------------------------------------------
 */
TCPdaytime(host, service)
char    *host;
char    *service;
{
        char    buf[LINELEN+1];              /* buffer for one line of text */
        int     s, n;                        /* socket, read count          */

        s = connectTCP(host, service);

        while( (n = read(s, buf, LINELEN)) > 0) {
                buf[n] = '\0';               /* insure null-terminated      */
                (void) fputs( buf, stdout );
        }
}
```

Notice how using *connectTCP* simplifies the code. Once a connection has been established, DAYTIME merely reads input from the connection and prints it, iterating until it detects an end of file condition.

7.11 Reading From A TCP Connection

The DAYTIME example illustrates an important idea: TCP offers a stream service that does not guarantee to preserve record boundaries. In practice, the stream paradigm means that TCP decouples the sending and receiving applications. For example, suppose the sending application transfers *64* bytes of data in a single call to *write*, followed by *64* bytes in a second call. The receiving application may receive all *128* bytes in a single call to *read*, or it may receive *10* bytes in the first call, *100* bytes in the second call, and *18* bytes in a third call. The number of bytes returned in a call depends on the size of datagrams in the underlying internet, the buffer space available, and the delays encountered when crossing the internet.

Because the TCP stream service does not guarantee to deliver data in the same blocks that it was written, an application receiving data from a TCP connection cannot depend on all data being delivered in a single transfer; it must repeatedly call read *until all data has been obtained.*

7.12 The TIME Service

TCP/IP defines a service that allows one machine to obtain the current date and time of day from another. Officially named *TIME*, the service is quite simple: a client program executing on one machine sends a request to a server executing on another. Whenever the server receives a request, it obtains the current date and time of day from the local operating system, encodes the information in a standard format, and sends it back to the client in a response.

To avoid the problems that occur if the client and server reside in different timezones, the TIME protocol specifies that all time and date information must be represented in *Universal Coordinated Time†*, abbreviated *UCT* or *UT*. Thus, a server converts from its local time to universal time before sending a reply, and a client converts from universal time to its local time when the reply arrives.

Unlike the DAYTIME service, which is intended for human users, the TIME service is intended for use by programs that store or manipulate times. The TIME protocol always specifies time in a 32-bit integer, representing the number of seconds since an *epoch date*. The TIME protocol uses midnight, January 1, 1900, as its epoch.

Using an integer representation allows computers to transfer time from one machine to another quickly, without waiting to convert it into a text string and back into an integer. Thus, the TIME service makes it possible for one computer to set its time-of-day clock from the clock on another system.

7.13 Accessing The TIME Service

Clients can use either TCP or UDP to access the TIME service at protocol port *37* (technically, the standards define two separate services, one for UDP and one for TCP). A TIME server built for TCP uses the presence of a connection to trigger output, much like the DAYTIME service discussed above. The client forms a TCP connection to a TIME server and waits to read output. When the server detects a new connection, it sends the current time encoded as an integer, and then closes the connection. The client does not send any data because the server never reads from the connection.

Clients can also access a TIME service with UDP. To do so, a client sends a request, which consists of a single datagram. The server does not process the incoming

---

†Universal Coordinated Time was formerly known as *Greenwich Mean Time*.

datagram, except to extract the sender's address and protocol port number for use in a reply. The server encodes the current time as an integer, places it in a datagram, and sends the datagram back to the client.

7.14 Accurate Times And Network Delays

Although the TIME service accommodates differences in timezones, it does not handle the problem of network latency. If it takes 3 seconds for a message to travel from the server to the client, the client will receive a time that is 3 seconds behind that of the server. Other, more complex protocols handle clock synchronization. However, the TIME service remains popular for three reasons. First, TIME is extremely simple compared to clock synchronization protocols. Second, most clients contact servers on a local area network, where network latency accounts for only a few milliseconds. Third, except when using programs that use timestamps to control processing, humans do not care if the clocks on their computers differ by small amounts.

In cases where more accuracy is required, it is possible to improve TIME or use an alternative protocol. The easiest way to improve the accuracy of TIME is to compute an approximation of network delay between the server and client, and then add that approximation to the time value that the server reports. For example, one way to approximate latency requires the client to compute the time that elapses during the round trip from client to server and back. The client assumes equal delay in both directions, and obtains an approximation for the trip back by dividing the round trip time in half. It adds the delay approximation to the time of day that the server returns.

7.15 A UDP Client For The TIME Service

File *UDPtime.c* contains code that implements a UDP client for the TIME service.

```
/* UDPtime.c - main */

#include <sys/types.h>

#include <stdio.h>

#define BUFSIZE 64

#define UNIXEPOCH      2208988800      /* UNIX epoch, in UCT secs      */
#define MSG            "what time is it?\n"

extern int     errno;
extern char    *sys_errlist[];

char    *ctime();
u_long  ntohl();

/*------------------------------------------------------------------------
 * main - UDP client for TIME service that prints the resulting time
 *------------------------------------------------------------------------
 */
int
main(argc, argv)
int     argc;
char    *argv[];
{
        char    *host = "localhost";    /* host to use if none supplied */
        char    *service = "time";      /* default service name         */
        time_t  now;                    /* 32-bit integer to hold time  */
        int     s, n;                   /* socket descriptor, read count*/

        switch (argc) {
        case 1:
                host = "localhost";
                break;
        case 3:
                service = argv[2];
                /* FALL THROUGH */
        case 2:
                host = argv[1];
                break;
        default:
                fprintf(stderr, "usage: UDPtime [host [port]]\n");
                exit(1);
        }
```

```
    s = connectUDP(host, service);

    (void) write(s, MSG, strlen(MSG));

    /* Read the time */

    n = read(s, (char *)&now, sizeof(now));
    if (n < 0)
            errexit("read failed: %s\n", sys_errlist[errno]);
    now = ntohl((u_long)now);         /* put in host byte order    */
    now -= UNIXEPOCH;                 /* convert UCT to UNIX epoch  */
    printf("%s", ctime(&now));
    exit(0);
}
```

The example code contacts the TIME service by sending a datagram. It then calls *read* to wait for a reply and extract the time value from it. Once *UDPtime* has obtained the time, it must convert the time into a form suitable for the local machine. First, it uses *ntohl* to convert the 32-bit value (a *long* in C) from network standard byte order into the local host byte order. Second, *UDPtime* must convert to the machine's local representation. The example code is designed for UNIX. Like the Internet protocols, UNIX represents time in a 32-bit integer and interprets the integer to be a count of seconds. Unlike the Internet, however, UNIX assumes an epoch date of January 1, 1970. Thus, to convert from the TIME protocol epoch to the UNIX epoch, the client must subtract the number of seconds between January 1, 1900 and January 1, 1970. The example code uses the conversion value *2208988800*. Once the time has been converted to a representation compatible with that of the local machine, *UDPtime* can invoke the library procedure *ctime*, which converts the value into a human readable form for output.

7.16 The ECHO Service

TCP/IP standards specify an *ECHO service* for both UDP and TCP protocols. At first glance, ECHO services seem almost useless because an ECHO server merely returns all the data it receives from a client. Despite their simplicity, ECHO services are important tools that network managers use to test reachability, debug protocol software, and identify routing problems.

The TCP ECHO service specifies that a server must accept incoming connection requests, read data from the connection, and write the data back over the connection until the client terminates the transfer. Meanwhile, the client sends input and then reads it back.

7.17 A TCP Client For The ECHO Service

File *TCPecho.c* contains a simple client for the ECHO service.

```
/* TCPecho.c - main, TCPecho */

#include <stdio.h>

extern int       errno;
extern char ,    *sys_errlist[];

#define LINELEN        128

/*------------------------------------------------------------
 * main - TCP client for ECHO service
 *------------------------------------------------------------
 */
int
main(argc, argv)
int     argc;
char    *argv[];
{
        char    *host = "localhost";   /* host to use if none supplied */
        char    *service = "echo";     /* default service name         */

        switch (argc) {
        case 1:
                host = "localhost";
                break;
        case 3:
                service = argv[2];
                /* FALL THROUGH */
        case 2:
                host = argv[1];
                break;
        default:
                fprintf(stderr, "usage: TCPecho [host [port]]\n");
                exit(1);
        }
        TCPecho(host, service);
        exit(0);
}
```

```
/*-------------------------------------------------------------------
 * TCPecho - send input to ECHO service on specified host and print reply
 *-------------------------------------------------------------------
 */
int
TCPecho(host, service)
char    *host;
char    *service;
{
        char    buf[LINELEN+1];        /* buffer for one line of text  */
        int     s, n;                  /* socket descriptor, read count*/
        int     outchars, inchars;     /* characters sent and received */

        s = connectTCP(host, service);

        while (fgets(buf, sizeof(buf), stdin)) {
                buf[LINELEN] = '\0';   /* insure line null-terminated  */
                outchars = strlen(buf);
                (void) write(s, buf, outchars);

                /* read it back */
                for (inchars = 0; inchars < outchars; inchars+=n ) {
                        n = read(s, &buf[inchars], outchars - inchars);
                        if (n < 0)
                                errexit("socket read failed: %s\n",
                                        sys_errlist[errno]);
                }
                fputs(buf, stdout);
        }
}
```

After opening a connection, *TCPecho* enters a loop that repeatedly reads one line of input, sends the line across the TCP connection to the ECHO server, reads it back again, and prints it. After all input lines have been sent to the server, received back, and printed successfully, the client exits.

7.18 A UDP Client For The ECHO Service

File *UDPecho.c* shows how a client uses UDP to access an ECHO service.

```c
/* UDPecho.c - main, UDPecho */

#include <stdio.h>

extern int      errno;
extern char     *sys_errlist[];

#define LINELEN         128

/*------------------------------------------------------------------------
 * main - UDP client for ECHO service
 *------------------------------------------------------------------------
 */
int
main(argc, argv)
int     argc;
char    *argv[];
{
        char    *host = "localhost";
        char    *service = "echo";

        switch (argc) {
        case 1:
                host = "localhost";
                break;
        case 3:
                service = argv[2];
                /* FALL THROUGH */
        case 2:
                host = argv[1];
                break;
        default:
                fprintf(stderr, "usage: UDPecho [host [port]]\n");
                exit(1);
        }
        UDPecho(host, service);
        exit(0);
}

/*------------------------------------------------------------------------
 * UDPecho - send input to ECHO service on specified host and print reply
 *------------------------------------------------------------------------
 */
int
```

```
UDPecho(host, service)
char    *host;
char    *service;
{
        char    buf[LINELEN+1];          /* buffer for one line of text  */
        int     s, nchars;              /* socket descriptor, read count*/

        s = connectUDP(host, service);

        while (fgets(buf, sizeof(buf), stdin)) {
                buf[LINELEN] = '\0';     /* insure null-terminated */
                nchars = strlen(buf);
                (void) write(s, buf, nchars);

                if (read(s, buf, nchars) < 0)
                        errexit("socket read failed: %s\n",
                                        sys_errlist[errno]);
                fputs(buf, stdout);
        }
}
```

The example UDP ECHO client follows the same general algorithm as the TCP version. It repeatedly reads a line of input, sends it to the server, reads it back from the server, and prints it. The biggest difference between the UDP and TCP versions lies in how they treat data received from the server. Because UDP is datagram-oriented, the client treats an input line as a unit and places each in a single datagram. Similarly, the ECHO server receives and returns complete datagrams. Thus, while the TCP client reads incoming data as a stream of bytes, the UDP client either receives an entire line back from the server or receives none of it; each call to *read* returns the entire line unless an error has occurred.

7.19 Summary

Programmers use the procedural abstraction to keep programs flexible and easy to maintain, to hide details, and to make it easy to port programs to new computers. Once a programmer writes and debugs a procedure, he or she places it in a library where it can be reused in many programs easily. A library of procedures is especially important for programs that use TCP/IP because they often operate on multiple computers.

This chapter presents an example library of procedures used to create client software. The primary procedures in our library, *connectTCP* and *connectUDP*, make it easy to allocate and connect a socket to a specified service on a specified host.

The chapter presents examples of a few client applications. Each example contains the code for a complete C program that implements a standard application protocol: DAYTIME (used to obtain and print the time of day in a human-readable format), TIME (used to obtain the time in 32-bit integer form), and ECHO (used to test network connectivity). The example code shows how a library of procedures hides many of the details associated with socket allocation and makes it easier to write client software.

FOR FURTHER STUDY

The application protocols described here are each part of the TCP/IP standard. Postel [RFC 867] contains the standard for the DAYTIME protocol, Postel and Harrenstien [RFC 868] contains the standard for the TIME protocol, and Postel [RFC 862] contains the standard for the ECHO protocol. Mills [RFC 1119] specifies the Network Time Protocol, NTP.

EXERCISES

7.1 Use program *TCPdaytime* to contact servers on several machines. How does each format the time and date?

7.2 The Internet standard represents time in a 32-bit integer that gives seconds past the epoch, midnight January 1, 1900. UNIX systems also represent time in a 32-bit integer that measures seconds, but UNIX uses January 1, 1970 as its epoch. What is the maximum date and time that can be represented in each system?

7.3 Improve the TIME client so it checks the date received to verify that it is greater than January 1, 1992 (or some other date you know to be in the recent past).

7.4 Modify the TIME client so it computes E, the time that elapses between when it sends the request and when it receives a response. Add one-half E to the time the server sends.

7.5 Build a TIME client that contacts two TIME servers, and reports the differences between the times they return.

7.6 Explain how deadlock can occur if a programmer changes the line size in the TCP ECHO client to be arbitrarily large (e.g., 20,000).

7.7 The ECHO clients presented in this chapter do not verify that the text they receive back from the server matches the text they sent. Modify them to verify the data received.

7.8 The ECHO clients presented in this chapter do not count the characters sent or received. What happens if a server incorrectly sends one additional character back that the client did not send?

7.9 The example ECHO clients in this chapter do not use *shutdown*. Explain how the use of *shutdown* can improve client performance.

7.10 Rewrite the code in *UDPecho.c* so it tests reachability by generating a message, sending it, and timing the reply. If the reply does not arrive in 5 seconds, declare the destination host to be unreachable. Be sure to retransmit the request at least once in case the internet happens to lose a datagram.

7.11 Rewrite the code in *UDPecho.c* so it creates and sends a new message once per second, checks replies to be sure they match transmissions, and reports only the round trip time for each reply without printing the contents of the message itself.

7.12 Explain what happens to *UDPecho* when the underlying network: duplicates a request sent from the client to the server, duplicates a response sent from the server to the client, loses a request sent from the client to the server, or loses a response sent from the server to the client. Modify the code to handle each of these problems.

8

Algorithms And Issues In Server Software Design

8.1 Introduction

This chapter considers the design of server software. It discusses fundamental issues, including: connectionless vs. connection-oriented server access, stateless vs. stateful applications, and iterative vs. concurrent server implementations. It describes the advantages of each approach, and gives examples of situations in which the approach is valid. Later chapters illustrate the concepts by showing complete server programs that each implement one of the basic design ideas.

8.2 The Conceptual Server Algorithm

Conceptually, each server follows a simple algorithm: it creates a socket and binds the socket to the well-known port at which it desires to receive requests. It then enters an infinite loop in which it accepts the next request that arrives from a client, processes the request, formulates a reply, and sends the reply back to the client.

Unfortunately, this unsophisticated, conceptual algorithm suffices only for the most trivial services. To understand why, consider a service like file transfer that requires substantial time to handle each request. Suppose the first client to contact the server requests the transfer of a giant file (e.g., 200 megabytes), while the second client to contact the server requests the transfer of a trivially small file (e.g., 20 bytes). If the server waits until the first transfer completes before starting the second transfer, the second client may wait an unreasonable amount of time for a small transfer. The second user would expect a small request to be handled immediately. Most practical servers do handle small requests quickly, because they handle more than one request at a time.

8.3 Concurrent Vs. Iterative Servers

We use the term *iterative server* to describe a server implementation that processes one request at a time, and the term *concurrent server* to describe a server that handles multiple requests at one time. Although most concurrent servers achieve apparent concurrency, we will see that a concurrent implementation may not be required – it depends on the application protocol. In particular, if a server performs small amounts of processing relative to the amount of I/O it performs, it may be possible to implement the server as a single process that uses asynchronous I/O to allow simultaneous use of multiple communication channels. From a client's perspective, the server appears to communicate with multiple clients concurrently. The point is:

> *The term* concurrent server *refers to whether the server handles multiple requests concurrently, not to whether the underlying implementation uses multiple concurrent processes.*

In general, concurrent servers are more difficult to design and build, and the resulting code is more complex and difficult to modify. Most programmers choose concurrent server implementations, however, because iterative servers cause unnecessary delays in distributed applications and can become a performance bottleneck that affects many client applications. We can summarize:

> *Iterative server implementations, which are easier to build and understand, may result in poor performance because they make clients wait for service. In contrast, concurrent server implementations, which are more difficult to design and build, yield better performance.*

8.4 Connection-Oriented Vs. Connectionless Access

The issue of connectivity centers around the transport protocol that a client uses to access a server. In the TCP/IP protocol suite, TCP provides a *connection-oriented* transport service, while UDP provides a *connectionless* service. Thus, servers that use TCP are, by definition, *connection-oriented servers*, while those that use UDP are *connectionless servers†*.

Although we apply the terminology to servers, it would be more accurate if we restricted it to application protocols, because the choice between connectionless and connection-oriented implementations depends on the application protocol. An application protocol designed to use a connection-oriented transport service may perform incorrectly or inefficiently when using a connectionless transport protocol. To summarize:

---

†The socket interface does permit an application to *connect* a UDP socket to a remote endpoint, but practical servers do not do so, and UDP is not a connection-oriented protocol.

When considering the advantages and disadvantages of various server implementation strategies, the designer must remember that the application protocol used may restrict some or all of the choices.

8.5 Connection-Oriented Servers

The chief advantage of a connection-oriented approach lies in ease of programming. In particular, because the transport protocol handles packet loss and out-of-order delivery problems automatically, the server need not worry about them. Instead, a connection-oriented server manages and uses *connections*. It accepts an incoming connection from a client, and then sends all communication across the connection. It receives requests from the client and sends replies. Finally, the server closes the connection after it completes the interaction.

While a connection remains open, TCP provides all the needed reliability. It retransmits lost data, verifies that data arrives without transmission errors, and reorders incoming packets as necessary. When a client sends a request, TCP either delivers it reliably or informs the client that the connection has been broken. Similarly, the server can depend on TCP to deliver responses or inform it that the connection has broken.

Connection-oriented servers also have disadvantages. Connection-oriented designs require a separate socket for each connection, while connectionless designs permit communication with multiple hosts from a single socket. Socket allocation and the resulting connection management can be especially important inside an operating system that must run forever without exhausting resources. For trivial applications, the overhead of the 3-way handshake used to establish and terminate a connection makes TCP expensive compared to UDP. The most important disadvantage arises because TCP does not send any packets across an idle connection. Suppose a client establishes a connection to a server, exchanges a request and a response, and then crashes. Because the client has crashed, it will never send further requests. However, because the server has already responded to all requests received so far, it will never send more data to the client. The problem with such a situation lies in resource use: the server has data structures (including buffer space) allocated for the connection and these resources cannot be reclaimed. Remember that a server must be designed to run forever. If clients crash repeatedly, the server will run out of resources (e.g., sockets, buffer space, TCP connections) and cease to operate.

8.6 Connectionless Servers

Connectionless servers also have advantages and disadvantages. While connectionless servers do not suffer from the problem of resource depletion, they cannot depend on the underlying transport for reliable delivery. One side or the other must take responsibility for reliable delivery. Usually, clients take responsibility for retransmitting requests if no response arrives. If the server needs to divide its response into multiple data packets, it may need to implement a retransmission mechanism as well.

Achieving reliability through timeout and retransmission can be extremely difficult. In fact, it requires considerable expertise in protocol design. Because TCP/IP operates in an internet environment where end-to-end delays change quickly, using fixed values for timeout does not work. Many programmers learn this lesson the hard way when they move their applications from local area networks (which have small delays with little variation) to wider area internets (which have large delays with greater variation). To accommodate an internet environment, the retransmission strategy must be adaptive. Thus, applications must implement a retransmission scheme as complex as the one used in TCP. As a result, novice programmers are encouraged to use connection-oriented transport.

> *Because UDP does not supply reliable delivery, connectionless tran-*
> *sport requires the application protocol to provide reliability, if need-*
> *ed, through a complex, sophisticated technique known as adaptive re-*
> *transmission. Adding adaptive retransmission to an existing applica-*
> *tion is difficult and requires considerable expertise.*

Another consideration in choosing connectionless vs. connection-oriented design focuses on whether the service requires broadcast or multicast communication. Because TCP offers point-to-point communication, it cannot supply broadcast or multicast communication; such services require UDP. Thus, any server that accepts or responds to multicast communication must be connectionless. In practice, most sites try to avoid broadcasting whenever possible; none of the standard TCP/IP application protocols currently require multicast. However, future applications could depend more on multicast.

8.7 Failure, Reliability, And Statelessness

As Chapter 2 states, information that a server maintains about the status of ongoing interactions with clients is called *state information*. Servers that do not keep any state information are called *stateless servers*, while those that maintain state information are called *stateful servers*.

The issue of statelessness arises from a need to ensure reliability, especially when using connectionless transport. Remember that in an internet, messages can be duplicated, delayed, lost, or delivered out of order. If the transport protocol does not guarantee reliable delivery, and UDP does not, the application protocol must be designed to ensure it. Furthermore, the server implementation must be done carefully so it does not introduce state dependencies (and inefficiencies) unintentionally.

8.8 Optimizing Stateless Servers

To understand the subtleties involved in optimization, consider a connectionless server that allows clients to read information from files stored on the server's computer. To keep the protocol stateless, the designer requires each client request to specify a file name, a position in the file, and the number of bytes to read. The most straightforward server implementation handles each request independently: it opens the specified file, seeks to the specified position, reads the specified number of bytes, sends the information back to the client, and then closes the file.

A clever programmer assigned to write a server observes that: (1) the overhead of opening and closing files is high, (2) the clients using this server may read only a dozen bytes in each request, and (3) clients tend to read files sequentially. Furthermore, the programmer knows from experience that the server can extract data from a buffer in memory several orders of magnitude faster than it can read data from a disk. So, to optimize server performance, the programmer decides to maintain a small table of file information as Figure 8.1 shows.

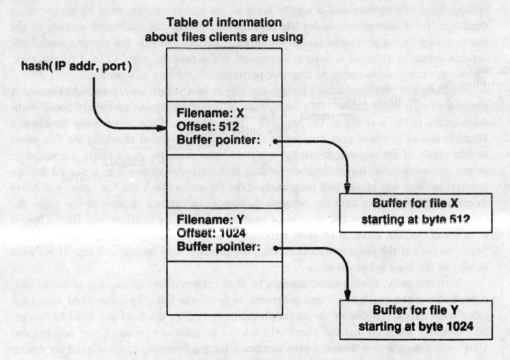

Figure 8.1 A table of information kept to improve server performance. The server uses the client's IP address and protocol port number to find an entry. This optimization introduces state information.

The programmer uses the client's IP address and protocol port number as an index into the table, and arranges for each table entry to contain a pointer to a large buffer of data from the file being read. When a client issues its first request, the server searches the table and finds that it has no record of the client. It allocates a large buffer to hold data from the file, allocates a new table entry to point to the buffer, opens the specified file, and reads data into the buffer. It then copies information out of the buffer when forming a reply. The next time a request arrives from the same client, the server finds the matching entry in the table, follows the pointer to the buffer, and extracts data from it without opening the file. Once the client has read the entire file, the server deallocates the buffer and the table entry, making the resources available for use by another client.

Of course, our clever programmer builds the software carefully so that it checks to make sure the requested data resides in the buffer and reads new data into the buffer from the file if necessary. The server also compares the file specified in a request with the file name in the table entry to verify that the client is still using the same file as the previous request.

If the clients follow the assumptions listed above and the programmer is careful, adding large file buffers and a simple table to the server can improve its performance dramatically. Furthermore, under the assumptions given, the optimized version of the server will perform at least as fast as the original version because the server spends little time maintaining the data structures compared to the time required to read from a disk. Thus, the optimization seems to improve performance without any penalty.

Adding the proposed table changes the server in a subtle way, however, because it introduces state information. Of course, state information chosen carelessly could introduce errors in the way the server responds. For example, if the server used the client's IP address and protocol port number to find the buffer without checking the file name or file offset in the request, duplicate or out-of-order requests could cause the server to return incorrect data. But remember we said that the programmer who designed the optimized version was clever and programmed the server to check the file name and offset in each request, just in case the network duplicates or drops a request or the client decides to read from a new file instead of reading sequentially from the old file. Thus, it may seem that the addition of state information does not change the way the server replies. In fact, if the programmer is careful, the protocol will remain correct. If so, what harm can the state information do?

Unfortunately, even a small amount of state information can cause a server to perform badly when machines, client programs, or networks fail. To understand why, consider what happens if one of the client programs fails (i.e., crashes) and must be restarted. Chances are high that the client will ask for an arbitrary protocol port number and UDP will assign a new protocol port number different from the one assigned for earlier requests. When the server receives a request from the client, it cannot know that the client has crashed and restarted, so it allocates a new buffer for the file and a new slot in the table. Consequently, it cannot know that the old table entry the client was using should be removed. If the server does not remove old entries, it will eventually run out of table slots.

It may seem that leaving an idle table entry around does not cause any problem as long as the server chooses an entry to delete when it needs a new one. For example, the server might choose to delete the *least recently used* (LRU) entry, much like the LRU page replacement strategy used in many virtual memory systems. However, in a network where multiple clients access a single server, frequent crashes can cause one client to dominate the table by filling it with entries that will never be reused. In the worst case, each request that arrives causes the server to delete an entry and reuse it. If one client crashes and reboots frequently enough, it can cause the server to remove entries for legitimate clients. Thus, the server expends more effort managing the table and buffers than it does answering requests†.

The important point here is that:

> *A programmer must be extremely careful when optimizing a stateless server because managing small amounts of state information can consume resources if clients crash and reboot frequently or if the underlying network duplicates or delays messages.*

8.9 Four Basic Types Of Servers

Servers can be iterative or concurrent, and can use connection-oriented transport or connectionless transport. Figure 8.2 shows that these properties group servers into four general categories.

iterative connectionless	iterative connection-oriented
concurrent connectionless	**concurrent connection-oriented**

Figure 8.2 The four general server categories defined by whether they offer concurrency and whether they use connection-oriented transport.

8.10 Request Processing Time

In general, iterative servers suffice only for the most trivial application protocols because they make each client wait in turn. The test of whether an iterative implementation will suffice focuses on the response time needed, which can be measured locally or globally.

We define the server's *request processing time* to be the total time the server takes to handle a single isolated request, and we define the client's *observed response time* as the total delay between the time it sends a request and the time the server responds. Obviously, the response time observed by a client can never be less than the server's request processing time. However, if the server has a queue of requests to handle, the observed response time can be much greater than the request processing time.

Iterative servers handle one request at a time. If another request arrives while the server is busy handling an existing request, the system enqueues the new request. Once the server finishes processing a request, it looks at the queue to see if it has a new request to handle. If N denotes the average length of the request queue, the observed response time for an arriving request will be approximately $N/2 + 1$ times the server's request processing time. Because the observed response time increases in proportion to N, most implementations restrict N to a small value (e.g., 5) and expect programmers to use concurrent servers in cases where a small queue does not suffice.

Another way of looking at the question of whether an iterative server suffices focuses on the overall load the server must handle. A server designed to handle K clients, each sending R requests per second must have a request processing time of less than $1/KR$ seconds per request. If the server cannot handle requests at the required rate, its queue of waiting requests will eventually overflow. To avoid overflow in servers that may have large request processing times, a designer should consider concurrent implementations.

8.11 Iterative Server Algorithms

An iterative server is the easiest to design, program, debug, and modify. Thus, most programmers choose an iterative design whenever iterative execution provides sufficiently fast response for the expected load. Usually, iterative servers work best with simple services accessed by a connectionless access protocol. As the next sections show, however, it is possible to use iterative implementations with both connectionless and connection-oriented transport.

8.12 An Iterative, Connection-Oriented Server Algorithm

Algorithm 8.1 presents the algorithm for an iterative server accessed via the TCP connection-oriented transport. The sections following the algorithm describe each of the steps in more detail.

Algorithm 8.1

1. Create a socket and bind to the well-known address for the service being offered.
2. Place the socket in passive mode, making it ready for use by a server.
3. Accept the next connection request from the socket, and obtain a new socket for the connection.
4. Repeatedly read a request from the client, formulate a response, and send a reply back to the client according to the application protocol.
5. When finished with a particular client, close the connection and return to step *3* to accept a new connection.

Algorithm 8.1 An iterative, connection-oriented server. A single process handles connections from clients one at a time.

8.13 Binding To A Well-Known Address Using INADDR_ANY

A server needs to create a socket and bind it to the well-known port for the service it offers. Like clients, servers use procedure *getportbyname* to map a service name into the corresponding well-known port number. For example, TCP/IP defines an *ECHO* service. A server that implements ECHO uses *getportbyname* to map the string ''echo'' to the assigned port, 7.

Remember that when *bind* specifies a connection endpoint for a socket, it uses structure *sockaddr_in*, which contains both an IP address and a protocol port number. Thus, *bind* cannot specify a protocol port number for a socket without also specifying an IP address. Unfortunately, selecting a specific IP address at which a server will accept connections can cause difficulty. For hosts that have a single network connection, the choice is obvious because the host has only one IP address. However, gateways and multi-homed hosts have multiple IP addresses. If the server specifies one particular IP address when binding a socket to a protocol port number, the socket will not accept communications that clients send to the machine's other IP addresses.

To solve the problem, the socket interface defines a special constant, *INADDR_ANY*, that can be used in place of an IP address. *INADDR_ANY* specifies a *wildcard address* that matches any of the host's IP addresses. Using *INADDR_ANY* makes it possible to have a single server on a gateway accept incoming communication addressed to any of the gateway's IP addresses. To summarize:

> *When specifying a local endpoint for a socket, servers use*
> INADDR_ANY, *instead of a specific IP address, to allow the socket*
> *to receive datagrams sent to any of the machine's IP addresses.*

8.14 Placing The Socket In Passive Mode

A TCP server calls *listen* to place a socket in passive mode. *Listen* also takes an argument that specifies the length of an internal request queue for the socket. The request queue holds the set of incoming TCP connection requests from clients that have each requested a connection with the server.

8.15 Accepting Connections And Using Them

A TCP server calls *accept* to obtain the next incoming connection request (i.e., extract it from the request queue). The call returns the descriptor of a socket to be used for the new connection. Once it has accepted a new connection, the server uses *read* to obtain application protocol requests from the client, and *write* to send replies back. Finally, once the server finishes with the connection, it calls *close* to release the socket.

8.16 An Iterative, Connectionless Server Algorithm

Recall that iterative servers work best for services that have a low request processing time. Because connection-oriented transport protocols like TCP have higher overhead than connectionless transport protocols like UDP, most iterative servers use connectionless transport. Algorithm 8.2 gives the general algorithm for an iterative server that uses UDP.

Creation of a socket for an iterative, connectionless server proceeds in the same way as for a connection-oriented server. The server's socket remains unconnected and can accept incoming datagrams from any client.

Algorithm 8.2

1. Create a socket and bind to the well-known address for the service being offered.
2. Repeatedly read the next request from a client, formulate a response, and send a reply back to the client according to the application protocol.

Algorithm 8.2 An iterative, connectionless server. A single process handles requests (datagrams) from clients one at a time.

8.17 Forming A Reply Address In A Connectionless Server

The socket interface provides two ways of specifying a remote endpoint. Chapters 6 and 7 discuss how clients use *connect* to specify a server's address. After a client calls *connect*, it can use *write* to send data because the internal socket data structure contains the remote endpoint address as well as the local endpoint address. A connectionless server cannot use *connect*, however, because doing so restricts the socket to communication with one specific remote host and port; the server cannot use the socket again to receive datagrams from arbitrary clients. Thus, a connectionless server uses an unconnected socket. It generates reply addresses explicitly, and uses the *sendto* socket call to specify both a datagram to be sent and an address to which it should go. *Sendto* has the form:

```
retcode = sendto(s, message, len, flags, toaddr, toaddrlen);
```

where *s* is an unconnected socket, *message* is the address of a buffer that contains the data to be sent, *len* specifies the number of bytes in the buffer, *flags* specifies debugging or control options, *toaddr* is a pointer to a *sockaddr in* structure that contains the endpoint address to which the message should be sent, and *toaddrlen* is an integer that specifies the length of the address structure.

The socket calls provide an easy way for connectionless servers to obtain the address of a client: the server obtains the address for a reply from the source address found in the request. In fact, the socket interface provides a call that servers can use to receive the sender's address along with the next datagram that arrives. The call, *recvfrom*, takes two arguments that specify two buffers. The system places the arriving datagram in one buffer and the sender's address in the second buffer. A call to *recvfrom* has the form:

```
retcode = recvfrom(s, buf, len, flags, from, fromlen);
```

where argument *s* specifies a socket to use, *buf* specifies a buffer into which the system will place the next datagram, *len* specifies the space available in the buffer, *from* specifies a second buffer into which the system will place the source address, and *fromlen* specifies the address of an integer. Initially, *fromlen* specifies the length of the *from* buffer. When the call returns, *fromlen* will contain the length of the source address the system placed in the buffer. To generate a reply, the server uses the address that *recvfrom* stored in the *from* buffer when the request arrived.

8.18 Concurrent Server Algorithms

The primary reason for introducing concurrency into a server arises from a need to provide faster response times to multiple clients. Concurrency improves response time if:

- forming a response requires significant I/O,
- the processing time required varies dramatically among requests, or
- the server executes on a computer with multiple processors.

In the first case, allowing the server to compute responses concurrently means that it can overlap use of the processor and peripheral devices, even if the machine has only one CPU. While the processor works to compute one response, the I/O devices can be transferring data into memory that will be needed for other responses. In the second case, timeslicing permits a single processor to handle requests that only require small amounts of processing without waiting for requests that take longer. In the third case, concurrent execution on a computer with multiple processors allows one processor to compute a response to one request while another processor computes a response to another. In fact, most concurrent servers adapt to the underlying hardware automatically – given more hardware resources (e.g., more processors) they perform better.

> *Concurrent servers achieve high performance by overlapping processing and I/O. They are usually designed so performance improves automatically if the server is run on hardware that offers more resources.*

8.19 Master And Slave Processes

Although it is possible for a server to achieve some concurrency using a single process, most concurrent servers use multiple processes. They can be divided into two types: a single *master server process* begins execution initially. The master process opens a socket at the well-known port, waits for the next request, and creates a *slave server process* to handle each request. The master server never communicates directly with a client – it passes that responsibility to a slave. Each slave process handles communication with one client. After the slave forms a response and sends it to the client, it exits. The next sections will explain the concept of master and slave in more detail, and will show how it applies to both connectionless and connection-oriented concurrent servers.

8.20 A Concurrent, Connectionless Server Algorithm

The most straightforward version of a concurrent, connectionless server follows Algorithm 8.3.

Algorithm 8.3

Master 1. Create a socket and bind to the well-known address for the service being offered. Leave the socket unconnected.

Master 2. Repeatedly call *recvfrom* to receive the next request from a client, and create a new slave process to handle the response.

Slave 1.   Receive a specific request upon creation as well as access to the socket.

Slave 2.   Form a reply according to the application protocol and send it back to the client using *sendto*.

Slave 3.   Exit (i.e., a slave process terminates after handling one request).

Algorithm 8.3 A concurrent, connectionless server. The master server process accepts incoming requests (datagrams) and creates a slave process to handle each.

Programmers should remember that although the exact cost of creating a process depends on the operating system and underlying architecture, the operation can be expensive. In the case of a connectionless protocol, one must consider carefully whether the cost of concurrency will be greater than the gain in speed. In fact:

> *Because process creation is expensive, few connectionless servers have concurrent implementations.*

8.21 A Concurrent, Connection-Oriented Server Algorithm

Connection-oriented application protocols use a connection as the basic paradigm for communication. They allow a client to establish a connection to a server, communicate over that connection, and then discard it. In most cases, the connection between client and server handles more than a single request: the protocol allows a client to repeatedly send requests and receive responses without terminating the connection or creating a new one. Thus,

Connection-oriented servers implement concurrency among connections rather than among individual requests.

Algorithm 8.4 specifies the steps that a concurrent server uses for a connection-oriented protocol.

Algorithm 8.4

Master 1. Create a socket and bind to the well-known address for the service being offered. Leave the socket unconnected.

Master 2. Place the socket in passive mode, making it ready for use by a server.

Master 3. Repeatedly call *accept* to receive the next request from a client, and create a new slave process to handle the response.

Slave 1. Receive a connection request (i.e., socket for the connection) upon creation.

Slave 2. Interact with the client using the connection: read request(s) and send back response(s).

Slave 3. Close the connection and exit. The slave process exits after handling all requests from one client.

Algorithm 8.4 A concurrent, connection-oriented server. The master server process accepts incoming connections and creates a slave process to handle each. Once the slave finishes, it closes the connection.

As in the connectionless case, the master server process never communicates with the client directly. As soon as a new connection arrives, the master creates a slave to handle that connection. While the slave interacts with the client, the master waits for other connections.

8.22 Using Separate Programs As Slaves

Algorithm 8.4 shows how a concurrent server creates a new process for each connection. In UNIX, the master server does so by calling the *fork* system call. For simple application protocols, a single server program can contain all the code needed for both the master and slave processes. After the call to *fork*, the original process loops back to accept the next incoming connection, while the new process becomes the slave and handles the connection. In some cases, however, it may be more convenient to have the slave process execute code from a program that has been written and compiled independently. UNIX can handle such cases easily because it allows the slave process to call *execve* after the call to *fork*. The general idea is:

> *For many services, a single program can contain code for both the master and server processes. In cases where an independent program makes the slave process easier to program or understand, the master program contains a call to* execve *after the call to* fork.

8.23 Apparent Concurrency Using A Single Process

Previous sections discuss concurrent servers implemented with concurrent processes. In some cases, however, it makes sense to use a single process to handle client requests concurrently. In particular, some operating systems make process creation so expensive that a server cannot afford to create a new process for each request or each connection. More important, many applications require the server to share information among all connections.

To understand the motivation for a server that provides *apparent concurrency* with a single process, consider the X window system. X allows multiple clients to paint text and graphics in windows that appear on a bit-mapped display. Each client controls one window, sending requests that update the contents. Each client operates independently, and may wait many hours before changing the display or may update the display frequently. For example, an application that displays the time by drawing a picture of a clock might update its display every minute. Meanwhile, an application that displays the status of a user's electronic mail waits until new mail arrives before it changes the display.

A server for the X window system integrates information it obtains from clients into a single, contiguous section of memory called the *display buffer*. Because data arriving from all clients contributes to a single, shared data structure and because BSD UNIX does not allow independent processes to share memory, the server cannot execute as separate UNIX processes. Thus, a conflict arises between a desire for concurrency among processes that share memory and a lack of support for such concurrency in UNIX.

Although it may not be possible to achieve *real concurrency* among processes that share memory, it may be possible to achieve *apparent concurrency* if the total load of requests presented to the server does not exceed its capacity to handle them. To do so, the server operates as a single UNIX process that uses the *select* system call for asynchronous I/O. Algorithm 8.5 describes the steps a single-process server takes to handle multiple connections.

Algorithm 8.5

1. Create a socket and bind to the well-known port for the service. Add socket to the list of those on which I/O is possible.
2. Use *select* to wait for I/O on existing sockets.
3. If original socket is ready, use *accept* to obtain the next connection, and add the new socket to the list of those on which
   I/O is possible.
4. If some socket other than the original is ready, use *read* to obtain the next request, form a response, and use *write* to send
   the response back to the client.
5. Continue processing with step 2 above.

Algorithm 8.5 A concurrent, connection-oriented server implemented by a
single process. The server process waits for the next descriptor that is ready, which could mean a new connection has arrived or that a client has sent a request on an existing connection.

8.24 When To Use Each Server Type

Iterative vs. Concurrent: Iterative servers are easier to design, implement, and
maintain, but concurrent servers can provide quicker response to requests. Use an iterative implementation if request processing time is short and an iterative solution produces response times that are sufficiently fast for the application.

Real vs. Apparent Concurrency: A single-process server must manage multiple
connections and use asynchronous I/O; a multi-process server allows the operating system to provide concurrency automatically. Use a single-process solution if the server
must share or exchange data among connections. Use a multi-process solution if each
slave can operate in isolation or to achieve maximal concurrency (e.g., on a multiprocessor).

Connection-Oriented vs. Connectionless: Because connection-oriented access
means using TCP, it implies reliable delivery. Because connectionless transport means
using UDP, it impiies unreliable delivery. Only use connectionless transport if the application protocol handles reliability (almost none do) or each client accesses its server
on a local area network that exhibits extremely low loss and no packet reordering. Use
connection-oriented transport whenever a wide area network separates the client and
server. Never move a connectionless client and server to a wide area environment
without checking to see if the application protocol handles the reliability problems.

8.25 A Summary of Server Types

Iterative, Connectionless Server

The most common form of connectionless server, used especially for services that require a trivial amount of processing for each request. Iterative servers are often stateless, making them easier to understand and less susceptible to failures.

Iterative, Connection-Oriented Server

A less common server type used for services that require a trivial amount of processing for each request, but for which reliable transport is necessary. Because the overhead associated with establishing and terminating connections can be high, the average response time can be non-trivial.

Concurrent, Connectionless Server

An uncommon type in which the server creates a new process to handle each request. On many systems, the added cost of process creation dominates the added efficiency gained from concurrency. To justify concurrency, either the time required to create a new process must be significantly less than the time required to compute a response or concurrent requests must be able to use many I/O devices simultaneously.

Concurrent, Connection-Oriented Server

The most general type of server because it offers reliable transport (i.e., it can be used across a wide area internet) as well as the ability to handle multiple requests concurrently. Two basic implementations exist: the most common implementation uses concurrent processes to handle connections; a far less common implementation relies on a single process and asynchronous I/O to handle multiple connections.

In a concurrent process implementation, the master server process creates a slave process to handle each connection. Using multiple processes makes it easy to execute a separately compiled program for each connection instead of writing all the code in a single, large server program.

In the single-process implementation, the server process manages multiple connections. It achieves apparent concurrency by using asynchronous I/O. The process repeatedly waits for I/O on any of the connections it has open and handles that request. Because a single process handles all connections, it can share data among them. However, because the server has only one process, it cannot handle requests faster than an iterative server, even on a computer that has multiple processors. The application must need data sharing or the processing time for each request must be short to justify this server implementation.

8.26 The Important Problem Of Server Deadlock

Many server implementations share an important flaw: namely, the server can be subject to deadlock†. To understand how deadlock can happen, consider an iterative, connection-oriented server. Suppose some client application, *C*, misbehaves. In the simplest case, assume *C* makes a connection to a server, but never sends a request. The server will accept the new connection, and call *read* to extract the next request. The server process blocks in the call to *read* waiting for a request that will never arrive.

Server deadlock can arise in a much more subtle way if clients misbehave by not consuming responses. For example, assume that a client *C* makes a connection to a server, sends it a sequence of requests, but never reads the responses. The server keeps accepting requests, generating responses, and sending them back to the client. At the server, TCP protocol software transmits the first few bytes over the connection to the client. Eventually, TCP will fill the client's receive window and will stop transmitting data. If the server application program continues to generate responses, the local buffer TCP uses to store outgoing data for the connection will become full and the server process will block.

Deadlock arises because processes block when the operating system cannot satisfy a system call. In particular, a call to *write* will block the calling process if TCP has no local buffer space for the data being sent; a call to *read* will block the calling process until TCP receives data. For concurrent servers, only the single slave process associated with a particular client blocks if the client fails to send requests or read responses. For a single-process implementation, however, the central server process will block. If the central server process blocks, it cannot handle other connections. The important point is that any server using only one process can be subject to deadlock.

> *A misbehaving client can cause deadlock in a single-process server if the server uses system functions that can block when communicating with the client. Deadlock is a serious liability in servers because it means the behavior of one client can prevent the server from handling other clients.*

8.27 Alternative Implementations

Chapters *9* through *12* provide examples of the server algorithms described in this chapter. Chapters *13* and *14* extend the ideas by discussing two important practical implementation techniques not described here: multiprotocol and multiservice servers. While both techniques provide interesting advantages for some applications, they have not been included here because they are best understood as simple generalizations of the single-process server algorithm illustrated in Chapter *12*.

---

†The term *deadlock* refers to a condition in which a program or set of programs cannot proceed because they are blocked waiting for an event that will never happen. In the case of servers, deadlock means that the server ceases to answer requests.

8.28 Summary

Conceptually, a server consists of a simple algorithm that iterates forever, waiting for the next request from a client, handling the request, and sending a reply. In practice, however, servers use a variety of implementations to achieve reliability, flexibility, and efficiency.

Iterative implementations work well for services that require little computation. When using a connection-oriented transport, an iterative server handles one connection at a time; for connectionless transport, an iterative server handles one request at a time.

To achieve efficiency, servers often provide concurrent service by handling multiple requests at the same time. A connection-oriented server provides for concurrency among connections by creating a process to handle each new connection. A connectionless server provides concurrency by creating a new process to handle each new request.

Any server implemented with a single process that uses synchronous system functions like *read* or *write* can be subject to deadlock. Deadlock can arise in iterative servers as well as in concurrent servers that use a single-process implementation. Server deadlock is especially serious because it means a single misbehaving client can prevent the server from handling requests for other clients.

FOR FURTHER STUDY

Stevens [1990] describes some of the server algorithms covered in this chapter and shows implementation details. BSD UNIX contains examples of many server algorithms; programmers often consult the UNIX source code for programming techniques.

EXERCISES

8.1   Calculate how long an iterative server takes to transfer a 200 megabyte file if the internet has a throughput of 2.3 Kbytes per second.

8.2   If 20 clients each send 2 requests per second to an iterative server, what is the maximum time that the server can spend on each request?

8.3   How long does it take a concurrent, connection-oriented server to accept a new connection and create a new process to handle it on the computers to which you have access?

8.4   Write an algorithm for a concurrent, connectionless server that creates one new process for each request.

8.5   Modify the algorithm in the previous problem so the server creates one new process per client instead of one new process per request. How does your algorithm handle process termination?

8.6 Connection-oriented servers provide concurrency among connections. Does it make sense for a concurrent, connection-oriented server to increase concurrency even further by having the slave processes create additional processes for each request? Explain.

8.7 Rewrite the TCP echo client so it uses a single process to concurrently handle input from the keyboard, input from its TCP connection, and output to its TCP connection.

8.8 Can clients cause deadlock or disrupt service in concurrent servers? Why or why not?

8.9 Look carefully at the *select* system call. How can a single-process server use *select* to avoid deadlock?

8.10 The *select* call takes an argument that specifies how many I/O descriptors it should check. Explain how the argument makes a single-process server program portable across many UNIX systems.

9

Iterative, Connectionless Servers (UDP)

9.1 Introduction

The previous chapter discusses many possible server designs, comparing the advantages and disadvantages of each. This chapter gives an example of an iterative server implementation that uses connectionless transport. The example server follows Algorithm 8.2†. Later chapters continue the discussion by providing example implementations of other server algorithms.

9.2 Creating A Passive Socket

The steps required to create a passive socket are similar to those required to create an active socket. They involve many details, and require the program to lookup a service name to obtain a well-known protocol port number.

To help simplify server code, programmers should use procedures to hide the details of socket allocation. As in the client examples, our example implementations use two high-level procedures, *passiveUDP* and *passiveTCP*, that allocate a passive socket and bind it to the server's well-known port. Each server invokes one of these procedures, with the choice dependent on whether the server uses connectionless or connection-oriented transport. This chapter considers *passiveUDP*; the next chapter shows the code for *passiveTCP*. Because the two procedures have many details in common, they both call the low-level procedure, *passivesock* to perform the work.

---

†See page 105 for a description of Algorithm 8.2.

A connectionless server calls function *passiveUDP* to create a socket for the service that it offers. If the server needs to use one of the ports reserved for well-known services (i.e., a port numbered below *1024*), the server process must have special privilege†. An arbitrary application program can use *passiveUDP* to create a socket for nonprivileged services. *PassiveUDP* calls *passivesock* to create a connectionless socket, and then returns the socket descriptor to its caller.

To make it easy to test client and server software, *passivesock* relocates all port values by adding the contents of global integer *portbase*. The importance of using *portbase* will become clearer in later chapters. However, the basic idea is fairly easy to understand:

> *If a new version of a client-server application uses the same protocol port numbers as an existing, production version, the new software cannot be tested while the production version continues to execute.*

Using *portbase* allows a programmer to compile a modified version of a server, and then to have the server look up the standard protocol port and compute a final port number as a function of the standard port and the value of *portbase*. If the programmer selects a unique value of *portbase* for each particular version of a client-server pair, the ports used by the new version will not conflict with the ports used by the production version. In fact, using *portbase* makes it possible to test multiple versions of a client-server pair at the same time without interference because each pair communicates independently of other pairs.

```
/* passiveUDP.c - passiveUDP */


/*------------------------------------------------------------------------
 * passiveUDP - create a passive socket for use in a UDP server
 *------------------------------------------------------------------------
 */
int
passiveUDP( service )
char    *service;          /* service associated with the desired port     */
{
        return passivesock(service, "udp", 0);
}
```

Procedure *passivesock* contains the socket allocation details, including the use of *portbase*. It takes three arguments. The first argument specifies the name of a service, the second specifies the name of the protocol, and the third (used only for TCP sockets) specifies the desired length of the connection request queue. *Passivesock* allocates either a datagram or stream socket, binds the socket to the well-known port for the service, and returns the socket descriptor to its caller.

---

†In UNIX, an application must execute as root (i.e., be the superuser) to have sufficient privilege to bind to a reserved port.

Recall that when a server binds a socket to a well-known port, it must specify the
address using structure *sockaddr_in*, which includes an IP address as well as a protocol
port number. *Passivesock* uses the constant *INADDR_ANY* instead of a specific local IP
address, enabling it to work either on hosts that have a single IP address or on gateways
and multi-homed hosts that have multiple IP addresses. Using *INADDR_ANY* means
that the server will receive communication addressed to its well-known port at any of
the machine's IP addresses.

```
/* passivesock.c - passivesock */

#include <sys/types.h>
#include <sys/socket.h>

#include <netinet/in.h>

#include <netdb.h>

extern int        errno;
extern char       *sys_errlist[];

u_short htons(), ntohs();

u_short portbase = 0;              /* port base, for non-root servers    */

/*------------------------------------------------------------------------
 * passivesock - allocate & bind a server socket using TCP or UDP
 *------------------------------------------------------------------------
 */
int
passivesock( service, protocol, qlen )
char    *service;       /* service associated with the desired port    */
char    *protocol;      /* name of protocol to use ("tcp" or "udp")    */
int     qlen;           /* maximum length of the server request queue  */
{
        struct servent *pse;    /* pointer to service information entry */
        struct protoent *ppe;   /* pointer to protocol information entry*/
        struct sockaddr_in sin; /* an Internet endpoint address         */
        int    s, type;         /* socket descriptor and socket type    */

        bzero((char *)&sin, sizeof(sin));
        sin.sin_family = AF_INET;
        sin.sin_addr.s_addr = INADDR_ANY;
```

```
    /* Map service name to port number */
        if ( pse = getservbyname(service, protocol) )
                sin.sin_port = htons(ntohs((u_short)pse->s_port)
                        + portbase);
        else if ( (sin.sin_port = htons((u_short)atoi(service))) == 0 )
                errexit("can't get \"%s\" service entry\n", service);

    /* Map protocol name to protocol number */
        if ( (ppe = getprotobyname(protocol)) == 0)
                errexit("can't get \"%s\" protocol entry\n", protocol);

    /* Use protocol to choose a socket type */
        if (strcmp(protocol, "udp") == 0)
                type = SOCK_DGRAM;
        else
                type = SOCK_STREAM;

    /* Allocate a socket */
        s = socket(PF_INET, type, ppe->p_proto);
        if (s < 0)
                errexit("can't create socket: %s\n", sys_errlist[errno]);

    /* Bind the socket */
        if (bind(s, (struct sockaddr *)&sin, sizeof(sin)) < 0)
                errexit("can't bind to %s port: %s\n", service,
                        sys_errlist[errno]);
        if (type == SOCK_STREAM && listen(s, qlen) < 0)
                errexit("can't listen on %s port: %s\n", service,
                        sys_errlist[errno]);
        return s;
}
```

9.3 Process Structure

Figure 9.1 illustrates the simple process structure used for an iterative, connection-less server.

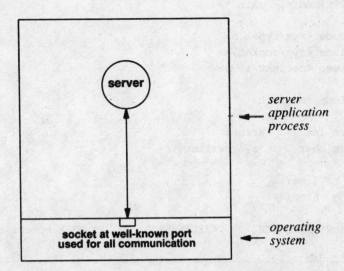

Figure 9.1 The process structure for an iterative, connectionless server. A single server process communicates with many clients using one socket.

The single server process executes forever. It uses a single passive socket that has been bound to the well-known protocol port for the service it offers. The server obtains a request from the socket, computes a response, and sends a reply back to the client using the same socket. The server uses the source address in the request as the destination address in the reply.

9.4 An Example TIME Server

An example will illustrate how a connectionless server process uses the socket allocation procedures described above. Recall from Chapter 7 that clients use the TIME service to obtain the current time of day from a server on another system. Because TIME requires little computation, an iterative server implementation works well. File *UDPtimed.c* contains the code for an iterative, connectionless TIME server.

```
/* UDPtimed.c - main */

#include <sys/types.h>
#include <sys/socket.h>
#include <netinet/in.h>

#include <stdio.h>

extern int      errno;
extern char     *sys_errlist[];

time_t  time();
u_long  htonl();

#define UNIXEPOCH       2208988800      /* UNIX epoch, in UCT secs       */

/*------------------------------------------------------------------------
 * main - Iterative UDP server for TIME service
 *------------------------------------------------------------------------
 */
int
main(argc, argv)
int     argc;
char    *argv[];
{
        struct sockaddr_in fsin;        /* the from address of a client */
        char    *service = "time";      /* service name or port number  */
        char    buf[1];                 /* "input" buffer; any size > 0 */
        int     sock;                   /* server socket                */
        time_t  now;                    /* current time                 */
        int     alen;                   /* from-address length          */

        switch (argc) {
        case    1:
                break;
        case    2:
                service = argv[1];
                break;
        default:
                errexit("usage: UDPtimed [port]\n");
        }

        sock = passiveUDP(service);
```

```
while (1) {
    alen = sizeof(fsin);
    if (recvfrom(sock, buf, sizeof(buf), 0,
                    (struct sockaddr *)&fsin, &alen) < 0)
        errexit("recvfrom: %s\n", sys_errlist[errno]);
    (void) time(&now);
    now = htonl((u_long)(now + UNIXEPOCH));
    (void) sendto(sock, (char *)&now, sizeof(now), 0,
                    (struct sockaddr *)&fsin, sizeof(fsin));
}
}
```

Like any server, the *UDPtimed* process must execute forever. Thus, the main body of code consists of an infinite loop that accepts a request, computes the current time, and sends a reply back to the client that sent the request.

The code contains several details. After parsing its arguments, *UDPtimed* calls *passiveUDP* to create a passive socket for the TIME service. It then enters the infinite loop. The TIME protocol specifies that a client can send an arbitrary datagram to trigger a reply. The datagram can be of any length and can contain any values because the server does not interpret its contents. The example implementation uses *recvfrom* to read the next datagram. *Recvfrom* places the incoming datagram in buffer *buf*, and places the endpoint address of the client that sent the datagram in structure *fsin*. Because it does not need to examine the data, the implementation uses a single-character buffer. If the datagram contains more than one byte of data, *recvfrom* discards all remaining bytes.

UDPtimed uses the UNIX system routine *time* to obtain the current time. Recall from Chapter 7 that UNIX uses a 32-bit integer to represent time, measuring from the epoch of midnight, January 1, 1970. After obtaining the time from UNIX, *UDPtimed* must convert it to a value measured from the Internet epoch and place the result in network byte order. To perform the conversion, it adds constant *UNIXEPOCH*, which is defined to have the value *2208988800*, the difference in seconds between the Internet epoch and the UNIX epoch. It then calls function *htonl* to convert the result to network byte order. Finally, *UDPtimed* calls *sendto* to transmit the result back to the client. *Sendto* uses the endpoint address in structure *fsin* as the destination address (i.e., it uses the address of the client that sent the datagram).

9.5 Summary

For simple services, where a server does little computation for each request, an iterative implementation works well. This chapter presented an example of an iterative server for the TIME service that uses UDP for connectionless access. The example illustrates how procedures hide the details of socket allocation and make the server code simpler and easier to understand.

FOR FURTHER STUDY

Harrenstien [RFC 738] specifies the TIME protocol. Mills [RFC 1119] describes the Network Time Protocol (NTP); Mills [September 1991] summarizes issues related to using NTP in practical networks. Marzullo and Owicki [July 1985] also discusses how to maintain clocks in a distributed environment.

EXERCISES

9.1 Instrument *UDPtimed* to determine how much time it expends processing each request. If you have access to a network analyzer, also measure the time that elapses between the request and response packets.

9.2 Suppose *UDPtimed* inadvertently clobbered the client's address between the time it received a request and sent a response (i.e., the server accidentally assigned *fsin* a random value before using it in the call to *sendto*). What would happen? Why?

9.3 Conduct an experiment to determine what happens if *N* clients all send requests to *UDPtimed* simultaneously. Vary both *N*, the number of senders, and the size of the datagram they send. Explain why the server fails to respond to all requests. (Hint: look at the manual page for *listen*.)

9.4 The example code in *UDPtimed.c* specifies a buffer size of *1* when it calls *recvfrom*. What happens if it specifies a buffer size of *0*?

9.5 Compute the difference between the UNIX time epoch and the Internet time epoch. Remember to account for leap years. Does the value you compute agree with the constant *UNIXEPOCH* defined in *UDPtimed*? If not, explain. (Hint: read about leap seconds.)

9.6 As a security check, the system manager asks you to modify *UDPtimed* so it keeps a written log of all clients who access the service. Modify the code to print a line on the console whenever a request arrives. Explain how logging can affect the service.

9.7 If you have access to a pair of machines connected by a wide-area internet, use the *UDPtime* client in Chapter 7 and the *UDPtimed* server in this chapter to see if your internet drops or duplicates packets.

10

Iterative, Connection-Oriented Servers (TCP)

10.1 Introduction

The previous chapter provides an example of an iterative server that uses UDP for connectionless transport. This chapter shows how an interactive server can use TCP for connection-oriented transport. The example server follows Algorithm 8.1†.

10.2 Allocating A Passive TCP Socket

Chapter 9 mentions that a connection-oriented server uses function *passiveTCP* to allocate a stream socket and bind it to the well-known port for the service being offered. *PassiveTCP* takes two arguments. The first argument, a character string, specifies the name or number of a service, and the second specifies the desired length of the incoming connection request queue. If the first argument contains a name, it must match one of the entries in the service database accessed by library function *getservbyname*. If the first argument specifies a port number, it must represent the number as a text string (e.g., "79").

---

†See page 103 for a description of Algorithm 8.1.

```
/* passiveTCP.c - passiveTCP */

/*------------------------------------------------------------------
 * passiveTCP - create a passive socket for use in a TCP server
 *------------------------------------------------------------------
 */
int
passiveTCP( service, qlen )
char    *service;       /* service associated with the desired port  */
int     qlen;           /* maximum server request queue length       */
{
        return passivesock(service, "tcp", qlen);
}
```

10.3 A Server For The DAYTIME Service

Recall from Chapter 7 that the DAYTIME service allows a user on one machine to obtain the current date and time of day from another machine. Because the DAYTIME service is intended for humans, it specifies that the server must format the date in an easily readable string of ASCII text when it sends a reply. Thus, the client can display the response for a user exactly as it is received.

Chapter 7 shows how a client uses TCP to contact a DAYTIME server and to display the text that the server sends back. Because obtaining and formatting a date requires little processing and one expects little demand for the service, a DAYTIME server need not be optimized for speed. If additional clients attempt to make connection requests while the server is busy handling a request, the protocol software enqueues the additional requests. Thus, an iterative implementation suffices.

10.4 Process Structure

As Figure 10.1 shows, an iterative, connection-oriented server consists of a single process. The process iterates forever, using one socket to handle incoming requests and a second, temporary socket to handle communication with a client.

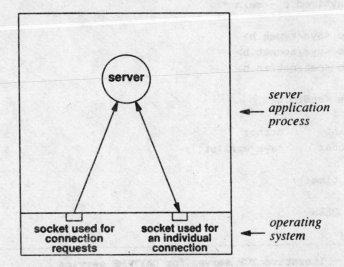

Figure 10.1 The process structure of an iterative, connection-oriented server. The server waits at the well-known port for a connection, and then communicates with the client over that connection.

A server that uses connection-oriented transport iterates on connections: it waits at the well-known port for the next connection to arrive from a client, accepts the connection, handles it, closes the connection, and then waits again. The DAYTIME service makes the implementation especially simple because the server does not need to receive an explicit request from the client – it uses the presence of an incoming connection to trigger a response. Because the client does not send an explicit request, the server does not read data from the connection.

10.5 An Example DAYTIME Server

File *TCPdaytimed.c* contains example code for an iterative, connection-oriented DAYTIME server.

```c
/* TCPdaytimed.c - main */

#include <sys/types.h>
#include <sys/socket.h>
#include <netinet/in.h>

#include <stdio.h>

extern int      errno;
extern char     *sys_errlist[];

long    time();

#define QLEN    5

/*------------------------------------------------------------------------
 * main - Iterative TCP server for DAYTIME service
 *------------------------------------------------------------------------
 */
int
main(argc, argv)
int     argc;
char    *argv[];
{
        struct  sockaddr_in fsin;       /* the from address of a client */
        char    *service = "daytime";   /* service name or port number  */
        int     msock, ssock;           /* master & slave sockets       */
        int     alen;                   /* from-address length          */

        switch (argc) {
        case    1:
                break;
        case    2:
                service = argv[1];
                break;
        default:
                errexit("usage: TCPdaytimed [port]\n");
        }

        msock = passiveTCP(service, QLEN);

        while (1) {
                ssock = accept(msock, (struct sockaddr *)&fsin, &alen);
                if (ssock < 0)
```

```
                                  errexit("accept failed: %s\n",sys_errlist[errno]);
                   (void) TCPdaytimed(ssock);
                   (void) close(ssock);
         }
}


/*------------------------------------------------------------------------
 * TCPdaytimed - do TCP DAYTIME protocol
 *------------------------------------------------------------------------
 */
int
TCPdaytimed(fd)
int     fd;
{
         char    *pts;                          /* pointer to time string      */
         time_t  now;                           /* current time                */
         char    *ctime();

         (void) time(&now);
         pts = ctime(&now);
         (void) write(fd, pts, strlen(pts));
         return 0;
}
```

Like the iterative, connectionless server described in the previous chapter, an iterative, connection-oriented server must run forever. After creating a socket that listens at the well-known port, the server enters an infinite loop in which it accepts and handles connections.

The code for the server is fairly short because the call to *passiveTCP* hides the details of socket allocation and binding. The call to *passiveTCP* creates a master socket associated with the well-known port for the DAYTIME service. The second argument specifies that the master socket will have a request queue length of *QLEN*, allowing the system to enqueue connection requests that arrive from *QLEN* additional clients while the server is busy replying to a request from a given client.

After creating the master socket, the server's main program enters an infinite loop. During each iteration of the loop, the server calls *accept* to obtain the next connection request from the master socket. To prevent the server from consuming resources while waiting for a connection from a client, the call to *accept* blocks the server process until a connection arrives. When a connection request arrives, the TCP protocol software engages in a 3-way handshake to establish a connection. Once the handshake completes and the system allocates a new socket for the incoming connection, the call to *accept* returns the descriptor of the new socket, allowing the server to continue execution. If no connection arrives, the server process remains blocked forever in the *accept* call.

Each time a new connection arrives, the server calls procedure *TCPdaytimed* to handle it. The code in *TCPdaytimed* centers around calls to the UNIX functions *time* and *ctime*. Procedure *time* returns a 32-bit integer that gives the current time in seconds since the UNIX epoch.* The UNIX library function *ctime* takes an integer argument that specifies a time in seconds since the UNIX epoch, and returns the address of an ASCII string that contains the time and date formatted so a human can understand it. Once the server obtains the time and date in an ASCII string, it calls *write* to send the string back to the client over the TCP connection.

Once the call to *TCPdaytimed* returns, the main program continues executing the loop, and encounters the *accept* call again. The *accept* call blocks the server until another request arrives.

10.6 Closing Connections

After it has written the response, the call to procedure *TCPdaytimed* returns. Once the call returns, the main program explicitly closes the socket on which the connection arrived.

Calling *close* requests a graceful shutdown. In particular, TCP guarantees that all data will be reliably delivered to the client and acknowledged before it terminates the connection. Thus, when calling *close*, a programmer does not need to worry about data being delivered.

Of course, TCP's definition of graceful shutdown means that the call to *close* may not return instantly – the call will block until TCP on the server receives a reply from TCP on the client. Once the client acknowledges both the receipt of all data and the request to terminate the connection, the *close* call returns.

10.7 Connection Termination And Server Vulnerability

The application protocol determines how a server manages TCP connections. In particular, the application protocol usually dictates the choice of the termination strategy. For example, arranging for the server to close connections works well for the DAYTIME protocol because the server knows when it has finished sending data. Applications that have more complex client-server interactions cannot choose to have the server close a connection immediately after processing one request because they must wait to see if the client chooses to send additional request messages. For example, consider an ECHO server. The client controls server processing because it determines the amount of data to be echoed. Because the server must process arbitrary amounts of data, it cannot close the connection after reading and writing once. Thus, the client must signal completion so the server knows when to terminate the connection.

Allowing a client to control connection duration can be dangerous because it allows clients to control resource use. In particular, misbehaving clients can cause the server to consume resources like sockets and TCP connections. It may seem that our example server will never run out of resources because it explicitly closes connections. Even our simple connection termination strategy can be vulnerable to misbehaving clients. To understand why, recall that TCP defines a connection timeout period of 2 times the maximum segment lifetime (2*MSL) after a connection closes. During the timeout, TCP keeps a record of the connection so it can correctly reject any old packets that may have been delayed. Thus, if clients make repeated requests rapidly, they can use up resources at the server. Although programmers may have little control over protocols, they should understand how protocols can make distributed software vulnerable to network failures and try to avoid such vulnerabilities when designing servers.

10.8 Summary

An iterative, connection-oriented server iterates once per connection. Until a connection request arrives from a client, the server remains blocked in a call to *accept*. Once the underlying protocol software establishes the new connection and creates a new socket, the call to *accept* returns the socket descriptor and allows the server to continue execution.

Recall from Chapter 7 that the DAYTIME protocol uses the presence of a connection to trigger a response from the server. The client does not need to send a request because the server responds as soon as it detects a new connection. To form a response, the server obtains the current time from the operating system, formats the information into a string suitable for humans to read, and then sends the response back to the client. The example server closes the socket that corresponds to an individual connection after sending a response. The strategy of closing the connection immediately works because the DAYTIME service only allows one response per connection. Servers that allow multiple requests to arrive over a single connection must wait for the client to close the connection.

FOR FURTHER STUDY

Postel [RFC 867] describes the DAYTIME protocol used in this chapter.

EXERCISES

10.1   Does a process need special privilege to run a DAYTIME server on your local system? Does it need special privilege to run a DAYTIME client?

10.2   What is the chief advantage of using the presence of a connection to trigger a response from a server? The chief disadvantage?

10.3   Some DAYTIME servers terminate the line of text by a combination of two characters: *carriage return* (*CR*) and *linefeed* (*LF*). Modify the example server to send *CR-LF* at the end of the line instead of sending only *LF*. How does the standard specify lines should be terminated?

10.4   TCP software usually allocates a fixed-size queue for additional connection requests that arrive while a server is busy, and allows the server to change the queue size using *listen*. How large is the queue that your local TCP software provides? How large can the server make the queue with *listen*?

10.5   Modify the example server code in *TCPdaytimed.c* so it does not explicitly close the connection after writing a response. Does it still work correctly? Why or why not?

10.6   Compare a connection-oriented server that explicitly closes each connection after sending a response to one that allows the client to hold a connection arbitrarily long before closing the connection. What are the advantages and disadvantages of each approach?

10.7   Assume that TCP uses a connection timeout of *4* minutes (i.e., keeps information for *4* minutes after a connection closes). If a DAYTIME server runs on a system that has 100 slots for TCP connection information, what is the maximum rate at which the server can handle requests without running out of slots?

11

Concurrent, Connection-Oriented Servers (TCP)

11.1 Introduction

The previous chapter illustrates how an iterative server uses a connection-oriented transport protocol. This chapter gives an example of a concurrent server that uses a connection-oriented transport. The example server follows Algorithm 8.4†, the design that programmers use most often when they build concurrent TCP servers. The server relies on the operating system's support for concurrent processing to achieve concurrency when computing responses. The system manager arranges to have the master server process start automatically when the system boots. The master server runs forever waiting for new connection requests to arrive from clients. The master creates a new slave process to handle each new connection, and allows each slave to handle all communication with its client.

Later chapters consider alternative implementations of concurrent servers, and show how to extend the basic ideas presented here.

11.2 Concurrent ECHO

Consider the ECHO service described in Chapter 7. A client opens a connection to a server, and then repeatedly sends data across the connection and reads the "echo" the server returns. The ECHO server responds to each client. It accepts a connection, reads from the connection, and then sends back the same data it receives.

---

†See page 108 for a description of Algorithm 8.4.

To allow a client to send arbitrary amounts of data, the server does not read the entire input before it sends a response. Instead, it alternates between reading and writing When a new connection arrives, the server enters a loop. On each iteration of the loop the server first reads from the connection and then writes the data back to the connection. The server continues iterating until it encounters an end-of-file condition, at which time it closes the connection.

11.3 Iterative Vs. Concurrent Implementations

An iterative implementation of an ECHO server can perform poorly because it requires a given client to wait while it handles all prior connection requests. If a client chooses to send large amounts of data (e.g., many megabytes), an iterative server will delay all other clients until it can satisfy the request.

A concurrent implementation of an ECHO server avoids long delays because it does not allow a single client to hold all resources. Instead, a concurrent server allows its communication with many clients to proceed simultaneously. Thus, from a client's point of view, a concurrent server offers better observed response time than an iterative server.

11.4 Process Structure

Figure 11.1 illustrates the process structure of a concurrent, connection-oriented server. As the figure shows, the master server process does not communicate with clients directly. Instead, it merely waits at the well-known port for the next connection request. Once a request has arrived, the system returns the socket descriptor of the new socket to use for that connection. The master server process creates a slave process to handle the connection, and allows the slave to operate concurrently. At any time, the server consists of one master process and zero or more slave processes.

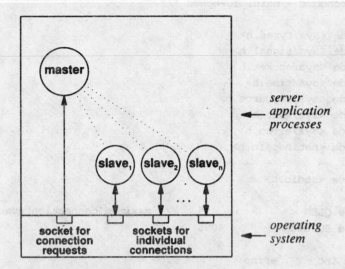

Figure 11.1 The process structure of a concurrent, connection-oriented server. A master server process accepts each incoming connection, and creates a slave process to handle it.

To avoid using CPU resources while it waits for connections, the master server uses a blocking call of *accept* to obtain the next connection from the well-known port. Thus, like the iterative server process in Chapter *10*, the master server process in a concurrent server spends most of its time blocked in a call to *accept*. When a connection request arrives, the call to *accept* returns, allowing the master process to execute. The master creates a slave to handle the request, and reissues the call to *accept*. The call blocks the server again until another connection request arrives.

11.5 An Example Concurrent ECHO Server

File *TCPechod.c* contains the code for an ECHO server that uses concurrent processes to provide concurrent service to multiple clients.

```
/* TCPechod.c - main, TCPechod */

#include <sys/types.h>
#include <sys/signal.h>
#include <sys/socket.h>
#include <sys/time.h>
#include <sys/resource.h>
#include <sys/wait.h>
#include <sys/errno.h>
#include <netinet/in.h>

#include <stdio.h>

#define QLEN                5    /* maximum connection queue length    */
#define BUFSIZE         4096

extern int      errno;
extern char     *sys_errlist[];

int     reaper();

/*------------------------------------------------------------------------
 * main - Concurrent TCP server for ECHO service
 *------------------------------------------------------------------------
 */
int
main(argc, argv)
int     argc;
char    *argv[];
{
        char    *service = "echo";      /* service name or port number */
        struct  sockaddr_in fsin;       /* the address of a client     */
        int     alen;                   /* length of client's address  */
        int     msock;                  /* master server socket        */
        int     ssock;                  /* slave server socket         */

        switch (argc) {
        case    1:
                break;
        case    2:
                service = argv[1];
                break;
        default:
                errexit("usage: TCPechod [port]\n");
        }
```

```
        msock = passiveTCP(service, QLEN);

        (void) signal(SIGCHLD, reaper);

        while (1) {
                alen = sizeof(fsin);
                ssock = accept(msock, (struct sockaddr *)&fsin, &alen);
                if (ssock < 0) {
                        if (errno == EINTR)
                                continue;
                        errexit("accept: %s\n", sys_errlist[errno]);
                }
                switch (fork()) {
                case 0:              /* child */
                        (void) close(msock);
                        exit(TCPechod(ssock));
                default:             /* parent */
                        (void) close(ssock);
                        break;
                case -1:
                        errexit("fork: %s\n", sys_errlist[errno]);
                }
        }
}


/*------------------------------------------------------------------------
 * TCPechod - echo data until end of file
 *------------------------------------------------------------------------
 */
int
TCPechod(fd)
int     fd;
{
        char    buf[BUFSIZ];
        int     cc;

        while (cc = read(fd, buf, sizeof buf)) {
                if (cc < 0)
                        errexit("echo read: %s\n", sys_errlist[errno]);
                if (write(fd, buf, cc) < 0)
                        errexit("echo write: %s\n", sys_errlist[errno]);
        }
        return 0;
}
```

```
/*-----------------------------------------------------------------------
 * reaper - clean up zombie children
 *-----------------------------------------------------------------------
 */
int
reaper()
{
        union wait      status;

        while (wait3(&status, WNOHANG, (struct rusage *)0) >= 0)
                /* empty */;

}
```

As the example shows, the calls that control concurrency occupy only a small portion of the code. A master server process begins executing at *main*. After it checks its arguments, the master server calls *passiveTCP* to create a passive socket for the well-known protocol port. It then enters an infinite loop.

During each iteration of the loop, the master server calls *accept* to wait for a connection request from a client. As in the iterative server, the call blocks until a request arrives. After the underlying TCP protocol software receives a connection request, the system creates a socket for the new connection, and the call to *accept* returns the socket descriptor.

After *accept* returns, the master server creates a slave process to handle the connection. To do so, the master process calls *fork* to divide itself into two processes†. The newly created child process first closes the master socket, and then calls procedure *TCPechod* to handle the connection. The parent process closes the socket that was created to handle the new connection, and continues executing the infinite loop. The next iteration of the loop will wait at the *accept* call for another new connection to arrive. Note that both the original and new processes have access to open sockets after the call to *fork()*, and that they both must close a socket before the system deallocates it. Thus, when the master process calls *close* for the new connection, the socket for that connection only disappears from the master process. Similarly, when the slave process calls *close* for the master socket, the socket only disappears from the slave process. The slave process continues to retain access to the socket for the new connection until the slave exits; the master server continues to retain access to the socket that corresponds to the well-known port.

After the slave closes the master socket, it calls procedure *TCPechod*, which provides the ECHO service for one connection. Procedure *TCPechod* consists of a loop that repeatedly calls *read* to obtain data from the connection and then calls *write* to send the same data back over the connection. Normally, *read* returns the (positive) count of bytes read. It returns a value less than zero if an error occurs (e.g., the network connec-

---

†Recall from Chapter 3 that *fork* creates two processes, both executing the same code. The return value distinguishes between the original parent process and the newly created child.

tion between the client and server breaks) or zero if it encounters an *end-of-file* condition (i.e., no more data can be extracted from the socket). Similarly, *write* normally returns the count of characters written, but returns a value less than zero if an error occurs. The slave checks the return codes, and uses *errexit* to print a message if an error occurs.

TCPechod returns zero if it can echo all data without error. When *TCPechod* returns, the main program uses the returned value as the argument in a call to *exit*. UNIX interprets the *exit* call as a request to terminate the process, and uses the argument as a process exit code. By convention, a process uses exit code zero to denote normal termination. Thus, the slave process exits normally after performing the ECHO service. When the slave exits, the system automatically closes all open descriptors, including the descriptor for the TCP connection.

11.6 Cleaning Up Errant Processes

Because concurrent servers generate processes dynamically, they introduce a potential problem of incompletely terminated processes. UNIX solves the problem by sending a *signal* to the parent whenever a child process exits. The exiting process remains in a *zombie* state until the parent executes a *wait3* system call. To terminate a child completely (i.e., to eliminate a zombie process), our example ECHO server catches the child termination signal and executes a signal handling function. The call

```
signal(SIGCHLD, reaper);
```

informs the operating system that the master server process should execute function *reaper* whenever it receives a signal that a child process has exited (signal *SIGCHLD*). After the call to *signal*, the system automatically invokes *reaper* each time the server process receives a *SIGCHLD* signal.

Function *reaper* calls system function *wait3* to complete termination for a child that exits. *Wait3* blocks until one or more children exit (for any reason). It returns a value in the status structure that can be examined to find out about the process that exited. Because the program calls *wait3* when a *SIGCHLD* signal arrives, it will always be called after a child has exited. To ensure that an erroneous call does not deadlock the server, the program uses argument *WNOHANG* to specify that *wait3* should not block waiting for a process to exit, but should return immediately, even if no process has exited.

11.7 Summary

Connection-oriented servers achieve concurrency by allowing multiple clients to communicate with the server. The straightforward implementation in this chapter uses the *fork* function to create a new slave process each time a connection arrives. The master process never interacts with any clients; it merely accepts connections and creates a slave to handle each of them.

Each slave process begins execution in the main program immediately following the call to *fork*. The master process closes its copy of the descriptor for the new connection, and the slave closes its copy of the master descriptor. A connection to a client terminates after the slave exits because the operating system closes the slave's copy of the socket.

FOR FURTHER STUDY

Postel [RFC 862] defines the ECHO protocol used in the example TCP server.

EXERCISES

11.1   Instrument the server so it keeps a log of the time at which it creates each slave process and the time at which the slave terminates. How many clients must you start before you can find any overlap between the slave processes?

11.2   How many clients can access the example concurrent server simultaneously before any client must be denied service? How many can access the iterative server in Chapter *10* before any is denied service?

11.3   Build an iterative implementation of an ECHO server. Conduct an experiment to determine if a human can sense the difference in response time between the concurrent and iterative versions.

11.4   Modify the example server so procedure *TCPechod* explicitly closes the connection before it returns. Explain why an explicit call to *close* might make the code easier to maintain.

12

Single-Process, Concurrent Servers (TCP)

12.1 Introduction

The previous chapter illustrates how most concurrent, connection-oriented servers operate. They use operating system facilities to create a separate process for each connection, and allow the operating system to timeslice the processor among the processes. This chapter illustrates a design idea that is interesting, but not obvious: it shows how a server can offer apparent concurrency to clients while using only a single process. First, it examines the general idea. It discusses why such an approach is feasible and when it may be superior to an implementation using multiple processes. Second, it considers how a single-process server uses the UNIX system calls to handle multiple connections concurrently. The example server follows Algorithm 0.5†.

12.2 Data-driven Processing In A Server

For applications where I/O dominates the cost of preparing a response to a request, a server can use asynchronous I/O to provide apparent concurrency among clients. The idea is simple: arrange for a single server process to keep TCP connections open to multiple clients, and have the server handle a given connection when data arrives. Thus, the server uses the arrival of data to trigger processing.

To understand why the approach works, consider the concurrent ECHO server described in the previous chapter. To achieve concurrent execution, the server creates a separate slave process to handle each new connection. In theory, the server depends on

†See page 110 for a description of Algorithm 8.5.

139

the operating system's timeslicing mechanism to share the CPU among the processes, and hence, among the connections.

In practice, however, an ECHO server seldom depends on timeslicing. If one were able to watch the execution of a concurrent ECHO server closely, one would find that the arrival of data often controls processing. The reason relates to data flow across an internet. Data arrives at the server in bursts, not in a steady stream, because the underlying internet delivers data in discrete packets. Clients add to the bursty behavior if they choose to send blocks of data so that the resulting TCP segments each fit into a single IP datagram. At the server, each slave process spends most of its time blocked in a call to *read* waiting for the next burst to arrive. Once the data arrives, the *read* call returns and the slave process executes. The slave calls *write* to send the data back to the client, and then calls *read* again to wait for more data. A CPU that can handle the load of many clients without slowing down must execute sufficiently fast to complete the cycle of reading and writing before data arrives for another slave.

Of course, if the load becomes so great that the CPU cannot process one request before another arrives, timesharing takes over. The operating system switches the processor among all slaves that have data to process. For simple services that require little processing for each request, chances are high that execution will be driven by the arrival of data. To summarize:

> *Concurrent servers that require little processing time per request often behave in a sequential manner where the arrival of data triggers execution. Timesharing only takes over if the load becomes so high that the CPU cannot handle it sequentially.*

12.3 Data-Driven Processing With A Single Process

Understanding the sequential nature of a concurrent server's behavior allows us to understand how a single process can perform the same task. Imagine a single server process that has TCP connections open to many clients. The process blocks waiting for data to arrive. As soon as data arrives on any connection, the process awakens, handles the request, and sends a reply. It then blocks again, waiting for more data to arrive from another connection. As long as the CPU is fast enough to satisfy the load presented to the server, the single process version handles requests as well as a version with multiple processes. In fact, because a single-process implementation requires less switching between process contexts, it may be able to handle a slightly higher load than an implementation that uses multiple processes.

The key to programming a single-process concurrent server lies in the use of asynchronous I/O through the operating system primitive *select*. A server creates a socket for each of the connections it must manage, and then calls *select* to wait for data to arrive on any of them. In fact, because *select* can wait for I/O on all possible sockets, it can also wait for new connections at the same time. Algorithm 8.5 lists the detailed steps a single-process server uses.

12.4 Process Structure Of A Single-Process Server

Figure 12.1 illustrates the process and socket structure of a single-process concurrent server. One process manages all sockets.

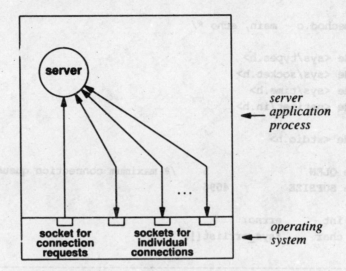

Figure 12.1 The process structure of a connection-oriented server that achieves concurrency with a single process. The process manages multiple sockets.

In essence, a single process server must perform the duties of both the master and slave processes. It maintains a set of sockets, with one socket in the set bound to the well-known port at which the master would accept connections. The other sockets in the set each correspond to a connection over which a slave would handle requests. The server passes the set of socket descriptors as an argument to *select*, and waits for activity on any of them. When *select* returns, it passes back a bit mask that specifies which of the descriptors in the set is ready. The server uses the order in which descriptors become ready to decide how to proceed.

To distinguish between master and slave operations, a single-process server uses the descriptor. If the descriptor that corresponds to the master socket becomes ready, the server performs the same operation the master would perform: it calls *accept* on the socket to obtain a new connection. If a descriptor that corresponds to a slave socket becomes ready, the server performs the operation a slave would perform: it calls *read* to obtain a request, and then answers it.

12.5 An Example Single-Process ECHO Server

An example will help clarify the ideas and explain how a single-process, concurrent server works. Consider file *TCPmechod.c*, which contains the code for a single-process server that implements the ECHO service.

```c
/* TCPmechod.c - main, echo */

#include <sys/types.h>
#include <sys/socket.h>
#include <sys/time.h>
#include <netinet/in.h>

#include <stdio.h>

#define QLEN             5       /* maximum connection queue length     */
#define BUFSIZE       4096

extern int      errno;
extern char     *sys_errlist[];

/*------------------------------------------------------------------------
 * main - Concurrent TCP server for ECHO service
 *------------------------------------------------------------------------
 */
int
main(argc, argv)
int     argc;
char    *argv[];
{
        char    *service = "echo";   /* service name or port number  */
        struct sockaddr_in fsin;     /* the from address of a client */
        int     msock;               /* master server socket         */
        fd_set  rfds;                /* read file descriptor set     */
        fd_set  afds;                /* active file descriptor set   */
        int     alen;                /* from-address length          */
        int     fd, nfds;

        switch (argc) {
        case    1:
                break;
        case    2:
                service = argv[1];
                break;
```

```
        default:
                errexit("usage: TCPmechod [port]\n");
        }

        msock = passiveTCP(service, QLEN);

        nfds = getdtablesize();
        FD_ZERO(&afds);
        FD_SET(msock, &afds);

        while (1) {
                bcopy((char *)&afds, (char *)&rfds, sizeof(rfds));

                if (select(nfds, &rfds, (fd_set *)0, (fd_set *)0,
                                (struct timeval *)0) < 0)
                        errexit("select: %s\n", sys_errlist[errno]);
                if (FD_ISSET(msock, &rfds)) {
                        int     ssock;

                        alen = sizeof(fsin);
                        ssock = accept(msock, (struct sockaddr *)&fsin,
                                &alen);
                        if (ssock < 0)
                                errexit("accept: %s\n",
                                        sys_errlist[errno]);
                        FD_SET(ssock, &afds);
                }
                for (fd=0; fd<nfds; ++fd)
                        if (fd != msock && FD_ISSET(fd, &rfds))
                                if (echo(fd) == 0) {
                                        (void) close(fd);
                                        FD_CLR(fd, &afds);
                                }

        }
}
/*------------------------------------------------------------------
 * echo - echo one buffer of data, returning byte count
 *------------------------------------------------------------------
 */
int
echo(fd)
int     fd;
{
```

```
char      buf[BUFSIZ];
int       cc;

cc = read(fd, buf, sizeof buf);
if (cc < 0)
        errexit("echo read: %s\n", sys_errlist[errno]);
if (cc && write(fd, buf, cc) < 0)
        errexit("echo write: %s\n", sys_errlist[errno]);
return cc;
}
```

The single-process server begins, like the master server in a multiple-process implementation, by opening a passive socket at the well-known port. It uses *FD_ZERO* and *FD_SET* to create a bit vector that corresponds to the socket descriptors that it wishes to test. The server then enters an infinite loop in which it calls *select* to wait for one or more of the descriptors to become ready.

If the master descriptor becomes ready, the server calls *accept* to obtain a new connection. It adds the descriptor for the new connection to the set it manages, and continues to wait for more activity. If a slave descriptor becomes ready, the server calls procedure *echo* which calls *read* to obtain data from the connection and *write* to send it back to the client. If one of the slave descriptors reports an end-of-file condition, the server closes the descriptor and uses macro *FD_CLR* to remove it from the set of descriptors *select* uses.

12.6 Summary

Execution in concurrent servers is often driven by the arrival of data and not by the timeslicing mechanism in the underlying operating system. In cases where the service requires little processing, a single-process implementation can use asynchronous I/O to manage connections to multiple clients as effectively as an implementation that uses multiple processes.

The single-process implementation performs the duties of the master and slave processes. When the master socket becomes ready, it accepts a new connection. When any other socket becomes ready, it reads a request and sends a reply. An example single-process server for the ECHO service illustrates the ideas and shows the programming details.

'OR FURTHER STUDY

A good protocol specification does not constrain the implementation. For example, the single-process server described in this chapter implements the ECHO protocol defined by Postel [RFC 862]. Chapter *11* shows an example of a multiple-process, concurrent server built from the same protocol specification.

EXERCISES

12.1 Conduct an experiment that proves the example ECHO server can handle connections concurrently.

12.2 Does it make sense to use the implementation discussed in this chapter for the DAY-TIME service? Why or why not?

12.3 Read the *UNIX Programmer's Manual* to find out the exact representation of descriptors in the list passed to *select*. Write the *FD_SET* and *FD_CLR* macros.

12.4 Compare the performance of single-process and multiple-process server implementations on a computer with multiple processors. Under what circumstances will a single-process version perform better than (or equal to) a multiple-process version?

12.5 Suppose a large number of clients (e.g., *100*) access the example server in this chapter at the same time. Explain what each client might observe.

12.6 Can a single-process server ever deprive one client of service while it repeatedly honors requests from another? Can a multiple-process implementation ever exhibit the same behavior? Explain.

OR FURTHER STUDY

A good protocol specification does not constrain the implementation. For example, the single-process server described in this chapter implements the ECHO protocol defined by Postel [RFC 862]. Chapter 11 shows an example of a multiple-process concurrent server built from the same protocol specification.

EXERCISES

11.1 Conduct an experiment that proves the example ECHO server can handle connections concurrently.

11.2 Does a timeout arise in implementation discussed in this chapter like the DAY TIME service? Why or why not?

11.3 Read the UNIX Programmer's Manual to find out the exact representation of keep alive. In the last paragraph to verify. Write the AD, ACT and TW CCR changes.

11.4 Compare the performance of single-process and multiple-process server implementations on a computer with small file phasespace. Under what circumstances will a single-process version perform better than (or equal to) a multiple-process version?

11.5 Suppose a large number of clients (e.g., 100) access the example ECHO server in this chapter at the same time. Explain what each client might observe.

11.6 Can a single-process server ever deprive one client of service while it repeatedly responds from another? Can a multiple-process implementation ever exhibit the same behavior? Explain.

13

Multiprotocol Servers (TCP, UDP)

13.1 Introduction

The previous chapter describes how to construct a single-process server that uses asynchronous I/O to provide apparent concurrency among multiple connections. This chapter expands the concept. It shows how a single-process server can accommodate multiple transport protocols. It illustrates the idea by showing a single process server that provides the DAYTIME service through both UDP and TCP. While the example server handles requests iteratively, the basic idea generalizes directly to servers that handle requests concurrently.

13.2 The Motivation For Reducing The Number Of Servers

In most cases, a given server handles requests for one particular service accessed through one particular transport protocol. For example, a computer system that offers the DAYTIME service often runs two servers – one server handles requests that arrive via UDP, while the other handles requests that arrive via TCP.

The chief advantage of using a separate server for each protocol lies in control: a system manager can easily control which protocols a computer offers by controlling which of the servers the system runs. The chief disadvantage of using one server per protocol lies in replication. Because many services can be accessed through either UDP or TCP, each service can require two servers. Furthermore, because both UDP and TCP servers use the same basic algorithm to compute a response, they both contain the code needed to perform the computation. If two programs both contain code to perform a given service, software management and debugging can become tedious. The programmer must ensure that both server programs remain the same when correcting bugs or when changing servers to accommodate new releases of system software. Furthermore, the system manager must coordinate execution carefully to ensure that the TCP and UDP servers executing at any time both supply exactly the same version of the service. Another disadvantage of running separate servers for each protocol arises from the use of resources: multiple server processes unnecessarily consume process table entries and other system resources. The magnitude of the problem becomes clear when one remembers that the TCP/IP standards define dozens of services.

13.3 Multiprotocol Server Design

A multiprotocol server consists of a single process that uses asynchronous I/O to handle communication over either UDP or TCP. The server initially opens two sockets: one that uses a connectionless transport (UDP) and one that uses a connection-oriented transport (TCP). The server then uses asynchronous I/O to wait for one of the sockets to become ready. If the TCP socket becomes ready, a client has requested a TCP connection. The server uses *accept* to obtain the new connection, and then communicates with the client over that connection. If the UDP socket becomes ready, a client has sent a request in the form of a UDP datagram. The server uses *recvfrom* to read the request and record the sender's endpoint address. Once it has computed a response, the server sends the response back to the client using *sendto*.

13.4 Process Structure

Figure 13.1 illustrates the process structure of an iterative, multiprotocol server.

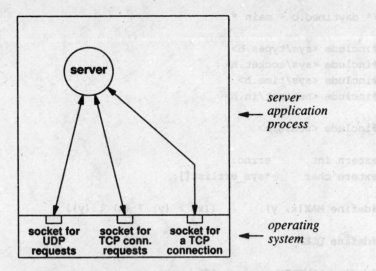

Figure 13.1 The process structure of an iterative, multiprotocol server. At
any time, the server has at most three sockets open: one for
UDP requests, one for TCP connection requests, and a temporary one for an individual TCP connection.

An iterative, multiprotocol server has at most three sockets open at any given time.
Initially, it opens one socket to accept incoming UDP datagrams and a second socket to
accept incoming TCP connection requests. When a datagram arrives on the UDP socket, the server computes a response and sends it back to the client using the same socket.
When a connection request arrives on the TCP socket, the server uses *accept* to obtain
the new connection. *Accept* creates a third socket for the connection, and the server
uses the new socket to communicate with the client. Once it finishes interacting, the
server closes the third socket and waits for activity on the other two.

13.5 An Example Multiprotocol DAYTIME Server

Program *daytimed* illustrates how a multiprotocol server operates. It consists of a
single process that provides the DAYTIME service for both UDP and TCP.

```
/* daytimed.c - main */

#include <sys/types.h>
#include <sys/socket.h>
#include <sys/time.h>
#include <netinet/in.h>

#include <stdio.h>

extern int       errno;
extern char      *sys_errlist[];

#define MAX(x, y)        ((x) > (y) ? (x) : (y))

#define QLEN             5

#define LINELEN          128

/*------------------------------------------------------------------------
 * main - Iterative server for DAYTIME service
 *------------------------------------------------------------------------
 */
int
main(argc, argv)
int      argc;
char     *argv[];
{
        char     *service = "daytime";    /* service name or port number */
        char     buf[LINELEN+1];          /* buffer for one line of text */
        struct sockaddr_in fsin;          /* the request from address    */
        int      alen;                    /* from-address length         */
        int      tsock;                   /* TCP master socket           */
        int      usock;                   /* UDP socket                  */
        int      nfds;
        fd_set   rfds;                    /* readable file descriptors   */

        switch (argc) {
        case     1:
                break;
        case     2:
                service = argv[1];
                break;
        default:
                errexit("usage: daytimed [port]\n");
        }
```

```
        tsock = passiveTCP(service, QLEN);
        usock = passiveUDP(service);
        nfds = MAX(tsock, usock) + 1;    /* bit number of max fd */


        FD_ZERO(&rfds);

        while (1) {
                FD_SET(tsock, &rfds);
                FD_SET(usock, &rfds);

                if (select(nfds, &rfds, (fd_set *)0, (fd_set *)0,
                                (struct timeval *)0) < 0)
                        errexit("select error: %s\n", sys_errlist[errno]);
                if (FD_ISSET(tsock, &rfds)) {
                        int       ssock;           /* TCP slave socket        */

                        alen = sizeof(fsin);
                        ssock = accept(tsock, (struct sockaddr *)&fsin,
                                &alen);
                        if (ssock < 0)
                                errexit("accept failed: %s\n",
                                                sys_errlist[errno]);
                        daytime(buf);
                        (void) write(ssock, buf, strlen(buf));
                        (void) close(ssock);
                }
                if (FD_ISSET(usock, &rfds)) {
                        alen = sizeof(fsin);
                        if (recvfrom(usock, buf, sizeof(buf), 0,
                                (struct sockaddr *)&fsin, &alen) < 0)
                                errexit("recvfrom: %s\n",
                                                sys_errlist[errno]);
                        daytime(buf);
                        (void) sendto(usock, buf, strlen(buf), 0,
                                (struct sockaddr *)&fsin, sizeof(fsin));
                }
        }
}

/*------------------------------------------------------------------------
 * daytime - fill the given buffer with the time of day
 *------------------------------------------------------------------------
 */
int
daytime(buf)
char    buf[];
```

```
{
        char    *ctime();
        time_t  time(), now;

        (void) time(&now);
        sprintf(buf, "%s", ctime(&now));
}
```

Daytimed takes an optional argument that allows the user to specify a service name or protocol port number. If the user does not supply an argument, *daytimed* uses the port for service *daytime*.

After parsing its arguments, *daytimed* calls *passiveTCP* and *passiveUDP* to create two passive sockets for use with TCP and UDP. Both sockets use the same service and, for most services, both will use the same protocol port number. Think of these as the master sockets – the server keeps them open forever, and all initial contact from a client arrives through one of them. The call to *passiveTCP* specifies that the system must en- queue up to *QLEN* connection requests.

After the server creates the master sockets, it prepares to use *select* to wait for one or both to be ready for I/O. First, it sets variable *nfds* to the index in the descriptor bit- mask of the larger of the two sockets and clears the bitmask (variable *rfds*). The server then enters an infinite loop. In each iteration of the loop, it uses macro *FD_SET* to build a bitmask with bits set for the descriptors that correspond to the two master sock- ets. It then uses *select* to wait for input activity on either of them.

When the *select* call returns, one or both of the master sockets is ready. The server uses macro *FD_ISSET* to check the TCP socket and again to check the UDP socket. The server must check both because if a UDP datagram happened to arrive at exactly the same time as a TCP connection request, both sockets would be ready.

If the TCP socket becomes ready, it means that a client initiated a connection re- quest. The server uses *accept* to establish the connection. *Accept* returns the descriptor of a new, temporary socket used only for the new connection. The server calls pro- cedure *daytime* to compute the response, *write* to send the response across the new con- nection, and *close* to terminate the connection and release resources.

If the UDP socket becomes ready, it means that a client sent a datagram to prompt for a DAYTIME response. The server calls *recvfrom* to read the incoming datagram and record the client's endpoint address. It uses procedure *daytime* to compute the response, and then calls *sendto* to send the response back to the client. Because it uses the master UDP socket for all communication, the server does not issue a *close* after sending the UDP response.

13.6 The Concept Of Shared Code

Our example server illustrates an important idea:

A multiprotocol server design permits the designer to create a single procedure that responds to requests for a given service and to call that procedure regardless of whether requests arrive via UDP or TCP.

In the DAYTIME example, of course, the shared code occupies only a few lines. It has been placed in a single procedure, *daytime*. In most practical servers, however, the code needed to compute a response can span hundreds or thousands of lines and usually involves many procedures. It should be obvious that keeping the code in a single place where it can be shared makes maintenance easier and guarantees that the service offered by both transport protocols will be identical.

13.7 Concurrent Multiprotocol Servers

Like the single-protocol DAYTIME servers shown earlier, the example multiprotocol DAYTIME server uses an iterative method to handle requests. The reason for using an iterative solution is the same as for the earlier servers that supply the DAYTIME service: an iterative server suffices because the DAYTIME service performs minimal computation for each request.

An iterative implementation may not suffice for other services that require more computation per request. In such cases, the multiprotocol design can be extended to handle the requests concurrently. In the simplest case, a multiprotocol server can create a new process to handle each TCP connection concurrently, while it handles UDP requests iteratively. The multiprotocol design can also be extended to use the single-process implementation described in Chapter 12. Such an implementation provides apparent concurrency among requests that arrive over multiple TCP connections or via UDP.

13.8 Summary

A multiprotocol server allows the designer to encapsulate all the code for a given service in a single program, eliminating replication and making it easier to coordinate changes. The multiprotocol server consists of a single process. The process opens master sockets for both UDP and TCP, and uses *select* to wait for either or both of them to become ready. If the TCP socket becomes ready, the server accepts the new connection and handles requests using it. If the UDP socket becomes ready, the server reads the request and responds.

The multiprotocol server design illustrated in this chapter can be extended to allow concurrent TCP connections or to use a single-process implementation that handles requests concurrently regardless of whether they arrive via TCP or UDP.

Multiprotocol servers eliminate replication of code by using a single procedure to compute the response for the service. They also eliminate unnecessary use of system resources, especially processes.

FOR FURTHER STUDY

Reynolds and Postel [RFC 1060] specifies a list of application protocols along with the UDP and TCP protocol ports assigned to each.

EXERCISES

13.1   Extend the example server in this chapter to handle requests concurrently.

13.2   Study some of the most common services defined for TCP/IP. Can you find examples where a multiprotocol server cannot use shared code to compute the responses? Explain.

13.3   The example code allows the user to specify a service name or protocol port number as an argument, and uses the argument when creating passive sockets for the service. Is there an example of a service that uses a different protocol port number for UDP than for TCP? Change the code to allow the user to specify a separate protocol port number for each protocol.

13.4   The example server does not allow the system manager to control which protocols it uses. Modify the server to include arguments that allow a manager to specify whether to offer the service for TCP, UDP, or both.

13.5   Consider a site that decides to implement security through an authorization scheme. The site provides each server with a list of authorized client machines, and makes the rule that the server must disallow requests that originate from machines other than those on the list. Implement the authorization scheme for the example multiprotocol server. (Hint: look carefully at the socket functions to see how to do it for TCP.)

14

Multiservice Servers (TCP, UDP)

14.1 Introduction

Chapter *12* describes how to construct a single-process server that uses asynchronous I/O to provide apparent concurrency among multiple connections, and Chapter *13* shows how a multiprotocol server supplies a service over both the TCP and UDP transport protocols. This chapter expands the concepts and combines them with some of the iterative and concurrent server designs discussed in earlier chapters. It shows how a single server can supply multiple services, and illustrates the idea using a single process server that handles a set of services.

14.2 Consolidating Servers

In most cases, programmers design an individual server to handle each service. The example servers in previous chapters illustrate the single-service approach – each waits at a well-known port and answers requests for the service associated with that port. Thus, a computer usually runs one server for the DAYTIME service, another for the ECHO service, and so on. The previous chapter discusses how a server that uses multiple protocols helps conserve system resources and makes maintenance easier. The same advantages that motivate multiprotocol servers motivate consolidating multiple services into a single, multiservice server.

To appreciate the cost of creating one server per service, one needs to examine the set of standardized services. TCP/IP defines a large set of *simple services* that are intended to help test, debug, and maintain a network of computers. Earlier chapters discuss a few examples like DAYTIME, ECHO, and TIME, but many other services exist. A system that runs one server for every standardized service can have dozens of server processes even though most of them will never receive a request. Thus, consolidating many services into a single server process can reduce the number of executing processes dramatically†. Furthermore, because many of the small services can be handled with a trivial computation, most of the code in a server handles the details of accepting requests and sending replies. Consolidating many services into a single server reduces the total code required.

14.3 A Connectionless, Multiservice Server Design

Multiservice servers can use either connectionless or connection-oriented transport protocols. Figure 14.1 illustrates one possible process structure for a connectionless, multiservice server.

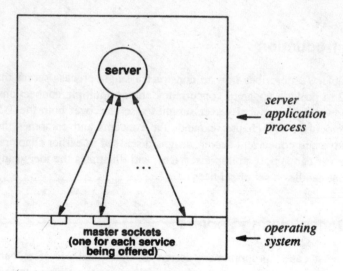

Figure 14.1 An iterative, connectionless, multiservice server. The server waits for a datagram on any of several sockets, where each socket corresponds to an individual service.

As Figure 14.1 shows, an iterative, connectionless, multiservice server usually consists of a single process that contains all the code needed for the services it supplies. The server opens a set of UDP sockets, and binds each to a well-known port for one of

---

†Because UNIX implementations limit the maximum number of sockets a single process can open, it may not be possible for a single server to offer all services. However, if a process can open *N* sockets, using multiservice servers can reduce the number of processes required by a factor of *N*.

the services being offered. It uses a small table to map sockets to services. For each socket descriptor, the table records the address of a procedure that handles the service offered on that socket. The server uses the *select* system call to wait for a datagram to arrive on any of the sockets.

When a datagram arrives, the server calls the appropriate procedure to compute a response and send a reply. Because the mapping table records the service offered by each socket, the server can easily map the socket descriptor to the procedure that handles the service.

14.4 A Connection-Oriented, Multiservice Server Design

A connection-oriented, multiservice server can also follow an iterative algorithm. In principle, such a server performs the same tasks as a set of iterative, connection-oriented servers. To be more precise, the single process in a multiservice server replaces the master server processes in a set of connection-oriented servers. At the top level, the multiservice server uses asynchronous I/O to handle its duties. Figure 14.2 shows the process structure.

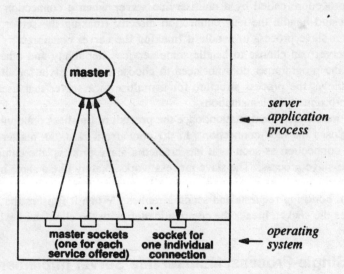

Figure 14.2 The process structure of an iterative, connection-oriented, multiservice server. At any time, the server has one socket open for each service and at most one additional socket open to handle a particular connection.

When it begins execution, the multiservice server creates one socket for each service it offers, binds each socket to the well-known port for the service, and uses *select* to wait for an incoming connection request on any of them. When one of the sockets becomes ready, the server calls *accept* to obtain the new connection that has arrived. *Accept* creates a new socket for the incoming connection. The server uses the new socket to interact with a client, and then closes it. Thus, besides one master socket for each service, the server has at most one additional socket open at any time.

As in the connectionless case, the server keeps a table of mappings so it can decide how to handle each incoming connection. When the server begins, it allocates master sockets. For each master socket, the server adds an entry to the mapping table that specifies the socket number and a procedure that implements the service offered by that socket. After it has allocated a master socket for each service, the server calls *select* to wait for a connection. Once a connection arrives, the server uses the mapping table to decide which of many internal procedures to call to handle the service that the client requested.

14.5 A Concurrent, Connection-Oriented, Multiservice Server

The procedure called by a multiservice server when a connection request arrives can accept and handle the new connection directly (making the server iterative), or it can create a slave process to handle it (making the server concurrent). In fact, a multiservice server can choose to handle some services iteratively and other services concurrently; the programmer does not need to choose a single style for all services. Figure 14.3 shows the process structure for a multiservice server that uses a concurrent, connection-oriented implementation.

In an iterative implementation, once the procedure finishes communicating with the client, it closes the new connection. In the concurrent case, the master server process closes the connection as soon as it has created a slave process; the connection remains open in the slave process. The slave process works exactly like a slave in a conventional, concurrent, connection-oriented server. It communicates with the client over the connection, honoring requests and sending replies. When it finishes the interaction, the slave closes the socket, breaks the communication with the client, and exits.

14.6 A Single-Process, Multiservice Server Implementation

It is possible, although uncommon, to manage all activity in a multiservice server with a single process, using a design exactly like the single-process server discussed in Chapter *12*. Instead of creating a slave process for each incoming connection, a single-process server adds the socket for each new connection to the set it uses with *select*. If one of the master sockets becomes ready, the single-process server calls *accept*; if one of the slave sockets becomes ready, the single-process server calls *read* to obtain an incoming request from the client, forms a response, and calls *write* to send the response back to the client.

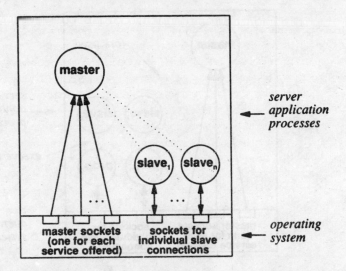

Figure 14.3 The process structure for a concurrent, connection-oriented, multiservice server. The master process handles incoming connection requests, while a slave process handles each connection.

14.7 Invoking Separate Programs From A Multiservice Server

One of the chief disadvantages of most of the designs discussed so far is their inflexibility: changing the code for any single service requires recompilation of the entire multiservice server. The disadvantage does not become important until one considers a server that handles many services. Any small change requires the programmer to recompile the server, terminate the executing server process, and restart the server process using the newly compiled code.

If a multiservice server offers many services, the chances are higher that at least one client will be communicating with it at any given time. Thus, terminating the server process may cause a problem for some clients. In addition, the more services a given server offers, the higher the probability that it will need to be modified.

Designers often choose to break a large, monolithic multiservice server into independent components by using independently compiled programs to handle each service. The idea is easiest to understand when applied to a concurrent, connection-oriented design.

Consider the concurrent, connection-oriented server illustrated in Figure 14.3. The master server process waits for a connection request from a set of master sockets. Once a connection request arrives, the master process calls *fork* to create a slave process that will handle the connection. The server must have the code for all services compiled into the master program. Figure 14.4 illustrates how the design can be modified to break the large server into separate pieces.

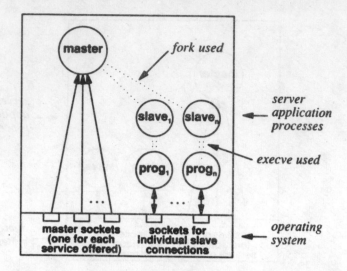

Figure 14.4 The process structure of a connection-oriented, multiservice
server that uses *execve* to execute a separate program to handle
each connection.

As the figure shows, the master server uses *fork* to create a new process to handle
each connection. Unlike the earlier design, however, the slave process calls *execve* to
replace the original code with a new program that handles all client communication.

Because *execve* retrieves the new program from a file, the design described above
allows a system manager to replace the file without recompiling the multiservice server,
terminating the server process, or restarting it. Conceptually, using *execve* separates the
programs that handle each service from the master server code that sets up connections.

> *In a multiservice server, the UNIX* execve *call makes it possible to
> separate the code that handles an individual service from the code
> that manages initial requests from clients.*

14.8 Multiservice, Multiprotocol Designs

Although it may seem natural to think of a multiservice server as either connectionless or connection-oriented, a multiprotocol design is also possible. As described in
Chapter *13*, a multiprotocol design allows a single server process to manage both a
UDP socket and a TCP socket for the same service. In the case of a multiservice
server, the server can manage UDP and TCP sockets for some or all of the services it
offers.

Many networking experts use the term *super server* to refer to a multiservice, multiprotocol server. In principle, a super server operates much the same as a conventional multiservice server. Initially, the server opens one or two master sockets for each service it offers. The master sockets for a given service correspond to connectionless transport (UDP) or connection-oriented transport (TCP). The server uses *select* to wait for any socket to become ready. If a UDP socket becomes ready, the server calls a procedure that reads the next request (datagram) from the socket, computes a response, and sends a reply. If a TCP socket becomes ready, the server calls a procedure that accepts the next connection from the socket and handles it. The server can handle the connection directly, making it iterative, or it can create a new process to handle the connection, making it concurrent.

14.9 An Example Multiservice Server

The multiservice server in file *superd.c* extends the single-process server implementation in Chapter *12*. After initializing data structures and opening sockets for each of the services it offers, the main program enters an infinite loop. Each iteration of the loop calls *select* to wait for one of the sockets to become ready. The *select* call returns when a request arrives.

When *select* returns, the server iterates through each possible socket descriptor and used macro *FD_ISSET* to test whether the descriptor is ready. If it finds a ready descriptor, the server invokes a function to handle the request. To do so, it first uses array *fd2sv* to map from the descriptor number to an entry in array *svent*.

Each entry in *svent* contains a structure of type *service* that maps a socket descriptor to a service. Field *sv_func* contains the address of a function to handle the service. After mapping the descriptor to an entry in *svent*, the program calls the selected function. For a UDP socket, the server calls the service handler directly; for a TCP socket, the server calls the service handler indirectly through procedure *doTCP*.

TCP services require the additional procedure because a TCP socket corresponds to the master socket in a connection-oriented server. When such a socket becomes ready, it means that a connection request has arrived at the socket. The server needs to create a new process to manage the connection. Thus, procedure *doTCP* calls *accept* to accept the new connection. It then calls *fork* to create a new slave process. After closing extraneous file descriptors, *doTCP* invokes the service handler function (*sv_func*). When the service function returns, the slave process exits.

```
/* superd.c - main */

#include <sys/types.h>
#include <sys/param.h>
#include <sys/socket.h>
#include <sys/time.h>
#include <sys/resource.h>
#include <sys/errno.h>
#include <sys/signal.h>
#include <sys/wait.h>
#include <netinet/in.h>

#include <stdio.h>

extern int          errno;
extern char         *sys_errlist[];

#define UDP_SERV     0
#define TCP_SERV     1

#define NOSOCK      -1          /* an invalid socket descriptor */

int     TCPechod(), TCPchargend(), TCPdaytimed(), TCPtimed(), reaper();

struct service {
        char    *sv_name;
        char    sv_useTCP;
        int     sv_sock;
        int     (*sv_func)();
} svent[] = {   { "echo", TCP_SERV, NOSOCK, TCPechod },
                { "chargen", TCP_SERV, NOSOCK, TCPchargend },
                { "daytime", TCP_SERV, NOSOCK, TCPdaytimed },
                { "time", TCP_SERV, NOSOCK, TCPtimed },
                { 0, 0, 0, 0 },
        };

#ifndef MAX
#define MAX(x, y)        ((x) > (y) ? (x) : (y))
#endif  /* MAX */

#define QLEN            5

#define LINELEN        128
```

```
extern  u_short portbase;            /* from passivesock() */

/*------------------------------------------------------------------------
 * main - Super-server main program
 *------------------------------------------------------------------------
 */
int
main(argc, argv)
int     argc;
char    *argv[];
{
        struct service  *psv,           /* service table pointer    */
                *fd2sv[NOFILE];         /* map fd to service pointer */
        int     fd, nfds;
        fd_set  afds, rfds;             /* readable file descriptors */

        switch (argc) {
        case 1:
                break;
        case 2:
                portbase = (u_short) atoi(argv[1]);
                break;
        default:
                errexit("usage: superd [portbase]\n");
        }

        nfds = 0;
        FD_ZERO(&afds);
        for (psv = &svent[0]; psv->sv_name; ++psv) {
                if (psv->sv_useTCP)
                        psv->sv_sock = passiveTCP(psv->sv_name, QLEN);
                else
                        psv->sv_sock = passiveUDP(psv->sv_name);
                fd2sv[psv->sv_sock] = psv;
                nfds = MAX(psv->sv_sock+1, nfds);
                FD_SET(psv->sv_sock, &afds);
        }
        (void) signal(SIGCHLD, reaper);

        while (1) {
                bcopy((char *)&afds, (char *)&rfds, sizeof(rfds));
                if (select(nfds, &rfds, (fd_set *)0, (fd_set *)0,
                                (struct timeval *)0) < 0) {
                        if (errno == EINTR)
```

```
                                            continue;
                               errexit("select error: %s\n", sys_errlist[errno]);
                    }
                    for (fd=0; fd<nfds; ++fd)
                         if (FD_ISSET(fd, &rfds)) {
                               psv = fd2sv[fd];
                               if (psv->sv_useTCP)
                                     doTCP(psv);
                               else
                                     psv->sv_func(psv->sv_sock);
                         }
     }
}


/*------------------------------------------------------------------------
 * doTCP - handle a TCP service connection request
 *------------------------------------------------------------------------
 */
int
doTCP(psv)
struct service  *psv;
{
        struct sockaddr_in fsin;          /* the request from address    */
        int     alen;                     /* from-address length         */
        int     fd, ssock;

        alen = sizeof(fsin);
        ssock = accept(psv->sv_sock, (struct sockaddr *)&fsin, &alen);
        if (ssock < 0)
                errexit("accept: %s\n", sys_errlist[errno]);
        switch (fork()) {
        case 0:
                break;
        case -1:
                errexit("fork: %s\n", sys_errlist[errno]);
        default:
                (void) close(ssock);
                return;           /* parent */
        }
        /* child */

        for (fd = NOFILE; fd >= 0; --fd)
                if (fd != ssock)
                        (void) close(fd);
```

```
        exit(*sv->sv_func(ssock));
}

/*--------------------------------------------------------------------
 * reaper - clean up zombie children
 *--------------------------------------------------------------------
 */
int
reaper()
{
        union wait      status;

        while (wait3(&status, WNOHANG, (struct rusage *)0) >= 0)
                /* empty */;
}
```

The example super server supplies four services: ECHO, CHARGEN, DAYTIME, and TIME. The services other than CHARGEN appear in examples in earlier chapters. Programmers use the CHARGEN service to test client software. Once a client forms a connection to a CHARGEN server, the server generates an infinite sequence of characters and sends it to the client.

File *sv_funcs.c* contains the code for the functions that handle each of the individual services.

```
/* sv_funcs.c - TCPechod, TCPchargend, TCPdaytimed, TCPtimed */

#include <sys/types.h>

#define BUFSIZ   4096              /* max read buffer size */

extern  int     errno;
extern  char    *sys_errlist[];

/*------------------------------------------------------------------------
 * TCPecho - do TCP ECHO on the given socket
 *------------------------------------------------------------------------
 */
int
TCPechod(fd)
int     fd;
{
        char    buf[BUFSIZ];
        int     cc;

        while (cc = read(fd, buf, sizeof buf)) {
                if (cc < 0)
                        errexit("echo read: %s\n", sys_errlist[errno]);
                if (write(fd, buf, cc) < 0)
                        errexit("echo write: %s\n", sys_errlist[errno]);
        }
        return 0;
}

#define LINELEN          72

/*------------------------------------------------------------------------
 * TCPchargend - do TCP CHARGEN on the given socket
 *------------------------------------------------------------------------
 */
int
TCPchargend(fd)
{
        char    c, buf[LINELEN+2];          /* print LINELEN chars + \r\n */

        c = ' ';
        buf[LINELEN] = '\r';
        buf[LINELEN+1] = '\n';
        while (1) {
```

```
                      int      i;

              for (i=0; i<LINELEN; ++i) {
                      buf[i] = c++;
                      if (c > '~')
                              c = ' ';
              }
              if (write(fd, buf, LINELEN+2) < 0)
                      break;
      }
      return 0;
}


/*------------------------------------------------------------------------
 * TCPdaytimed - do TCP DAYTIME protocol
 *------------------------------------------------------------------------
 */
int
TCPdaytimed(fd)
int     fd;
{
      char    buf[LINELEN], *ctime();
      time_t  time(), now;

      (void) time(&now);
      sprintf(buf, "%s", ctime(&now));
      (void) write(fd, buf, strlen(buf));
      return 0;
}

#define UNIXEPOCH        2208900000      /* UNIX epoch, in UCT secs      */

/*------------------------------------------------------------------------
 * TCPtimed - do TCP TIME protocol
 *------------------------------------------------------------------------
 */
int
TCPtimed(fd)
int     fd;
{
      time_t  now, time();
      u_long  htonl();

      (void) time(&now);
```

```
        now = htonl((u_long)(now + UNIXEPOCH));
        (void) write(fd, (char *)&now, sizeof(now));
        return 0;
}
```

Code for most of the individual functions should seem familiar; it has been derived from the example servers in earlier chapters. The code for the CHARGEN service can be found in procedure *TCPchargend*; it is straightforward. The procedure consists of a loop that repeatedly creates a buffer filled with ASCII characters and calls *write* to send the contents of the buffer to the client.

14.10 The BSD UNIX Super Server, Inetd

In practice, many implementations of TCP/IP supply the skeleton of a super server to which system administrators can add additional services. In fact, the system may already have a super server process running. Thus, it may be possible for a manager to add new services to an existing multiservice server without creating a new process.

The BSD UNIX program *inetd* is perhaps the most well-known super server. It supplies many of the small TCP/IP services that network managers use for testing. *Inetd* uses a configuration file to make the addition of new services easier.

14.11 Summary

When designing a server, a programmer can choose among a myriad of possible implementations. While most servers offer only a single service, the programmer can choose a multiservice implementation to reduce the number of server processes. Among multiservice servers, most use a single transport protocol. However, multiple transport protocols can be used to combine connectionless and connection-oriented services into a single server. Finally, the programmer can choose to implement a concurrent, multiservice server with concurrent processes or with a single process that uses asynchronous I/O to provide apparent concurrency.

The example server presented in this chapter illustrates how a multiservice server uses asynchronous I/O to replace a set of master servers.

FOR FURTHER STUDY

Section *8* of the *UNIX Programmer's Manual* describes the *inetd* super server. It also describes the syntax of entries in the *inetd* configuration file, */etc/inetd.conf*.

EXERCISES

14.1   If a connection-oriented, concurrent, multiservice server handles K services, what is the maximum number of sockets it will use?

14.2   How many sockets can a single process create on your local computer system?

14.3   Consider a single-process implementation of a multiservice server. Write an algorithm that shows how the server manages connections.

14.4   Add a UDP service to the example multiservice server described in this chapter.

14.5   Read RFC 1288 to find out about the FINGER service. Add FINGER to the example multiservice server described in this chapter.

14.6   Design a super server that allows new services to be added without recompiling or restarting processes.

14.7   For each of the iterative and concurrent multiservice server designs discussed in this chapter, write an expression for the maximum number of sockets the server allocates. Express your answer as a function of the number of services offered and the number of requests handled concurrently.

14.8   What is the chief disadvantage of a super server that forks a process to handle each connection and then uses *execve* to run a program that supplies the service?

14.9   Consult the *UNIX Programmer's Manual* and find out how to add a new service to *inetd*. How much effort is involved? Which programs must be recompiled? Does one need to restart the server?

14.10   Look at the configuration file on a BSD UNIX machine to find out which services *inetd* offers.

14.11   Read the manual page that describes the *inetd* program and its configuration. Explain the relationship between its use of the *wait* option and concurrency in servers.

15

Uniform, Efficient Management Of Server Concurrency

15.1 Introduction

Earlier chapters present specific server designs, and show how each design uses iterative or concurrent processing. The previous chapter considers how some of the designs can be combined to create a multiservice server.

This chapter considers concurrent servers in a broader sense. It examines the issues underlying server design and several techniques for managing concurrency that can apply to many of the previous designs. The techniques increase design flexibility and allow a designer to optimize server performance. Although the two main approaches presented here may seem contradictory, they can each improve server performance in some circumstances. Furthermore, we will see that both techniques arise from a single concept.

15.2 Choosing Between An Iterative And A Concurrent Design

The server designs discussed so far have been partitioned into two categories: those that handle requests iteratively and those that handle them concurrently. The discussions in previous chapters imply that the designer must make a clear choice between the two basic approaches before the server is constructed.

171

The choice between iterative and concurrent implementations is fundamental because it influences the entire program structure, the perceived response time, and the ability of a server to handle multiple requests. If the designer makes an incorrect decision early in the design process, the cost to change can be high; much of the program may need to be rewritten.

How can a programmer know whether concurrency is warranted? How can a programmer know which server design is optimal? More important, how can a programmer estimate demand or service times? These questions are not easy to answer because networks change: experience shows that networks tend to grow rapidly and unexpectedly. Once users hear about the available services, they want access. As the set of connected users increases, the demand on individual servers increases. At the same time, new technologies and products continually improve communication and processing speeds. However, increases in communication and processing capabilities do not usually occur at the same rate. First one, then the other, becomes faster.

One might wonder exactly how a designer can make a fundamental design choice in a world that is constantly changing. The answer usually comes from experience and intuition: a designer makes the best estimate possible by looking at recent trends. In essence, the designer extrapolates from recent history to formulate an estimate for the near future. Of course, designers can only provide an approximation: as technologies and user demands change, the designer must reevaluate the decisions and, possibly, change the design. The point is:

> *Choosing between iterative and concurrent server designs can be difficult because user demands, processing speeds, and communication capabilities change rapidly. Most designers extrapolate from recent trends when making a choice.*

15.3 Level Of Concurrency

Consider one of the details of concurrent server implementation: the level of concurrency permitted. We define the *level of concurrency* for a server to be the total number of processes the server has running at a given time. The level of concurrency varies over time as the server creates a process to handle an incoming request or as a slave completes a request and exits. Programmers and system administrators are not concerned with tracking the level of concurrency at any given instant, but they do care about the maximum level of concurrency a server exhibits over its lifetime.

Only a few of the designs presented so far require the designer to specify the maximum level of concurrency for a server. Most of the designs permit the master server process to create as many concurrent slave processes as needed to handle incoming requests.

Usually, a concurrent, connection-oriented server creates one process for each connection it receives from a client. Of course, a practical server cannot handle arbitrarily many connections. Each implementation of TCP places a bound on the number of active connections possible, and each operating system places a bound on the number of processes available (the system must restrict either the number of processes available per user or the total number available). When the server reaches one of these limits, the system will deny its requests for more processes.

To increase server flexibility, many programmers avoid placing a fixed upper bound on the maximum level of concurrency in the program. If the server code does not have a predefined maximum level of concurrency, the single implementation can operate either in an environment that does not demand much concurrency or in an environment that has much demand. The programmer does not need to change the code or recompile when moving a server from the former type of environment to the latter. However, servers that do not bound concurrency are a risk in an environment that presents a heavy load. Concurrency can increase until the server's operating system becomes swamped with processes.

15.4 Demand-Driven Concurrency

To achieve flexibility, most of the concurrent server designs presented in earlier chapters use incoming requests to trigger an increase in concurrency. We call such schemes *demand-driven*, and say that the level of concurrency increases *on demand*.

Servers that increase concurrency on demand may seem optimal because they do not use system resources (e.g., process table slots or buffers) unless needed. Thus, demand-driven servers do not use resources unnecessarily. However, demand-driven servers provide low observed response times because they can handle multiple requests without waiting for processing to complete on an existing request.

15.5 The Cost Of Concurrency

While the general motivation for demand-driven concurrency is laudable, the implementations presented in earlier chapters may not produce optimal results. To understand why, we must consider the subtleties of process creation and scheduling as well as the details of server operation. The central issue is one of how to measure the costs and benefits. In particular, one must consider the cost of concurrency as well as its benefits.

15.6 Overhead And Delay

The server designs presented in earlier chapters all use incoming requests as a measure of demand and as a trigger for increased concurrency. The master server waits for a request, and creates a new slave process to handle it immediately after the request arrives. Thus, the level of concurrency at any instant reflects the number of requests the server has received, but has not finished processing.

Despite the apparent simplicity of the request-driven scheme, creating a new process for each request can be expensive. Whether the server uses connectionless or connection-oriented transport, the operating system must inform the master server that a message or a connection has arrived. The master must then ask the system to create a slave process.

Receiving a request from a network and creating a new process can take considerable time. In addition to delaying request processing, creating a process consumes system resources. Thus, on a conventional uniprocessor, the server will not execute while the operating system creates a new process and switches process context.

15.7 Small Delays Can Matter

Does the short delay incurred while creating new processes matter? Figure 15.1 shows how it can.

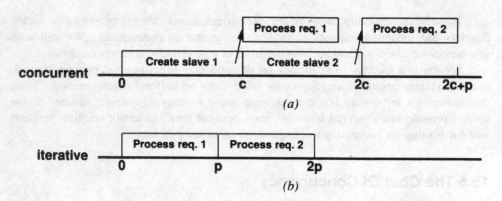

Figure 15.1 (a) The time required to process two requests in a concurrent server and (b) in an iterative version of the server. The iterative version has lower delay because the time required to process a request, p, is less than the time required to create a process, c.

The figure shows an example in which the time required to process a request is less than the time required to create a new process. Let p denote the processing time, and let c denote the time required to create a process. Assume that two requests arrive in a burst at time 0. The concurrent version completes processing the first request after $c+p$ time units, and it finishes processing the second after $2c+p$ time units. Thus, it requires an average of $3c/2 + p$ time units per request. An iterative server completes processing the first request at time p and the second at time $2p$, yielding an average of only $3p/2$ time units per request. Thus, the iterative server design exhibits lower average delay than the concurrent version.

The small additional delay may seem unimportant when considering only a few requests. However, the delay can be significant if one considers the continuous operation of a server under heavy load. If many requests arrive close to the same time, they must wait while the server creates processes to handle them. If additional requests arrive faster than the server can process them, the delays accumulate.

In the short term, small delays in the server affect the observed response time but not the overall throughput. If a burst of requests arrives at or near the same time, protocol software in the operating system will place them in a queue until the server can extract and process them. For example, if the server uses a connection-oriented transport, TCP will enqueue connection requests. If the server uses a connectionless transport, UDP will enqueue incoming datagrams.

In the long term, extra delays can cause requests to be lost. To see how, imagine a server that takes c time units to create a process, but only p time units ($p<c$) to process a request. A concurrent implementation of the server can handle an average of $1/c$ requests per unit time, while an iterative version can handle $1/p$ requests per unit time.

A problem arises when the rate at which requests arrive exceeds $1/c$, but remains less than $1/p$. An iterative implementation can handle the load, but a concurrent implementation spends too much time creating processes. In the concurrent version, queues in the protocol software eventually become full and the software begins rejecting further requests.

In practice, few servers operate close to their maximum throughput. Furthermore, few designers use concurrent servers when the cost of creating a process exceeds the cost of processing. Thus, request delay or loss does not occur in many applications. However, servers designed to provide optimum response under heavy load must consider alternatives to on-demand concurrency.

15.8 Process Preallocation

A straightforward technique can be used to control delay, limit the maximum level of concurrency, and maintain high throughput in concurrent servers when process creation time is significant. The technique consists of preallocating concurrent processes to avoid the cost of creating them.

To use the preallocation technique, a designer programs the master server to create N slave processes when it begins execution. Each process uses facilities available in the operating system to wait for a request to arrive. When a request arrives, one of the waiting slave processes begins execution and handles the request. When it finishes handling a request, the slave does not exit. Instead, it returns to the code that waits for another request.

The chief advantage of preallocation arises from lower operating system overhead. Because the server does not need to create a process when a request arrives, it can handle requests faster. The technique is especially important when request processing involves more I/O than computation. Preallocation allows the server system to switch to

176   Uniform, Efficient Management Of Server Concurrency   Chap. 15

another process and begin to handle the next request while waiting for I/O activity associated with the previous request. To summarize:

> *When using preallocation, a server creates concurrent slave processes*
> *at startup. Preallocation can lower server delay because it avoids the*
> *cost of creating a process each time a request arrives and allows pro-*
> *cessing of one request to overlap I/O activity associated with another.*

15.8.1 Preallocation In UNIX

Some operating systems make the interaction between the master and preallocated slave processes easy because the system offers shared memory or message passing facilities. In UNIX, processes do not share memory. However, process preallocation is still possible. Coordination relies on shared sockets:

> *When a UNIX process calls* fork, *the newly created child process re-*
> *ceives a copy of all open descriptors, including descriptors that*
> *correspond to sockets.*

To take advantage of socket sharing, a master server process opens the necessary socket before it preallocates slave processes. In particular, when it starts, the master server process opens a socket for the well-known port at which it will receive requests. The master then calls *fork* to create as many slave processes as desired. Because each process inherits copies of socket descriptors from the parent, all slaves have access to the socket for the well-known port. The next sections discuss the details of how UNIX handles preallocation for connection-oriented and connectionless servers.

15.8.2 Preallocation In A Connection-Oriented Server

If a concurrent server uses TCP for communication, the level of concurrency depends on the number of active connections. Each incoming connection request must be handled by an independent process. Fortunately, the UNIX implementation provides mutual exclusion for multiple processes that all attempt to accept a connection from the same socket. Each slave calls *accept*, which blocks awaiting receipt of an incoming connection request to the well-known port. When a connection request arrives, the system unblocks exactly one of the slave processes. In an individual slave process, when the call to *accept* returns, it provides a new file descriptor used for the incoming connection. The slave handles the connection, closes the new socket, and then calls *accept* to wait for the next request. Figure 15.2 shows the process structure.

As the figure shows, all slaves inherit access to the socket for the well-known port. An individual slave receives a new socket used for an individual connection when its call to *accept* returns. Although the master creates the socket that corresponds to the well-known port, it does not use the socket for other operations. The dashed line in the diagram denotes the difference between the master's use of the socket and the slaves' use.

Although Figure 15.2 shows a master process running at the same time as the slaves, the distinction between master and slave is somewhat blurred. In practice, the master has no role after it preallocates the slave processes. Thus, the master process can simply exit once the slaves have been started†. A clever programmer can even arrange for the master process to create all except the last slave process. The master process then becomes the last slave, thereby saving the cost of one extra process creation. In UNIX, the code required to do so is trivial.

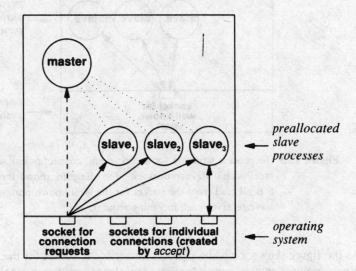

Figure 15.2 The process structure in a concurrent, connection-oriented server that preallocates slave processes. The example shows three preallocated slaves with one of them actively handling a connection. The master opens the socket for the well-known port, but does not use it.

15.8.3 Preallocation In A Connectionless Server

If a concurrent server uses connectionless transport, the level of concurrency depends on the number of requests that arrive. Each incoming request arrives in a separate UDP datagram, and each must be given to a separate process. Concurrent, connectionless designs usually arrange for a master server to create a separate slave process when a request arrives.

UNIX permits a connectionless server to preallocate slave processes using the same preallocation strategy as is used in connection-oriented servers. Figure 15.3 shows the process structure.

---

†In practice, if the master exits, the slaves will be owned by the UNIX *init* process. The master can eliminate *zombie processes* if it enters a loop that repeatedly calls the system function *wait3*.

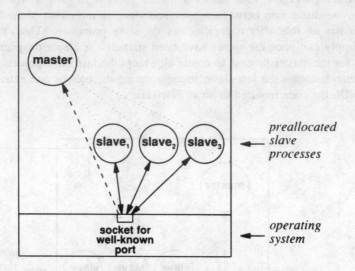

preallocated
slave
processes

operating
system

Figure 15.3 The process structure for a concurrent, connectionless server that
preallocates slave processes. The diagram shows three slaves
that all read from the socket for the well-known port. Only one
slave receives each incoming request.

As the figure shows, each slave process inherits the socket for the well-known port.
Because communication is connectionless, the slaves can use a single socket to send
responses as well as to receive incoming requests. A slave calls *recvfrom* to obtain the
sender's address as well as a datagram from that sender; it calls *sendto* to transmit a reply.

As in a connection-oriented server that uses preallocation, the master process for
the connectionless case has little to do after it opens the socket for the well-known port
and preallocates the slaves. Thus, it can either exit or choose to transform itself into the
last slave to avoid the overhead of creating the last process.

15.8.4 Preallocation, Bursty Traffic, And NFS

Experience has shown that because most implementations of UDP do not provide
large queues for arriving datagrams, bursts of incoming requests can easily overrun a
queue. UDP merely discards datagrams that arrive after the receiver's queue has filled,
so bursts of traffic can cause loss.

The problem of overrun is especially difficult because UDP software often resides
in the operating system. Thus, application programmers cannot always modify it easily.
However, application programmers can preallocate slave processes. The preallocation is
usually sufficient to eliminate loss.

Many implementations of NFS use preallocation to avoid datagram loss. If one examines a system running NFS, one often finds a set of preallocated server processes all reading from the same UDP socket. In fact, preallocation can mean the difference between a usable and an unusable implementation of NFS.

15.8.5 Process Preallocation On A Multiprocessor

Preallocation on a multiprocessor has a special purpose. It permits the designer to relate the level of concurrency in a server to the hardware's capability. If the machine has K processors, the designer can preallocate K slave processes. Because multiprocessor operating systems give each process to a separate processor, a preallocation ensures that the level of concurrency matches the hardware. When a request arrives, the operating system passes it to one of the preallocated processes and assigns that process to a processor. Because the process has been preallocated, little time is required to start it running. Thus, the system will distribute requests quickly. If a burst of requests arrives, each processor will handle one request, giving the maximum possible speed.

15.9 Delayed Process Allocation

Although preallocation can improve efficiency, it does not solve all problems. Surprisingly, in some circumstances efficiency can be improved by using the opposite approach: namely, delaying slave process allocation.

To understand how delay can help, recall that process creation requires time and resources. Creating additional processes can only be justified if doing so will somehow increase the system throughput or lower delay. Creating a process not only takes time, it also adds overhead to the operating system component that must manage processes. In addition, preallocating processes that all attempt to receive incoming requests may add overhead to the networking code.

We said that concurrency will lower delay if the cost of creating a process is smaller than the cost of processing a request. An iterative solution works best if the cost of processing a request is smaller. However, a programmer cannot always know how the costs will compare because the time required may depend on the request (e.g., the time required to search a database may depend on the query).

In addition, the programmer may not know whether an error will be found quickly. To understand why, consider how most server software works. When a request arrives, the server software checks the message to verify that the fields contain appropriate values and that the client is authorized to make a request. Verification can take a few microseconds, or it may involve further network communication that can take several orders of magnitude longer. On one hand, if the server detects an error in the message, it will reject the request quickly, making the total time required to process the message negligible. On the other hand, if the server receives a valid request, it may take considerable processing time. In cases where processing time is short, concurrent processing is unwarranted; an iterative server exhibits lower delay and higher throughput.

How can designers optimize delay and throughput when they do not know whether concurrent processing is justified? The answer lies in a technique for *delayed process allocation*. The idea is straightforward: instead of choosing an iterative or concurrent design, allow a server to measure processing cost and choose between iterative handling or concurrent handling dynamically. The choice is dynamic because it can vary from one request to the next.

To implement dynamic, delayed allocation, servers usually estimate processing cost by measuring elapsed time. The master server receives a request, sets a timer, and begins processing the request (iteratively). If the server finishes processing the request before the timer expires, the server cancels the timer. If the timer expires before the server finishes processing the request, the server creates a slave process and allows the slave to handle the request. To summarize:

> *When using delayed process allocation, a server begins processing each request iteratively. The server creates a concurrent process to handle the request only if processing takes substantial time. Doing so allows the master to check for errors and handle short requests before it creates a process or switches context.*

In UNIX, delayed allocation is easy. Because UNIX includes an *alarm* mechanism, the master process can set a timer and arrange to execute a procedure when the timer expires. Because the UNIX *fork* function permits a newly created process to inherit open sockets as well as a copy of the executing program and data from its parent, the master can create a slave that continues processing exactly at the point where the master was executing when the timer expired.

15.10 The Uniform Basis For Both Techniques

It may seem that the techniques of slave preallocation and delayed slave allocation have nothing in common. In fact, they seem to be exact opposites. However, they share much in common because they both arise from the same conceptual principle: it is possible to improve the performance of some concurrent servers by relaxing the interval between request arrival and slave process creation. Preallocation increases the level of server concurrency before requests arrive; delayed allocation increases server concurrency after requests arrive. The idea can be summarized:

> *Preallocation and delayed allocation arise from a single principle: by detaching the level of server concurrency from the number of currently active requests, the designer can gain flexibility and improve server efficiency.*

15.11 Combining Techniques

The techniques of delayed allocation and preallocation can be combined. A server can begin with no preallocated processes and can use delayed allocation. It waits for a request to arrive, and only creates a slave if processing takes a long time (i.e., if its timer expires). Once a slave has been created, however, the slave need not exit immediately; it can consider itself permanently allocated and persist. After processing one request, the slave can wait for the next incoming request to arrive.

The biggest problem with a combined system arises from the need to control concurrency. It is easy to know when to create additional slave processes, but more difficult to know when a slave should exit instead of persisting. One possible solution arranges for the master to specify a maximum propagation value, M, when creating a slave. The slave can create up to M additional slaves, each of which can create zero more. Thus, the system begins with only a master process, but eventually reaches a fixed maximum level of concurrency. Another technique for controlling concurrency involves arranging for a slave to exit after a period of inactivity. The slave starts a timer before it waits for the next request. If the timer expires before a request arrives, the slave exits.

In some systems, the slaves can use facilities like shared memory to coordinate their activities. They can store a shared integer that records the level of concurrency at any instant, and can use that value to determine whether to persist or exit after handling a request. In systems that permit an application to find out the number of requests enqueued at a socket, a slave can also use the queue length to help it decide the level of concurrency.

15.12 Summary

Two main techniques permit a designer to improve concurrent server performance: preallocation and delayed allocation of slave processes.

Preallocation optimizes delay by arranging to create slave processes before they are needed. The master server opens a socket for the well-known port it will use and then preallocates all slave processes. Because the slaves inherit access to the socket, they can all wait for a request to arrive. The system hands each incoming request to one process. Preallocation is important for concurrent, connectionless servers because the time required to process a request is usually small, making the overhead of process creation significant. Preallocation also makes concurrent, connectionless designs efficient on multiprocessor systems.

Delayed allocation uses a lazy approach to process allocation. A master server begins processing each request iteratively, but sets a timer. It creates a concurrent process to handle the request if the timer expires before the master finishes. Delayed allocation works well in cases where processing times vary among requests or when a server must check a request for correctness (i.e., to verify that the client is authorized). Delayed allocation eliminates process creation overhead for short requests or requests that contain errors.

Although they appear to be opposite, both optimization techniques arise from the same basic principle: they relax the strict coordination between the level of concurrency in the server and the number of pending requests. Doing so can improve server performance.

FOR FURTHER STUDY

Chapters *23* and *24* describe the *Network File System* (NFS). Many implementations of NFS use preallocation to help avoid loss of requests.

EXERCISES

15.1 Modify one of the example servers in previous chapters to use preallocation. How does the performance change?

15.2 Modify one of the example servers in previous chapters to use delayed allocation. How does the performance change?

15.3 Test a connectionless server that uses preallocation on a multiprocessor. Be sure to arrange for clients that transmit bursts of requests. How does the useful level of concurrency relate to the number of processors? If the two are not the same, explain why.

15.4 Write a server algorithm that combines delayed allocation with preallocation. How can you limit the maximum level of concurrency?

15.5 In the previous question, if your operating system offered a message passing facility, how could you use it to control the level of concurrency?

15.6 What advantages can one obtain by combining the techniques discussed in this chapter with a concurrent, single-process server?

15.7 How can a designer use the techniques discussed in this chapter with a multiservice server?

16

Concurrency In Clients

16.1 Introduction

The previous chapters show how servers can handle requests concurrently. This chapter considers the issue of concurrency in client software. It discusses how a client can benefit from concurrency and how a concurrent client operates. Finally, it shows an example client that illustrates concurrent operation.

16.2 The Advantages Of Concurrency

Servers use concurrency for two main reasons:

- Concurrency can improve the observed response time (and therefore the overall throughput to all clients).
- Concurrency can eliminate potential deadlocks.

In addition, a concurrent implementation permits the designer to create multiprotocol or multiservice servers easily. Finally, concurrent implementations that use multiple processes are extremely flexible because they operate well on a variety of hardware platforms. When ported to a computer that has a single CPU, they work correctly. When ported to a computer that has multiple processors, they operate more efficiently because they take advantage of the additional processing power without any changes to the code.

It may seem that clients could not benefit from concurrency, primarily because a client usually performs only one activity at a time. Once it sends a request to a server,

183

the client cannot proceed until it receives a response. Furthermore, the issue of client efficiency and deadlock are not as serious as the issue of server deadlock because if a client slows or ceases to execute, it stops only itself – other clients continue to operate.

Despite appearances, concurrency does have advantages in clients. First, concurrent implementations can be easier to program because they separate functionality into conceptually separate components. Second, concurrent implementations can be easier to maintain and extend because they make the code modular. Third, concurrent clients can contact several servers at the same time either to compare response times or to merge the results the servers return. Fourth, concurrency can allow the user to change parameters, inquire about the client status, or control processing dynamically. This chapter will focus on the idea of interacting with multiple servers at the same time.

> *The key advantage of using concurrency in clients lies in asynchrony.*
> *It allows a client to handle multiple tasks simultaneously without im-*
> *posing a strict execution order on them.*

16.3 The Motivation For Exercising Control

One possible use of asynchrony arises from the need to separate control functions from normal processing. For example, consider a client used to query a large demographic database. Assume a user can generate queries like:

> *Find all people who live on Elm Street.*

If the database contains information for a single town, the response could include fewer than *100* names. If the database contains information about all people in the United States, however, the response could contain hundreds of thousands of names. Furthermore, if the database system consists of many servers distributed across a wide geographic area, the lookup could take many minutes.

The database example illustrates an important idea underlying many client-server interactions: a user who invokes a client may have little or no idea how long it will take to receive a response or how large that response will be.

Most client software merely waits until a response arrives. Of course, if the server malfunctions, deadlock occurs and the client will block attempting to read a response that will never arrive. Unfortunately, the user cannot know if a true deadlock has occurred or if processing is merely slow because network delays are high or the server is overloaded. Furthermore, the user cannot know whether the client has received any messages from the server.

If a user becomes impatient or decides that a particular response requires too much time, the user has only one option: abort the client program and try again later. In such situations, concurrency can help because an appropriately designed concurrent client can permit the user to continue to interact with the client while the client waits for a response. The user can find out whether any data has been received, choose to send a different request, or terminate the communication gracefully.

As an example, consider the hypothetical database client described above. A concurrent implementation can read and process commands from the user's keyboard concurrently with database lookup. Thus, a user can type a command like *status* to determine whether the client has successfully opened a connection to the server and whether the client has sent a request. The user can type *abort* to stop communication, or the user can type *newserver* to instruct the client to terminate the existing communication and attempt to communicate with another server.

Separating client control from normal processing allows a user to interact with a client even if the normal input for the client comes from a file. Thus, even after the user starts a client handling a large input file, he or she can interact with the running client program to find out how processing has progressed. Similarly, a concurrent client can proceed to place responses in an output file while keeping its interaction with the user separate.

16.4 Concurrent Contact With Multiple Servers

Concurrency can allow a single client to contact several servers at the same time and to report to the user as soon as it receives a response from any of them. For example, a concurrent client for the TIME service can send to multiple servers and either accept the first response that arrives or take the average of several responses.

Consider a client that uses the ECHO service to measure the throughput to a given destination. Assume the client forms a TCP connection to an ECHO server, sends a large volume of data, reads the echo back, computes the total time required for the task, and reports the throughput in bytes per second. A user can invoke such a client to determine the current network throughput.

Now consider how concurrency can enhance a client that uses ECHO to measure throughput. Instead of measuring one connection at a time, a concurrent client can access multiple destinations at the same time. It can send to any of them and read from any of them concurrently. Because it performs all measurements concurrently, it executes faster than a non-concurrent client. Furthermore, because it makes all measurements at the same time, they are all affected equally by the loads on the CPU and the local network.

16.5 Implementing Concurrent Clients

Like concurrent servers, most concurrent client implementations follow one of two basic approaches:

- The client divides into two or more processes that each handle one function, or

- The client consists of a single process that uses *select* to handle multiple input and output events asynchronously.

Some operating systems support interprocess memory sharing and interprocess communications. Figure 16.1 illustrates how the multiple process approach can be used in such systems to support a connection-oriented application protocol.

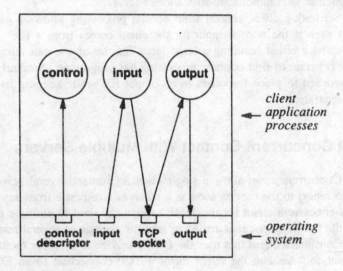

Figure 16.1 One possible process structure for a connection-oriented client that uses multiple processes to achieve concurrent processing. One process handles input and sends requests to the server, while another retrieves responses and handles output.

As Figure 16.1 illustrates, multiple processes allow the client to separate input and output processing. The figure shows how the processes interact with file descriptors and a socket descriptor. An *input process* reads from standard input, formulates requests, and sends them to the server over the TCP connection, while a separate *output process* receives responses from the server and writes them to standard output. Meanwhile, a third *control process* accepts commands from the user that control processing.

16.6 Single-Process Implementations

Unfortunately, most UNIX implementations do not allow separate processes to share memory. Thus, the multiple process implementation does not work well under UNIX. Instead, concurrent clients built for UNIX usually implement concurrency with a single-process algorithm similar to Algorithm 8.5† and the examples in Chapters *12* through *14*. Figure 16.2 illustrates the process structure.

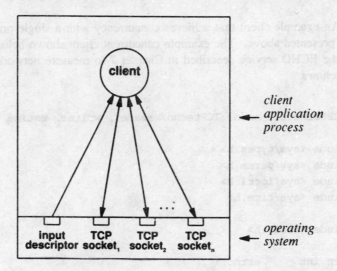

Figure 16.2 The process structure most often used with UNIX to provide apparent concurrency in a single-process, connection-oriented client. The client uses *select* to handle multiple connections concurrently.

A single-process client uses asynchronous I/O like a single-process server. The client creates socket descriptors for its TCP connections to multiple servers. It may also have a descriptor from which it obtains input. The body of a client program consists of a loop that uses *select* to wait for one of its descriptors to become ready. If the input descriptor becomes ready, the client reads the input and either stores it for later use or acts on it immediately. If a TCP connection becomes ready for output, the client prepares and sends a request across the TCP connection. If a TCP connection becomes ready for input, the client reads the response that the server has sent and handles it.

Of course, a single-process concurrent client shares many advantages and disadvantages with a single-process server implementation. The client reads input or responses from the server at whatever rate they are generated. Local processing will continue even if the server delays for a short time. Thus, the client will continue to read and honor control commands even if the server fails to respond.

---

†See page 110 for a description of Algorithm 8.5.

A single-process client can become deadlocked if it invokes a system function that blocks. Thus, the programmer must be careful to ensure that the client process does not block indefinitely waiting for an event that will not occur. Of course, the programmer may choose to ignore some cases and to allow the user to detect that deadlock problems have occurred. It is important for the programmer to understand the subtleties and to make conscious decisions about each case.

16.7 An Example Concurrent Client That Uses ECHO

An example client that achieves concurrency with a single process will clarify the ideas presented above. The example concurrent client shown below in file *TCPtecho.c* uses the ECHO service described in Chapter 7 to measure network throughput to a set of machines.

```
/* TCPtecho.c - main, TCPtecho, reader, writer, mstime */


#include <sys/types.h>
#include <sys/param.h>
#include <sys/ioctl.h>
#include <sys/time.h>

#include <stdio.h>

extern int      errno;
extern char     *sys_errlist[];

#define BUFSIZE        4096             /* write buffer size          */
#define CCOUNT         64*1024          /* default character count    */

#define USAGE     "usage: TCPtecho [ -c count ] host1 host2...\n"

char    *hname[NOFILE];                 /* fd to host name mapping    */
int     rc[NOFILE], wc[NOFILE];         /* read/write character counts */
char    buf[BUFSIZE];                   /* read/write data buffer     */
long    mstime();


/*------------------------------------------------------------------------
 * main - concurrent TCP client for ECHO service timing
 *------------------------------------------------------------------------
 */
int
main(argc, argv)
```

```
int     argc;
char    *argv[];
{
        int     ccount = CCOUNT;
        int     i, hcount, maxfd, fd;
        int     one = 1;
        fd_set  afds;

        hcount = 0;
        maxfd = -1;
        for (i=1; i<argc; ++i) {
                if (strcmp(argv[i], "-c") == 0) {
                        if (++i < argc && (ccount = atoi(argv[i])))
                                continue;
                        errexit(USAGE);
                }
                /* else, a host */

                fd = connectTCP(argv[i], "echo");
                if (ioctl(fd, FIONBIO, (char *)&one))
                        errexit("can't mark socket nonblocking: %s\n",
                                sys_errlist[errno]);
                if (fd > maxfd)
                        maxfd = fd;
                hname[fd] = argv[i];
                ++hcount;
                FD_SET(fd, &afds);
        }
        TCPtecho(&afds, maxfd+1, ccount, hcount);
        exit(0);
}


/*------------------------------------------------------------------------
 * TCPtecho - time TCP ECHO requests to multiple servers
 *------------------------------------------------------------------------
 */
int
TCPtecho(pafds, nfds, ccount, hcount)
fd_set  *pafds;
int     nfds, ccount, hcount;
{
        fd_set  rfds, wfds;             /* read/write fd sets          */
        fd_set  rcfds, wcfds;           /* read/write fd sets (copy)   */
        int     fd, i;
```

```
        for (i=0; i<BUFSIZE; ++i)           /* echo data    */
                buf[i] = 'D';
        bcopy((char *)pafds, (char *)&rcfds, sizeof(rcfds));
        bcopy((char *)pafds, (char *)&wcfds, sizeof(wcfds));
        for (fd=0; fd<nfds; ++fd)
                rc[fd] = wc[fd] = ccount;

        (void) mstime((long *)0);           /* set the epoch */

        while (hcount) {
                bcopy((char *)&rcfds, (char *)&rfds, sizeof(rfds));
                bcopy((char *)&wcfds, (char *)&wfds, sizeof(wfds));

                if (select(nfds, &rfds, &wfds, (fd_set *)0,
                                (struct timeval *)0) < 0)
                        errexit("select failed: %s\n",sys_errlist[errno]);
                for (fd=0; fd<nfds; ++fd) {
                        if (FD_ISSET(fd, &rfds))
                                if (reader(fd, &rcfds) == 0)
                                        hcount--;
                        if (FD_ISSET(fd, &wfds))
                                writer(fd, &wcfds);
                }
        }


/*------------------------------------------------------------------------
 * reader - handle ECHO reads
 *------------------------------------------------------------------------
 */
int
reader(fd, pfdset)
int     fd;
fd_set *pfdset;
{
        long    now;
        int     cc;

        cc = read(fd, buf, sizeof(buf));
        if (cc < 0)
                errexit("read: %s\n", sys_errlist[errno]);
        if (cc == 0)
                errexit("read: premature end of file\n");
```

```
                rc[fd] -= cc;
                if (rc[fd])
                        return 1;
                (void) mstime(&now);
                printf("%s: %d ms\n", hname[fd], now);
                (void) close(fd);
                FD_CLR(fd, pfdset);
                return 0;
}


/*-----------------------------------------------------------------------
 * writer - handle ECHO writes
 *-----------------------------------------------------------------------
 */
int
writer(fd, pfdset)
int     fd;
fd_set  *pfdset;
{
        int     cc;

        cc = write(fd, buf, MIN(sizeof(buf), wc[fd]));
        if (cc < 0)
                errexit("read: %s\n", sys_errlist[errno]);
        wc[fd] -= cc;
        if (wc[fd] == 0) {
                (void) shutdown(fd, 1);
                FD_CLR(fd, pfdset);
        }
}

/*-----------------------------------------------------------------------
 * mstime - report the number of milliseconds since Jan 1, 1970
 *-----------------------------------------------------------------------
 */
long
mstime(pms)
long    *pms;
{
        static struct timeval   epoch;
        struct timeval          now;

        if (gettimeofday(&now, (struct timezone *)0))
                errexit("gettimeofday: %s\n", sys_errlist[errno]);
```

```
        if (!pms) {
                epoch = now;
                return 0;
        }
        *pms = (now.tv_sec - epoch.tv_sec) * 1000;
        *pms += (now.tv_usec - epoch.tv_usec + 500)/ 1000;
        return *pms;
}
```

16.8 Execution Of The Concurrent Client

TCPtecho accepts multiple machine names as arguments. For each machine, it opens a TCP connection to the ECHO server on that machine, sends *ccount* characters (bytes) across the connection, reads the bytes it receives back from each server, and prints the total time required to complete the task. Thus, *TCPtecho* can be used to measure the current throughput to a set of machines.

TCPtecho begins by initializing the character count variable to the default value, *CCOUNT*. It then parses its arguments to see if the user typed the *-c* option. If so, *TCPtecho* converts the specified count to an integer and stores it in variable *ccount* to replace the default.

TCPtecho assumes all arguments other than the *-c* flag specify the name of a machine. For each such argument, it calls *connectTCP* to form a TCP connection to the ECHO server on the named machine. *TCPtecho* records the machine name in array *hname*, and calls macro *FD_SET* to set the bit in the file descriptor mask that corresponds to the socket. It also records the maximum descriptor number in *maxfd* (needed for the call to *select*).

Once it has established a TCP connection for each machine specified in the arguments, the main program calls procedure *TCPtecho* to handle the transmission and reception of data. *TCPtecho* handles all connections concurrently. It fills buffer *buf* with data to be sent (the letter *D*), and then calls *select* to wait for any TCP connection to become ready for input or for output. When the *select* call returns, *TCPtecho* iterates through all descriptors to see which are ready.

When a connection becomes ready for output, *TCPtecho* calls procedure *writer*, which sends as much data from the buffer as TCP will accept in a single call to *write*. If *write* finds that the entire buffer has been sent, it calls *shutdown* to close the descriptor for output and removes the descriptor from the output set used by *select*.

When a descriptor becomes ready for input, *TCPtecho* calls procedure *reader*, which accepts as much data from the connection as TCP can deliver and place in the buffer. Procedure *reader* reads data into the buffer and decrements the count of characters remaining. If the count reaches zero (i.e., the server has received as many characters as it sent), procedure *reader* computes how much time has elapsed since data transmission started, prints a message, and closes the connection. It also removes the descriptor from the input set used by *select*. Thus, a message that reports the total time required to echo data appears on the output each time a connection completes.

After performing a single input or output operation on a connection, procedures *reader* and *writer* each return and the loop in *TCPtecho* continues to iterate, calling *select* again. *Reader* returns a value of *0* if it detected an end of file condition and closed a connection, and a value of *1*, otherwise. *TCPtecho* uses *reader*'s return code to determine whether it should decrement the count of active connections. When the count of connections reaches zero, the loop in *TCPtecho* terminates, *TCPtecho* returns to the main program, and the client process exits.

Figure 16.3 shows sample output from three separate executions of *TCPtecho*. The first invocation shows that *TCPtecho* only requires *311* milliseconds to send data to the ECHO server on the local machine. The command line has a single argument, *localhost*. Because the second invocation has three arguments (*ector*, *arthur*, and *merlin*), it causes *TCPtecho* to interact with all three machines concurrently. The third invocation measures the time required to reach machine *sage*, but the command line specifies that *TCPtecho* should only send *1000* characters instead of the default (64K).

```
% TCPtecho localhost
localhost: 311 ms

% TCPtecho ector arthur merlin
arthur:   601 ms
merlin: 4921 ms
ector: 11791 ms

% TCPtecho -c 1000 sage
sage: 80 ms
```

Figure 16.3 An example of the output from three separate executions of *TCPtecho* for machines at Purdue University. A machine requires more time if it is further away from the client or has a slower processor.

16.9 Concurrency In The Example Code

A concurrent implementation of *TCPtecho* improves the program in two ways. First, a concurrent implementation obtains a more accurate measure of the time required for each connection because it measures the throughput on all connections during the same time interval. Thus, congestion affects all connections equally. Second, a concurrent implementation makes *TCPtecho* more appealing to users. To understand why, look again at the times reported in the sample output for the second trial. The output message for machine *arthur* appears in a little over one half of a second, the message for machine *merlin* appears after about five seconds, and the final message, for *ector*, appears after about twelve seconds. If the user had to wait for all tests to run sequentially, the total execution would require approximately eighteen seconds. When measuring machines further away on the Internet, individual times can be substantially longer, making the concurrent version much faster. In many circumstances, using a sequential client implementation to measure N machines can take approximately N times longer than a concurrent version.

16.10 Summary

Concurrent execution provides a powerful tool that can be used in clients as well as servers. Concurrent client implementations can offer faster response time and can avoid deadlock problems. Finally, concurrency can help designers separate control and status processing from normal input and output.

We studied an example connection-oriented client that measures the time required to access the ECHO server on one or more machines. Because the client executes concurrently, it can avoid the differences in throughput caused by network congestion by making all measurements during the same time interval. The concurrent implementation also appeals to users because it overlaps the measurements instead of making the user wait to perform them sequentially.

EXERCISES

16.1 Notice that the example server checks ready file descriptors sequentially. If many descriptors become ready simultaneously, the server will handle the descriptors with lowest numbers first, and then iterate through the others. After handling all ready descriptors, it again calls *select* to wait until another descriptor becomes ready. Consider the time that elapses between handling a ready descriptor and calling *select*. Less time elapses after operations on descriptors with higher numbers than elapses after operations on descriptors with low numbers. Can the difference lead to starvation? Explain.

16.2 Modify the example server to avoid the unfairness discussed in the previous exercise.

16.3 For each of the iterative and concurrent client designs discussed in this chapter, write an expression that gives the maximum number of sockets used.

17

Tunneling At The Transport
And Application Levels

17.1 Introduction

Previous chapters describe the design of client and server software for cases where a TCP/IP internet interconnects all communicating machines. Many of the designs presented assume that clients and servers will run on reasonably powerful computers that have operating system support for concurrent processes as well as full support for TCP/IP protocols.

This chapter begins to explore the techniques system managers and programmers use to exploit alternative topologies. In particular, it examines techniques that allow computers to use a high-level protocol service to carry IP traffic and designs that use IP to carry traffic for other protocol systems.

17.2 Multiprotocol Environments

In an ideal world, programmers using TCP/IP only need to build client and server software for computers that connect directly to a TCP/IP internet and provide full support for TCP/IP protocols. In reality, however, not all machines provide complete TCP/IP support, and not all organizations use TCP/IP exclusively to interconnect computers. For example, an organization may have small personal computers with insufficient capacity to run server software, or it may have groups of machines connected to networks that use protocols like *DECNET*, *SNA*, or *X.25*. In fact, networking in most organizations has grown over time as the organization has added new networks to interconnect existing groups of computers. Usually, network managers choose a hardware technology and a protocol suite for each group of computers independently. They use factors such as cost, distance, desired speed, and vendor availability when making a choice. Organizations that installed networks before TCP/IP protocols were available may have selected a vendor-specific protocol suite. As a result of such network evolution, most large organizations have several groups of machines, with each group using its own protocol suite. The point is:

> *Because networking has evolved slowly over many years, because vendors promoted proprietary network systems, and because TCP/IP was not always available, large organizations often have groups of computers using alternative protocol systems to communicate. Furthermore, to minimize expense, organizations often continue to use older network systems until they can phase in new technologies.*

For example, Figure 17.1 illustrates an organization that uses three networks at its two sites. Each site has its own Ethernet. A single wide area network that uses X.25 protocols interconnects hosts at the two sites. As the figure shows, a subset of machines connect to each network.

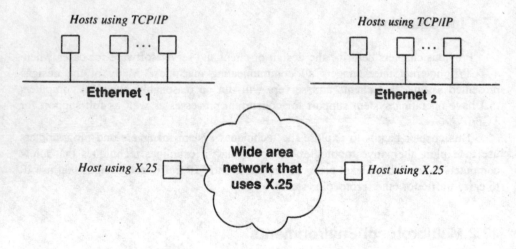

Figure 17.1 An example organization with three networks. All computers connected to the wide area network use the X.25 protocol while all computers connected to the local area networks use TCP/IP.

The chief disadvantages of having multiple network systems arise from duplication of effort and limitations on interoperability. Hosts that connect to an X.25 wide area network must use X.25 protocols instead of TCP/IP protocols. Thus, if a client and server run on hosts connected to the X.25 network shown in Figure 17.1, they must use

an X.25 virtual circuit for communication. Meanwhile, clients and servers running on
an Ethernet use TCP virtual circuits.

17.3 Mixing Network Technologies

Usually, a TCP/IP internet consists of a set of hosts on physical networks interconnected by gateways (routers). All hosts and gateways in the internet must use TCP/IP
protocols. Similarly, a network running the DECNET protocols consists of physical
links and computers that use DECNET exclusively, while a network running SNA protocols usually consists of physical links and computers that use SNA exclusively. However, because a transport-level service can deliver packets from one point to another as
easily as packet-switching hardware can, it should be possible to substitute any
transport-level switching service in place of a single physical link in another packet
switching system.

Many internets have been built that use transport-level switching services instead
of physical networks. For example, consider the networks shown in Figure 17.1 again.
Assume the organization decides to interconnect its two Ethernets to form a single
TCP/IP internet that will allow all the hosts attached to the Ethernets to communicate.
The most obvious strategy involves installing two gateways between them. However, if
a large geographic distance separates the two Ethernets, the cost of adding a dedicated
leased line to interconnect the two networks may be prohibitive. The additional cost
may be especially difficult to justify because the organization already has an X.25 network connecting the two sites.

Figure 17.2 illustrates how the organization shown in Figure 17.1 can use existing
X.25 network connectivity to provide a TCP/IP internet connection between its two
sites.

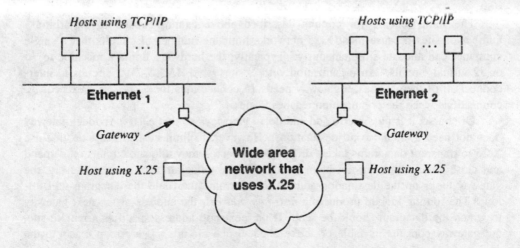

Figure 17.2 IP gateways using an X.25 transport-level service in place of a
physical network.

The organization installs a new gateway at each site. Each of the new gateways connects to the X.25 network and to the local Ethernet at its site. When the gateways boot, they use X.25 to form a conventional, transport-level virtual circuit to one another across the X.25 wide area network. Each gateway arranges its routing table so it routes nonlocal traffic across the X.25 circuit. The gateways use the X.25 protocol to send IP datagrams to one another. From the viewpoint of the gateways, X.25 merely provides a link over which datagrams can be sent. From the viewpoint of the X.25 network, IP software on the two gateways acts exactly like application software on other hosts. The X.25 service does not know that the data being sent across the virtual circuit consists of IP datagrams.

With the two gateways in place, a user on any host can invoke standard TCP/IP client software that contacts a server on any other host. Client-server interactions may cross a single Ethernet or may traverse the X.25 network to reach the other site. Neither the user nor the client-server applications needs to know that datagrams pass across an X.25 network when they travel from the Ethernet at one site to the Ethernet at the other. The two Ethernets merely form part of a TCP/IP internet. Furthermore, hosts using X.25 protocols on the wide area network do not need to change. They can continue to communicate without interference from the TCP/IP traffic because the virtual circuits they use will remain independent of the new connection between the gateways.

17.4 Dynamic Circuit Allocation

In the example topology that Figure 17.2 illustrates, the TCP/IP internet traffic needs only one X.25 virtual circuit through the X.25 network because the organization only has two sites. If the organization expands by adding additional sites, it can extend the topology by placing a gateway at each new site and creating additional circuits through the X.25 network to interconnect each new gateway to the gateways at existing sites.

The static scheme for circuits described above cannot expand to an arbitrary number of sites because most X.25 networks limit the number of circuits that a single computer can allocate simultaneously. Typically, the hardware limits a machine to *16* or *32* virtual circuits. An organization with N sites needs $(N*(N-1))/2$ circuits to interconnect all of them. Thus, a gateway needs *15* connections for *6* sites, and exceeds *32* connections when the organization reaches *9* sites.

Of course, it is possible to add additional gateways so that each individual gateway does not need a circuit to all destinations. However, to limit costs, most sites that use X.25 to transport datagrams take a different approach – they allocate circuits on demand and close circuits that are not being used. When a datagram arrives at a gateway, the gateway looks up the destination address to determine the route the datagram will follow. The routing lookup produces a *next-hop address*, the address of the next gateway to which the datagram should be sent. If the next hop address specifies a remote site, the gateway consults its table of active X.25 virtual circuits. If a circuit exists to the next-hop, the gateway forwards the datagram across the circuit. If no circuit exists, the gateway opens a new circuit to the desired destination dynamically.

If the gateway does not have an unused circuit when it needs to open a new circuit, the gateway must close an existing circuit to make one available. The problem becomes one of choosing which circuit to close. Usually, a gateway follows the same policy that a demand paging system uses: it closes the *least recently used* (LRU) circuit. After sending its datagram across the new circuit, the gateway leaves the circuit open. Often the outgoing datagrams will cause the receiver to reply, so keeping the circuit open helps minimize delay and cost.

By dynamically opening and closing virtual circuits, a gateway can limit the number of simultaneous connections it needs without losing the ability to communicate with all sites. The gateway only needs to have one circuit open for each site with which communication is currently in progress.

17.5 Encapsulation And Tunneling

The term *encapsulation* describes the process of placing an IP datagram inside a network packet or frame so that it can be sent across an underlying network. Encapsulation refers to how the network interface uses packet switching hardware. For example, two hosts that communicate across an Ethernet using IP encapsulate each datagram in a single Ethernet packet for transmission. The encapsulation standard for TCP/IP specifies that an IP datagram occupies the data portion of the Ethernet packet and that the Ethernet packet type must be set to a value that specifies IP.

By contrast, the term *tunneling* refers to the use of a high-level transport network service to carry packets or messages from another service. The example in Figure 17.2 shows that gateways can tunnel through an X.25 service to send IP datagrams to one another. The key difference between tunneling and encapsulation lies in whether IP transmits datagrams in hardware packets or uses a high-level transport service to deliver them.

> *IP encapsulates each datagram in a packet when it uses the hardware directly. It creates a tunnel when it uses a high-level transport delivery service to send datagrams from one point to another.*

17.6 Tunneling Through An IP Internet

After TCP/IP was first defined, researchers experimented to see how they could make IP software tunnel through existing networks (like X.25) to deliver datagrams. The motivation should be clear: many organizations had existing networks in place. Surprisingly, the trend has turned around. Most tunneling now occurs because vendors use IP protocols to deliver packets from non-TCP/IP protocols.

Understanding the change in tunneling requires us to understand a change in networking. As TCP/IP became popular, the TCP/IP internet became the universal packet delivery mechanism for many groups. In fact, IP now provides the widest connectivity among the computers at most organizations.

To see how the availability of IP affects other protocols, suppose two computers in an organization need to communicate using a vendor-specific protocol. Instead of adding additional physical network connections between the two computers, a manager can think of the organization's IP internet as a large network, and can allow the protocol software on the two computers to exchange messages by sending them in IP datagrams. Software is currently available that uses IP to carry IPX traffic (Novell), SNA traffic (IBM), and traffic from other high-level protocols. In addition, researchers have devised ways to allow IP networks to carry OSI traffic, allowing vendors to build and debug high-level OSI protocols before they have working implementations of lower layers.

17.7 Application-Level Tunneling Between Clients And Servers

Although the general notion of tunneling refers to the use of one transport-level protocol suite by another, programmers can extend the idea to client-server interactions. The programmer can use *application-level tunneling* to provide a communication path between a client and a server.

To understand how application-level tunneling works, think of two computers that attach to an X.25 network. Suppose a programmer wishes to run a UDP client application on one and a UDP server application on the other. Often, application programmers cannot make changes to the operating system software because they are only permitted to build application programs. Therefore, if the operating systems on the two computers do not support TCP/IP protocols and transport-level tunneling, a programmer may find it inconvenient or impossible to use UDP or to make IP datagrams tunnel through the X.25 network.

In such cases, application-level tunneling makes it possible for clients and servers to communicate across an X.25 network. To do so, the programmer must build a library of procedures that simulates the socket interface. The simulation library must allow an application to create an active or passive UDP socket and to send or receive UDP datagrams. Procedures in the socket simulation library translate calls to the standard socket routines (e.g., *socket*, *send*, and *receive*) into operations that allocate and manipulate local data structures and transmit the message across the X.25 network. When the client calls *socket* to create a socket, the *socket* library routine creates an X.25 connection to the server. When the client or server calls *send* to transmit a message, the *send* library routine transfers the UDP datagram across the X.25 connection.

Once a socket simulation library has been created, programmers can compile any UDP client or server program, link the compiled program using the simulation library, and then run the resulting application. Figure 17.3 illustrates the resulting software structure.

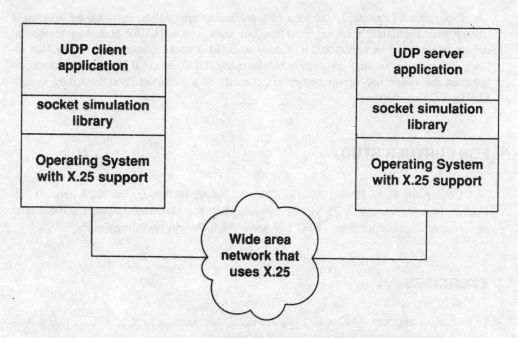

Figure 17.3 Conceptual organization of software in a client and server using
application-level tunneling through an X.25 network. The sock-
et simulation library allows the client and server to exchange
UDP datagrams across a non-TCP/IP transport service.

17.8 Summary

Tunneling consists of sending packets between computers using a transport-level
packet delivery system instead of sending them directly across physical networks. Early
work on tunneling IP through existing network systems was motivated by organizations
that already had large wide area networks in place. These organizations wanted to
avoid the cost of adding new physical connections to run IP. Researchers devised ways
to allow IP to use the existing networks to transfer packets without changing the networks. IP treats the transport service as a single hardware link; the transport service
treats IP traffic the same as traffic sent by any application.

IP has become the delivery system that provides the most interoperability. Consequently, current work on tunneling concentrates on finding ways to use IP as a packet
delivery system that carries packets for other network protocols. Many vendors have
announced software that enables their proprietary networking systems to communicate
across an underlying IP internet.

Programmers can apply the idea of tunneling to application software by building a library that simulates a socket interface but uses a non-TCP/IP transport service to deliver messages. In particular, it is easy to build a socket simulation library that allows clients and servers to communicate using UDP, even if the only connection between the client and server computers consists of a transport-level switching system like an X.25 network.

FOR FURTHER STUDY

Comer and Korb [1983] describes how to tunnel IP through an X.25 network, including how to manage X.25 virtual circuits when the hardware imposes a fixed limit on simultaneous connections. RFC 877 gives the technical encoding details.

EXERCISES

17.1   Read RFC 877. How does a gateway that tunnels through an X.25 network map a destination IP address to an equivalent X.25 address?

17.2   Many transport-level services use their own retransmission scheme to provide reliable delivery. What can happen if both TCP and the underlying network protocols retransmit messages?

17.3   We said that a gateway uses dynamic virtual circuit allocation to tunnel through X.25, and that it usually applies an LRU heuristic when it needs to close an existing circuit to make one available. Explain what happens in a gateway if its X.25 interface allows K simultaneous circuits and the gateway attempts to communicate with $K+1$ other sites simultaneously.

17.4   Build a socket simulation library that allows client and server applications to exchange UDP datagrams over a non-TCP/IP transport-level protocol. Test it by arranging for a UDP ECHO client to communicate with a UDP ECHO server.

18

Application Level Gateways

18.1 Introduction

The previous chapter examines tunneling, a technique that allows one protocol suite to use the transport-level delivery service from another protocol suite in place of a physical network. From an application programmer's viewpoint, tunneling makes it possible for a client and server to communicate using TCP/IP even if the only path between them includes a non-TCP/IP network.

This chapter continues the exploration of techniques that clients and servers use to communicate across environments that do not provide full TCP/IP connectivity. It shows how clients operating on systems with limited protocol support can use an application program on an intermediate machine to forward requests, and how the use of such intermediaries can expand the range of available services.

18.2 Clients And Servers In Constrained Environments

18.2.1 The Reality Of Multiple Technologies

Not all computer systems have direct access to a TCP/IP internet. Furthermore, access limitations can complicate client and server software because they arise for economic and political reasons as well as technical ones. Chapter 17 points out that networking has evolved slowly in many organizations. As a result, subgroups may each have their own network and the networks may each use a different protocol suite. More important, a group of users may become accustomed to the application software available from a particular vendor or a particular computer. If the application software only operates with one set of protocols, the users may want to keep the network in place.

203

Network technologies can also gain inertia as managers gain expertise. As a technology becomes entrenched, an organization invests in training for personnel who install, manage, or operate the network. In addition to people who plan and manage the physical network, programmers invest time learning how to write software that uses the network. Once a manager learns the details and subtleties of a given technology, it becomes easier to expand the existing network than to replace it with a new technology. Thus, organizations that have multiple groups, each managing an independent network, often find that the initial cost of consolidation can be high because many groups must retrain their personnel.

For programmers, multiple network technologies often result in incompatible systems that do not provide interoperability. Unless the organization provides tunneling, programmers cannot depend on end-to-end transport-level connectivity. Thus, they cannot use a single transport protocol, nor can they easily communicate between clients and servers on arbitrary machines. Finally, programmers often build and maintain programs that duplicate functionality for each network technology. For example, programmers must maintain multiple electronic mail systems.

18.2.2 Computers With Limited Functionality

In addition to contending with multiple networks, programmers must sometimes create software for computers that offer limited network functionality. For example, many organizations have groups of small personal computers that lack operating system facilities for concurrent processing or asynchronous I/O. Such computers cannot support the concurrent server algorithms discussed in Chapter 8 or the concurrent client algorithms discussed in Chapter 15.

18.2.3 Connectivity Constraints That Arise From Security

Organizations may institute security policies that also constrain how clients and servers communicate. Some organizations partition computers into *secure* and *unsecure* subsets. To prevent client and server programs from compromising security, the network manager places policy constraints on connectivity. The manager restrains computers in the secure partition so they can communicate among themselves, but they can neither initiate contact to servers nor accept requests from clients on computers in the unsecure partition. Although such policies ensure security, they can make it difficult for programmers to design applications that use client-server interactions. In particular, computers in one partition cannot directly access services available on computers in the other partition.

18.3 Using Application Gateways

Programmers who need to design client-server interactions in restricted environments usually rely on a single, powerful technique to overcome connectivity constraints. The technique consists of adding application programs that run on intermediate machines, and enabling the applications to relay information between a client and the desired server. An intermediate program that provides such service is known as an *application gateway†*. If the intermediate machine has been dedicated to running one particular application gateway program, programmers or network managers sometimes refer to the machine as a *gateway machine*. For example, a computer dedicated to running a progra n that passes electronic mail between two groups may be called a *mail gateway*. Technically, of course, the term *application gateway* refers to the running program – programmers stretch the terminology when they refer to a machine as an application gateway.

Figure 18.1 illustrates a common use of an application gateway as an intermediary between two electronic mail systems.

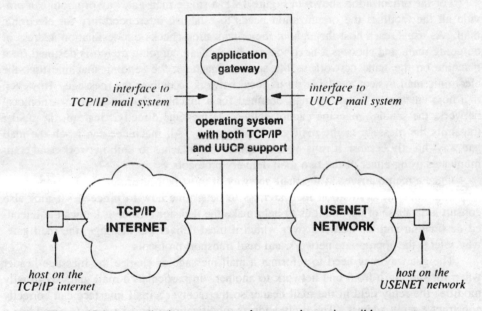

Figure 18.1 An application program used to pass electronic mail between two
network systems. The application gateway understands the syntax and semantics of both mail systems, and translates messages
between them.

---

†Use of the term *gateway* is unfortunate because IP uses the term to refer to computers that route datagrams. To avoid confusion, one should always distinguish the two carefully.

The organization depicted in Figure 18.1 has access to two main network systems: the USENET network and a TCP/IP internet. Each network system has its own electronic mail system. In a broad conceptual sense, the two mail systems provide the same services. Each system allows a user to compose and transmit an outgoing message or to receive and read an incoming message. However, the two systems cannot interoperate directly because each has its own destination address syntax and its own mail transport protocol.

To allow users on one network system to send mail to users on the other, the organization has installed an application program that serves as a mail gateway. In the example, the mail gateway program runs on a computer that attaches to both networks. The mail gateway must be designed carefully so it can communicate with any host in the organization. It must understand how to send messages using either of the two mail systems, and it must have logical connections to both networks.

18.4 Interoperability Through A Mail Gateway

For the organization shown in Figure 18.1, a single mail gateway program can provide all the facilities the organization needs to establish interoperability for electronic mail. As usual, each host throughout the organization checks the destination address of outgoing mail, and chooses a next-hop machine. If an outgoing memo is destined for a machine on the same network as the sending machine, the sending machine uses the electronic mail system available on its local network to deliver the message. However, if a host encounters outgoing mail destined for a machine that attaches to a nonlocal network, the sending machine cannot deliver the message directly. Instead, the sender transmits the message to the mail gateway program. All machines can reach the mail gateway directly because it runs on a computer that attaches to both networks and communicates using either of the two mail delivery protocols.

Once a memo arrives at the mail gateway, it must be routed again. The mail gateway examines the destination mail address to determine how to proceed. It may also consult a database of destinations to help make the decision. Once it knows the intended destination and the network over which it must deliver the message, the mail gateway selects the appropriate network and mail transport protocols.

The gateway may need to reformat a mail message or change the message header when forwarding it from one network to another. In particular, a mail gateway usually modifies the reply field in the mail header so the receiver's mail interface can correctly construct a reply address. The reply address modification may be trivial (e.g., adding a suffix that identifies the sender's network), or it may be complicated (e.g., adding information that identifies the mail gateway as an intermediate machine that will lead back to the source).

18.5 Implementation Of A Mail Gateway

In theory, a single process suffices to implement a mail gateway. In practice, however, most implementations divide the functionality into two processes. One process handles incoming mail messages, while the other manages outgoing mail. The process that handles incoming mail never sends a message. It computes a reply address, routes the mail to its destination, and then deposits the outgoing message in a queue to await transmission. The process that handles outgoing messages does not accept incoming messages directly. Instead, it scans the output queue periodically. For each message it finds in the output queue, the output process makes a network connection to the destination, and sends the message. If it cannot make a connection to the destination (e.g., because the destination machine has crashed), the output process leaves the message in the output queue and continues processing with the next message in the queue. Later, when it rescans the queue, the output process will try again to contact the destination and deliver the message. If a message remains in the output queue for an extended time (e.g., three days), the output process reports a delivery error to the user who originally sent the message.

Separating the mail gateway into input and output components allows each component to proceed independently. The output process can try to deliver a message, wait to see if the connection attempt succeeds, and then go on to the next message without coordinating its activities with those of the input process. If the connection attempt succeeds, the output process can send a message without regard to its length. It does not need to interrupt transmission to accept incoming messages because the input process handles them. Meanwhile, the input process can continue to accept incoming messages, route them, and store them for later transmission. Because the components operate independently, a long output message does not block input processing, nor does a long input message interfere with output processing.

18.6 A Comparison Of Application Gateways And Tunneling

The previous chapter showed that designers could choose tunneling to provide interoperability in a heterogeneous environment. It may be difficult to choose between tunneling and application gateways because neither technique solves all problems well and each technique provides advantages in some situations.

The chief advantage of using an application gateway instead of tunneling arises because programmers can create application gateways without modifying the computer's operating system. In many circumstances, programmers cannot modify the system either because they do not have access to the source code or because they do not have the expertise required. An application gateway can be built using conventional programming tools; the gateway does not require any change to the underlying protocol software. Furthermore, once an application gateway is in place, the site can use standard client and server programs.

Using application gateways has a secondary advantage: it allows all existing network systems to continue operation undisturbed. Managers do not need to learn about new network technologies, nor do they need to change any physical network connections. Similarly, users do not need to learn a new interface for services; each user continues to use existing client software associated with the networks to which they are accustomed.

Application gateways do have some disadvantages. The application gateway technique requires programmers to construct a separate application gateway program for each service. A mail gateway interconnects the mail services of two separate systems, but does not supply remote file access or remote login capabilities. Each time the organization adds a new service to its network systems, programmers must construct a new application gateway that interconnects the new service between multiple networks.

Application gateways may also require additional hardware resources. The organization may need to purchase new computers, or it may need to add network connections to existing computers. Adding new network connections may mean acquiring additional software as well as additional hardware. Because the translation required when forwarding a message or data can be complex, application gateways can use large amounts of CPU or memory. Thus, it may be necessary for an organization to purchase additional computers or upgrade existing machines to handle the load as it adds new services. The demand for CPU resources also introduces computational delay, which adds to the delay between the client and server. If the delay becomes too long, clients may timeout and resend a message.

In contrast to the application gateway approach, tunneling does not require any changes when new services appear. Once in place, a transport-level tunnel becomes part of the underlying network structure. Because applications remain unaware of the tunnel, it can be used for any application service. Tunneling also provides uniformity because it means the organization can use a single transport protocol.

Tunneling does have some disadvantages when compared to the application gateway solution. To install a transport-level tunnel that provides full functionality, the site must modify the operating system that runs on the gateway connecting the two network systems. Surprisingly, the organization may also need to modify software on hosts that use the tunnel. To understand how the need for modifications arises, imagine an X.25 network configured to serve as a tunnel for IP traffic. Consider a host connected to the network. Before an application can use the IP tunnel, it must have access to TCP/IP protocol software, and the IP software must know how to tunnel datagrams through the X.25 network. Thus, the host operating system must supply an IP interface (i.e., a socket-level interface) for application programs and must route traffic across the tunnel. If the operating system does not contain TCP/IP protocol software, it must be added. If existing IP protocol software does not know how to route through a tunnel, it must be changed.

Tunneling can also have a dramatic impact on users. Organizations adopt tunneling as a way to provide uniform transport services over heterogeneous networks. Once the organization establishes a tunnel, all hosts can begin using a single transport protocol for client-server interactions. For example, if an organization chooses to use IP and creates a tunnel through an X.25 network to provide connectivity, computers throughout the organization can use TCP/IP for transport connections. As an immediate consequence, all computers can support client-server interactions that use TCP/IP.

Unfortunately, a change in the underlying network protocols usually results in changes to client software with which users interact. Most organizations purchase commercially available client software for standard applications like electronic mail. Thus, the organization must use whatever software is available for a given transport protocol. If the organization adopts a universal transport protocol, it must purchase new client software that uses the new protocol suite. From the user's point of view, changing to the new software means learning a new interface. Unless the new interface offers all the functionality of the existing interface, users may be dissatisfied.

To avoid changing the users' environment, many organizations choose the application gateway solution. Programmers construct the application gateway carefully so it does not require changes to the user interface on any network. For example, after an organization adds an application gateway for electronic mail, users can use the old client software to send and receive mail. The mail system can use the destination address syntax to distinguish between messages sent to local destinations and those sent to foreign networks. Doing so allows users to use old addresses for local destinations, and only requires them to learn new addresses for new destinations.

18.7 Application Gateways And Limited Functionality Systems

Application gateways can increase the range of services accessible from small computers. For example, consider the network of personal computers shown in Figure 18.2.

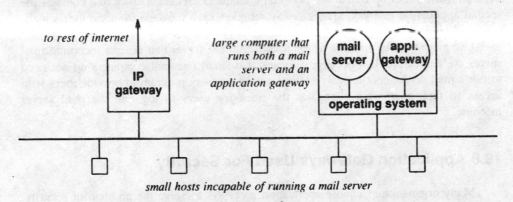

Figure 18.2 A network of personal computers incapable of running a concurrent mail server and the application gateway that they use to receive electronic mail.

The operating systems on small personal computers often provide limited facilities that do not include support for concurrent processing. The lack of concurrent processing limits client-server interactions because the computer must be dedicated to a single task at any time. In particular, it is often impossible for a user to run a server in the background while using the computer for other processing.

To understand how the lack of background processing limits client-server interaction, consider electronic mail. A personal computer can support mail client software because it can wait until the user decides to send a message before executing client software. Furthermore, once the user composes a message, the client program can make the user wait while it transmits the message to its destination. However, a computer system that does not support concurrent processing cannot run server software in the background. Thus, it cannot have a server ready to accept incoming mail until the user decides to run the server. Unfortunately, users cannot run any other application while the mail server operates because the machine must stop receiving mail while performing any other task. As a result, users seldom use such computers to run electronic mail servers.

An organization that has many personal computers can use an application gateway to solve the server problem. Consider the computers in Figure 18.2 again. The organization has purchased one large, powerful computer on which it runs a standard server that accepts incoming electronic mail. The server, which runs in the background, remains available to accept mail at all times. When a message arrives, the server places it in a file on disk. Files that store mail are often called *mailbox files* or *mailboxes*. The system may have one mailbox file for each user, or may place each message in a separate file. Usually, implementations that use a separate file for each message collect the files together into directories, where each directory corresponds to a single user.

In addition to the standard mail server, the computer must also run a specialized application gateway that allows users on personal computers to access their mailboxes. To read mail, a user on one of the personal computers invokes a client that contacts the special application gateway. The gateway retrieves each message from the user's mailbox, and sends it to the personal computer for the user to read.

Using a powerful machine to run a conventional server that accepts incoming mail solves the server problem because it means that small personal computers do not need to run a mail server continuously. Using a mail gateway program to provide users with access to their mailboxes eliminates the need for users to log into the mail server machine.

18.8 Application Gateways Used For Security

Many organizations choose application gateways to solve the problem of security. For example, suppose an organization needs to restrict remote login. Imagine that the organization classifies its employees as either authorized or unauthorized for remote login. Figure 18.3 illustrates how the organization can use an application gateway to implement its security policy.

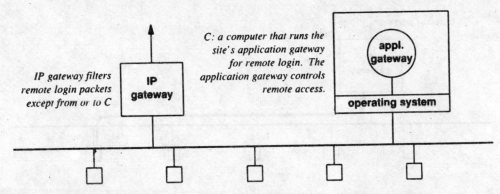

conventional hosts prohibited from sending remote login packets except through application gateway

Figure 18.3 An application gateway used to implement a remote login security policy. A user must communicate with remote machines through the application gateway which enforces authorization controls.

The organization depicted in the figure uses a conventional IP gateway filter to block all datagrams that contain remote login connection requests unless they originate from the host that runs the application gateway. To form a remote login connection, a user on any host in the organization invokes a client that first connects to the application gateway. After the user obtains authorization, the application gateway connects the user to the desired destination.

18.9 Application Gateways And The Extra Hop Problem

The *extra hop problem* refers to a situation in which datagrams pass across the same network twice on their way to a final destination. The problem is usually caused by incorrect routing tables.

Introduction of an application gateway into an existing network can also create a form of the extra hop problem. To understand why, consider the network topology that Figure 18.4a illustrates. The figure shows the path a message would travel from a host to a remote server if the host supported the same transport protocol as the server. Now assume that the existing host wishes to access a service that is only available through some protocol other than the one the host uses. Interoperability can be achieved by introducing an application gateway as Figure 18.4b shows. The application gateway accepts requests using one protocol system and sends them to the remote server using another. Unfortunately, each message traverses the network twice. The figure is realistic: network managers often acquire a new physical computer for each application gateway program because they want to avoid overloading existing machines.

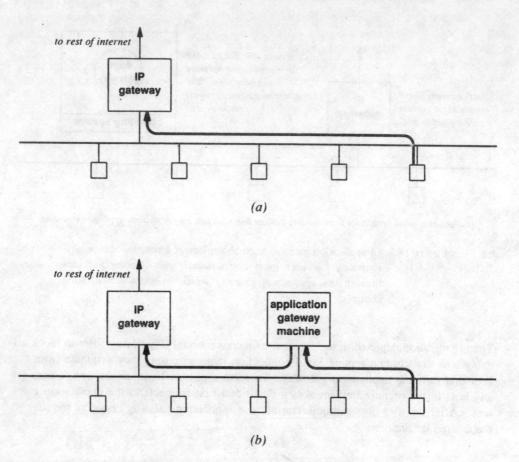

Figure 18.4 (a) A set of hosts and a gateway. The darkened arrow shows the
path a message takes from a host to a remote server and (b) the
path of a message after an application gateway is introduced.
The new gateway causes each message to traverse the network
twice.

Once the application gateway has been introduced, clients executing on existing
hosts use the application gateway to access the service it offers. A client sends its request to the application gateway using one protocol, which forwards the request on to
the remote server using another protocol. When the server returns its result to the application gateway, the gateway sends a response back to the client. The system appears to
work well. Existing protocol software on the hosts need not be changed. After the application gateway has been installed, a client executing on an arbitrary host will be able
to access the desired service through the gateway.

Unfortunately, close examination of the underlying network reveals that the configuration in Figure 18.4b does not make good use of network resources. It creates the extra hop problem. Each request must pass across the local area network twice: once when it travels from the original host to the application gateway machine, and once when it travels from the application gateway machine on toward the ultimate server. If the server lies in the TCP/IP internet beyond the IP gateway, the second transmission occurs when the message passes from the application gateway machine to the IP gateway. If the server lies on the local net, the second transmission occurs when the message passes from the application gateway machine to the machine running the server.

For services that do not require much network traffic, the extra hop may be unimportant. Indeed, several vendors build products that use the topology Figure 18.4b illustrates. If the network is heavily loaded, however, or if the service requires significant network traffic, the extra hop may make such a solution too expensive. Thus, designers need to calculate expected load carefully before they adopt the application gateway approach.

18.10 An Example Application Gateway

An application gateway can extend services by providing access to client machines that do not run all protocols. For example, consider a user on a host that has access to electronic mail but has no access to file transfer protocols like FTP. Such restrictions may arise from economic considerations (i.e., the cost of FTP software is too high), commercial realities (i.e., no one sells FTP client software for the computer in question), or security reasons (e.g., the site decides to reduce its security risk by prohibiting high-speed data transfer).

Suppose users on a restricted machine need access to the *Request For Comments* documents (RFCs). The application gateway technique can solve the access problem by allowing the organization to interconnect electronic mail and FTP services, while controlling access and ensuring authorization.

To provide RFC access from electronic mail, an application gateway must connect to both services. To use the gateway, a user must send the gateway an e-mail message that specifies the desired RFC. The application gateway verifies that the user is authorized to access RFCs, makes an FTP connection, obtains a copy of the RFC, and sends the RFC document back to the user in an e-mail message.

For example, imagine an application gateway located at e-mail address *rfc* on machine *somewhere.com*. Imagine that the application gateway accepts a mail message that mentions an RFC number on the subject line, uses FTP to retrieve that RFC, and mails the results back to the sender.

To use such a gateway, a user would create a mail message addressed to *rfc@somewhere.com*:

```
To: rfc@somewhere.com
From: user@elsewhere.edu
Subject: 791


Body of message (possibly empty).
```

This mail message requests RFC 791 from the application gateway. Because the gateway only looks at the number on the *Subject:* line, the text in the message body is irrelevant; it can be empty.

18.11 Implementation Of An Application Gateway

To implement the example application gateway described above, a programmer needs three facilities: a machine that has access to both electronic mail and FTP, a program that will act as the application gateway, and a mechanism that passes each incoming electronic mail message for a specified destination to the gateway program.

UNIX systems permit a system administrator to establish the necessary components easily. The administrator can create a special mail destination, *rfc*, by adding it to the e-mail alias file, or the administrator can create an account for a fictitious user named *rfc* and arrange to forward all mail for that user to a program. In fact, most UNIX systems allow an individual user to redirect their incoming e-mail to a program, so it is possible for a nonprivileged user to build and test an e-mail application gateway.

Among other tasks, the application gateway needs to retrieve an RFC. Our example implementation uses a separate program to retrieve an RFC document. The program, shown in file *rfc* below, is a UNIX shell script.

```
#! /bin/sh
#
# rfc:          retrieve an RFC document given its number
#
# operation:    check the local cache for a copy of the requested
#               document and use FTP to obtain a copy from the NIC if
#               none present.  Store a copy in the local cache when
#               retrieving from the NIC.
#
# method:       keep the local cache in directory /usr/tmp/RFC; use in-line
#               commands to invoke the ftp command.  Assume any file name t
#               ends in .Z contains a compressed file and run zcat to
#               decompress it.
#
HOST=nic.ddn.mil
PATH=/bin:/usr/bin:/usr/ucb
PUB=/usr/tmp/RFC
```

```
umask 022

if test ! -d $PUB
then
        mkdir $PUB
        chmod 777 $PUB
fi
for i
do
        if test $i = "index"
        then
                i="-index"
        fi
        if test ! -r $PUB/$i -a ! -r $PUB/$i".Z" -o $i = "-index"
        then
            trap "rm -f $PUB/$i;
                echo int - $PUB/$i removed;exit 1" 1 2 3 13 15 24 25
                ftp -n ${HOST}  >/dev/null <<!
user anonymous guest
binary
get rfc/rfc$i.txt $PUB/$i
quit
!
                trap 1 2 3 13 15 24 25
        fi

        if test -r $PUB/$i
        then
                cat $PUB/$i
        elif test -r $PUB/$i".Z"
        then
                zcat $PUB/$i
        else
                echo Could not retrieve RFC $i
        fi
done
chmod 666 $PUB/-index >/dev/null 2>&1
```

The *rfc* script takes an argument that specifies either an RFC number or the word *index* (to denote the RFC index). It creates the needed FTP commands and then invokes the *ftp* program. The commands instruct *ftp* to open a connection to the Network Information Center and retrieve a copy of the specified RFC.

The *rfc* script is more complex than necessary because it contains an optimization. The code caches a copy of each RFC it retrieves in directory */usr/tmp/RFC*. Before it retrieves an RFC, *rfc* checks to see if a copy currently resides in the cache. If it does, the script retrieves the copy from the cache, avoiding unnecessary network traffic.

18.12 Code For The Application Gateway

Once the *rfc* script has been installed in a system, building an application gateway that accesses RFCs is straightforward. File *rfcd* contains the code. Like the *rfc* program above, it is a shell script. *Rfcd* uses the *rfc* program to retrieve an RFC document; it uses a conventional e-mail program (*/usr/ucb/mail*) to send the results back to the user who requested it.

```
#!/bin/sh
#
# rfcd:          an application gateway between e-mail and FTP
#
# operation:     receive an e-mail message, extract an RFC number from the
#                subject line, invoke a program that obtains a copy of the
#                RFC, and send it back to the user that sent the e-mail
#
# method:        use awk to parse the input, extract information, and form
#                a shell program; pipe the program directly into the shell
#                to execute it.
#
PATH=/bin:/usr/bin
RFCPROG=/usr/local/bin/rfc
awk "
     BEGIN      { fnd = 0 }

     /^From:/   { retaddr = substr(\$0, 6) ; next }

     /^Subject:/{ rfcnum = substr(\$0, 9) ; fnd++ ; next }

     /^ *\$/    { if (fnd==0 || rfcnum!~/^[0-9 ]*$/) exit
                  cmd = \"$RFCPROG \"rfcnum
                  cmd = cmd \" | /usr/ucb/mail -s 'RFC \"rfcnum\" ' \"
                  cmd = cmd \" '\"retaddr\" ' \"
                  print cmd ; exit
                }" | /bin/sh
```

Although the details may seem complex to readers unfamiliar with shell scripts and the UNIX *awk* utility, it should be apparent that little programming effort was required to create the script.

In essence, the *rfcd* script reads a mail message and extracts the contents of the *From:* and *Subject:* lines. It uses an *awk* program to do most of the work. The *awk* program scans each line of the incoming mail message. It assumes the *Subject:* line contains an RFC number and the *From:* line contains the e-mail address of the sender. The sender's address becomes the destination when *rfcd* generates a reply.

Once the *awk* program in *rfcd* detects an empty line, it knows that it has reached the end of the mail headers. It stops processing and forms and prints a shell program. Because *rfcd* feeds the output of the *awk* program directly into the command interpreter (*sh*), the generated program will be executed immediately.

If the incoming message contains a valid *Subject:* line in its headers, the generated program calls */usr/local/bin/rfc* to obtain the specified RFC and */usr/ucb/mail* to mail it back to whoever sent the request. If the mail message contains no subject or if the subject line contains anything other than digits or blanks, the *awk* program exits without generating any output. When the *awk* program exits early, *rfcd* does not attempt to obtain an RFC and does not send any mail (i.e., this version does not even send back an error message).

18.13 An Example Gateway Exchange

An example will clarify the steps. Suppose user *comer* decides to request RFC *1094*. *Comer* sends mail to the application gateway address, *rfc@somewhere.com*, specifying a *Subject:* line of *1094*. The message contains:

```
To: rfc@somewhere.com
From: comer
Subject: 1094

Body of message (possibly empty).
```

The mail system on *somewhere.com* has been configured to pass the incoming message to the *rfcd* script.

When *rfcd* runs, the *awk* code extracts *1094* from the *Subject:* line in the mail message and stores it in variable *rfcnum*. It extracts *comer* from the *From:* line and stores it in variable *retaddr*. When *rfcd* encounters the empty line that separates the header from the body of the message, it generates the following command line:

```
/usr/local/bin/rfc 1094 | /usr/ucb/mail -s 'RFC 1094' 'comer'
```

UNIX users will recognize this line as valid input to the UNIX command interpreter, *sh*. It specifies that the command interpreter should run the program in file */usr/local/bin/rfc* with argument *1094*, and then connect the output to the program in file */usr/ucb/mail* using the UNIX *pipe* mechanism. The mail program has three arguments: *-s*, *RFC 1094*, and *comer*. The first two specify that the subject consists of the string *RFC 1094*. The third argument specifies that the recipient is *comer*. The body of the message consists of the RFC document retrieved by the *rfc* script.

Because *rfcd* sends the output of the *awk* program directly to the command interpreter, the command interpreter will execute the command line shown above. It will run the *rfc* program, and then mail the results to user *comer*.

18.14 Using Rfcd With UNIX's .forward

An individual user can use his or her own e-mail account to test *rfcd*. To do so, the user creates a file named *.forward* in his or her home directory. Each time the mail system receives a message, it extracts the recipient's name from the *To:* field and examines that user's home directory for a *.forward* file. If it finds one, the mail system reads the *.forward* file and honors the specification in it. For example, suppose a user wishes the mailer to send each of his or her incoming messages to a program with the full path name */usr/XXX/Q*. The user places a single line in his or her *.forward* file:

```
| "/usr/XXX/Q"
```

The mail system interprets this line to mean: *invoke program /usr/XXX/Q with the incoming mail message as standard input*. Thus, to invoke the e-mail application gateway shown above, a user must place the *rfcd* script in a file, make the file executable, and make the *.forward* entry reference it. Of course, a user should not install a *.forward* entry without testing the program it specifies or mail could be lost.

18.15 Summary

Although tunneling allows one protocol system to use another high-level protocol as a transport device, tunneling is restricted to cases where the designer has access to the operating system code. The application gateway technique, an alternative to tunneling, permits application programmers to interconnect heterogeneous systems without changing the operating system.

An application gateway is a program that accepts requests using one high-level protocol and fulfills requests using another high-level protocol. In essence, each application gateway is a server for one service and a client of another.

We examined an application gateway that accepts a request for an RFC from an electronic mail message, uses FTP to obtain the specified RFC, and returns the RFC to the original requester using electronic mail. The example shows that application gateways need not be complex nor written in a low-level language. Our example code consists of a UNIX shell script and an *awk* program.

Many sites use application gateways to implement authorization and security checks. Because the gateway operates as a conventional application program, little effort is required to program the gateway to filter unwanted access or to keep a record of all requests.

FOR FURTHER STUDY

More information on the UNIX shell and the *awk* programming language can be found in the documentation that accompanies the operating system. Aho, Kernighan, and Weinberger [1988] describes *awk* programming in detail. Bolsky and Korn [1989] describes a more advanced UNIX shell and shows examples of shell programs.

The BSD UNIX program *sendmail* handles e-mail transfers over a variety of transport protocols; it can be configured to act as an application gateway. Information on *sendmail* can be found in the *UNIX Programmer's Manual*.

EXERCISES

18.1   Add authorization checks to the example application gateway in this chapter that permit a system administrator to limit access.

18.2   Add a logging mechanism to the example application gateway in this chapter that accumulates a list of all users who request RFCs.

18.3   How can a sender request a copy of the RFC index through the application gateway in this chapter?

18.4   Observe that if a user invokes the *rfc* script to request an RFC at exactly the same time the application gateway is using it to request the same RFC, the user may obtain an empty or partial file. Modify the script to correct this weakness.

18.5   How does the *sendmail* system permit a system administrator to establish an application gateway?

19

External Data
Representation (XDR)

19.1 Introduction

Previous chapters describe algorithms, mechanisms, and implementation techniques for client and server programs. This chapter begins a discussion of the concepts and techniques that help programmers use the client-server paradigm and the mechanisms that provide programming support for these concepts. In particular, it examines a *de facto* standard for external data representation and presentation as well as a set of library procedures used to perform data conversion.

This chapter describes the general motivations for using an external data representation and the details of one particular implementation. The next chapter shows how an external data representation standard helps simplify client and server communication, and illustrates how a standard makes it possible to use a single, uniform remote access mechanism for client-server communication.

19.2 Representations For Data In Computers

Each computer architecture provides its own definition for the representation of data. Some computers store the least significant byte of an integer at the lowest memory address, others store the most significant byte at the lowest address, and others do not store bytes contiguously in memory. For example, Figure 19.1 shows the two most popular representations for 32-bit integers.

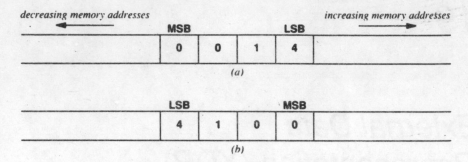

Figure 19.1 Two representations for the value *260* stored as a 32-bit binary
integer: (a) "big endian" order with the most significant byte at
the lowest memory address and (b) "little endian" order with
the least significant byte at the lowest memory address.
Numbers give the decimal value of each 8-bit byte.

Programmers who write programs for a single computer do not need to think about
data representation because a given computer usually only permits one representation.
When a programmer declares a variable to be an integer (e.g., by using Pascal's *integer*
declaration or C's *int* declaration), the compiler uses the computer's *native data
representation* when it allocates storage for the integer or when it generates code to
fetch, store, or compare values.

Programmers who create client and server software must contend with data
representation, however, because both endpoints must agree on the exact representation
for all data sent across the communication channel between them. If the native data
representations on two machines differ, data sent from a program on one machine to a
program on the other must be converted.

19.3 The N-Squared Conversion Problem

The central issue underlying data representation is software portability. At one ex-
treme, a programmer could choose to embed knowledge of the computers' architecture
in each client-server pair so the client and server agree on which side will convert the
data. Designs that convert directly from the client's representation to the server's
representation use *asymmetric data conversion* because one side or the other performs
conversion. Unfortunately, using asymmetric data conversion means that the programmer must write a different version of the client-server pair for each pair of architectures
on which they will be used.

To understand why building separate client-server pairs for each architecture combination can be costly, consider a set of *N* computers. If each computer uses a different
data representation to store floating point numbers, a programmer must construct a total
of

$$(N^2 - N)/2$$

versions of any client-server program that exchanges floating point values. We call this the *n-squared conversion problem†* to emphasize that the programming effort is proportional to the square of the number of different data representations.

Another way to view the n-squared conversion problem is to imagine the effort required to add a new architecture to an existing set of N machines. Each time a new computer arrives, the programmer must build N new versions of each client-server pair before the new computer can interoperate with each of the existing computers.

Even if the programmer uses conditional compilation (e.g., the C preprocessor's *ifdef* construct), creating, testing, maintaining, and managing N^2 versions of a program can be difficult. Furthermore, users may need to distinguish among versions when they invoke a client. To summarize:

> *If client-server software is designed to convert from the client's native data representation directly to the server's native data representation asymmetrically, the number of versions of the software grows as the square of the number of architectures.*

To avoid the problems inherent in maintaining N-squared versions of a client-server program, programmers try to avoid asymmetric data conversion. Instead, they write client and server software in such a way that each source program can be compiled and executed on a variety of machines without change. Doing so makes programming easier because it results in a highly portable program. It also makes accessing a service easier because users only need to remember how to invoke one version of the client.

19.4 Network Standard Byte Order

How can a single source program compile and execute correctly on a variety of architectures if the architectures use multiple representations for data? More important, how can a client or server program send data to a program on another machine if the two machines use a different data representation? Chapter 5 describes how TCP/IP solves the representation problem for simple integer data by using functions that convert from the computer's native byte order to a network standard byte order and vice versa.

Conceptually, the use of a standard representation for data sent across a network in protocol headers means the TCP/IP protocol software employs *symmetric data conversion*. Both ends perform the required conversion. As a result, only one version of the protocol software is needed because all protocol headers represent data in a standard, machine-independent form.

Most programmers adopt the same symmetric data conversion technique when they build client-server application software. Instead of converting directly from one machine's representation to the other's, both client and server perform a data conver-

---

†Some literature refers to the problem as the $n * m$ problem to emphasize that clients can operate on n architectures while servers can operate on m architectures.

sion. Before sending across the network, they convert data from the sending computer's native representation into a standard, machine-independent representation. Likewise, they convert from the machine-independent representation to the receiving computer's native representation after receiving data from the network. The standard representation used for data traversing the network is known as the *external data representation*.

Using a standard external data representation has both advantages and disadvantages. The chief advantage lies in flexibility: neither the client nor the server needs to understand the architecture of the other. A single client can contact a server on an arbitrary machine without knowing the machine architecture. The total programming effort required will be proportional to the number of machine architectures instead of the square of that number.

The chief disadvantage of symmetric conversion is computational overhead. In cases where the client and server both operate on computers that have the same architecture, the cost seems unwarranted. One end converts all data from the native architecture's representation to the external representation before sending it, and the other end converts from the external representation back to the original representation after receiving it.

Even if the client and server machines do not share a common architecture, using an intermediate form introduces additional computation. Instead of converting directly from the sender's representation to the receiver's, the client and server must each spend CPU time converting between their local representations and the external representation. Furthermore, because the external representation may add information to the data or align it on word boundaries, the conversion may result in a larger stream of bytes than necessary.

Despite the additional overhead and network bandwidth required, most programmers agree that using symmetric conversion is worthwhile. It simplifies programming, reduces errors, and increases interoperability among programs. It also makes network management and debugging easier because the network manager can interpret the contents of packets without knowing the architectures of the sending and receiving machines.

19.5 A De Facto Standard External Data Representation

Sun Microsystems, Incorporated devised an external data representation that specifies how to represent common forms of data when transferring data across a network. Known by the initials *XDR*, Sun's *eXternal Data Representation* has become a *de facto* standard for most client-server applications.

XDR specifies data formats for most of the data types that clients and servers exchange. For example, XDR specifies that 32-bit binary integers should be represented in "big endian" order (i.e., with the most significant byte in the lowest memory address).

19.6 XDR Data Types

The table in Figure 19.2 lists the data types for which XDR defines a standard representation.

Data Type	Size	Description
int	32 bits	32-bit signed binary integer
unsigned Int	32-bits	32-bit unsigned binary integer
bool	32 bits	Boolean value (*false* or *true*) represented by *0* or *1*
enum	arb.	Enumeration type with values defined by integers (e.g., *RED=1, WHITE=2, BLUE=3*)
hyper	64 bits	64-bit signed binary integer
unsigned hyper	64-bits	64-bit unsigned binary integer
float	32 bits	Single precision floating point number
double	64 bits	Double precision floating point number
opaque	arb.	Unconverted data (i.e., data in the sender's native representation)
string	arb.	String of ASCII characters
fixed array	arb.	A fixed-size array of any other data type
counted array	arb.	Array in which the type has a fixed upper limit, but individual arrays may vary up to that size
structure	arb.	A data aggregate, like C's *struct*
discriminated union	arb.	A data structure that allows one of several alternative forms, like C's *union* or Pascal's variant record
void	0	Used if no data is present where a data item is optional (e.g., in a structure)
symbolic constant	arb.	A symbolic constant and associated value
optional data	arb.	Allows zero or one occurrences of an item

Figure 19.2 The types for which XDR defines an external representation. The standard specifies how data items for each type should be encoded when sent across a network.

The types in Figure 19.2 cover most of the data structures found in application programs because they allow the programmer to compose aggregate types from other types. For example, in addition to allowing an array of integers, XDR allows an array of structures, each of which can have multiple fields that can each be an array, structure, or union. Thus, XDR provides representations for most of the structures that a C programmer can specify.

19.7 Implicit Types

The XDR standard specifies how a data object should be encoded for each of the data types listed in Figure 19.2. However, the encodings contain only the data items and not information about their types. For example, XDR specifies using "big-endian" order for 32-bit binary integers (the same encoding used in TCP/IP protocol headers). If an application program uses XDR representation to encode a 32-bit integer, the result occupies exactly 32 bits; the encoding does not contain additional bits to identify it as an integer or to specify its length. Thus, clients and servers using XDR must agree on the exact format of messages they will exchange. A program cannot interpret an XDR-encoded message unless it knows the exact format and the types of all data fields.

19.8 Software Support For Using XDR

Programmers who choose to use the XDR representation for symmetric data conversion must be careful to place each data item in external form before sending it across a network. Similarly, a receiving program must be careful to convert each incoming item to native representation. Chapter 5 shows one method programmers can use to perform the conversion: insert a function call in the code to convert each data item in a message to external form before sending the message, and insert a function call to convert each data item to internal form when a message arrives.

Most programmers could write the required XDR conversion functions with little effort. However, some conversions require considerable expertise (e.g., converting from a computer's native floating point representation to the XDR standard without losing precision may require an understanding of basic numerical analysis). To eliminate potential conversion errors, an implementation of XDR includes library routines that perform the necessary conversions.

19.9 XDR Library Routines

XDR library routines for a given machine can convert data items from the computer's native representation to the XDR standard representation and vice versa. Most implementations of XDR use a *buffer paradigm* that allows a programmer to create a complete message in XDR form.

19.10 Building A Message One Piece At A Time

The buffer paradigm XDR uses requires a program to allocate a buffer large enough to hold the external representation of a message and to add items (i.e., fields) one at a time. For example, the version of XDR available under the SunOS operating system provides conversion routines that each append an external representation to the end of a buffer in memory. A program first invokes procedure *xdrmem_create* to allocate a buffer in memory and inform XDR that it intends to compose an external representation in it. *Xdrmem_create* initializes the memory so it represents an *XDR stream* that can be used to encode (convert to standard representation) or decode (convert to native representation) data. The call initializes the XDR stream to be empty by assigning the address of the beginning of the buffer to an internal pointer. *Xdrmem_create* returns a pointer to the stream, which must then be used in successive calls to XDR routines. The declarations and calls needed to create an XDR stream using C are:

```
#include <rpc/xdr.h>
#define BUFSIZE 4000              /* size of memory for encoding */

    XDR     *xdrs;                /* pointer to an XDR "stream"  */
    char    buf[BUFSIZE];         /* memory area to hold XDR data */

    xdrmem_create(xdrs, buf, BUFSIZE, XDR_ENCODE);
```

Once a program has created an XDR stream, it can call individual XDR conversion routines to convert native data objects into external form. Each call encodes one data object and appends the encoded information on the end of the stream (i.e., places the encoded data in the next available locations in the buffer and then updates the internal stream pointer). For example, procedure *xdr_int* converts a 32-bit binary integer from the native representation to the standard XDR representation and appends it to an XDR stream. A program invokes *xdr_int* by passing it a pointer to an XDR stream and a pointer to an integer:

```
    int     i;               /* integer in native representation    */
    . . .                    /* assume stream initialized for ENCODE */
    i = 260;                 /* assign integer value to be converted */
    xdr_int(xdrs, &i);       /* convert integer and append to stream */
```

Figure 19.3 illustrates how the call to *xdr_int* shown in the sample code adds four bytes of data to the XDR stream.

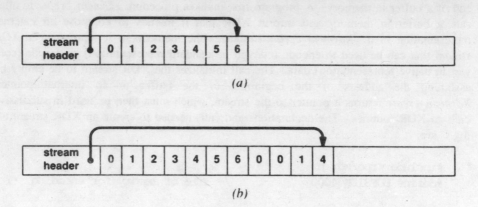

Figure 19.3 (a) An XDR stream that has been initialized for *ENCODE* and already contains 7 bytes of data, and (b) the same XDR stream after a call to *xdr_int* appends a 32-bit integer with value *260*.

19.11 Conversion Routines In The XDR Library

The table in Figure 19.4 lists the XDR conversion routines.

Procedure	arguments	Data Type Converted
xdr_bool	xdrs, ptrbool	Boolean (*int* in C)
xdr_bytes	xdrs, ptrstr, strsize, maxsize	Counted byte string
xdr_char	xdrs, ptrchar	Character
xdr_double	xdrs, ptrdouble	Double precision floating point
xdr_enum	xdrs, ptrint	Variable of enumerated data type (an *int* in C)
xdr_float	xdrs, ptrfloat	Single precision floating point
xdr_int	xdrs, ip	32-bit integer
xdr_long	xdrs, ptrlong	64-bit integer
xdr_opaque	xdrs, ptrchar, count	Bytes sent without conversion
xdr_pointer	xdrs, ptrobj, objsize, xdrobj	A pointer (used in linked data structures like lists or trees)
xdr_short	xdrs, ptrshort	16-bit integer
xdr_string	xdrs, ptrstr, maxsize	A C string
xdr_u_char	xdrs, ptruchar	Unsigned 8-bit integer
xdr_u_int	xdrs, ptrint	Unsigned 32-bit integer
xdr_u_long	xdrs, ptrulong	Unsigned 64-bit integer
xdr_u_short	xdrs, ptrushort	Unsigned 16-bit integer
xdr_union	xdrs, ptrdiscrim, ptrunion, choicefcn, default	Discriminated union
xdr_vector	xdrs, ptrarray, size, elemsize, elemproc	Fixed length array
xdr_void	-none-	Not a conversion (used to denote empty part of a data structure)

Figure 19.4 The XDR data conversion routines found in an XDR library. The routines can convert in either direction because most arguments are pointers to data objects and not data values.

To form a message, the application calls XDR conversion routines for each data item in the message. After encoding each data item and placing it in an XDR stream, the application can send the message by sending the resulting stream. The receiving application must reverse the entire process. It calls *xdrmem_create* to create a memory buffer that will hold an XDR stream, and places the incoming message in a buffer area. XDR records the direction of conversion in the stream itself where the conversion routines can access it. The receiver specifies *XDR_DECODE* as the third argument of *xdrmem_create* when creating an XDR stream that will be used for input. As a result, whenever the receiver calls an individual conversion routine on an input stream, the routine extracts an item from the stream and converts it to native mode. For example, if the receiver has established an XDR stream used for input (i.e., the call specified

XDR_DECODE), it can extract a 32-bit integer and convert it to the native representation by calling *xdr_int*:

```
        int     i;              /* integer using native representation  */
        . . .                   /* assume stream initialized for DECODE */

        xdr_int(xdrs, &i);  /* extract integer from stream              */
```

Thus, unlike the conversion routines *htons* and *ntohs* found in BSD UNIX, individual XDR conversion routines do not specify the direction of conversion. Instead, they require the program to specify the direction when creating the XDR stream. To summarize:

> *Individual XDR conversion routines do not specify the direction of conversion. Instead, a single routine that can convert in either direction determines the direction of the conversion by examining the XDR stream being used.*

19.12 XDR Streams, I/O, and TCP

The code fragments above create an XDR stream associated with a buffer in memory. Using memory to buffer data can make a program efficient because it allows the application to convert large amounts of data to external form before sending it across a network. After items have been converted to external form and placed in the buffer, the application must call an I/O function like *write* to send it across a TCP connection.

It is possible to arrange to have XDR conversion routines send data across a TCP connection automatically each time they convert a data item to external form. To do so, an application program first creates a TCP socket, and then calls *fdopen* to attach a UNIX *standard I/O stream* to the socket. Instead of calling *xdrmem_create*, the application calls *xdrstdio_create* to create an XDR stream and connect it to the existing I/O descriptor. XDR streams attached to a TCP socket do not require explicit calls to *write* or *read*. Each time the application calls an XDR conversion routine, the conversion routine automatically performs a buffered *read* or *write* operation using the underlying descriptor. A *write* causes TCP to transmit outgoing data to the socket; a *read* causes TCP to read incoming data from the socket. The application can also call conventional functions from the UNIX standard I/O library to act on the I/O stream. For example, if output is desired, the application can use *fflush* to flush the output buffer after only a few bytes of data have been converted.

19.13 Records, Record Boundaries, And Datagram I/O

As described, the XDR mechanism works well when connected to a TCP socket because both XDR and TCP implementations use the stream abstraction. To make XDR work with UDP as easily as it works with TCP, the designers added a second interface. The alternative design provides an application with a *record-oriented interface*.

To use the record-oriented interface, a program calls function *xdrrec_create* when creating an XDR stream. The call includes two arguments, *inproc* and *outproc*, that specify an input procedure and an output procedure. When converting to external form, each conversion routine checks the buffer. If the buffer becomes full, the conversion routine calls *outproc* to send the existing buffer contents and make space for the new data. Similarly, each time the application calls a conversion routine to convert from external form to the native representation, the routine checks the buffer to see if it contains data. If the buffer is empty, the conversion routine calls *inproc* to obtain more data.

To use XDR with UDP, an application creates a record-oriented XDR stream. It arranges for the input and output procedures associated with the stream to call *read* and *write* (or *recv* and *send*). When the application fills a buffer, the conversion routines call *write* to transmit the buffer in a single UDP datagram. Similarly, when an application calls a conversion routine to extract data, the conversion routine calls *read* to obtain the next incoming datagram and place it in the buffer.

XDR streams created by *xdrrec_create* differ from other XDR streams in several ways. Record-oriented streams allow an application to mark record boundaries. Furthermore, the sender can specify whether to send the record immediately or to wait for the buffer to fill before sending it. The receiver can detect record boundaries, skip a fixed number of records in the input, or find out whether additional records have been received.

19.14 Summary

Because computers do not use a common data representation, client and server programs must contend with representation issues. To solve the problem, client-server interaction can be *asymmetric* or *symmetric*. Asymmetric conversion requires either the client or the server to convert between its own representation and the other machine's native representation. Symmetric conversion uses a standard network representation, and requires both the client and server to convert between the network standard and the local representation.

The chief problem with asymmetric interaction arises because multiple versions of each program are required. If the network supports N architectures, asymmetric interaction requires programming effort proportional to N^2. While symmetric designs may require slightly more computational overhead, they provide interoperability with one program per architecture. Thus, most designers choose symmetric solutions because they require programming effort proportional to N.

Sun Microsystems, Incorporated has defined an external data representation that has become, *de facto*, a standard. Known as XDR, the Sun standard provides definitions for data aggregates (e.g., arrays and structures) as well as for basic data types (e.g., integers and character strings). XDR library routines provide conversion from a computer's native data representation to the external standard and vice versa. Client and server programs can use XDR routines to convert data to external form before sending it and to internal form after receiving it. The conversion routines can be associated with input and output using TCP or UDP.

FOR FURTHER STUDY

Sun Microsystems, Incorporated [RFC 1014] defines the XDR encoding and the standard XDR conversion routines. Additional information can be found in the *Network Programming Guide* that accompanies the SunOS operating system.

International Organization for Standardization [1987a and 1987b] defines an alternative external data representation known as *Abstract Syntax Notation One* (*ASN.1*). Although some protocols in the TCP/IP suite use the ASN.1 representation, most application programmers use XDR. Partridge and Rose [1989] shows that XDR and ASN.1 have equivalent expressive power.

Padlipsky [1983] discusses the problem of asymmetric conversion and points out that it requires $n * m$ possible conversions.

EXERCISES

19.1   Construct a version of *ntohs* and conduct an experiment that compares the execution time of your version to the execution time of the version in your system's library or *include* files. Explain the results.

19.2   How does XDR's use of the buffer paradigm make programming easier?

19.3   Design an external data representation that includes a type field before each data item. What is the chief advantage of such a solution? What is the chief disadvantage?

19.4   Read the *UNIX Programmer's Manual* to find out more about the format of an XDR stream. What information is kept in the header?

19.5   Argue that programs would be easier to read if the designers of XDR had chosen to use separate conversion routines for encoding and decoding instead of recording the conversion direction in the stream header. What is the disadvantage of keeping separate conversion routines?

19.6   Under what circumstances might a programmer need to pass *opaque* data objects between a client and a server?

20

Remote Procedure Call
Concept (RPC)

20.1 Introduction

The previous chapter begins a discussion of techniques and mechanisms that help programmers use the client-server paradigm. It considers the advantages of using symmetric data conversion, and describes how the XDR external data representation standard and associated library routines provide symmetric conversion.

This chapter continues the discussion. It introduces the remote procedure call concept in general, and describes a particular implementation of a remote procedure call that uses the XDR standard for data representation. It shows how the remote procedure concept simplifies the design of client-server software and makes the resulting programs easier to understand. The next two chapters complete the discussion of remote procedure call by describing a tool that generates much of the C code needed to implement a program that uses remote calls. They contain a complete working example that shows how the tool can generate a client and a server that use remote procedure calls.

20.2 Remote Procedure Call Model

So far, we have described client-server programs by examining the structure of the client and server components separately. However, when programmers build a client-server application, they cannot focus exclusively on one component at a time. Instead, they must consider how the entire system will function and how the two components will interact.

233

To help programmers design and understand client-server interaction, researchers have devised a conceptual framework for building distributed programs. Known as the *remote procedure call model* or *RPC model*, the framework uses familiar concepts from conventional programs as the basis for the design of distributed applications.

20.3 Two Paradigms For Building Distributed Programs

A programmer can use one of two approaches when designing a distributed application:

- **Communication-Oriented Design**
  Begin with the communication protocol. Design a message format and syntax. Design the client and server components by specifying how each reacts to incoming messages and how each generates outgoing messages.

- **Application-Oriented Design**
  Begin with the application. Design a conventional application program to solve the problem. Build and test a working version of the conventional program that operates on a single machine. Divide the program into two or more pieces, and add communication protocols that allow each piece to execute on a separate computer.

A communication-oriented design sometimes leads to problems. First, by focusing on the communication protocol, the programmer may miss important subtleties in the application and may find that the protocol does not provide all the needed functionality. Second, because few programmers have experience and expertise with protocol design, they often produce awkward, incorrect, or inefficient protocols. Small oversights in protocol design can lead to fundamental errors that remain hidden until the programs run under stress (e.g., the possibility of deadlock). Third, because the programmer concentrates on communication, it usually becomes the centerpiece of the resulting programs, making them difficult to understand or modify. In particular, because the server is specified by giving a list of messages and the actions required when each message arrives, it may be difficult to understand the intended interaction or the underlying motivations.

The remote procedure call model uses the application-oriented approach, which emphasizes the problem to be solved instead of the communication needed. Using the remote procedure call model, a programmer first designs a conventional program to solve the problem, and then divides the program into pieces that run on two or more computers. The programmer can follow good design principles that make the code modular and maintainable.

In an ideal situation, the remote procedure call model provides more than an abstract concept. It allows a programmer to build, compile, and test a conventional version of the program to ensure that it solves the problem correctly before dividing the program into pieces that operate on separate machines. Furthermore, because RPC divides programs at procedure boundaries, the split into local and remote parts can be made without major modifications to the program structure. In fact, it may be possible to move some of the procedures from a program to remote machines without changing or even recompiling the main program itself. Thus, RPC separates the solution of a problem from the task of making the solution operate in a distributed environment.

> *The remote procedure call paradigm for programming focuses on the application. It allows a programmer to concentrate on devising a conventional program that solves the problem before attempting to divide the program into pieces that operate on multiple computers.*

20.4 A Conceptual Model For Conventional Procedure Calls

The remote procedure call model draws heavily from the procedure call mechanism found in conventional programming languages. Procedures offer a powerful abstraction that allows programmers to divide programs into small, manageable, easily-understood pieces. Procedures are especially useful because they have a straightforward implementation that provides a conceptual model of program execution. Figure 20.1 illustrates the concept.

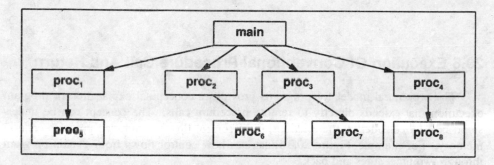

Figure 20.1 The procedure concept. A conventional program consists of one or more procedures, usually arranged in a hierarchy of calls. An arrow from procedure *n* to procedure *m* denotes a call from *n* to *m*.

20.5 An Extension Of the Procedural Model

The remote procedure call model uses the same procedural abstraction as a conventional program, but allows a procedure call to span the boundary between two computers. Figure 20.2 illustrates how the remote procedure call paradigm can be used to divide a program into two pieces that each execute on a separate computer. Of course, a conventional procedure call cannot pass from one computer to another. Before a program can use remote procedure calls, it must be augmented with protocol software that allows it to communicate with the remote procedure.

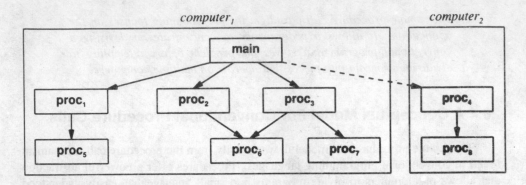

Figure 20.2 A distributed program that shows how the program from Figure 20.1 can be extended to use the remote procedure call paradigm. The division occurs between the main program and procedure 4. A communication protocol is required to implement the remote call.

20.6 Execution Of Conventional Procedure Call And Return

The procedural model for programs provides a conceptual explanation of program execution that extends directly to remote procedure calls. The concept can be understood best by considering the relationship of control flow to compiled program code in memory. For example, Figure 20.3 illustrates how control flows from a main program through two procedures and back.

According to the procedural execution model, a single *thread of control* or *thread of execution* flows through all procedures. The computer begins execution in a *main* program and continues until it encounters a *procedure call*. The call causes execution to branch to code in the specified procedure and continue. If it encounters another call, the computer branches to a second procedure.

Execution continues in the called procedure until the computer encounters a *return* statement. The return statement causes execution to resume at a point just after the last call. For example, in Figure 20.3, executing the return in procedure *B* causes control to pass back to procedure *A* at a point just after the call to *B*.

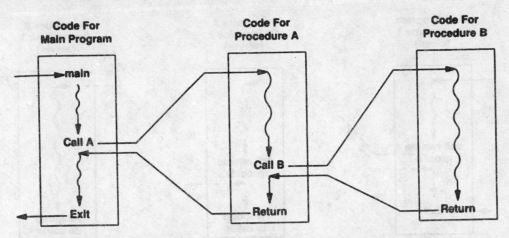

Figure 20.3 A conceptual model of execution that explains flow of control during procedure call and return. A single thread of control begins in the main program, passes through procedures *A* and *B*, and eventually returns to the main program.

In the conceptual model, only one thread of execution continues at any time. Therefore, the execution of one procedure must "stop" temporarily while the computer executes the call to another procedure. The computer suspends the calling procedure, leaving the values in all variables frozen during the call. Later, when execution returns from the procedure call, the computer resumes execution in the caller with the values in all variables available again. A called procedure may make further procedure calls because the computer remembers the sequence of calls and always returns to the most recently executing caller.

20.7 The Procedural Model In Distributed Systems

The execution model of procedure calls that programmers use when thinking about conventional computer programs can help us to understand how execution proceeds in a distributed program. Instead of thinking about a client program and a server program exchanging messages, imagine that each server implements a (remote) procedure and that the interactions between a client and a server correspond to a procedure call and return. A request sent from a client to a server corresponds to a call of a remote procedure, and a response sent from a server back to a client corresponds to the execution of a return instruction. Figure 20.4 illustrates the analogy.

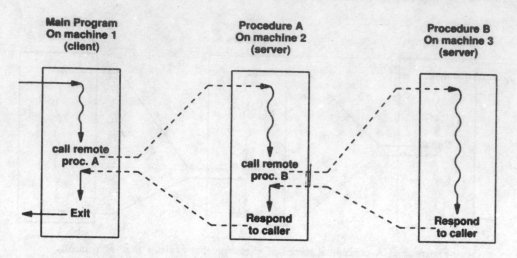

Figure 20.4 The model of execution used with remote procedure calls. A single thread of control executes in a distributed environment. Dashed lines show how control passes from a client to a server during a remote procedure call, and how it passes back when the server responds.

20.8 Analogy Between Client-Server And RPC

The remote procedure call concept provides a strong analogy that allows programmers to think about client-server interactions in a familiar context. Like a conventional procedure call, a remote procedure call transfers control to the called procedure. Also like a conventional procedure call, the system suspends execution of the calling procedure during the call and only allows the called procedure to execute.

When a remote program issues a response, it corresponds to the execution of a *return* in a conventional procedure call. Control flows back to the caller, and the called procedure ceases to execute. The notion of nested procedure calls also applies to remote procedure calls. One remote procedure may call another remote procedure. As Figure 20.4 illustrates, nested remote procedure calls correspond to a server that becomes a client of another service.

Of course, the analogy between remote procedure call and client-server interaction does not explain all the details. For example, we know that a conventional procedure remains completely inactive until the flow of control passes to it (i.e., until it is called). In contrast, a server process must exist in the remote system and be waiting to compute a response before it receives the first request from a client. Further differences arise in the way data flows to a remote procedure. Conventional procedures usually accept a few arguments and return only a few results. However, a server can accept or return arbitrary amounts of data (i.e., it can accept or return an arbitrary stream over a TCP connection).

Although it would be ideal if local and remote procedure calls behaved identically, several practical constraints prevent it. First, network delays can make a remote procedure call several orders of magnitude more expensive than a conventional procedure call. Second, because the called procedure operates in the same address space as the calling procedure, conventional programs can pass pointers as arguments. A remote procedure call cannot have pointers as arguments because the remote procedure operates in a completely different address space than the caller. Third, because a remote procedure does not share the caller's environment, it does not have direct access to the caller's I/O descriptors or operating system functions. For example, a remote procedure cannot write error messages directly to the caller's standard error file.

20.9 Distributed Computation As A Program

The key to appreciating remote procedure call is to understand that, despite its practical limitations, the paradigm helps programmers design distributed programs easily. To see how, imagine that each distributed computation consists of an individual program that runs in a distributed environment. Instead of thinking about the client and server software that implements communication, imagine how easy it would be to build distributed programs if a program simply invoked a procedure when it needed access to a remote service. Imagine that the program's thread of execution could pass across the network to the remote machine, execute the remote procedure on that machine, and then return back to the caller. From the programmer's point of view, remote services would be as easy to access as local procedures or local operating system services. In short, distributed programs would become as easy to construct as conventional programs because they could draw on the programmer's intuition and experience with conventional procedure calls. Furthermore, programmers familiar with the procedure parameter mechanism could define client-server communication precisely without any need for a special notation or language. To summarize:

> Thinking of a distributed computation as a single program in which control passes across the network to a remote procedure and back helps programmers specify client-server interactions; it relates the interaction of distributed computations to the familiar notions of procedure call and return.

20.10 Sun Microsystems' Remote Procedure Call Definition

Sun Microsystems, Incorporated has defined a specific form of remote procedure call. Known as *Sun RPC*, or simply *RPC*†, Sun's remote procedure call definition has received wide acceptance in the industry. It has been used as an implementation mechanism for many applications, including Sun's Network File System (NFS‡).

Sun RPC defines the format of messages that the caller (client) sends to invoke a remote procedure on a server, the format of arguments, and the format of results that the called procedure returns to the caller. It permits the calling program to use either UDP or TCP to carry messages, and uses XDR to represent procedure arguments as well as other items in an RPC message header. Finally, in addition to the protocol specification, Sun RPC includes a compiler system that helps programmers build distributed programs automatically.

20.11 Remote Programs And Procedures

Sun RPC extends the remote procedure call model by defining a remote execution environment. It defines a *remote program* as the basic unit of software that executes on a remote machine. Each remote program corresponds to what we think of as a server, and contains a set of one or more remote procedures plus global data. The procedures inside a remote program all share access to its global data. Thus, a set of cooperative remote procedures can share state information. For example, one can implement a simple remote database by constructing a single remote program that includes data structures to hold shared information and three remote procedures to manipulate it: *insert*, *delete*, and *lookup*. As Figure 20.5 illustrates, all remote procedures inside the remote program can share access to the single database.

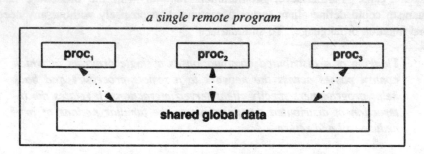

Figure 20.5 Conceptual organization of three remote procedures in a single remote program that implements a database. All three procedures share access to global data in the program, just as conventional procedures share access to global data in a conventional program.

---

†We will use the term *RPC* throughout the remainder of this text to refer to Sun RPC unless otherwise noted.

‡Chapter *23* discusses NFS in detail.

20.12 Reducing The Number Of Arguments

Because most programming languages use positional notation to represent arguments, a procedure call that contains more than a handful of arguments can be difficult to read. Programmers can reduce the problem by collecting many arguments into a single data aggregate (e.g., a C *struct*) and passing the resulting aggregate as a single argument. The caller assigns each field in the structure a value before passing the structure to the called procedure; the caller extracts return values from the structure after the call returns. To summarize:

> *Using a structure instead of multiple arguments makes the program*
> *more readable because the structure field names serve as keywords*
> *that tell the reader how each argument will be used.*

Because we will assume throughout the remainder of this discussion that all programs using RPC collect their arguments into a structure, each remote procedure will need only a single argument.

20.13 Identifying Remote Programs And Procedures

The Sun RPC standard specifies that each remote program executing on a computer must be assigned a unique 32-bit integer that the caller uses to identify it. Furthermore, Sun RPC assigns an integer identifier to each remote procedure inside a given remote program. The procedures are numbered sequentially: *1, 2, ..., N*†. Conceptually, a specific remote procedure on a given remote computer can be identified by a pair:

$$(prog, proc)$$

where *prog* identifies the remote program and *proc* identifies a remote procedure within the program. To help ensure that program numbers defined by separate organizations do not conflict, Sun RPC has divided the set of program numbers into eight groups as Figure 20.6 shows.

---

†By convention, the number *0* is always reserved for an echo procedure that can be used to test whether the remote program can be reached.

From		To	Values Assigned By
0x00000000	-	0x1fffffff	Sun Microsystems, Inc.
0x20000000	-	0x3fffffff	The system manager at a user's site
0x40000000	-	0x5fffffff	Transient (temporary)
0x60000000	-	0x7fffffff	Reserved
0x80000000	-	0x9fffffff	Reserved
0xa0000000	-	0xbfffffff	Reserved
0xc0000000	-	0xdfffffff	Reserved
0xe0000000	-	0xffffffff	Reserved

Figure 20.6 The division into eight groups of 32-bit numbers that Sun RPC uses to identify remote programs. Each remote program is assigned a unique number.

Sun Microsystems, Incorporated administers the first group of identifiers, allowing anyone to apply for a standard RPC program number. Because Sun publishes the assignments, all computers that run RPC use the standard values. Of the 2^{29} program numbers available in the first group, Sun has only assigned a handful of numbers. Figure 20.7 summarizes some of the assignments.

20.14 Accommodating Multiple Versions Of A Remote Program

In addition to a program number, Sun RPC includes an integer *version number* for each remote program. Usually, the first version of a program is assigned version *1*. Later versions each receive a unique version number.

Version numbers provide the ability to change the details of a remote procedure call without obtaining a new program number. In practice, each RPC message identifies the intended recipient on a given computer by a triple:

$$(prog, vers, proc)$$

where *prog* identifies the remote program, *vers* specifies the version of the program to which the message has been sent, and *proc* identifies a remote procedure within that remote program. The RPC specification permits a computer to run multiple versions of a remote program simultaneously, allowing for graceful migration during changes. The idea can be summarized:

> Because all Sun RPC messages identify a remote program, the version of that program, and a remote procedure in the program, it is possible to migrate from one version of a remote procedure to another gracefully and to test a new version of the server while an old version continues to operate.

Name	assigned number	Description
portmap	100000	port mapper
rstatd	100001	rstat, rup, and perfmeter
rusersd	100002	remote users
nfs	100003	network file system
ypserv	100004	yp (now called NIS)
mountd	100005	mount, showmount
dbxd	100006	DBXprog (debugger)
ypbind	100007	NIS binder
walld	100008	rwall, shutdown
yppasswdd	100009	yppasswd
etherstatd	100010	ethernet statistics
rquotad	100011	rquotaprog, quota, rquota
sprayd	100012	spray
selection_svc	100015	selection service
dbsessionmgr	100016	unify, netdbms, dbms
rexd	100017	rex, remote_exec
office_auto	100018	alice
lockd	100020	klmprog
lockd	100021	nlmprog
statd	100024	status monitor
bootparamd	100026	bootstrap
pcnfsd	150001	NFS for PC

Figure 20.7 Example RPC program numbers currently assigned by Sun Microsystems, Inc.

20.15 Mutual Exclusion For Procedures In A Remote Program

The Sun RPC mechanism specifies that at most one remote procedure in a remote program can be invoked at a given time. Thus, RPC provides automatic mutual exclusion among procedures within a given remote program. Such exclusion can be important for remote programs that maintain shared data accessed by several procedures. For example, if a remote database program includes remote procedures for *insert* and *delete* operations, the programmer does not need to worry about two remote procedure calls interfering with one another because the mechanism only permits one call to execute at a time. The system blocks other calls until the current call finishes. To summarize:

Sun RPC provides mutual exclusion among remote procedures within a single remote program; at most one remote procedure call can execute in a remote program at one time.

20.16 Communication Semantics

When choosing the semantics for Sun RPC, the designers had to choose between two possibilities. On one hand, to make a remote procedure call behave as much like a local procedure call as possible, RPC should use a reliable transport like TCP and should guarantee reliability to the programmer. The remote procedure call mechanism should either transfer the call to the remote procedure and receive a reply, or it should report that communication is impossible. On the other hand, to allow programmers to use efficient, connectionless transport protocols, the remote procedure call mechanism should support communication through a datagram protocol like UDP.

Sun RPC does not enforce reliable semantics. It allows each application to choose TCP or UDP as a transport protocol. Furthermore, the standard does not specify additional protocols or mechanisms to achieve reliable delivery. Instead, it defines RPC semantics as a function of the semantics of the underlying transport protocol. For example, because UDP permits datagrams to be lost or duplicated, Sun RPC specifies that remote procedure calls using UDP may experience loss or duplication.

20.17 At Least Once Semantics

Sun RPC defines the semantics of a remote procedure call in the simplest way by specifying that a program should only draw the weakest possible conclusion from any interaction. For example, when using UDP, a request or reply message (call to a remote procedure or return from one) can be lost or duplicated. If a remote procedure call does not return, the caller cannot conclude that the remote procedure has not been called because the reply could have been lost, even if the request was not. If a remote procedure call does return, the caller can conclude that the remote procedure was called *at least once*. However, the calling procedure cannot conclude that the remote procedure was called exactly once because the request could have been duplicated or a reply message could have been lost.

The Sun RPC standard uses the term *at least once semantics* to describe RPC execution when the caller receives a reply, and *zero or more semantics* to describe the behavior of a remote procedure call when the caller does not receive a reply.

RPC's zero-or-more semantics imposes an important responsibility on the programmer:

Programmers who choose to use UDP as the transport protocol for a Sun RPC application must build the application to tolerate zero-or-more execution semantics.

In practice, zero-or-more semantics usually means that a programmer makes each remote procedure call *idempotent†*. For example, consider a remote file access application. A remote procedure that appends data to a file is not idempotent because repeated executions of the procedure will append data repeatedly. On the other hand, a remote procedure that writes data to a specified position in a file is idempotent because repeated executions will always write data to the same position.

20.18 RPC Retransmission

The library software supplied with Sun's RPC implementation includes a simple timeout and retransmission strategy, but does not guarantee reliability in the strict sense. The default timeout mechanism implements a fixed (nonadaptive) timeout with a fixed number of retries. When the RPC library software sends a message that corresponds to a remote procedure call, it starts a timer. The software retransmits the request if the timer expires before a response arrives. Programmers can adjust the timeout and retry limits for a given application, but the software does not adapt automatically to long network delays or to changes in delay over time.

Of course, a simple retransmission strategy does not guarantee reliability, nor does it guarantee that the calling application can draw a correct conclusion about execution of the remote procedure. For example, if the network loses all responses, the caller may retransmit the request several times and each request may result in an execution of the remote procedure. Ultimately, however, library software on the caller's machine will reach its retry limit and declare that the remote procedure cannot be executed. Most important, an application cannot interpret failure as a guarantee that the remote procedure was never executed (in fact, it may have executed several times).

20.19 Mapping A Remote Program To A Protocol Port

UDP and TCP transport protocols use 16-bit protocol port numbers to identify communication endpoints. Earlier chapters describe how a server creates a passive socket, binds the socket to a well-known protocol port, and waits for client programs to contact it. To make it possible for clients and servers to rendezvous, we assume that each service is assigned a unique protocol port number and that the assignments are well-known. Thus, both the server and client agree on the protocol port at which the server accepts requests because they both consult a published list of port assignments.

---

†The term is taken from mathematics, where an operation is said to be idempotent if repeated applications of the operation produce the same result.

Sun RPC introduces an interesting problem: because it uses 32-bit numbers to identify remote programs, RPC programs can outnumber protocol ports. Thus, it is impossible to map RPC program numbers onto protocol-ports directly. More important, because RPC programs cannot all be assigned a unique protocol port, programmers cannot use a scheme that depends on well-known protocol-port assignments.

Although the potential number of RPC programs rules out well-known port assignments, RPC does not differ dramatically from other services. At any given time, a single computer executes only a small number of remote programs. Thus, as long as the port assignments are temporary, each RPC program can obtain a protocol port number and use it for communication.

If an RPC program does not use a reserved, well-known protocol port, clients cannot contact it directly. To see why, think of the server and client components. When the server (remote program) begins execution, it asks the operating system to allocate an unused protocol port number. The server uses the newly allocated protocol port for all communication. The system may choose a different protocol port number each time the server begins (i.e., the server may have a different port assigned each time the system boots).

The client (the program that issues the remote procedure call) knows the machine address and RPC program number for the remote program it wishes to contact. However, because the RPC program (server) only obtains a protocol port after it begins execution, the client cannot know which protocol port the server obtained. Thus, the client cannot contact the remote program directly.

20.20 Dynamic Port Mapping

To solve the port identification problem, a client must be able to map from an RPC program number and a machine address to the protocol port that the server obtained on the destination machine when it started. The mapping must be dynamic because it can change if the machine reboots or if the RPC program starts execution again.

To allow clients to contact remote programs, the Sun RPC mechanism includes a dynamic mapping service. Each machine that offers an RPC program (i.e., that runs a server) maintains a database of port mappings and provides a mechanism that allows a caller to map RPC program numbers to protocol ports. Called the *RPC port mapper* or sometimes simply the *port mapper*, the RPC port mapping mechanism uses a server to maintain a small database on each machine. Figure 20.8 illustrates that the port mapper operates as a separate server process.

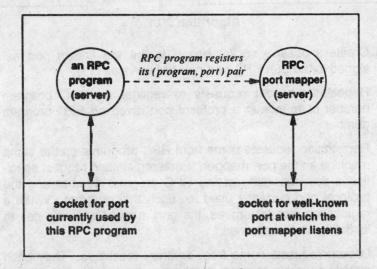

Figure 20.8 The Sun RPC port mapper. Each RPC program registers its program number and protocol port number with the port mapper on its local machine. A caller always contacts the port mapper on a machine to find the protocol port to use for a given RPC program on that machine.

20.21 RPC Port Mapper Algorithm

One port mapper operates on each machine using Algorithm 20.1. The port mapper allows clients to reach remote programs even though the remote programs dynamically allocate protocol ports. Whenever a remote program (i.e., a server) begins execution, it allocates a local protocol port that it will use for communication. The remote program then contacts the port mapper on its local machine and adds a pair of integers to the database:

$$(RPC\ prog\ number,\ protocol\ port\ number)$$

Once an RPC program has registered itself, callers on other machines can find its protocol port by sending a request to the port mapper.

Algorithm 20.1

1. Create a passive socket bound to the well-known port assigned to the Sun RPC port mapper service (*111*).

2. Repeatedly accept requests to register an RPC program number or to lookup a protocol port given an RPC program number.

   Registration requests come from RPC programs on the same machine as the port mapper. Each registration request specifies a pair consisting of the RPC program number and the protocol port currently used to reach that program. When a registration request arrives, the port mapper adds the pair to its database of mappings.

   Lookup requests come from arbitrary machines. They each specify a remote program number, and request the number of a protocol port that can be used to reach the remote program. The port mapper looks up the remote program in its database, and responds by returning the corresponding protocol port for that program.

Algorithm 20.1 The Sun RPC port mapper algorithm. One port mapper server runs on each machine that implements the server side of an RPC program.

The port mapper on a given machine works like directory assistance in the U.S. telephone system: a caller can ask the port mapper how to reach a particular RPC program on that machine. To contact a remote program, a caller must know the address of the machine on which the remote program executes as well as the RPC program number assigned to the program. The caller first contacts the RPC port mapper on the target machine, and then sends the port mapper an RPC program number. The port mapper returns the protocol port number that the specified program is currently using. A caller can always reach the port mapper because the port mapper communicates using the well-known protocol port, *111*. Once a caller knows the protocol port number the target program is using, it can contact the remote program directly.

20.22 Sun RPC Message Format

Unlike many TCP/IP protocols, Sun RPC does not use a fixed format for messages. The protocol standard defines the general format of RPC messages as well as the data items in each field using a language known as the *XDR Language*. Because XDR language resembles data structure declarations in C, programmers familiar with C can usually read and understand the language without much explanation. In general, the language specifies how to assemble a sequence of data items that comprise a message. Each item is encoded using the XDR representation standard.

A message type field in the RPC message header distinguishes between messages that a client uses to initiate a remote procedure call and messages that a remote procedure uses to reply. Constants used in the message type field can be defined using XDR language. For example, the declarations:

```
enum msg_type {              /* RPC message type constants */
     CALL  = 0;
     REPLY = 1;
};
```

declare the symbolic constants *CALL* and *REPLY* to be the values of an enumerated type, *msg_type*.

Data structures in XDR language can be considered a sequence of XDR types, and can be interpreted as instructions for assembling a message by composing data using XDR. For example, once values have been declared for symbolic constants, the XDR language can define the format of an RPC message:

```
struct rpc_msg {                 /* Format of an RPC message     */
     unsigned int mesgid;        /* used to match reply to call  */
     union switch (msg_type mesgt) {
          case CALL:
               call_body cbody;
          case REPLY:
               rply_body rbody;
     } body;
```

The declaration specifies that an RPC message, *rpc_msg* consists of an integer message identifier, *mesgid*, followed by the XDR representation of a discriminated union. Using the XDR representation, each union begins with an integer, *mesgt* in this case. *Mesgt* determines the format of the remainder of the RPC message; it contains a value that defines the message to be either a *CALL* or a *REPLY*. A CALL message contains further information in the form of a *call_body*; a REPLY contains information in the form of a *rply_body*. The declarations for *call_body* and *rply_body* must be given elsewhere. For example, RPC defines a *call_body* to have the form:

```
struct call_body {              /* format of RPC CALL           */
    unsigned int rpcvers;       /* which version of RPC?        */
    unsigned int rprog;         /* number of remote program     */
    unsigned int rprogvers;     /* version number of remote prog*/
    unsigned int rproc;         /* number of remote procedure   */
    opaque_auth  cred;          /* credentials for called auth. */
    opaque_auth  verf;          /* authentication verifier      */
    /* ARGS */                  /* arguments for remote proc.   */
};
```

The first few items in the body of a remote procedure call present no surprises. The caller must supply the RPC protocol version number in field *rpcvers* to ensure that both client and server are using the same message format. Integer fields *rprog*, *rprogvers*, and *rproc* identify the remote program being called, the desired version of that program, and the remote procedure within that program. Fields *cred* and *verf* contain information that the called program can use to authenticate the caller's identity.

20.23 Marshaling Arguments For A Remote Procedure

Fields in an RPC message following the authentication information contain arguments for the remote procedure. The number of arguments and the type of each depend on the remote procedure being called.

RPC must represent all arguments in an external form that allows them to be transferred between computers. In particular, if any of the arguments passed to the remote procedure consists of a complex data structure like a linked list, it must be encoded into a compact representation that can be sent across the network. We use the terms *marshal*, *linearize*, or *serialize* to denote the task of encoding arguments. We say that the client side of RPC marshals arguments into the message and the server side unmarshals them. A programmer must remember that although RPC allows an RPC call to contain complex data objects, marshaling and unmarshaling large data structures can require significant CPU time and network bandwidth. Thus, most programmers avoid passing linked structures as arguments.

20.24 Authentication

RPC defines several possible forms of authentication, including a simple authentication scheme that relies on UNIX and a more complex scheme that uses the *Data Encryption Standard* (*DES*) originally published by The National Bureau Of Standards†. Authentication information can have one of the four types shown in the following declaration:

---

†NBS has changed its name to the National Institute For Standards and Technology (NIST).

```
            enum auth_type {              /* possible forms of auth.      */
                AUTH_NULL  = 0;           /* no authentication           */
                AUTH_UNIX  = 1;           /* UNIX machine name authentic. */
                AUTH_SHORT = 2;           /* Used for short form auth. in */
                                          /*   messages after the first  */
                AUTH_DES   = 3;           /* NIST's (NBS's) DES standard  */
            };
```

In each case, RPC leaves the format and interpretation of the authentication information up to the authentication subsystem. Therefore, the declaration of the authentication structure in an RPC message uses the keyword *opaque* to indicate that it appears in the message without any interpretation:

```
            struct opaque_auth {          /* structure for authent. info. */
                auth_type atype;          /* which type of authentication */
                opaque body<400>;         /* data for the type specified  */
            };
```

Of course, each authentication method uses a specific format for encoding data. For example, most sites that send RPC messages use the UNIX operating system. UNIX authentication defines the structure of its authentication information to contain several fields:

```
            struct auth_unix {            /* format of UNIX authentication*/
                unsigned int timestamp;   /* integer timestamp           */
                string smachine<255>;     /* name of sender's machine    */
                unsigned int userid;      /* user id of user making req.  */
                unsigned int grpid;       /* group id of user making req. */
                unsigned int grpids<10>;  /* other group ids for the user */
            };
```

UNIX authentication relies on the client machine to supply its name in field *smachine* and the numeric identifier of the user making the request in field *userid*. The client also specifies its local time in field *timestamp*, which can be used to sequence requests. Finally, the client sends the main numeric group identifier and secondary group identifiers of the sending user in fields *grpid* and *grpids*.

20.25 An Example Of RPC Message Representation

XDR defines the size and external format of each field in an RPC message. For example, XDR specifies that an integer (either signed or unsigned) occupies 32 bits and is stored in big-endian byte order.

Figure 20.9 shows the size of fields in an example RPC *CALL* message.

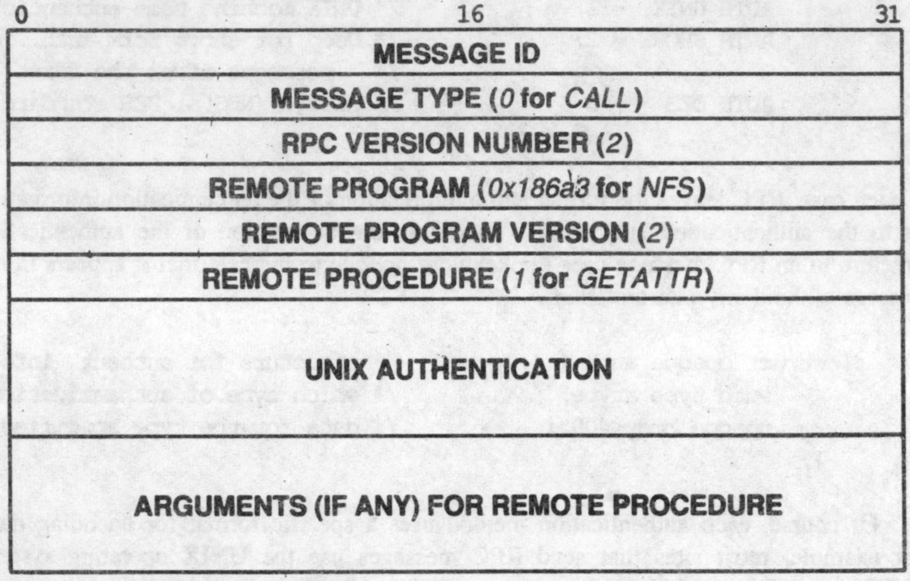

0	16	31
MESSAGE ID		
MESSAGE TYPE (*0* for *CALL*)		
RPC VERSION NUMBER (*2*)		
REMOTE PROGRAM (*0x186a3* for *NFS*)		
REMOTE PROGRAM VERSION (*2*)		
REMOTE PROCEDURE (*1* for *GETATTR*)		
UNIX AUTHENTICATION		
ARGUMENTS (IF ANY) FOR REMOTE PROCEDURE		

Figure 20.9 An example of the external format used for an RPC *CALL* message. The first fields of the message have a fixed size, but the sizes of later fields vary with their content.

20.26 An Example Of The UNIX Authentication Field

The size of the authentication field in an RPC message depends on its contents. For example the second field in a UNIX authentication structure is a machine name in a variable-length format. XDR represents a variable-length string as a 4-byte integer length followed by the bytes of the string itself. Figure 20.10 shows an example of the representation for a UNIX authentication field. In the example, the computer's name, *merlin.cs.purdue.edu*, contains *20* characters.

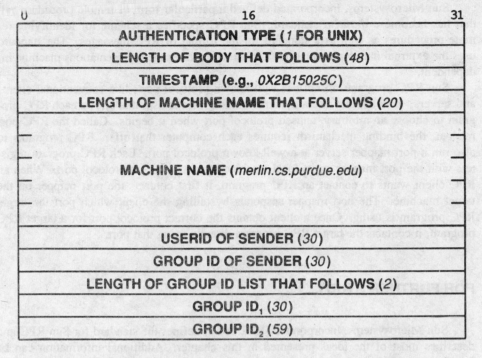

0	16	31

AUTHENTICATION TYPE (*1* FOR UNIX)
LENGTH OF BODY THAT FOLLOWS (*48*)
TIMESTAMP (e.g., *0X2B15025C*)
LENGTH OF MACHINE NAME THAT FOLLOWS (*20*)
MACHINE NAME (*merlin.cs.purdue.edu*)
USERID OF SENDER (*30*)
GROUP ID OF SENDER (*30*)
LENGTH OF GROUP ID LIST THAT FOLLOWS (*2*)
GROUP ID₁ (*30*)
GROUP ID₂ (*59*)

Figure 20.10 Example representation for UNIX authentication within a Sun
RPC message. The example values are taken from a message
sent by a user with numeric login identifier *30* on machine
merlin.cs.purdue.edu.

20.27 Summary

The remote procedure model helps make distributed programs easy to **design and**
understand because it relates client-server communication to conventional **procedure**
calls. The remote procedure call model views each server as implementing one or more
procedures. A message sent from a client to a server corresponds to a "call" of a remote procedure, and a response from the server to the client corresponds to a "return"
from a procedure call.

Like conventional procedures, remote procedures accept arguments and **return one**
or more results. The arguments and results passed between the caller and the **called**
procedure provide a precise definition of the communication between the client **and the**
server.

Using the remote procedure call model helps programmers focus on the **application**
instead of the communication protocol. The programmer can build and test a **conven-**
tional program that solves a particular problem, and then can divide the program **into**
parts that execute on two or more computers.

Sun Microsystems, Incorporated defined a particular form of remote procedure call that has become a *de facto* standard. Sun RPC specifies a scheme for identifying remote procedures as well as a standard for the format of RPC messages. The standard uses the external data representation, XDR, to keep message representations machine independent.

Sun RPC programs do not use well-known protocol ports like conventional clients and servers. Instead, they use a dynamic binding mechanism that allows each RPC program to choose an arbitrary, unused protocol port when it begins. Called the RPC port mapper, the binding mechanism requires each computer that offers RPC programs to also run a port mapper server at a well-known protocol port. Each RPC program registers with the port mapper on its local machine after it obtains a protocol port. When an RPC client wants to contact an RPC program, it first contacts the port mapper on the target machine. The port mapper responds by telling the client which port the target RPC program is using. Once a client obtains the correct protocol port for a target RPC program, it contacts the target RPC program directly using that port.

FOR FURTHER STUDY

Sun Microsystems, Incorporated [RFC 1057] defines the standard for Sun RPC and describes most of the ideas presented in this chapter. Additional information can be found in the *Network Programming Guide* that accompanies the SunOS operating system.

EXERCISES

20.1   Read the Sun RPC specification and create a diagram that shows the size of the fields in a typical return message.

20.2   Conduct an experiment to measure the overhead that using a port mapper introduces.

20.3   A client can avoid needless overhead by caching protocol port bindings. That is, after a client contacts the port mapper to obtain a protocol port for the target RPC program, it can store the binding in a cache to avoid looking it up again. How long will a binding remain valid?

20.4   Can the port mapper concept be extended to services other than RPC? Explain your answer.

20.5   What are the major advantages and disadvantages of using a port mapper instead of well-known ports?

20.6   When an RPC client contacts a port mapper, it must either specify or learn whether the target program has opened a UDP port or a TCP port. Read the specification carefully to find out how an RPC client distinguishes between the two.

21

Distributed Program Generation (Rpcgen Concept)

21.1 Introduction

The previous chapter presents the principles underlying the remote procedure call model. It describes the remote procedure call concept, and explains how programmers can use remote procedure calls to build programs that operate in the client-server paradigm. Finally, it describes the Sun RPC mechanism.

This chapter continues the discussion. It focuses on the structure of programs that use RPC, and shows how programs can be divided along procedural boundaries. It introduces the stub procedure concept and a program generator tool that automates much of the code generation associated with Sun RPC. It also discusses a library of procedures that makes it easy to build servers that offer remote procedures and clients that call them.

The next chapter completes the discussion of the generator. It shows the sequence of steps a programmer takes to create a conventional program and then to divide the program into local and remote components. It presents a simple example application, and then uses the example to follow through the process of constructing a distributed program. The example in the next chapter complements the conceptual description in this chapter by illustrating many of the details and showing the code that the generator produces.

21.2 Using Remote Procedure Calls

The remote procedure call model is general. A programmer can choose to use the remote procedure paradigm in any of the following ways:

- As a program specification technique only. To do so, the programmer follows the RPC model and specifies all interaction between a client and server as either a remote procedure call or a return. Procedure arguments specify the data passed between the client and server. The programmer can ignore the procedural structure when designing the client and server, but use the procedural specification to verify the correctness of the resulting system.

- For both program specification and as an abstraction during program design. To implement this approach, think about remote procedure calls when designing the application programs and the communication protocol. Design a communication protocol in which each message corresponds closely to one of the remote procedure calls.

- For the conceptual design and explicitly in the implementation. To include RPC in the implementation, the programmer designs a generalized RPC message format and a protocol for passing control to a remote procedure. The programmer follows the procedural specification precisely when passing data between the client and server. The program uses a standard external data representation to encode arguments, and follows the exact data type specifications given in the design. It calls standard library routines to convert between the computer's native representation and the external representation used when crossing a network.

- For design and implementation, constructing all software from scratch. The programmer builds a conventional application that solves the problem, and then divides it into pieces along procedural boundaries, moving the pieces to separate machines. The program uses the Sun RPC message format (including the XDR data representation) and the Sun RPC program numbering scheme when calling a remote procedure. The programmer builds the implementation from the RPC specifications alone, using the Sun RPC port mapper to bind a remote program number to the corresponding protocol port.

- For design and implementation, using standard libraries. The programmer builds an application and divides it into pieces using the Sun RPC specification, but relies on existing RPC library routines whenever possible. For example, the programmer uses library routines to register with the port mapper, to compose and send a remote procedure call message, and to compose a reply.

- For an automated implementation. The programmer follows the Sun RPC specification completely, and uses an automatic program generator tool to help automate construction of the necessary pieces of client and server code and the calls to RPC library routines that perform tasks like registering a program with the port mapper, constructing a message, and dispatching a call to the appropriate remote procedure in a remote program.

21.3 Programming Mechanisms To Support RPC

Sun RPC specifications are both extensive and complicated. Building an application that implements RPC without using any existing software can be tedious and time consuming. Most programmers prefer to avoid duplicating the effort for each application. Instead, they rely on library routines and programming tools to handle much of the work.

Implementations of Sun RPC provide significant help for those who wish to avoid unnecessary programming. Assistance comes in four forms:

1. XDR library routines that convert individual data items from internal form to the XDR standard external representation
2. XDR library routines that format the complex data aggregates (e.g., arrays and structures) used to define RPC messages
3. RPC run-time library routines that allow a program to call a remote procedure, register a service with the port mapper, or dispatch an incoming call to the correct remote procedure inside a remote program
4. A program generator† tool that produces many of the C source files needed to build a distributed program that uses RPC

The RPC run-time library has procedures that supply most of the functionality needed for RPC. For example, procedure *callrpc* sends an RPC message to a server. It has the form:

```
callrpc(host, prog, progver, procnum, inproc, in, outproc, out);
```

Argument *host* points to a character string that contains the name of a machine on which the remote procedure executes. Arguments *prog*, *progver*, and *procnum* identify the remote program number, the version of the program to use, and the remote procedure number. Argument *inproc* gives the address of a local procedure that can be called to marshal arguments into an RPC message, and argument *in* gives the address of the arguments for the remote procedure. Argument *outproc* gives the address of a local procedure that can be called to decode the results, and *out* gives the address in memory where the results should go.

While *callrpc* handles many of the chores required to send an RPC message, the Sun RPC library contains many other procedures. For example, a client calls function:

```
handle = clnt_create(host, prog, vers, proto);
```

to create an integer identifier that can be used to send RPC messages. RPC calls the integer identifier a *handle*; several RPC library procedures take a handle as one of their arguments. Arguments to *clnt_create* specify the name of a remote host, a remote program on that host, the version of that program, and a protocol (TCP or UDP).

---

†Programmers often refer to the program generator as a *stub generator*. The reason that such terminology has become popular will become apparent when we review how the generator works.

The library also contains routines that create, store, and manipulate authentication information. For example, procedure:

        authunix_create (host, uid, gid, len, aup_gids);

creates an authentication handle for a given user on a given host computer. Arguments specify a remote host, the user's login and primary group identifiers, and a set of groups to which the user belongs, *aup_gids*. Argument *len* specifies the number of items in the set.

Although programmers can write applications that call the RPC library routines directly, few programmers do. Most rely on the program generator tool discussed later in this chapter. The code it generates contains many calls to the library procedures.

21.4 Dividing A Program Into Local And Remote Procedures

To understand how the RPC programming tools work, it is necessary to understand how a program can be divided into local and remote procedures. Think of the procedure calls in a conventional application. Figure 21.1 illustrates one such call.

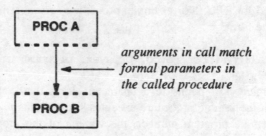

Figure 21.1 An example procedure call that illustrates the procedural interface used by a calling procedure and a called procedure. The dashed lines denote a match between arguments in the procedure call and parameters in the called procedure.

Each procedure has a set of formal parameters, and each procedure call specifies a set of arguments. The total number of arguments in the caller must equal the total number of formal parameters in the called procedure, and the type of each argument must match the declared type of the corresponding formal parameter. In other words, the parameters define the interface between a calling procedure and a called procedure.

21.5 Adding Code For RPC

Moving one or more procedures to a remote machine requires a programmer to add code between the procedure call and the remote procedure. On the client side, the new code must marshal arguments and translate them to a machine-independent representation, create an RPC *CALL* message, send the message to the remote program, wait for the results, and translate the resulting values back to the client's native representation. On the server side, the new code must accept an incoming RPC request, translate arguments to the server's native data representation, dispatch the message to the appropriate procedure, form a reply message by translating values to the machine-independent data representation, and send the result back to the client.

To keep the program structure intact and to isolate the code that handles RPC from the code that handles the application, the additional code required for RPC can be added in the form of two extra procedures that completely hide the communication details. The new procedures can add the required functionality without changing the interface between the original calling and called procedures. Preserving the original interface helps reduce the chance for errors because it keeps the communication details separate from the original application.

21.6 Stub Procedures

The additional procedures added to a program to implement RPC are called *stub procedures*. The easiest way to understand stub procedures is to imagine a conventional program being divided into two programs with an existing procedure being moved to a remote machine. On the caller's (client) side, a stub procedure replaces the called procedure. On the remote procedure's (server) side, a stub procedure replaces the caller. The two stubs implement all the communication required for the remote procedure call, leaving the original calling and called procedures unchanged. Figure 21.2 illustrates the stub concept, showing how stub procedures allow the procedure call shown in Figure 21.1 to be separated into local and remote parts.

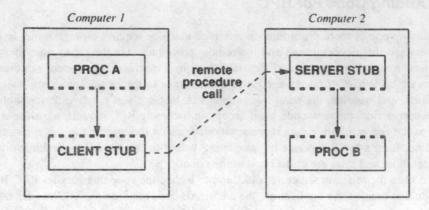

Figure 21.2 Stub procedures added to a program implement a remote procedure call. Because stubs use the same interface as the original
call, adding them does not require a change to either the original
calling procedure or the called procedure.

21.7 Multiple Remote Procedures And Dispatching

Figure 21.2 presents a simplified view of RPC because it only shows a single remote procedure call. In practice, a given server process usually includes several remote
procedures in a single remote program. Each RPC call consists of a message that identifies a specific remote procedure. When an RPC message arrives, the server uses the
remote procedure number in the message to *dispatch* the call to the correct procedure.
Figure 21.3 illustrates the concept.

The figure shows how RPC relates to a conventional client-server implementation.
The remote program consists of a single server process that must be running before any
messages arrive. A remote procedure call, which can originate from any client, must
specify the address of the machine on which the server operates as well as the number
of the remote procedure to call on that machine. The server program consists of a
dispatcher routine plus the remote procedures and server-side stub procedures. The
dispatcher understands how the remote procedure numbers correspond to the server-side
stubs, and uses the correspondence to forward each incoming remote procedure call to
an appropriate stub.

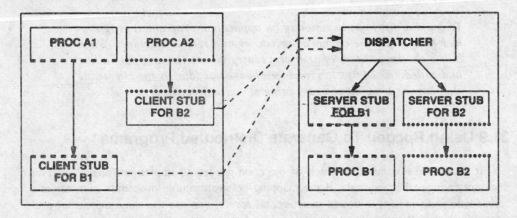

Figure 21.3 Message dispatch in an RPC server. Clients send RPC requests
to a single server program. The server uses the remote procedure number in a message to decide which procedure should
receive the call. In the example, procedure *A1* calls procedure
B1, and *A2* calls *B2*. Dashed and dotted lines show which interface each procedure uses.

21.8 Name Of The Client-Side Stub Procedure

The transition from a conventional application to a distributed program can be
trivial if the programmer chooses to name the client stub the same as the called procedure. To see why, consider again the stub procedures shown in Figure 21.3. The original caller, procedure *A1*, contains a call to procedure *B1*. After the program has been
divided, *A1* becomes part of the client and must call a stub to communicate with the remote procedure. If the programmer names the client-side stub *B1* and builds it to have
exactly the same interface as the original procedure *B1*, the calling procedure (*A1*) does
not need to change. In fact, it may even be possible to make the change without recompiling procedure *A1*. The original compiled binary for *A1* can be linked with the new
client-side stub for *B1* to produce a valid client. Adding a client-side stub without
changing the original caller isolates the RPC code from the original application program
code, making programming easier and reducing the chance of introducing errors.

Of course, naming the client stub *B1* makes source code management more difficult because it means that the distributed version of the program will have two procedures named *B1*: the client-side stub and the original procedure that becomes part of
the server. The two versions of *B1* are never part of the same linked program. In most
cases, they will not execute on the same computer. Thus, as long as the programmer
exercises caution when building object programs, the stub approach works well. To
summarize:

*To build a distributed version of an application program, a program-
mer must move one or more procedures to a remote machine. When
doing so, the addition of stub procedures allows the original calling
and called procedures to remain unchanged as long as the client-side
stub has the same name as the original called procedure.*

21.9 Using Rpcgen To Generate Distributed Programs

It should be obvious that much of the code needed to implement an RPC server
does not change. For example, if the mapping between remote procedure numbers and
server-side stubs is kept in a data structure, all servers can use the same dispatcher routine. Similarly, all servers can use the same code to register their services with the port
mapper.

To avoid unnecessary programming, implementations of Sun RPC include a tool
that generates much of the code needed to implement a distributed program automatically. Called *rpcgen*, the tool reads a specification file as input and generates files of C
source code as output. The specification file contains the declarations for constants,
global data types, global data, and remote procedures (including the procedure argument
and result types). The files that rpcgen produces contain most of the source code needed to implement the client and server programs that provide the specified remote procedure calls. In particular, rpcgen generates code for the client-side and server-side stub
procedures, including the code to marshal arguments, to send an RPC message, to
dispatch an incoming call to the correct procedure, to send a reply, and to translate arguments and results between the external representation and native data representation.
When combined with an application program and a few files that the programmer
writes, the rpcgen output produces complete client and server programs.

Because rpcgen produces source code as output, the programmer can choose to edit
the code (e.g., to hand-optimize the code to improve performance) or to combine it with
other files. In most cases, programmers use rpcgen to handle as many of the details as
possible. They try to avoid changing the output by hand to keep the entire process of
generating a client and server automated. If the program specifications change or new
remote procedure calls are needed, the programmer can modify the specifications and
use rpcgen again to produce a new client and server without manual intervention.

21.10 Rpcgen Output And Interface Procedures

To maintain flexibility and to allow automatic generation of significant portions of
the stub code, rpcgen separates each stub procedure into two parts. One part, common
to almost all applications that use RPC, provides basic client-server communication; the
other part provides an interface to the application program. Rpcgen produces the communication portion of the stub automatically from a description of the remote procedure

and its arguments. Because rpcgen produces code for the communication stub, it specifies the arguments required on the client side and the calling sequence on the server
side. The programmer must accept rpcgen calling conventions when using the communication stubs that rpcgen generates.

The idea behind separating the stub into communication and interface routines is
simple: it allows rpcgen to choose the calling conventions the communication stubs use,
while it allows the programmer to choose the calling conventions the remote procedures
use. The programmer creates interface stubs to map between the remote procedure calling conventions and the convensions provided by the communication stub procedures
that rpcgen generates. Figure 21.4 illustrates how all the routines interact.

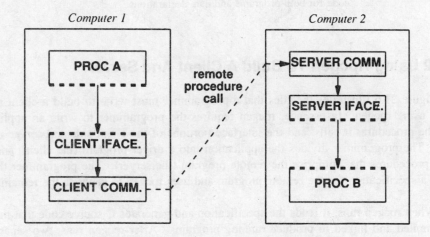

Figure 21.4 The form of a distributed program created using rpcgen. Rpcgen
generates the basic communication stubs automatically; the programmer supplies the two interface procedures.

As Figure 21.4 illustrates, the two parts of a stub each consist of two separate procedures. On the client side, the interface procedure calls the communication procedure.
On the server side, the communication procedure calls the interface procedure. If the
stub interface procedures are defined carefully, the original caller and the original called
procedure can remain unchanged.

21.11 Rpcgen Input And Output

Rpcgen reads an input file that contains a specification of a remote program. It
produces four output files, each of which contains source code. Rpcgen derives names
for the output files from the name of the input file. If the specification file has name
Q.x, all output files will begin with Q. The table in Figure 21.5 lists the output files
and describes their contents.

File Name	Contents
Q.h	Declarations of constants and types used in the code generated for both the client and server
Q_xdr.c	XDR procedure calls used in the client and server to marshal arguments
Q_clnt.c	Client-side communication stub procedure
Q_svc.c	Server-side communication stub procedure

Figure 21.5 The output files produced by rpcgen for an input file named Q.x. As their names imply, the output files contain the C source code for both programs and data declarations.

21.12 Using Rpcgen To Build A Client And Server

Figure 21.6 illustrates the files that a programmer must write to build a client and server using rpcgen. In essence, rpcgen requires the programmer to write an application, the procedures it calls, and the interface portions of the client-side and server-side stubs. The programmer divides the application into a driver program (the client) and a set of procedures that comprise the remote program (the server). The programmer then writes a specification for the remote program and uses rpcgen to generate the remaining pieces.

When rpcgen runs, it reads the specification and generates C source code that must be compiled and linked to produce running programs. After rpcgen runs, two separate compile-and-link steps occur. One produces the executable client program and the other produces an executable server.

Figure 21.6 only provides an overview of rpcgen input and output. The next chapter provides additional details on its use. The chapter presents a simple example application, and shows the steps a programmer takes to transform it into a distributed program. The chapter describes the specification file rpcgen takes as input as well as the code rpcgen produces.

21.13 Summary

RPC is a broad concept that can help programmers design client-server software. A programmer can use RPC to help specify or implement a distributed program. When using Sun RPC, the programmer can choose to follow the specification while building code from scratch, to use procedures found in the RPC library, or to use an automatic program generation tool called *rpcgen*.

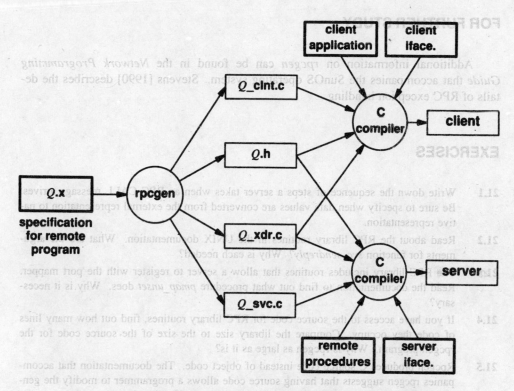

Figure 21.6 The files required to build a client and server from the output of rpcgen, and the compilation steps required to process them. Darkened boxes show the input that the programmer supplies.

RPC allows a programmer to construct a conventional program and then to transform it into a distributed program by moving some procedures to a remote machine. When doing so, the programmer can minimize changes and reduce the chance of introducing errors by adding stub procedures to the program. The stub procedures implement the necessary communication. Using stubs allows the original calling and called procedures to remain unchanged.

Because most distributed programs using RPC follow the same general architecture, rpcgen can generate much of the required code automatically. In addition to creating a specification file, the programmer only needs to supply a pair of interface procedures and the procedures associated with the application. Rpcgen generates the rest of the client and server programs, including procedures that register the server with the port mapper, provide communication between client and server, and dispatch incoming calls to the correct remote procedure.

FOR FURTHER STUDY

Additional information on *rpcgen* can be found in the *Network Programming Guide* that accompanies the SunOS operating system. Stevens [1990] describes the details of RPC exception handling.

EXERCISES

21.1 Write down the sequence of steps a server takes when an RPC CALL message arrives. Be sure to specify when data values are converted from the external representation to native representation.

21.2 Read about the RPC library routines in the UNIX documentation. What are the arguments for function *svc_sendreply*? Why is each needed?

21.3 The RPC library includes routines that allow a server to register with the port mapper. Read the documentation to find out what procedure *pmap_unset* does. Why is it necessary?

21.4 If you have access to the source code for RPC library routines, find out how many lines of code they occupy. Compare the library size to the size of the source code for the rpcgen program. Why is rpcgen as large as it is?

21.5 Rpcgen produces C source code instead of object code. The documentation that accompanies rpcgen suggests that having source code allows a programmer to modify the generated code. Why might a programmer make such modifications?

21.6 Refer to the previous question. What are the disadvantages of modifying the rpcgen output?

21.7 It is possible to design a remote procedure call mechanism that combines all procedures from a remote program into a single procedure by using an additional argument to decide which procedure to call (e.g., the remote procedure consists of a C *switch* statement that uses the new argument to make a choice among alternative actions). What are the chief advantages of such an approach compared to the Sun RPC approach? What are the chief disadvantages?

21.8 If the server side of a Sun RPC program uses sockets, what are the possible methods it can use to implement mutual exclusion (i.e., how can it guarantee that only one remote procedure will be called at any time)? What are the advantages and disadvantages of each method? Hint: consider the socket options and the creation of a file.

22

Distributed Program Generation (Rpcgen Example)

22.1 Introduction

The previous chapters present the principles underlying the remote procedure call model and the Sun RPC mechanism. They discuss the remote procedure call concept and explain how programs can be divided along procedure call boundaries. They also describe how the rpcgen tool and associated library routines automate much of the code generation for programs that use Sun RPC.

This chapter completes the discussion of rpcgen. It presents the sequence of steps a programmer takes to first create a conventional program and then divide the program into local and remote components. It uses an example application to follow through each step of the process. It shows the output from rpcgen and the additional code required to create the client and server components of a distributed program that uses RPC.

22.2 An Example To Illustrate Rpcgen

An example will clarify how rpcgen works and will illustrate most of the details. Because the point of the example is to explain how rpcgen works, we have selected an extremely simple application. In practice, of course, few RPC programs are as trivial or easy to follow as our example. Thus, one should think of the example as a tutorial and not question whether the application warrants a distributed solution.

22.3 Dictionary Lookup

As an example of using rpcgen, consider an application that implements a simple database. The database offers four basic operations: *initialize* to initialize the database (i.e., erase all previously stored values), *insert* to insert a new item, *delete* to remove an item, and *lookup* to search for an item. We will assume that items in the database are individual words. Thus, the database will function as a dictionary. The application inserts a set of valid words, and then uses the database to check new words to see if each is in the dictionary.

To keep the example simple, we will assume that input to the application is a text file, where each line contains a one-letter command followed by a word. The table in Figure 22.1 lists the commands, and gives the meaning of each:

one-letter command	Argument	Meaning
I	-none-	**Initialize the database by removing all words**
i	**word**	**insert** *word* **into the database**
d	**word**	**delete** *word* **from the database**
l	**word**	**lookup** *word* **in the database**
q	-none-	**quit**

Figure 22.1 Input commands for the example database application and their meanings. Some commands must be followed by a word that can be thought of as an argument to the command.

For example, the following input contains a sequence of data commands. The commands initialize the dictionary, insert names of computer vendors, delete some of the names, and look up three names:

```
I
i  Navy
i  IBM
i  RCA
i  Encore
```

```
i  Digital
d  RCA
d  Navy
l  IBM
d  Encore
l  CDC
l  Encore
q
```

When this file of commands is presented as input, the dictionary application should find *IBM* in the dictionary, but it should not find *Encore* or *CDC*.

22.4 Eight Steps To A Distributed Application

Figure 21.6† shows the input required for rpcgen and the output files it generates. To create the required files and combine them into a client and server, a programmer takes the following eight steps:

1. Build and test a conventional application that solves the problem.
2. Divide the program by choosing a set of procedures to move to a remote machine. Place the selected procedures in a separate file.
3. Write an rpcgen specification for the remote program, including names and numbers for the remote procedures and the declarations of their arguments. Choose a remote program number and a version number (usually *1*).
4. Run rpcgen to check the specification and, if valid, generate the four source code files that will be used in the client and server.
5. Write stub interface routines for the client side and server side.
6. Compile and link together the client program. It consists of four main files: the original application program (with the remote procedures removed), the client-side stub (generated by rpcgen), the client-side interface stub, and the XDR procedures (generated by rpcgen). When all these files have been compiled and linked together, the resulting executable program becomes the client.
7. Compile and link together the server program. It consists of four main files: the procedures taken from the original application that now comprise the remote program, the server-side stub (generated by rpcgen), the server-side interface stub, and the XDR procedures (generated by rpcgen). When all these files have been compiled and linked together, the resulting executable program becomes the server.
8. Start the server on the remote machine, and then invoke the client on the local machine.

---

†Figure 21.6 can be found on page 265.

The next sections examine each step in more detail and use the dictionary application to illustrate the subtleties.

22.5 Step 1: Build A Conventional Application Program

The first step in building a distributed version of the example dictionary application requires the programmer to construct a conventional program that solves the problem. File *dict.c* contains an application program for the dictionary problem written in the C language.

```
/* dict.c - main, initw, nextin, insertw, deletew, lookupw */

#include <stdio.h>
#include <ctype.h>

#define MAXWORD 50                /* maximum length of a command or word */
#define DICTSIZ 100               /* maximum number of entries in diction.*/
char    dict[DICTSIZ][MAXWORD+1];/* storage for a dictionary of words    */
int     nwords = 0;              /* number of words in the dictionary     */

/*------------------------------------------------------------------------
 * main - insert, delete, or lookup words in a dictionary as specified
 *------------------------------------------------------------------------
 */
int
main(argc, argv)
int     argc;
char    *argv[];
{
        char    word[MAXWORD+1]; /* space to hold word from input line   */
        char    cmd;
        int     wrdlen;          /* length of input word                 */

        while (1) {
            wrdlen = nextin(&cmd, word);
            if (wrdlen < 0)
                    exit(0);
            switch (cmd) {
            case 'I':       /* "initialize" */
                    initw();
                    printf("Dictionary initialized to empty.\n");
                    break;
            case 'i':       /* "insert" */
```

```
                                insertw(word);
                                printf("%s inserted.\n",word);
                                break;
                case 'd':           /* "delete" */
                                if (deletew(word))
                                        printf("%s deleted.\n",word);
                                else
                                        printf("%s not found.\n",word);
                                break;
                case 'l':           /* "lookup" */
                                if (lookupw(word))
                                        printf("%s was found.\n",word);
                                else
                                        printf("%s was not found.\n",word);
                                break;
                case 'q':           /* quit */
                                printf("program quits.\n");
                                exit(0);
                default:            /* illegal input */
                                printf("command %c invalid.\n", cmd);
                                break;
                }
        }
}


/*-------------------------------------------------------------------------
 * nextin - read a command and (possibly) a word from the next input line
 *-------------------------------------------------------------------------
 */
int
nextin(cmd, word)
char    *cmd, *word;
{
        int     i, ch;

        ch = getc(stdin);
        while (ch == ' ')
                ch = getc(stdin);
        if (ch == EOF)
                return -1;
        *cmd = (char) ch;
        ch = getc(stdin);
        while (ch == ' ')
                ch = getc(stdin);
```

```
            if (ch == EOF)
                    return -1;
            if (ch == '\n')
                    return 0;
            i = 0;
            while ((ch != ' ') && (ch != '\n')) {
                    if (++i > MAXWORD) {
                            printf("error: word too long.\n");
                            exit(1);
                    }
                    *word++ = ch;
                    ch = getc(stdin);
            }
            return i;
    }
    /*-----------------------------------------------------------------
     * initw - initialize the dictionary to contain no words at all
     *-----------------------------------------------------------------
     */
    int
    initw()
    {
            nwords = 0;
            return 1;
    }
    /*-----------------------------------------------------------------
     * insertw - insert  a word in the dictionary
     *-----------------------------------------------------------------
     */
    int
    insertw(word)
    char    *word;
    {
            strcpy(dict[nwords], word);
            nwords++;
            return nwords;
    }
    /*-----------------------------------------------------------------
     * deletew - delete  a word from the dictionary
     *-----------------------------------------------------------------
     */
```

```
int
deletew(word)
char    *word;
{
        int     i;

        for (i=0 ; i<nwords ; i++)
                if (strcmp(word, dict[i]) == 0) {
                        nwords--;
                        strcpy(dict[i], dict[nwords]);
                        return 1;
                }
        return 0;
}

/*-------------------------------------------------------------------
 * lookupw - look up a word in the dictionary
 *-------------------------------------------------------------------
 */
int
lookupw(word)
char    *word;
{
        int     i;

        for (i=0 ; i<nwords ; i++)
                if (strcmp(word, dict[i]) == 0)
                        return 1;
        return 0;
}
```

To keep the application simple and easy to understand, the conventional program in file *dict.c* uses a two-dimensional array to store words. A global variable, *nwords*, counts the number of words in the dictionary at any time. The main program contains a loop that reads and processes one line of input on each iteration. It calls procedure *nextin* to read a command (and possibly a word) from the next input line, and then uses a C *switch* statement to select one of six possible cases. The cases correspond to the five valid commands plus a default case that handles illegal input.

Each case in the main program calls a procedure to handle the details. For example, the case that corresponds to an insertion command, *i*, calls procedure *insertw*. Procedure *insertw* inserts a new word at the end of the array and increments *nwords*.

The other procedures operate as expected. Procedure *deletew* searches for the word to be deleted. If it finds the word, *deletew* replaces it with the last word in the dictionary and decrements *nwords*. Finally, *lookupw* searches the array sequentially to determine if the specified word is present. It returns *1* if the word is present in the dictionary and *0* otherwise.

To produce an executable binary for the application, the programmer invokes the C compiler. Most UNIX systems use the command:

```
cc -o dict dict.c
```

to produce an executable binary file named *dict* from the source program in file *dict.c*.

22.6 Step 2: Divide The Program Into Two Parts

Once a conventional application has been built and tested, it can be partitioned into local and remote components. Programmers must have a conceptual model of a program's procedure call graph before they can partition the program. For example, Figure 22.2 shows the procedural organization of the original dictionary application.

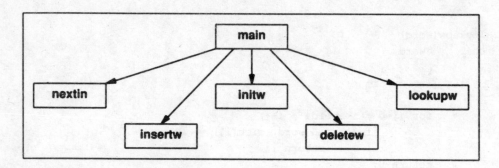

Figure 22.2 The procedure call graph for the original, conventional program that solves the dictionary problem. A call graph represents a program's procedural organization.

When considering which procedures can be moved to a remote machine, the programmer must consider the facilities that each procedure needs. For example, procedure *nextin* reads and parses the next input line each time it is called. Because it needs access to the program's standard input file, *nextin* must be kept with the main program. To summarize:

> *Procedures that perform I/O or otherwise access file descriptors cannot be moved to a remote machine easily.*

The programmer must also consider the location of data that each procedure accesses. For example, procedure *lookupw* needs to access the entire database of words. If *lookupw* executes on a machine other than the machine where the dictionary resides, the RPC call to *lookupw* must pass the entire dictionary as an argument.

Passing large data structures as arguments to remote procedures is extremely inefficient because the RPC mechanism must read and encode the entire data structure for each remote procedure call. In general:

> *Procedures should execute on the same machine as the data they access. Passing large data structures as arguments to remote procedures is inefficient.*

After considering the original dictionary program and the data each procedure accesses, it should be obvious that procedures *insertw*, *deletew*, *initw*, and *lookupw* belong on the same machine as the dictionary itself.

Assume that the programmer decides to move the dictionary storage and associated procedures to a remote machine. To help understand the consequences of moving some procedures to a remote machine, programmers usually create a mental image, or even a sketch, of the distributed program and data structures. Figure 22.3 illustrates the new structure of the dictionary application with the data and access procedures moved to a remote machine.

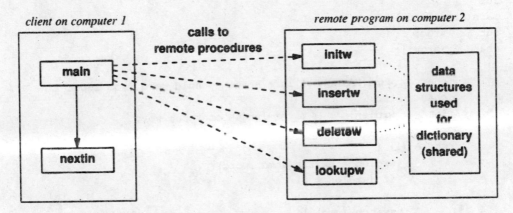

Figure 22.3 The conceptual division of the dictionary program into local and remote components. The remote component contains the data for the dictionary and the procedures that access and search it.

A simple drawing like the one in Figure 22.3 can help a programmer think about the division of a program into local and remote components. The programmer must consider whether each procedure has access to the data and services it needs, and must consider the arguments that each remote procedure will require along with the cost of passing that information across a network. Finally, the diagram helps the programmer assess how network delays will affect program performance.

Assuming the programmer chooses a conceptual division and decides to proceed, the next step is to divide the source program into two components. The programmer identifies the constants and data structures used by each component, and places each component in a separate file. In the dictionary example, the division is straightforward because the original source file can be divided between procedure *nextin* and procedure *initw*. File *dict1.c* contains the main program and procedure *nextin*:

```
/* dict1.c - main, nextin */


#include <stdio.h>
#include <ctype.h>

#define MAXWORD 50              /* maximum length of a command or word */
/*------------------------------------------------------------------------
 * main - insert, delete, or lookup words in a dictionary as specified
 *------------------------------------------------------------------------
 */
int
main(argc, argv)
int     argc;
char    *argv[];
{
        char    word[MAXWORD+1]; /* space to hold word from input line */
        char    cmd;
        int     wrdlen;          /* length of input word                */

        while (1) {
                wrdlen = nextin(&cmd, word);
                if (wrdlen < 0)
                        exit(0);
                switch (cmd) {
                case 'I':        /* "initialize" */
                        initw();
                        printf("Dictionary initialized to empty.\n");
                        break;
                case 'i':        /* "insert" */
                        insertw(word);
                        printf("%s inserted.\n",word);
                        break;
                case 'd':        /* "delete" */
                        if (deletew(word))
```

```
                                        printf("%s deleted.\n",word);
                                 else
                                        printf("%s not found.\n",word);
                                 break;
                        case 'l':        /* "lookup" */
                                 if (lookupw(word))
                                        printf("%s was found.\n",word);
                                 else
                                        printf("%s was not found.\n",word);
                                 break;
                        case 'q':        /* quit */
                                 printf("program quits.\n");
                                 exit(0);
                        default:         /* illegal input */
                                 printf("command %c invalid.\n", cmd);
                                 break;
                        }
                }
        }
```

```
/*-----------------------------------------------------------------------
 * nextin - read a command and (possibly) a word from the next input line
 *-----------------------------------------------------------------------
 */
int
nextin(cmd, word)
char    *cmd, *word;
{
        int     i, ch;

        ch = getc(stdin);
        while (ch == ' ')
                ch = getc(stdin);
        if (ch == EOF)
                return -1;
        *cmd = (char) ch;
        ch = getc(stdin);
        while (ch == ' ')
                ch = getc(stdin);
        if (ch == EOF)
                return -1;
        if (ch == '\n')
                return 0;
        i = 0;
```

```
        while ((ch != ' ') && (ch != '\n')) {
                if (++i > MAXWORD) {
                        printf("error: word too long.\n");
                        exit(1);
                }
                *word++ = ch;
                ch = getc(stdin);
        }
        return i;
}
```

File *dict2.c* contains the procedures from the original application that will become part
of the remote program. In addition, it contains declarations for the global data that the
procedures will share. At this point, the file does not contain a complete program – the
remaining code will be added later.

```
/* dict2.c - initw, insertw, deletew, lookupw */

#define MAXWORD 50              /* maximum length of a command or word  */
#define DICTSIZ 100             /* maximum number of entries in diction.*/
char    dict[DICTSIZ][MAXWORD+1];/* storage for a dictionary of words   */
int     nwords = 0;             /* number of words in the dictionary    */

/*------------------------------------------------------------------------
 * initw - initialize the dictionary to contain no words at all
 *------------------------------------------------------------------------
 */
int
initw()
{
        nwords = 0;
        return 1;
}


/*------------------------------------------------------------------------
 * insertw - insert  a word in the dictionary
 *------------------------------------------------------------------------
 */
int
insertw(word)
char    *word;
{
        strcpy(dict[nwords], word);
```

```
        nwords++;
        return nwords;
}

/*------------------------------------------------------------------------
 * deletew - delete  a word from the dictionary
 *------------------------------------------------------------------------
 */
int
deletew(word)
char    *word;
{
        int     i;

        for (i=0 ; i<nwords ; i++)
                if (strcmp(word, dict[i]) == 0) {
                        nwords--;
                        strcpy(dict[i], dict[nwords]);
                        return 1;
                }
        return 0;
}


/*------------------------------------------------------------------------
 * lookupw - look up a word in the dictionary
 *------------------------------------------------------------------------
 */
int
lookupw(word)
char    *word;
{
        int     i;

        for (i=0 ; i<nwords ; i++)
                if (strcmp(word, dict[i]) == 0)
                        return 1;
        return 0;
}
```

Note that the definition of symbolic constant *MAXWORD* appears in both components because they both declare variables used to store words. Only file *dict2.c* contains the declarations for data structures used to store the dictionary, however, because only the remote program will include the dictionary data structures.

From a practical point of view, separating the application into twc files makes it possible to compile the client and server pieces separately. The compiler checks for problems like symbolic constants referenced by both parts, and the linker checks to see that all data structures have been collected together with the procedures that reference them. On a UNIX system, the commands:

```
cc -c dict1.c
cc -c dict2.c
```

produce object files (not complete programs) for the two components. The components must be linked together to produce an executable program, but that is not the immediate reason to compile them: the compiler checks that both files are syntactically correct.

When thinking about the utility of having a compiler check the code, remember that most distributed programs are much more complex than our trivial example. A compilation may find problems in a large program that escape the programmer's attention. Catching such problems before additional code has been inserted makes them easier to repair.

22.7 Step 3: Create An Rpcgen Specification

Once the programmer selects a structure for the distributed program, he or she can prepare an rpcgen specification. In essence, an rpcgen specification file contains a declaration of a remote program, including the data structures it uses.

The specification file contains constants, type definitions, and declarations for the client and server programs. More precisely, the specification file contains:

- declarations for constants used in the client or, more often, in the server (remote program),
- declarations of data types used (especially in arguments to remote procedures), and
- declarations of remote programs, the procedures contained in each program, and the types of their parameters.

Recall that RPC uses numbers to identify remote programs and the remote procedures within them. The program declaration in a specification file defines such details as a program's RPC number, its version number, and the numbers assigned to each procedure within the program.

All specifications must be given in the RPC programming language, not C. While the differences are minor, they can be frustrating. For example, RPC language uses the keyword *string* to denote null-terminated character strings, while C uses *char* *. Even experienced programmers may require multiple iterations to produce a correct specification.

File *rdict.x* illustrates an rpcgen specification. It contains example declarations for the RPC version of the dictionary program.

```
/* rdict.x */

/* RPC declarations for dictionary program */

const    MAXWORD = 50;          /* maximum length of a command or word */
const    DICTSIZ = 100;         /* number of entries in dictionary      */


struct example {                /* unused structure declared here to    */
        int     exfield1;       /* illustrate how rpcgen builds XDR     */
        char    exfield2;       /* routines to convert structures.      */
};


/*-------------------------------------------------------------------------
 * RDICTPROG - remote program that provides insert, delete, and lookup
 *-------------------------------------------------------------------------
 */
program RDICTPROG {                 /* name of remote program (not used)    */
    version RDICTVERS {             /* declaration of version (see below)   */
        int INITW(void)     = 1;/* first procedure in this program      */
        int INSERTW(string) = 2;/* second procedure in this program     */
        int DELETEW(string) = 3;/* third procedure in this program      */
        int LOOKUPW(string) = 4;/* fourth procedure in this program     */
    } = 1;                          /* definition of the program version    */
} = 0x30090949;                     /* remote program number (must be       */
                                    /* unique)                              */
```

An rpcgen specification file does not contain entries for all declarations found in the original program. Instead, it only defines those constants and types shared across the client and server or needed to specify arguments.

The example specification file begins by defining constants *MAXWORD* and *DICTSIZE*. In the original application, both were defined to be symbolic constants using a C preprocessor *define* statement. RPC language does not use C symbolic constant declarations. Instead it requires symbolic constants to be declared with the *const* keyword and assigned a value using the equal symbol (=).

Following suggested conventions, the specification file uses upper case names to define procedures and programs. As we will see later, the names become symbolic constants that can be used in C programs. Using upper case is not absolutely required, but it helps avoid name conflicts.

22.8 Step 4: Run Rpcgen

After the specification has been completed, the programmer runs rpcgen to check for syntax errors and generate four† files of code as Figure 21.6 shows‡. On most UNIX systems, the command syntax is:

```
rpcgen rdict.x
```

Rpcgen uses the name of the input file when generating the names of the four output files. For example, because the input file began with *rdict*, the output files will be named: *rdict.h*, *rdict_clnt.c*, *rdict_svc.c*, and *rdict_xdr.c*.

22.9 The .h File Produced By Rpcgen

Figure 22.4 shows the contents of file *rdict.h*, which contains valid C declarations for any constants and data types declared in the specification file. In addition, rpcgen adds definitions for the remote procedures. In the example code, rpcgen defines upper case *INSERTW* to be 2 because the specification declared procedure *INSERTW* to be the second procedure in the remote program.

The external procedure declarations in *rdict.h* require an explanation. The declared procedures comprise the interface portion of the server-side stub. Procedure names have been generated by taking the declared procedure names, mapping them to lower case, and appending an underscore followed by the program version number. For example, the sample specification file declares that the remote program contains procedure *DELETEW*, so *dict.h* contains an *extern* declaration for procedure *deletew_1*. To understand why rpcgen declares these interface routines, recall the purpose of the interface portion of the stub: it allows rpcgen to choose its own calling conventions, while allowing the original called procedure to remain unchanged.

As an example of interface stub naming, consider procedure *insertw*. The original procedure will become part of the server and will remain unchanged. Thus, the server will have a procedure named *insertw* that has the same arguments as in the original application. To avoid a naming conflict, the server must use a different name for the interface stub procedure. Rpcgen arranges for the server-side communication stub to call an interface stub procedure named *insertw_1*. The call uses rpcgen's choice of arguments, and allows the programmer to design *insertw_1* so that it calls *insertw* using the correct arguments.

---

†If a particular output file would be empty, rpcgen will not create it. Therefore, some specifications produce fewer than four files.

‡Figure 21.6 can be found on page 265.

```
#define MAXWORD 50
#define DICTSIZ 100

struct example {
        int exfield1;
        char exfield2;
};
typedef struct example example;
bool_t xdr_example();


#define RDICTPROG ((u_long)0x30090949)
#define RDICTVERS ((u_long)1)
#define INITW ((u_long)1)
extern int *initw_1();
#define INSERTW ((u_long)2)
extern int *insertw_1();
#define DELETEW ((u_long)3)
extern int *deletew_1();
#define LOOKUPW ((u_long)4)
extern int *lookupw_1();
```

Figure 22.4 File *rdict.h* – an example *.h* file that rpcgen produces.

22.10 The XDR Conversion File Produced By Rpcgen

Rpcgen produces a file that contains calls to routines that perform XDR conversions for all data types declared in the remote program. For example, file *rdict_xdr.c* contains calls to conversion routines for the data types declared in the dictionary program.

```
#include <rpc/rpc.h>
#include "rdict.h"


bool_t
xdr_example(xdrs, objp)
        XDR *xdrs;
        example *objp;
{
        if (!xdr_int(xdrs, &objp->exfield1)) {
                return (FALSE);
        }
        if (!xdr_char(xdrs, &objp->exfield2)) {
                return (FALSE);
        }
        return (TRUE);
}
```

Figure 22.5 File *rdict_xdr.c* – an example file of XDR conversion routines
that rpcgen produces.

In our example, the only type declaration that appears in the specification file has
the name *example*. It defines a structure that has one integer field and one character
field. File *rdict_xdr.c* contains the code needed to convert a structure of type *example*
between the native data representation and the external data representation. The code,
which has been generated automatically by rpcgen, calls routines from the XDR library
for each field of the structure. Once a declaration has been given, the declared type can
be used for arguments to remote procedures. If one of the remote procedures did use an
example structure as an argument, rpcgen would generate code in both the client and
server to call procedure *xdr_example* to convert the representation.

22.11 The Client Code Produced By Rpcgen

For the example dictionary application, rpcgen produces file *rdict_clnt.c*, a source
program that will become the client-side communication stub in the distributed version
of the program.

```
#include <rpc/rpc.h>
#include <sys/time.h>
#include "rdict.h"

/* Default timeout can be changed using clnt_control() */
static struct timeval TIMEOUT = { 25, 0 };

int *
initw_1(argp, clnt)
        void *argp;
        CLIENT *clnt;
{

        static int res;

        bzero((char *)&res, sizeof(res));
        if (clnt_call(clnt, INITW, xdr_void, argp, xdr_int, &res, TIMEOUT)
                != RPC_SUCCESS) {
                return (NULL);
        }
        return (&res);

}


int *
insertw_1(argp, clnt)
        char **argp;
        CLIENT *clnt;
{

        static int res;

        bzero((char *)&res, sizeof(res));
        if (clnt_call(clnt, INSERTW, xdr_wrapstring, argp, xdr_int, &res,
                TIMEOUT) != RPC_SUCCESS) {
                return (NULL);
        }
        return (&res);
}

int *
deletew_1(argp, clnt)
        char **argp;
        CLIENT *clnt;
{
```

```
        static int res;

        bzero((char *)&res, sizeof(res));
        if (clnt_call(clnt, DELETEW, xdr_wrapstring, argp, xdr_int, &res,
                TIMEOUT) != RPC_SUCCESS) {
                return (NULL);
        }
        return (&res);
}


int *
lookupw_1(argp, clnt)
        char **argp;
        CLIENT *clnt;
{
        static int res;

        bzero((char *)&res, sizeof(res));
        if (clnt_call(clnt, LOOKUPW, xdr_wrapstring, argp, xdr_int, &res,
                TIMEOUT) != RPC_SUCCESS) {
                return (NULL);
        }
        return (&res);
}
```

Figure 22.6 File *rdict_clnt.c* – an example of the client stub that rpcgen produces.

The file contains a communication stub procedure for each of the procedures in the remote program. As with the server, names have been chosen to avoid conflicts.

22.12 The Server Code Produced By Rpcgen

For the dictionary example, rpcgen produces a fourth file, *rdict_svc.c*, that contains
the code needed for a server. The file contains a main program that executes when the
server begins. It obtains a protocol port, registers the RPC program with the port
mapper, and then waits to receive RPC calls. It dispatches each call to the appropriate
server-side stub interface routine. When the called procedure responds, the server
creates an RPC reply and sends it back to the client.

```
#include <stdio.h>
#include <rpc/rpc.h>
#include "rdict.h"

static void rdictprog_1();

main()
{
        SVCXPRT *transp;

        (void)pmap_unset(RDICTPROG, RDICTVERS);

        transp = svcudp_create(RPC_ANYSOCK);
        if (transp == NULL) {
                (void)fprintf(stderr, "cannot create udp service.\n");
                exit(1);
        }
        if (!svc_register(transp, RDICTPROG, RDICTVERS, rdictprog_1,
                IPPROTO_UDP)) {
                (void)fprintf(stderr,
                    "unable to register (RDICTPROG,RDICTVERS, udp).\n");
                exit(1);
        }

        transp = svctcp_create(RPC_ANYSOCK, 0, 0);
        if (transp == NULL) {
                (void)fprintf(stderr, "cannot create tcp service.\n");
                exit(1);
        }
        if (!svc_register(transp, RDICTPROG, RDICTVERS, rdictprog_1,
                IPPROTO_TCP)) {
                (void)fprintf(stderr,
                    "unable to register (RDICTPROG, RDICTVERS, tcp).\n");
                exit(1);
        }
        svc_run();
        (void)fprintf(stderr, "svc_run returned\n");
        exit(1);
}

static void
rdictprog_1(rqstp, transp)
        struct svc_req *rqstp;
        SVCXPRT *transp;
```

```
{
        union {
                char *insertw_1_arg;
                char *deletew_1_arg;
                char *lookupw_1_arg;
        } argument;
        char *result;
        bool_t (*xdr_argument)(), (*xdr_result)();
        char *(*local)();

        switch (rqstp->rq_proc) {
        case NULLPROC:
                (void)svc_sendreply(transp, xdr_void, (char *)NULL);
                return;

        case INITW:
                xdr_argument = xdr_void;
                xdr_result = xdr_int;
                local = (char *(*)()) initw_1;
                break;

        case INSERTW:
                xdr_argument = xdr_wrapstring;
                xdr_result = xdr_int;
                local = (char *(*)()) insertw_1;
                break;

        case DELETEW:
                xdr_argument = xdr_wrapstring;
                xdr'result = xdr_int;
                local = (char *(*)()) deletew_1;
                break;

        case LOOKUPW:
                xdr_argument = xdr_wrapstring;
                xdr_result = xdr_int;
                local = (char *(*)()) lookupw_1;
                break;

        default:
                svcerr_noproc(transp);
                return;
        }
        bzero((char *)&argument, sizeof(argument));
```

```
      if (!svc_getargs(transp, xdr_argument, &argument)) {
            svcerr_decode(transp);
            return;
      }
      result = (*local)(&argument, rqstp);
      if (result != NULL && !svc_sendreply(transp, xdr_result, result)) {
            svcerr_systemerr(transp);
      }
      if (!svc_freeargs(transp, xdr_argument, &argument)) {
            (void)fprintf(stderr, "unable to free arguments\n");
            exit(1);
      }
}
```

Figure 22.7 File *rdict_svc.c* – an example server stub that rpcgen produces.

Once the files have been generated, they can be compiled and kept in object form. In UNIX, the commands to compile all three files that contain generated code are:

cc -c dict_clnt.c

cc -c dict_svc.c

cc -c dict_xdr.c

Each command takes a C source file and produces a corresponding object file. Object file names have ".o" in place of the ".c" suffix†. For example, the compiled version of *rdict_clnt.c* will be placed in file *rdict_clnt.o*.

22.13 Step 5: Write Stub Interface Procedures

22.13.1 Client-Side Interface Routines

The files that rpcgen produces do not form complete programs. They require client-side and server-side interface routines that the programmer must write. One interface procedure must exist for each remote procedure in the remote program.

On the client side, the original application program controls processing. It calls interface procedures using the same procedure names and argument types as it originally used to call those procedures which have become remote in the distributed version. Each interface procedure must convert its arguments to the form used by rpcgen, and must then call the corresponding client-side communication procedure. For example, because the original program contained a procedure named *insertw* that takes a pointer to a character string as an argument, the client-side interface must contain such a pro-

---

†UNIX programmers sometimes refer to object files as "dot oh" files.

cedure. The interface procedure calls *insertw_1*, the client-side communication stub generated by rpcgen.

   The chief difference between conventional procedure parameters and the parameters used by the communication stubs is that the arguments for all procedures produced by rpcgen use indirection. For example, if the original procedure had an integer argument, the corresponding argument in the communication stub for that procedure must be a pointer to an integer. In the dictionary program, most procedures require a character string argument, declared in C to be a character pointer (*char **). The corresponding communication stubs all require that their arguments be a pointer to a character pointer (*char ***).

   File *rdict_cif.c* illustrates how interface routines convert arguments to the form expected by the code produced by rpcgen. The file contains one client-side interface procedure for each of the remote procedures in the program.

```
/* rdict_cif.c - initw, insertw, deletew, lookupw */

#include <rpc/rpc.h>

#include <stdio.h>

#include "rdict.h"

/* Client-side stub interface routines written by programmer */

extern  CLIENT  *handle;                 /* handle for remote procedure  */

/*-------------------------------------------------------------------------
 * initw - client interface routine that calls initw_1
 *-------------------------------------------------------------------------
 */
int
initw()
{
        return *initw_1(handle);
}

/*-------------------------------------------------------------------------
 * insertw - client interface routine that calls insertw_1
 *-------------------------------------------------------------------------
 */
int
insertw(word)
char    *word;
{
```

```
        char    **arg,                        /* pointer to argument */
        arg = &word;
        return *insertw_1(arg, handle);
}


/*--------------------------------------------------------------------
 * deletew - client interface routine that calls deletew_1
 *--------------------------------------------------------------------
 */
int
deletew(word)
char    *word;
{
        char    **arg;                        /* pointer to argument */

        arg = &word;
        return *deletew_1(arg, handle);
}


/*--------------------------------------------------------------------
 * lookupw - client interface routine that calls lookupw_1
 *--------------------------------------------------------------------
 */
int
lookupw(word)
char    *word;
{
        char    **arg;                        /* pointer to argument */

        arg = &word;
        return *lookupw_1(arg, handle);
}
```

22.13.2 Server-Side Interface Routines

On the server side, the interface routines accept calls from the communication stubs that rpcgen produces, and pass control to the procedure that implements the specified call. As with the client side, server-side interface routines must translate from argument types chosen by rpcgen to the argument types that the called procedures use. In most cases, the difference lies in an extra indirection – rpcgen passes a pointer to an object instead of the object itself. To convert an argument, an interface procedure only needs to apply the C indirection operator (*). File *rdict_sif.c* illustrates the concept. It contains the server-side interface routines for the dictionary program.

```c
/* rdict_sif.c - init_1, insert_1, delete_1, lookup_1 */

#include <rpc/rpc.h>

#include "rdict.h"

/* Server-side stub inteface routines written by programmer */

static  int retcode;

/*-------------------------------------------------------------------------
 * insertw_1 -  server side interface to remote procedure insertw
 *-------------------------------------------------------------------------
 */
int     *
insertw_1(w)
char    **w;
{
        retcode = insertw(*w);
        return &retcode;
}


/*-------------------------------------------------------------------------
 * initw_1 -  server side interface to remote procedure initw
 *-------------------------------------------------------------------------
 */
int     *
initw_1()
{
        retcode = initw();
        return &retcode;
}


/*-------------------------------------------------------------------------
 * deletew_1 -  server side interface to remote procedure deletew
 *-------------------------------------------------------------------------
 */
int     *
deletew_1(w)
char    **w;
{
        retcode = deletew(*w);
        return &retcode;
}
```

```
/* ---------------------------------------------------------------
 * lookupw_1 -  server side interface to remote procedure lookupw
 *---------------------------------------------------------------
 */
int     *
lookupw_1(w)
char    **w;
{
        retcode = lookupw(*w);
        return &retcode;
}
```

22.14 Step 6: Compile And Link The Client Program

Once the client interface routines have been written and placed in a source file, they can be compiled. For example, file *rdict_cif.c* contains all the interface routines for the dictionary example. On UNIX systems, the command needed to compile the result is:

cc -c rdict_cif.c

The compiler produces output file *rdict_cif.o*. To complete the client, the programmer needs to add a few details to the original main program. Because the new version uses RPC, it needs the C *include* file for RPC declarations. It also needs to include file *rdict.h* because that file contains definitions for constants used by both the client and server.

The client program also needs to declare and initialize a *handle* that the RPC communication routines can use to communicate with the server. Most clients declare the handle using the defined type *CLIENT*, and initialize the handle by calling the RPC library routine, *clnt_create*. File *rdict.c* shows an example of the necessary code:

```
/* rdict.c - main, nextin */

#include <rpc/rpc.h>

#include <stdio.h>
#include <ctype.h>

#include "rdict.h"

#define RMACHINE        "localhost"      /* name of remote machine    */
CLIENT  *handle;                         /* handle for remote procedure */

/*------------------------------------------------------------------------
 * main - insert, delete, or lookup words in a dictionary as specified
 *------------------------------------------------------------------------
 */
int
main(argc, argv)
int     argc;
char    *argv[];
{
        char    word[MAXWORD+1]; /* space to hold word from input line  */
        char    cmd;
        int     wrdlen;                 /* length of input word          */

    /* set up connection for remote procedure call  */

        handle = clnt_create(RMACHINE, RDICTPROG, RDICTVERS, "tcp");
        if (handle == 0) {
                printf("Could not contact remote program.\n");
                exit(1);
        }

        while (1) {
                wrdlen = nextin(&cmd, word);
                if (wrdlen < 0)
                        exit(0);
                switch (cmd) {
                case 'I':       /* "initialize" */
                        initw();
                        printf("Dictionary initialized to empty.\n");
                        break;
                case 'i':       /* "insert" */
                        insertw(word);
```

```
                                printf("%s inserted.\n",word);
                                break;
                    case 'd':        /* "delete" */
                            if (deletew(word))
                                    printf("%s deleted.\n",word);
                            else
                                    printf("%s not found.\n",word);
                            break;
                    case 'l':        /* "lookup" */
                            if (lookupw(word))
                                    printf("%s was found.\n",word);
                            else
                                    printf("%s was not found.\n",word);
                            break;
                    case 'q':        /* quit */
                            printf("program quits.\n");
                            exit(0);
                    default:         /* illegal input */
                            printf("command %c invalid.\n", cmd);
                            break;
                    }
            }
}

/*------------------------------------------------------------------------
 * nextin - read a command and (possibly) a word from the next input line
 *------------------------------------------------------------------------
 */
int
nextin(cmd, word)
char    *cmd, *word;
{
        int     i, ch;

        ch = getc(stdin);
        while (ch == ' ')
                ch = getc(stdin);
        if (ch == EOF)
                return -1;
        *cmd = (char) ch;
        ch = getc(stdin);
        while (ch == ' ')
                ch = getc(stdin);
        if (ch == EOF)
```

```
                return -1;
        if (ch == '\n')
                return 0;
        i = 0;
        while ((ch != ' ') && (ch != '\n')) {
                if (++i > MAXWORD) {
                        printf("error: word too long.\n");
                        exit(1);
                }
                *word++ = ch;
                ch = getc(stdin);
        }
        return i;
}
```

Compare *rdict.c* with *dict1.c*† from which it was derived to see how little code has been added. The sample code uses symbolic constant *RMACHINE* to specify the domain name of the remote machine. To make testing easy *RMACHINE* has been defined to be *localhost*, which means the client and server will operate on the same machine. Of course, once testing has been completed on a distributed program, the programmer will change the definition to specify the permanent location of the server.

Clnt_create attempts to make a connection to a specified remote machine. If the connection attempt fails, *clnt_create* returns the value *NULL*, allowing the application to report an error to the user. Our sample code exits if *clnt_create* reports an error. In practice, a client may choose to try repeatedly, or may maintain a list of machines and try each of them.

Like other C source files, *rdict.c* can be compiled with a single command:

```
cc -c rdict.c
```

Once the object program for *rdict.c* has been compiled, all files that comprise the client can be linked together into an executable program. The UNIX *cc* command invokes the linker for .o files. It can be invoked with the *-o* option to put the output in a named file. For example, the command line below links the .o files together and places the resulting executable client program in file *rdict*:

```
cc -o rdict rdict.o rdict_clnt.o rdict_xdr.o rdict_cif.o
```

---

†File *dict1.c* can be found on page 276.

22.15 Step 7: Compile And Link The Server Program

The output generated by rpcgen includes most of the code needed for a server. The programmer supplies two additional files: the server interface routines (which we have chosen to place in file *rdict_sif.c*) and the remote procedures themselves. For the dictionary example, the final version of the remote procedures appears in file *rdict_srp.c*. The code for the procedures has been derived from the code in the original application.

```
/* rdict_srp.c - initw, insertw, deletew, lookupw */

#include <rpc/rpc.h>

#include "rdict.h"

/* Server-side remote procedures and the global data they use */

char    dict[DICTSIZ][MAXWORD+1];/* storage for a dictionary of words   */
int     nwords = 0;                   /* number of words in the dictionary   */

/*-----------------------------------------------------------------
 * initw - initialize the dictionary to contain no words at all
 *-----------------------------------------------------------------
 */
int
initw()
{
        nwords = 0;
        return 1;
}


/*-----------------------------------------------------------------
 * insertw - insert  a word in the dictionary
 *-----------------------------------------------------------------
 */
int
insertw(word)
char    *word;
{
        strcpy(dict[nwords], word);
        nwords++;
        return nwords;
}
```

```
/*------------------------------------------------------------------
 * deletew - delete  a word from the dictionary
 *------------------------------------------------------------------
 */
int
deletew(word)
char    *word;
{
        int     i;

        for (i=0 ; i<nwords ; i++)
                if (strcmp(word, dict[i]) == 0) {
                        nwords--;
                        strcpy(dict[i], dict[nwords]);
                        return 1;
                }
        return 0;
}


/*------------------------------------------------------------------
 * lookupw - look up a word in the dictionary
 *------------------------------------------------------------------
 */
int
lookupw(word)
char    *word;
{
        int     i;

        for (i=0 ; i<nwords ; i++)
                if (strcmp(word, dict[i]) == 0)
                        return 1;
        return 0;
}
```

Once the file containing remote procedures has been compiled using command:

cc -c rdict_srp.c

the object programs that comprise the server can be linked together into an executable
file with the command:

```
cc -o rdictd rdict_svc.o rdict_xdr.o rdict_sif.o rdict_srp.o
```

When the command runs, it leaves the executable code in file *rdictd*†.

22.16 Step 8: Start The Server And Execute The Client

The first serious test of the entire system occurs when both the client and server components operate together on the same machine. The server must begin execution before the client attempts to contact it or the client will print the message:

Could not contact remote program.

and halt. On a UNIX system, the command:

```
./rdictd &
```

starts the server running in the background and leaves the user's terminal free to accept other commands. One can invoke the client interactively by typing its name and then typing the input. Alternatively, one can redirect the input from a file when invoking the client.

22.17 Using The UNIX Make Utility

Managing all the files associated with a distributed program can become tiresome. The UNIX utility program *make* helps because it automates the task of determining which programs should be recompiled after a change has been made. *Make* reads a specification file that lists dependencies among files and gives commands to run to rebuild complicated programs automatically. While the details of *make* are beyond the scope of this book, it is instructive to see how a simple input to *make* can specify all the files and commands needed to build the original or distributed versions of the dictionary program. File *Makefile* contains the specifications:

---

†UNIX systems often name servers with a trailing ''*d*'' to stand for *daemon*, the technical term UNIX applies to programs that run in the background.

```
#
#  Makefile for example dictionary application (conventional and RPC)
#
all:           dict dict1.o dict2.o rdict rdictd

install:       all
               @echo nothing to install.

clean:
               rm *.o dict rdict rdictd


#
# Original (conventional) application
#
dict:          dict.c
               cc -o dict dict.c


#
# Test division into two parts to see if they compile
#
dict1.o:       dict1.c
               cc -c dict1.c

dict2.o:       dict2.c
               cc -c dict2.c

#
# Dependencies for files generated by rpcgen
#
rdict_clnt.c:  rdict.h rdict.x

rdict_svc.c:   rdict.h rdict.x

rdict_xdr.c:   rdict.h rdict.x

rdict.h:       rdict.x
               rpcgen rdict.x


#
# Link client-side files for RPC version
#
rdict:         rdict_clnt.o rdict_cif.o rdict.o rdict_xdr.o
               cc -o rdict rdict_clnt.o rdict_cif.o rdict.o \
                     rdict_xdr.o
```

```
                    chmod 755 rdict


#
# Link server-side files for RPC version
#
rdictd:         rdict_svc.o rdict_sif.o rdict_srp.o rdict_xdr.o
                cc -o rdictd rdict_svc.o rdict_sif.o rdict_srp.o \
                        rdict_xdr.o
                chmod 755 rdictd


#
# Individual object file dependencies
#
rdict.o:        rdict.c rdict.h rdict.x
                cc -c rdict.c


rdict_clnt.o:   rdict_clnt.c rdict.h rdict.x
                cc -c rdict_clnt.c


rdict_svc.o:    rdict_svc.c rdict.h rdict.x
                cc -c rdict_svc.c


rdict_xdr.o:    rdict_xdr.c rdict.h rdict.x
                cc -c rdict_xdr.c


rdict_cif.o:    rdict_cif.c rdict.h rdict.x
                cc -c rdict_cif.c


rdict_sif.o:    rdict_sif.c rdict.h rdict.x
                cc -c rdict_sif.c


rdict_srp.o:    rdict_srp.c rdict.h rdict.x
                cc -c rdict_srp.c
```

Once the *Makefile* has been established, recompilation of the client and server are completely automatic. For example, if one starts in a directory that contains the rpcgen specification file, the *Makefile*, and all the source files described in this chapter, invoking *make* in that directory executes the following sequence of commands:

```
            cc -o dict dict.c
            cc -c dict1.c
            cc -c dict2.c
            rpcgen rdict.x
            cc -c rdict_clnt.c
```

```
cc -c rdict_cif.c
cc  -c rdict.c
cc  -c rdict_xdr.c
cc -o rdict rdict_clnt.o rdict_cif.o rdict.o  rdict_xdr.o
chmod 755 rdict
cc -c rdict_svc.c
cc  -c rdict_sif.c
cc -c rdict_srp.c
cc -o rdictd rdict_svc.o rdict_sif.o rdict_srp.o  rdict_xdr.o
chmod 755 rdictd
```

Thus, running *make* produces an executable client, *rdict*, and an executable server, *rdictd*.

22.18 Summary

Constructing a distributed program using rpcgen consists of eight steps. The programmer begins with a conventional application program to solve the problem, decides how to partition the program into components that execute locally and remotely, divides the application into two physical parts, creates a specification file that describes the remote program, and runs rpcgen to produce needed files. The programmer then writes client-side and server-side interface routines and combines them with the code produced by rpcgen. Finally, the programmer compiles and links the client-side files and the server-side files to produce executable client and server programs.

Although rpcgen eliminates much of the coding required for RPC, building a distributed program requires careful thought. When considering how to partition a program into local and remote components, the programmer must examine the data accessed by each piece to minimize data movement. The programmer must also consider the delay that each remote procedure call will introduce as well as how each piece will access I/O facilities.

The example dictionary application in this chapter shows how much effort is required to transform a trivial application into a distributed program. More complicated applications require substantially more complex specifications and interface procedures. In particular, applications that pass structured data to remote procedures or that check client authorizations can require substantially more code.

FOR FURTHER STUDY

Information about rpcgen can be found in the *Network Programming Guide* that accompanies the SunOS operating system. The *UNIX Programmer's Manual* describes the details of the *make* utility.

EXERCISES

22.1 Modify the example program from this chapter so the client interface routine keeps a cache of recently referenced words and searches the cache before making a remote procedure call. How much additional computational overhead does the cache require? How much time does the cache save when an entry can be found locally?

22.2 Build a distributed application that provides access to files on the remote machine. Include remote procedures that permit the client to *read* or *write* data to a specified location in a specified file.

22.3 Build a distributed program that passes a linked list as an argument to a remote procedure. Hint: use relative pointers instead of absolute memory addresses.

22.4 Try to modify the example dictionary program so the remote procedures can write error messages on the client's standard error file. What problems did you encounter? How did you solve them?

22.5 Rpcgen could have been designed so it automatically assigns each remote procedure a unique number, 1, 2, and so on. What are the advantages of having the programmer assign remote procedure numbers manually in the specification file instead of assigning them automatically? What are the disadvantages?

22.6 What limitations does rpcgen have? Hint: consider trying to build a server that is also a client for another service.

22.7 Look carefully at the code in *rdict_clnt.c*. What steps does the client take when it begins execution?

22.8 Try building and testing two versions of the distributed dictionary program simultaneously. Would it be possible to test new versions if the server side used well-known port numbers? Explain.

22.9 The example dictionary program recognizes blanks as separator characters in the input. Revise procedure *nextin* to allow tabs as well as blanks.

23

Network File System
Concepts (NFS)

23.1 Introduction

The previous chapters describe the Sun RPC facility, explain the relationship between RPC and client-server interaction, and show how RPC can be used to create a distributed version of an application program. This chapter and the next focus on an application and a protocol that is specified, designed, and implemented using RPC. This chapter describes the general concept of remote file access, and reviews the concepts underlying a particular remote file access mechanism. Because the mechanism derives many ideas and details from UNIX, this chapter reviews the UNIX file system and the semantics of file operations. It discusses hierarchical directory structures and path names, and shows how a remote file access mechanism implements operations on hierarchies. The next chapter provides additional details about the protocol, and shows how the protocol specification uses RPC to define remote file operations.

23.2 Remote File Access Vs. Transfer

Many early network systems provided *file transfer* services that permitted users to move a copy of a file from one machine to another. More recent network systems provide *file access* services that permit an application program to access a file from a remote machine. A remote file access mechanism keeps one copy of each file, and allows one or more application programs to access the copy on demand.

Applications that use a remote file mechanism to access a file can execute on the machine where the file resides, or they can execute on remote machines. When an application accesses a file that resides on a remote machine, the program's operating system invokes client software that contacts a server on the remote machine and performs the requested operations on the file. Unlike a file transfer service, the application's system does not retrieve or store an entire file at once. Instead, it requests transfers of one small block of data at a time.

To provide remote access to some or all of the files that reside on a computer, the system manager must arrange for the computer to run a server that responds to access requests. The server checks each request to verify that the client is authorized to access the specified file, performs the specified operation, and returns a result to the client.

Sun Microsystems, Incorporated defined a remote file access mechanism that has become widely accepted throughout the computer industry. Known as Sun's *Network File System*, or simply *NFS*, the mechanism allows a computer to run a server that makes some or all of its files available for remote access, and allows applications on other computers to access those files.

23.3 Operations On Remote Files

NFS provides the same operations on remote files that one expects to use on local files. An application can *open* a remote file to obtain access, *read* data from the file, *write* data to the file, *seek* to a specified position in the file (either at the beginning, the end, or elsewhere), and *close* the file when finished using it.

23.4 File Access Among Heterogeneous Computers

Providing remote file access can be nontrivial. In addition to the basic mechanisms for reading and writing files, a file access service must provide ways to create and destroy files, peruse directories, authenticate requests, honor file protections, and translate information between the representations used on various computers. Because a remote file access service connects two machines, it must handle differences in the way the client and server systems name files, denote paths through directories, and store information about files. More important, the file access software must accommodate differences in the semantic interpretation of file operations.

NFS was designed to accommodate heterogeneous computer systems. From the beginning, the NFS protocol, operations, and semantics were chosen to allow a variety of systems to interact. Of course, NFS cannot provide all the file system subtleties available in all possible operating systems. Instead, it tries to define file operations that accommodate as many systems as possible without becoming inefficient or hopelessly complex. In practice, most of the choices work well.

23.5 Stateless Servers

The NFS design stores state information at the client site, allowing servers to remain stateless. Because the server is stateless, disruptions in service will not affect client operation. In theory, for example, a client will be able to continue file access after a stateless server crashes and reboots; the application program, which runs on the client system, can remain unaware of the server reboot. Furthermore, because a stateless server does not need to allocate resources for each client, a stateless design can scale to handle many more clients than a stateful design.

NFS's stateless server design affects both the protocol and its implementation. Most important, a server cannot keep any notion of *position*, whether in a file or directory. We will see how NFS achieves a stateless design after examining the operations that NFS provides.

23.6 NFS And UNIX File Semantics

Although NFS was designed to accommodate heterogeneous file systems, the UNIX file system strongly influenced its overall design, the terminology used, and many of the protocol details. The NFS designers adopted UNIX file system semantics when defining the meaning of individual operations. Thus, to understand NFS, one must begin with the UNIX file system.

Chapter *3* contains a brief description of UNIX I/O; the next section expands that description. It discusses file storage and access under UNIX, concentrating on those concepts and details that are most pertinent to NFS. Later sections show how NFS borrowed many ideas from the UNIX file system directly and adopted many of the details with only slight modifications. To summarize:

> *Understanding the UNIX file system is essential to understanding NFS because NFS uses the UNIX file system terminology and semantics.*

23.7 Review Of The UNIX File System

23.7.1 Basic Definitions

From the user's point of view, UNIX defines a *file* to consist of a sequence of bytes. In theory, a UNIX file can grow arbitrarily large; in practice, a file is limited by the space available on the physical storage device. UNIX files can grow dynamically. The file system does not require predeclaration of the expected size or preallocation of space. Instead, a file grows automatically to accommodate whatever data an application writes into it.

Conceptually, UNIX numbers the bytes in a file starting at zero. At any time, the *size* of a file is defined to be the number of bytes in it. The UNIX file system permits random access to any file, using the byte numbers as a reference. It allows an application to move to any byte position in a file and to access data at that position.

23.7.2 A Byte Sequence Without Record Boundaries

Each UNIX file is a sequence of bytes; the system does not provide any additional structure for a file beyond the data itself. In particular, UNIX does not have notions of *record boundaries*, *record blocking*, *indexed files*, or *typed files* found in other systems. Of course, it is possible for an application to create a file of records and to access them later. The point is that the file system itself does not understand the file contents: applications that use a file must agree on the format.

23.7.3 A File's Owner And Group Identifiers

UNIX systems provide accounts for multiple users, and assign each user a numeric user identifier used for accounting and authentication throughout the system. Each UNIX file has a single *owner*, represented by the numeric identifier of the user who created the file. Ownership information is stored with the file (i.e., as opposed to the directory system).

In addition to user identifiers, UNIX provides for file sharing among groups of users by allowing the system manager to assign a subset of users a numeric *group identifier*. At any time, a given user can belong to one or more UNIX groups. When a user runs an application program (e.g., a spreadsheet program or a text editor), the running program inherits the user's owner and group identifiers. Each UNIX file belongs to one group and has its numeric group identifier stored with it. The system compares the owner and group identifiers stored with a file to the user and group identifiers of a particular application process to determine what operations that program can perform on the file.

23.7.4 Protection And Access

The UNIX access protection mechanism allows a file's owner to control file access separately for the owner, members of the file's group, and all other users. For each of the three sets, the protection mechanism allows the owner to specify whether the users in that set have permission to *read*, *write*, or *execute* the file. Figure 23.1 shows that the UNIX file access permissions can be viewed as a matrix of protection bits.

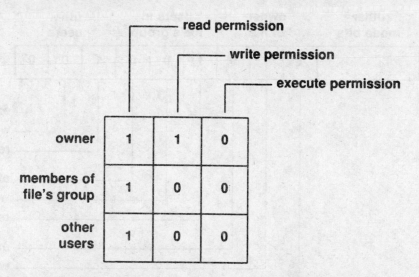

Figure 23.1 UNIX file access permissions viewed as a matrix of protection bits.

UNIX encodes the file access protection matrix in the low-order bits of a single binary integer, and uses the terms *file mode* or *file access mode* when referring to the integer that encodes the protection bits. Figure 23.2 illustrates how UNIX encodes file protection bits into the 9 low-order bits of a file mode integer. In addition to the protection bits illustrated in Figure 23.2, UNIX defines additional bits of the mode integer to specify other properties of the file (e.g., mode bits specify whether the file is a regular file or a directory).

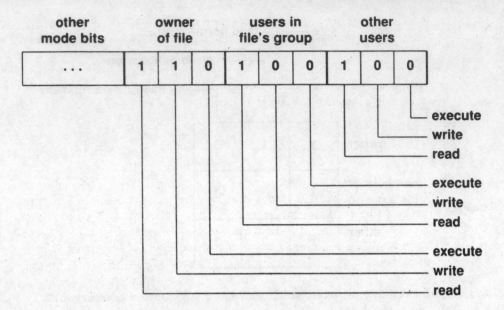

Figure 23.2 UNIX file access permissions stored in the low-order nine bits of the mode integer. A value of *1* grants permission; a value of *0* denies it. When written in octal, the protections illustrated have the value *0644*.

When the value of the protection integer is written in octal, the rightmost three digits give the protections for the owner, members of the file's group, and other users. Thus, a protection value of *0700* specifies that the owner can read, write, or execute the file, but no other users can have access. A protection mode value of *0644* specifies that all users can read the file, but only the owner can write to it.

23.7.5 The Open-Read-Write-Close Paradigm

Under UNIX, applications use the *open-read-write-close* to access files. To establish access to a file, an application must call function *open*, passing it the name of the file and an argument that describes the desired access. *Open* returns an integer file descriptor that the application uses for all further operations on the file. For example, the code:

```
fdesc = open("filename", O_CREAT | O_RDWR, 0644);
```

opens a file with name *filename*. The value *O_CREAT* in the second argument specifies that the file should be created if it does not already exist, and the value *O_RDWR* specifies that the file should be created for both reading and writing. The octal value *0644* specifies protection mode bits to assign to the file if it is created. Other values for the second argument can be used to specify whether the file should be truncated and whether it should be opened for reading, writing, or both.

23.7.6 Data Transfer

An application uses *read* to transfer data from a file into memory, and uses *write* to transfer data from memory to a file. The *read* function takes three arguments: the descriptor for an open file, a buffer address, and the number of bytes to read. For example, the following code requests that the system read *24* bytes of data from the file with descriptor *fdesc*:

$$n = read(fdesc, buff, 24);$$

Both *read* and *write* begin transfer at the current file position, and both operations update the file position when they finish. For example, if an application opens a file, moves to position *0*, and reads *10* bytes from the file, the file position will be *10* after the *read* operation completes. Thus, a program can extract all data from a file sequentially by starting at position zero and calling *read* repeatedly.

If an application attempts to *read* more bytes than the file contains, the *read* function extracts as many bytes as the file contains and returns the number read as its result. If the file is positioned at the end of a file when an application calls *read*, the *read* call returns zero to indicate an *end-of-file* condition.

23.7.7 Permission To Search A Directory

UNIX organizes files into a *hierarchy* using *directories*† to hold files and other directories. The system uses the same 9-bit protection mode scheme for directories as it uses for regular data files. The *read* permission bits determine whether an application can obtain a list of the files in a directory; and the *write* permission bits determine whether an application can insert or delete files in the directory. Each individual file has a separate set of permission bits that determine which operations are allowed on the contents of the file. The directory permissions only specify which operations are allowed on the directory itself.

Directories can contain application programs, but they do not consist of compiled code themselves. Thus, they cannot be executed like an application program, so *execute* permission is meaningless for a directory. UNIX interprets the *execute* permission bits for directories to mean *search permission*. If an application has search permission, it can reference a file that lies in a directory; otherwise, the system will not permit any references to the file. Search permission can be used to hide or uncover an entire subtree of the file hierarchy without modifying the permissions on individual files in the subtree.

23.7.8 Random Access

When a file is opened, the position can be set to the beginning of the file (e.g., to access the file sequentially) or to the end of the file (e.g., to append data to an existing file). After a file has been opened, the position can be changed by calling function

---

†Other systems sometimes use the term *folder* to denote what UNIX calls a *directory*.

lseek. *Lseek* takes three arguments that specify a file descriptor, an offset, and a measure for the offset. The third argument allows an application to specify whether the offset gives an absolute location in the file (e.g., byte 512), a new location relative to the current position (e.g., a byte that is 64 beyond the current position), or a position relative to the end of the file (e.g., 2 bytes before the end of the file). For example, the constant *L_SET* specifies that the system should interpret the offset as an absolute value. Thus, the call:

```
lseek(fdesc, 100L, L_SET);
```

specifies that the current position of the file with descriptor *fdesc* should be moved to byte number *100*.

23.7.9 Seeking Beyond The End Of File

The UNIX file system permits an application to move to any position in a file, even if the specified position lies beyond the current end of the file. If the application seeks to an existing byte position and writes new data, the new data replaces the old data at that position. If the application seeks beyond the end of the file and writes new data, the file system extends the file size. From the user's point of view, the system appears to fill any gap between existing data and new data with null bytes (bytes with value zero). Later, if an application attempts to read from the byte positions that comprise the gap, the file system will return bytes with zeros in them. Figure 23.3 illustrates the concept:

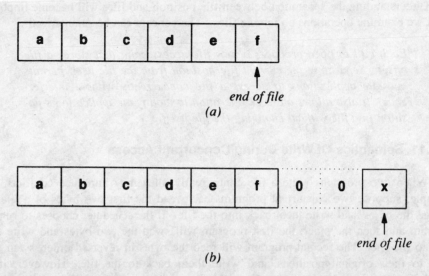

(a)

(b)

Figure 23.3 (a) a UNIX file that contains 6 bytes consisting of the characters
a through *f* and (b) the file after an application seeks to position
8 and writes a byte containing the character *x*. Unwritten bytes
appear to contain zeroes.

Although the file system appears to fill gaps with null bytes, the storage structure makes
it possible to simulate null bytes without representing them on the physical medium.
Thus, the file size records the highest byte position into which data has been written,
not the total number of bytes written.

23.7.10 File Position And Concurrent Access

The UNIX file system permits multiple application programs to access a file concurrently. The descriptor for each open file references a data structure that records a
current position in the file. When a process calls *fork* to create a new process, the child
inherits copies of all file descriptors the parent had open at the time of the fork. The
descriptors point to a common underlying data structure used to access the file. Thus, if
one of the two processes changes the file position, the position changes for the other
process as well.

Each call to *open* generates a new descriptor with a file position that is independent of that obtained by previous calls to *open*. Thus, if two applications both call *open*
on the same file, they can each maintain an independent position in the file. One application can move to the end of the file, while the other remains at the beginning. Programmers must decide when designing an application whether it needs to share the file
position with another process or have a separate position.

Understanding the separation between file position and files will become important when we examine operations on remote files. The concept can be summarized:

> *Each call to* open *produces a new file access point that stores a file offset. Separating the current file position from the file itself permits multiple applications to access a file concurrently without interference. It also allows an* lseek *operation to modify an application's position in a file without changing the file itself.*

23.7.11 Semantics Of Write During Concurrent Access

When two programs write a file concurrently, they may introduce conflicts. For example, suppose two concurrent programs each read the first two bytes of a file, exchange the bytes, and write them back into the file. If the scheduler chooses to run one program and then the other, the first program will swap the two bytes and write them back to the file. The second program will read the bytes in reversed order, swap them back to their original positions, and write them back to the file. However, if the scheduler starts both programs running, and allows them each to read from the file before either writes to it, they will both read the bytes in original order and then both write the bytes in reverse order. As a consequence, the byte order in the file depends on how the system scheduler chooses to delegate the CPU to the two programs.

UNIX does not provide mutual exclusion or define the semantics of concurrent access except to specify that a file always contains the data written most recently. Responsibility for correctness falls to the programmer†. A programmer must be careful to construct concurrent programs in such a way that they always produce the same results.

23.7.12 File Names And Paths

UNIX provides a hierarchical file namespace. Each file and directory in a UNIX file system has an individual name that can be represented by an ASCII string. In addition, each directory or file has a *full path name* that denotes the position of the file within the hierarchy. Figure 23.4 illustrates the names of files and directories for a small example of a UNIX hierarchy.

---

†Some versions of UNIX offer an advisory lock mechanism such as *flock* or *lockf*; others offer exclusive access with argument *O_EXCL* in the *open* call.

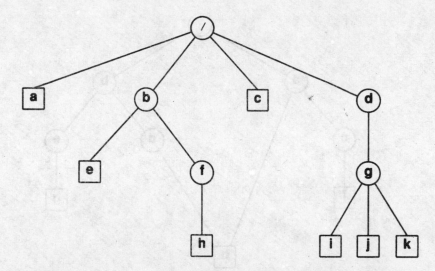

Figure 23.4 An example hierarchical file system. Circles denote directories
and squares denote files. In this example, the top level directory
contains two files (*a* and *c*) and two directories (*b* and *d*). In
practice, UNIX files seldom have single-character names.

As the figure shows, the top directory of the file system, called the *root*, has full
path name / (usually pronounced "slash"). The full path name of a file can be thought
of as the concatenation of labels on the path in the hierarchy from the root to the file,
using / as a separator character. For example, the file with name *a* that appears in the
root directory has full path name /*a*. The file with name *e* that appears in directory *b*
has full path name /*b*/*e*, and the file with name *k* has full path name /*d*/*g*/*k*.

23.7.13 Inode: Information Stored With A File

In addition to the data itself, UNIX stores information about each file on stable
storage. The information is kept in a structure known as the file's *inode†*. The inode
contains many fields, including: the owner and group identifiers, the mode integer
(described in Section 23.7.4), the time of last access, the time of last modification, the
file size, the disk device and file system on which the file resides, the number of directory entries for the file, the number of disk blocks currently used by the file, and the
basic type (e.g., regular file or directory).

The inode concept helps explain several features of the UNIX file system that are
also used in NFS. First, UNIX separates information such as ownership and file protection bits from the directory entry for a file. Doing so makes it possible to have two
directory entries that point to the same file. UNIX uses the term *link* or *hard link* to
refer to a directory entry for a file. As Figure 23.5 illustrates, when a file has more than
one hard link, it appears in more than one directory.

---

†*Inode*, usually pronounced "eye-node," is an abbreviation for *index node*.

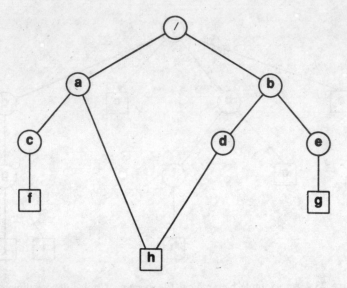

Figure 23.5 An illustration of hard links. File *h* has two links, one from
directory *a* and one from directory *d*. File *h* can be accessed by
path name */a/h* or path name */b/d/h*.

Files with multiple hard links can be accessed by more than one full path name.
For example, in Figure *23.5*, file *h* can be accessed by full path name */a/h* because it appears in directory *a*. It can also be accessed by full path name */b/d/h* because it appears
in directory *d*. As the example shows, the path names for a file with multiple links can
differ in length.

Because UNIX stores information about a file in its inode and not in the directory,
ownership and protection information for file *h* remain consistent no matter which name
an application uses to access the file. If the owner changes the protection mode of file
/a/h, the protection mode will also change on file */b/d/h*.

23.7.14 Stat Operation

The UNIX system function *stat* extracts information about a file from its inode and
returns the information to the caller. The call takes two arguments: the path name of a
file and the address of a structure into which it places the results:

```
stat( pathname, &result_struct );
```

The second argument must be the address of an area in memory large enough to hold the following structure:

```
struct stat {                          /* structure returned by stat   */
        dev_t    st_dev;               /* device on which inode resides*/
        ino_t    st_ino;               /* file's inode number          */
        u_short  st_mode;              /* protection bits              */
        short    st_nlink;             /* total hard links to the file */
        short    st_uid;               /* user id of file's owner      */
        short    st_gid;               /* group id assigned to file    */
        dev_t    st_rdev;              /* used for devices, not files   */
        long     st_size;              /* total size of file in bytes  */
        time_t   st_atime;             /* time of last file access     */
        int      st_unused1;           /* not used                     */
        time_t   st_mtime;             /* time of last modification    */
        int      st_unused2;           /* not used                     */
        time_t   st_ctime;             /* time of last inode change    */
};
```

Any user can call *stat* to obtain information about a file, even if the file itself is not readable. However, the caller must have permission to search all the directories along the path to the specified file or *stat* will return an error.

23.7.15 The File Naming Mechanism

Although users imagine all files and directories to be part of a single hierarchy, the hierarchy is achieved through a file naming mechanism. The naming mechanism allows a system manager to piece together a single, conceptual hierarchy out of several smaller hierarchies. Users seldom understand the underlying file system structure or how the various components form the UNIX hierarchy because the naming mechanism hides the structure completely. We will see that when NFS runs under UNIX, it takes advantage of the UNIX naming mechanism to integrate remote files with local ones.

The original motivation for the UNIX naming mechanism arose because computer systems have multiple physical storage devices (i.e., multiple hard disks). Instead of forcing users to identify a disk as well as a file, the UNIX designers invented the idea of allowing the system manager to attach the hierarchy on one disk to the hierarchy on another. The result is a single, unified file namespace that permits the user to work without knowing the location of files. The naming mechanism operates as follows:

- The manager designates the hierarchy on one of the disks to be the root.
- The manager creates an empty directory in the root hierarchy. Let the full path name of the empty directory be given by a string /α.
- The manager instructs the naming mechanism to overlay a new hierarchy (usually one from some other disk) over directory /α.

Once the manager has attached the new hierarchy, the naming mechanism automatically maps names of the form /α/β to the file or subdirectory with path β in the attached hierarchy. The important concept is:

> *The UNIX naming mechanism provides users and application pro-*
> *grams with a single, uniform file hierarchy even though the underly-*
> *ing files span multiple physical disks.*

In fact, the UNIX system is more general than a system that attaches entire disks as part of the hierarchy. It allows a system manager to partition a single physical disk into one or more *file systems*. Each file system is an independent hierarchy; it includes both files and directories. A file system can be attached to the unified hierarchy at any point. The example in the next section will clarify the naming mechanism.

23.7.16 File System Mounts

The UNIX naming mechanism relies on the *mount* system call to construct the uni-fied hierarchy. The system manager uses *mount* to specify how a file system on one disk should be attached in the hierarchy. Usually, the manager arranges to perform necessary mounts automatically at system startup. Figure 23.6 illustrates three file sys-tems that have been mounted to form a single hierarchy.

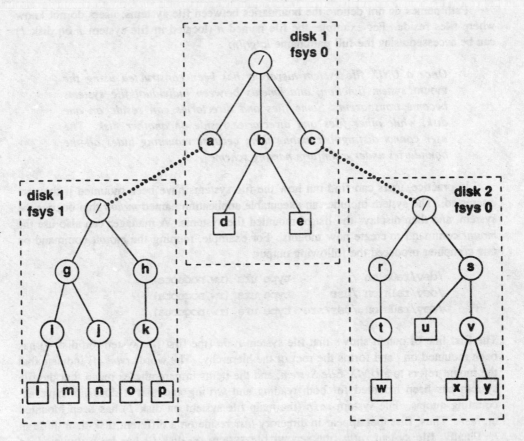

Figure 23.6 Three UNIX file systems mounted to form a single, uniform hierarchy. After the mounts, the boundaries between disks become invisible. For example, file system *0* on disk *2* appears to be directory */c*.

In the figure, file system *0* on disk *1* has been mounted on the root of the hierarchy. File system *1* on the same disk has been mounted on directory */a*, and file system *0* on disk *2* has been mounted on directory */c*. A mount completely overlays an original directory with a new file system. Usually, the system administrator creates a directory to be used for mounting. However, if the directory on which a file system is mounted contains any files before the mount occurs, they will be completely hidden (i.e., inaccessible, even to system administrators) until the file system is unmounted again.

From the user's point of view, the mounts are completely invisible†. If the user lists the contents of directory */*, the system reports three subdirectories: *a*, *b*, and *c*. If the user lists the contents of directory */a*, the system reports two directories: *g* and *h*. If the user lists the contents of directory */c/s*, the system reports a file, *u*, and a directory, *v*.

---

†Users cannot create hard links that cross file system boundaries.

Path names do not denote the boundaries between file systems; users do not know where files reside. For example, the file named *n* (located in file system *l* on disk *l*) can be accessed using the full path name */a/g/j/n*.

> *Once a UNIX file system hierarchy has been constructed using the mount system function, attachments between individual file systems become transparent. Some files and directories can reside on one disk, while other files and directories reside on another disk. The user cannot distinguish among them because mounting hides all the boundaries under a uniform naming scheme.*

In practice, users can find out how the file systems have been mounted if they are interested. The system includes an executable application named *mount* that queries the system, and then displays the list of mounted file systems. A manager can also use the *mount* command to create new mounts. For example, running the *mount* command on one computer produced the following output:

```
/dev/ra0a on /          type ufs (rw,noquota)
/dev/ra1h on /usr       type ufs (rw,noquota)
/dev/ra0b on /usr/src   type ufs (rw,noquota)
```

The first line of output shows that file system *ra0a* (the first file system on disk *0*) has been mounted on / and forms the root of the hierarchy. The words *type ufs* indicate that the mount refers to a *UNIX File System*, and the items in parentheses mean that the file system has been mounted for both reading and writing and that it does not have accounting quotas. File system *ra1h* (the main file system on disk *1*) has been mounted on */usr*. Thus, files that appear in directory */usr* reside on a different disk than those in */*. Finally, file system *ra0b* (the second file system on disk *0*) has been mounted on */usr/src*. The third mount provides an interesting twist because it means that although most files in */usr* reside on disk *1*, files in the subtree */usr/src* reside on disk *0*. The point is that the *mount* mechanism permits a manager to combine many file systems on many disks into a single, uniform directory hierarchy; a user or an application program uses the uniform hierarchy without knowing the location of files.

The concept of mounting file systems to form a single hierarchy provides incredible flexibility. It allows managers to choose an allocation of files to disks for economy, to reduce access contention, or to keep directories isolated in case of accidental loss. As we will see, it also provides a convenient way to introduce remote files into a UNIX hierarchy.

23.7.17 UNIX File Name Resolution

When presented with a full path name, the UNIX file system mechanism traces through the conceptual hierarchy to *resolve* the name. In UNIX, name resolution means finding the inode that identifies a file. To resolve a full path name, the file system begins at the root of the hierarchy and traces through directories one at a time. For example, given a name like /a/b/c/d, the file system opens the root directory and searches in it for a subdirectory named *a*. Once it finds /a, it opens that directory and searches it for a subdirectory named *b*. Similarly, it searches in *b* for a directory named *c*, and searches in *c* for a file or subdirectory named *d*. The name resolution software can extract one component of the full path name at each step because the slash character always separates individual components.

While the details of UNIX file name resolution are unimportant, the concept is essential:

> *UNIX resolves a path name one component at a time. It begins at the root of the hierarchy and at the beginning of the path. It repeatedly extracts the next component from the path and finds a file or subdirectory with that name.*

We will see that NFS takes the same approach as UNIX when resolving a name.

23.7.18 Symbolic Links

Later versions of the UNIX file system permit a special file type known as a *symbolic link*. A symbolic link is a special text file that contains the name of another file. For example, one can create a file named /a/b/c that contains a symbolic link with value /a/q. If a program opens file /a/b/c, the system finds that it contains a symbolic link and automatically switches to file /a/q.

The chief advantage of symbolic links lies in their generality: because a symbolic link can contain an arbitrary string, it can name any file or directory. For example, although the file system forbids making a hard link to a directory, it permits a user to create a symbolic link to a directory. Furthermore, because a symbolic link can refer to an arbitrary path, it can be used to abbreviate a long path name or to make a directory in a distant part of the hierarchy appear to be much closer.

The chief disadvantage of symbolic links arises from their lack of consistency and reliability. One can create a symbolic link to a file and then remove the file, leaving the symbolic link naming a nonexistent object. In fact, one can create a symbolic link to a nonexistent file because the system does not check the contents of a symbolic link when creating it. One can also create a set of symbolic links that forms a cycle or two symbolic links that point to one another. Calling *open* on such a link results in a run-time error.

23.8 Files Under NFS

NFS uses many of the UNIX file system definitions. It views a file as a sequence of bytes, permits files to grow arbitrarily large, and allows random access using byte positions in the file as a reference. It honors the same open-read-write-close paradigm as UNIX, and offers most of the same services.

Like UNIX, NFS assumes a hierarchical naming system. The NFS hierarchy uses UNIX terminology; it considers the file hierarchy to be composed of *directories* and *files*. A directory can contain files and other directories.

NFS has also adopted many of the UNIX file system details, leaving some unchanged, and making minor modifications to others. The next sections describe several features of NFS and show how they relate to the UNIX file system described earlier.

23.9 NFS File Types

NFS uses the same basic file types as UNIX. It defines enumerated values that a server can use when specifying a file type:

```
enum ftype {
        NFNON = 0,              /* Specified name is not a file */
        NFREG = 1,              /* Regular data file           */
        NFDIR = 2,              /* Directory                   */
        NFBLK = 3,              /* Block-oriented device       */
        NFCHR = 4,              /* Character-oriented device   */
        NFLNK = 5               /* Symbolic link               */
};
```

The set of types, including *NFBLK* and *NFCHR*, come directly from UNIX. In particular, UNIX permits system managers to configure I/O devices in the file system namespace, making it possible for application programs to open an I/O device and transfer data to or from it using the conventional open-read-write-close paradigm. NFS has adopted UNIX's terminology that divides I/O devices into block-oriented (e.g., a disk that always transfers data in 512-byte blocks) and character-oriented (e.g., an ASCII terminal device that transfers data one character at a time) devices. NFS literature sometimes uses the UNIX term *special file* to denote device names. A file name that corresponds to a block-oriented device has type *block-special*, while a name that corresponds to a character-oriented device has type *character-special*.

23.10 NFS File Modes

Like UNIX, NFS assumes that each file or directory has a *mode* that specifies its type and access protection. Figure 23.7 lists individual bits of the NFS mode integer and gives their meanings. The table uses octal values to represent bits; the definitions correspond directly to those returned by the UNIX *stat* function.

Mode Bit	Meaning
0040000	This is a directory; the "type" should be *NFDIR*.
0020000	This is a character-special file; the "type" should be *NFCHR*.
0060000	This is a block-special file; the type should be *NFBLK*
0100000	This is a regular file; the type should be *NFREG*
0120000	This is a symbolic link; the type should be *NFLNK*
0140000	This is a named socket; the type should be *NFNON*
0004000	Set user id on execution
0002000	Set group id on execution
0001000	Save swapped text after use
0000400	Read permission for owner
0000200	Write permission for owner
0000100	Execute or directory search permission for owner
0000040	Read permission for group
0000020	Write permission for group
0000010	Execute or directory search permission for group
0000004	Read permission for others
0000002	Write permission for others
0000001	Execute or directory search permission for others

Figure 23.7 The meaning of bits in the NFS *mode* integer. The definitions
have been taken directly from UNIX.

Although NFS defines file types for devices, it does not permit remote device access (e.g., a client may not *read* or *write* a remote device). Thus, while it is possible for a client to obtain information about a file name, it is not possible for a client to manipulate devices, even if the protection modes permit it.

> *Although NFS defines file protection bits that determine whether a client can read or write a particular file, NFS denies a remote machine access to all devices, even if the protection bits specify that access is allowed.*

23.11 NFS File Attributes

Similar to UNIX, NFS assumes that it is possible to obtain information about a file. NFS uses the term *file attributes* when referring to file information. Structure *fattr* describes the file attributes that NFS provides:

```
struct fattr {                        /* NFS file attributes      */
        ftype        type;            /* type: file, directory, etc  */
        unsigned int mode;            /* file's protection bits      */
        unsigned int nlink;           /* total hard links to the file */
```

```
        unsigned int userid;     /* user id of file's owner    */
        unsigned int groupid;    /* group id assigned to file  */
        unsigned int size;       /* total size of file in bytes */
        unsigned int blocksize;  /* block size used to store file*/
        unsigned int devnum;     /* dev. num. if file is device */
        unsigned int blocks;     /* number of blocks file uses */
        unsigned int fsid;       /* file system id for file    */
        unsigned int fileid;     /* unique id for file         */
        timeval      atime;      /* time of last file access   */
        timeval      mtime;      /* time of last modification  */
        timeval      ctime;      /* time of last inode change  */
    };
```

As the structure shows, the concept and most of the details have been derived from the information that the UNIX *stat* function returns.

23.12 NFS Client And Server

An *NFS server* runs on a machine that has a local file system. The server makes some of the local files available to remote machines. An *NFS client* runs on an arbitrary machine, and accesses the files on machines that run NFS servers. Often, an organization will choose to dedicate a computer that has large disks to the server function. Such a machine is often called a *file server*. Forbidding users from running application programs on an NFS file server machine helps keep the load low and guarantees faster response to access requests. Dedicating a computer to the file server function also guarantees that remote file access traffic will not reduce the CPU time available for application programs.

Most NFS client implementations integrate NFS files with the computer's native file system, hiding file locations from application programs and users. For example, consider an *MS-DOS* environment. MS-DOS files have names of the form: $X:\alpha$, where X is a single-character disk identifier and α denotes a path name on that disk. MS-DOS uses the backslash character (\) to separate components in the path. Thus, the MS-DOS name $C:\D\E\F$ denotes file F in subdirectory E in directory D on the system's hard disk. If an NFS client is added to the system and configured to access files on a remote server, it can use the MS-DOS naming scheme. For example, the manager might choose names of the form $R:\beta$ for all remote files, where β denotes a path on the remote file system.

When an application program calls *open* to obtain access to a file, the operating system uses the syntax of the path name to choose between local and remote file access procedures. If the path refers to a remote file, the system uses NFS client software to access the remote file. If the path refers to a local file, the system uses the computer's standard file system software to access the file. Figure 23.8 illustrates how the modules in an operating system interact when making the choice.

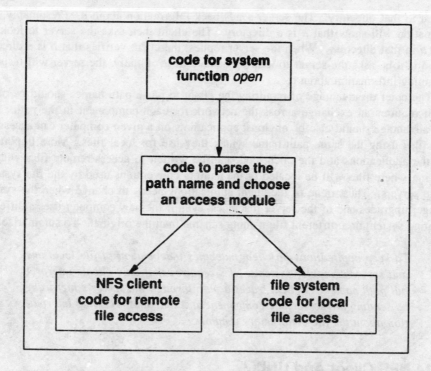

Figure 23.8 Procedures in an operating system that are called when an application opens a file. The system uses the path name syntax to choose between NFS, which will open a remote file, or the standard file system, which will open a local one.

23.13 NFS Client Operation

Recall that NFS was designed to accommodate heterogeneous computer systems. When system managers install NFS client code in an operating system, they try to integrate it into the system's file naming scheme. However, the path name syntax used by the remote file system may differ from that of the client machine. For example, when NFS client code running on a machine that uses MS-DOS connects to an NFS server running on a machine that uses UNIX, the client's system uses backslash (\) as a separator character, while the server's file system uses slash (/).

To accommodate potential differences between the client and server path name syntax, NFS follows a simple rule: only the client side interprets full path names. To trace a full path name through the server's hierarchical directory system, the client sends each individual path name component one at a time. For example, if a client that uses slash as a separator needs to look up path name /a/b/c on a server, it begins by obtaining information about the server's root directory. It then asks the server to look up name *a* in that directory. The server sends back information about *a*. Presumably, the information will show that *a* is a directory. The client then asks the server to look up name *b* in that directory. When the server replies, the client verifies that *b* is a directory, and if it is, asks the server to look up name *c* in it. Finally, the server will respond by sending information about *c*.

The chief disadvantage of requiring the client to parse path names should be obvious: it requires an exchange across the network for each component in the path. The chief advantage should also be obvious: applications on a given computer can access remote files using the same path name syntax they use for local files. More important, both the applications and the client code can be written to access remote files without knowing where files will be located or the naming conventions used by the file systems on the servers. Thus, none of the client applications needs to change when the system manager upgrades one of the server machines, even if the new computer uses a different operating system or a different file naming scheme than the original. To summarize:

> *To keep applications on client machines independent of file locations and server computer systems, NFS requires that only clients interpret full path names. A client traces a path through the server's hierarchy by sending the server one component at a time and receiving information about the file or directory it names.*

23.14 NFS Client And UNIX

Recall that UNIX uses the *mount* mechanism to construct a single, unified naming hierarchy from individual file systems on multiple disks. UNIX implementations of NFS client code use an extended version of the *mount* mechanism to integrate remote file systems into the naming hierarchy along with local file systems. From the application program's perspective, the chief advantage of using the *mount* mechanism is consistency: all file names have the same form. An application program cannot tell whether a file is local or remote from the name syntax alone. When an application opens a remote file, it receives an integer descriptor for the file exactly as it would for a local file. Internal information associated with the descriptor specifies that the file is a remote file accessible through NFS.

Whenever an application performs an operation on a file descriptor (e.g., *read*), the system checks to see whether the descriptor refers to a local file or a remote file. If the file is local, the operating system handles the operation as usual. If the file is remote, the operating system calls NFS client code that translates the operation into an equivalent NFS operation and places a remote procedure call to the server.

23.15 NFS Mounts

When managers add NFS mount entries to a UNIX mount table, they must specify a remote machine that operates an NFS server, a hierarchy on that server, a local directory onto which the mount will be added, and information that specifies details about the mount. For example, the following output from the UNIX *mount* command shows some of the NFS mounts used on a UNIX system at Purdue (non-NFS mounts have been deleted):

```
arthur:/p1 on /p1    type nfs (rw,grpid,intr,bg,noquota)
arthur:/p4 on /p4    type nfs (rw,grpid,intr,bg,noquota)
ector:/u4  on /u4    type nfs (rw,grpid,soft,bg,noquota)
gwen:/     on /gwen  type nfs (rw,grpid,soft,bg,noquota)
gwen:/u5   on /u5    type nfs (rw,grpid,soft,bg,noquota)
```

In this output, each line corresponds to a single NFS file system mount. The first field of each line specifies a machine that runs an NFS server and a hierarchy on that server, while the third field specifies a local directory on which the remote file system has been mounted. For example, *arthur:/p1* specifies the */p1* hierarchy on machine *arthur*. It has been mounted on the local directory named */p1*. The system manager chose to mount arthur's */p1* file system on a local directory with the same name so users on both machines could access the files using identical names.

All mounts shown in the example above have type *nfs*, which means they refer to remote file systems available via NFS. In addition, the parenthesized parameters on each line specify further details about the mount. Like mounts for local file systems, the remote file system mounts can specify whether to allow *reading* and *writing* (*rw*) or reading only (*r*).

NFS defines two basic paradigms for remote mounts in UNIX. Using a *soft mount* specifies that an NFS client should implement a timeout mechanism and consider the server offline if the timeout expires. Using a *hard mount* specifies that an NFS client should not use a timeout mechanism.

UNIX administrators usually arrange to have all mounts created automatically at system startup. Once an NFS mount has been created, application programs and users cannot distinguish between local and remote files. The user can use a conventional application program to manipulate a remote file as easily as the program can manipulate a local file. For example, a user can run a standard text editor to edit a remote file; the editor operates on the file the same way it operates on a local file. Furthermore, the user can change to a remote directory or back to a local directory simply by giving a path name that crosses one of the mount points.

23.16 File Handle

Once a client has identified and opened a file, it needs a way to identify that file for subsequent operations (e.g., *read* and *write*). Furthermore, a client needs a way to identify an individual directory or file as it traces through the server's hierarchy. To solve these problems, NFS arranges for a server to assign each file a unique *file handle* that it uses as an identifier. The server makes up a handle and sends it to the client when the client first *open*s the file. The client sends the handle back to the server when it requests operations on the file.

From the client's point of view, the file handle consists of a 32-byte string that the server uses to identify a file. From the server's point of view, a file handle can be chosen to be any convenient set of bytes that uniquely identify an individual file. For example, a file handle can encode information that allows the server to decode a handle and locate a file quickly.

In NFS terminology, a file handle is *opaque* to the client, meaning that a client cannot decode the handle or fabricate a handle itself. Only servers create file handles, and servers only recognize handles that they create. Furthermore, secure implementations of NFS servers use a sophisticated encoding to prevent a client from guessing the handle for a file. In particular, servers choose some of the bits in a handle at random to help ensure that clients cannot fabricate a valid handle.

To improve security, servers can also limit the time a handle can be used. Doing so makes it impossible for a client to keep a handle forever. To limit a handle's lifetime, the server encodes a *timestamp* in the handle. If the handle expires, the server refuses to perform further operations on a file using it. The client must obtain a fresh handle before it can continue access. In practice, NFS timestamps are usually long enough to permit any reasonable access. Applications that have legitimate use of a file can always obtain a fresh handle (the transactions required can be hidden from the application completely).

23.17 Handles Replace Path Names

To understand why handles are needed, consider naming files in a remote directory hierarchy. Recall that to isolate clients from the server's path name syntax and to allow heterogeneous machines to access hierarchical files, NFS requires that the client perform all path name interpretation. As a consequence, a client cannot use a full path name to specify a file when requesting an operation on that file. Instead, the client must obtain a handle that it can use to reference the file.

Having the server provide handles for directories as well as files permits a client to trace a path through the server's hierarchy. To see how, consider Figure 23.9, which illustrates the exchange between a client and server as the client looks up a file with path /a/b/c in the server's hierarchy.

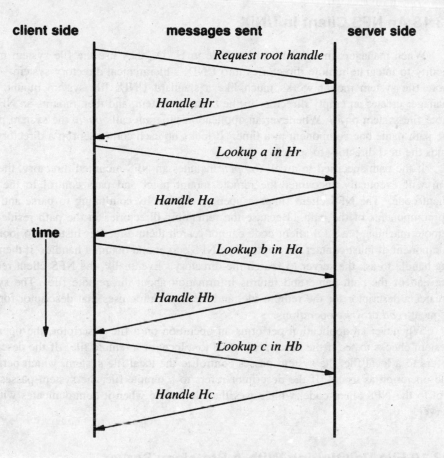

Figure 23.9 The messages a client and a server exchange as the client looks
up a file that has full path name /a/b/c, where "/" denotes the
client's component separator. The handle for a file or directory
named x is denoted Hx. In practice, a separate protocol provides
the root handle.

The figure shows that the server returns a handle for each directory along the path.
The client uses each handle in the next remote procedure call. For example, once the
client obtains a handle for directory a, it sends that handle back to the server and requests that the server search for b in directory a. The client cannot reference the file as
/a/b nor can it reference the directory as /a because the client does not know the
server's path name syntax.

23.18 An NFS Client In UNIX

When managers install NFS client code in UNIX, they use the file system mount facility to integrate remote directories into UNIX's hierarchical directory system. A remote file system mount works much like a standard UNIX file system mount. The manager creates an empty directory in the existing system, and then mounts an NFS remote file system on it. Whenever an application program calls *open*, the system parses the path name one component at a time. It looks up each component in a directory and finds the next directory to search.

If the path specified in a call to *open* includes an NFS-mounted directory, the system will eventually encounter the remote mount point and pass control to the NFS client code. The NFS client finishes opening the file by continuing to parse and look up components of the path. Because the remaining directories in the path reside on a remote machine, the NFS client code cannot search them directly. Instead, to lookup a component, it must contact the appropriate NFS server and obtain a handle. It then uses the handle to ask the server to search the directory. Eventually, the NFS client reaches the end of the path name and returns information about the remote file. The system creates a descriptor for the remote file, and the application uses that descriptor for subsequent *read* or *write* operations.

Whenever an application performs an operation on a file descriptor, the operating system checks to see if the descriptor refers to a local or a remote file. If the descriptor refers to a local file, the system passes control to the local file system, which performs the operation as usual. If the descriptor refers to a remote file, the system passes control to the NFS client code, which uses the file handle when it communicates with the server.

23.19 File Positioning With A Stateless Server

Because NFS uses a stateless server design, the server cannot store a file position for each application that is using a file. Instead, the client stores all file position information, and each request sent to the server must specify the file position to use. Storing position information at the client also helps optimize operations that change the file position. For example, in a UNIX implementation, NFS uses the local file table to store the position for a remote file just as UNIX uses it to store the position in a local file. If the client calls *lseek*, the system records the new file position in the table without sending a message to the server. Any subsequent access operation extracts the file position from the table and sends it to the server along with the access request. Because *lseek* does not send any messages across the network, seeking in a remote file is as efficient as seeking in a local one.

23.20 Operations On Directories

Conceptually, NFS defines a directory to consist of a set of pairs, where each pair contains a file name and a pointer to the named file. A directory can be arbitrarily large; there is no preset limit on its size.

NFS provides operations that permit a client to: *insert* a file in a directory, *delete* a file from a directory, *search* a directory for a name, and *read* the contents of a directory.

23.21 Reading A Directory Statelessly

Because directories can be arbitrarily large and communication networks impose a fixed limit on the size of a single message, reading the contents of a directory may require multiple requests. Because NFS servers are stateless, the server cannot keep a record of each client's position in the directory.

The NFS designers chose to overcome the limitations of stateless servers by arranging for an NFS server to return a *position identifier* when it answers a request for an entry from a directory. The client uses the position identifier in the next request to specify which entries it has already received and which it still needs. Thus, when a client wishes to read entries from a remote directory, it steps through the directory by making repeated requests that each specify the position identifier returned in the previous request.

Using informal terminology popular among systems programmers, NFS calls its directory position identifier a *magic cookie*. The term is meant to imply that the client does not interpret the identifier, nor can it fabricate an identifier itself. Only a server can create a magic cookie (hence the term *magic*); a client can only use a magic cookie that has been supplied by a server.

A magic cookie does not guarantee atomicity, nor does it lock the directory. Thus, two applications that perform operations on a directory may interfere with one another. For example, imagine a server that is handling requests from two or more clients concurrently. Suppose that after reading three directory entries from some directory, *D*, the first client receives a magic cookie that refers to a position before the fourth entry. Then suppose another client performs a series of operations that *insert* and *delete* files in directory *D*. If the first client attempts to read remaining entries from *D* using the old magic cookie, it may not receive all the changes.

In practice, the potential problems of concurrent directory access seldom affect users because they do not depend on instantaneous insertion or deletion of files. In fact, many conventional operating systems exhibit the same behavior as NFS; users seldom understand the details of how the system interprets concurrent directory operations because they rarely need to know.

23.22 Multiple Hierarchies In An NFS Server

Recall that to make NFS interoperate across heterogeneous machines, the designers chose to have the client parse all path names. Doing so allows both the client and server to each use the file naming scheme native to its operating system without requiring either of them to understand the other's environment.

Restricting the use of full path names has little effect on most file operations. However, it does introduce a serious problem because it means that a client cannot use a full path name to identify a remote file system or directory.

Early versions of the NFS protocol assumed that each server only provided access to a single 'remote hierarchy. The original protocol included a function named *NFSPROC_ROOT* that a client could call to obtain the handle for the root directory in the server's hierarchy. Once the client had a handle for the root, it could read directory entries and follow an arbitrary path through the hierarchy.

Later versions of NFS allow a single server to provide remote access to files located in several hierarchies. In such cases, a procedure that returns the handle of a single root directory does not suffice. To enable a single server to handle multiple hierarchies, NFS requires an additional mechanism. The additional mechanism allows a client to specify one of the possible hierarchies and obtain a handle for its root.

23.23 The Mount Protocol

The current version of NFS uses a separate protocol to handle the problem of finding a root directory. Called the *mount protocol*, it is defined using RPC. However, the mount protocol is not part of the NFS remote program. Although it is required for an NFS server, the mount protocol operates as a separate remote program.

The mount protocol provides four basic services that clients need before they can use NFS. First, it allows the client to obtain a list of the directory hierarchies (i.e., file systems) that the client can access through NFS. Second, it accepts full path names that allow the client to identify a particular directory hierarchy. Third, it authenticates each client's request and validates the client's permission to access the requested hierarchy. Fourth, it returns a file handle for the root directory of the hierarchy a client specifies. The client uses the root handle obtained from the mount protocol when making NFS calls.

The name and idea for the mount protocol come from UNIX: a UNIX system uses the mount protocol when it creates a remote file system mount in its namespace. A client system uses the mount protocol to contact a server and verify access to the remote file system before adding the remote mount to its local hierarchical namespace. If the mount protocol denies access, the client code reports an error to the system manager. If the mount protocol approves access, the client code stores the handle for the root of the remote file system so it can use the handle later when an application tries to open a file on that file system.

23.24 Summary

Sun Microsystems, Incorporated defined a remote file access mechanism called NFS that has become an industry standard. To allow many clients to access a server and to keep the servers isolated from client crashes, NFS uses stateless servers.

Because NFS is designed for a heterogeneous environment, a client cannot know the path name syntax on all servers. To accommodate heterogeneity, NFS requires the client to parse path names and look up each component individually. When a client looks up a particular component name, the server returns a 32-byte file handle that the client uses as a reference to the file or directory in subsequent operations.

Most of the NFS definitions and file system semantics have been derived from UNIX. NFS supports a hierarchical directory system, views a file as a sequence of bytes, allows files to grow dynamically, provides sequential or random access, and provides information about files almost identical to the information provided by the UNIX stat function.

Many of the conceptual file operations used in NFS have been derived from operations provided by the UNIX file system. NFS adopted the open-read-write-close access paradigm used in UNIX, along with basic file types and file protection modes.

A companion to NFS, the mount protocol makes it possible for a single NFS server to provide access to multiple directory hierarchies. The mount protocol implements access authentication, and allows a client to obtain the handle for the root of a particular directory hierarchy. Once the client obtains a handle for the root, it can use NFS procedures to access directories and files in that hierarchy. UNIX systems use the mount protocol when the system manager installs remote mounts in the UNIX hierarchical namespace.

FOR FURTHER STUDY

Ritchie and Thompson [1974] explains the original UNIX file system, and discusses the implementation of files using inodes and descriptors. Bach [1986] covers Unix file system semantics. McKusick et. al. [August 1984] describes the fast file system used in later releases of BSD UNIX. Sun Microsystems, Incorporated [RFC 1094] specifies the details of both NFS and the mount protocol. It mentions most of the concepts presented here.

EXERCISES

23.1   Build a program that obtains a magic cookie from an NFS server. Use the program to obtain magic cookies for several directories on several servers and print their contents in hexadecimal. Try to guess what information the cookie contains and how the server encodes it.

23.2   Use a network analyzer to watch messages exchanged between an NFS client and a
             server. How many packets are exchanged for each of the following operations: *open* a
             file not in the top level directory, *read 10* bytes from the file, and *close* the file?

23.3   Suppose the network that connects an NFS client and an NFS server delivers packets out
             of order. What errors can result from reordering NFS operations?

23.4   Suppose the network that connects an NFS client and an NFS server can duplicate pack-
             ets as well as deliver packets out of order. What errors can result from duplicating and
             reordering NFS operations? Compare your answer to your response for the previous ex-
             ercise. Does packet duplication introduce any additional error conditions? Why or why
             not?

24

Network File System Protocol (NFS, Mount)

24.1 Introduction

The previous chapter describes the concepts underlying Sun's Network File System (NFS), and shows that much of the terminology and many of the details were derived from the UNIX file system. This chapter continues the discussion of NFS by describing the protocol. It shows how NFS is defined to be a remote program using Sun RPC and how each operation on a file corresponds to a remote procedure call.

24.2 Using RPC To Define A Protocol

Chapters *20* through *22* show how RPC can be used to divide a program into components that execute on separate machines. Most programmers use RPC in the exact way described in those chapters: they first write a conventional program, and then use RPC to form a distributed version. This chapter takes another approach. It shows how RPC can be used to define a protocol without tying it to any particular program.

The chief difference between using RPC to construct a distributed version of a program and a general-purpose protocol arises in the way the designer thinks about the issues. When building a distributed version of a program, the programmer starts from an existing program that includes both procedures and data structures. When devising a protocol, the programmer starts from a set of desired services and devises abstract procedures that support them.

335

Designing a protocol requires thought about how services will be used as well as thought about how programmers will implement programs that supply those services. The designer must choose a protocol definition that strikes a balance between precision and freedom. The protocol must be precise enough to guarantee interoperability among programs that adhere to it, but it must be general enough to permit a wide variety of implementations.

Thinking about protocol design in a vacuum is seldom sufficient. Successful protocol specification requires the designer to be proficient with the technical details of communication and to have good intuition about the design. The intuition required usually arises from extensive experience with computer systems, application programs, and other communication protocols. Thus, protocol design can be more difficult than it appears. In particular, one should not confuse the apparent simplicity of a protocol like NFS with the notion that the design did not take much thought. The point is:

> *Although RPC provides a convenient way to specify a protocol, it does not make protocol design easier nor does it guarantee efficiency.*

24.3 Defining A Protocol With Data Structures And Procedures

To specify a protocol using RPC, one must:

- provide declarations for the constants, types, and data structures used as procedure arguments or function results,
- provide a declaration for each remote procedure that specifies the arguments, results, and semantics of the action it performs, and
- define the semantics for each remote procedure by specifying how it processes its arguments and computes a return value.

Conceptually, a protocol specified using RPC defines a server to be a single remote program. An operation sent from the client to the server corresponds to a remote procedure call, and a message returned from the server to the client corresponds to a procedure return. Thus, in any RPC-defined protocol, the client must initiate all operations; a server can only respond to individual client requests.

For NFS, requiring the client to initiate each operation makes sense because a file access protocol can be designed to be driven from the client. A server offers procedures that permit a client to: *create* or *delete* files, directories, and symbolic links; *read* or *write* data; *search* a directory for a named file; and obtain *status* information about an entire remote file system or about an individual file or directory. Although other application protocols may not lend themselves to RPC specification as directly as NFS, experience shows that most client-server interactions can be cast into the remote procedure call paradigm with modest effort.

NFS provides an interesting example of RPC specification because the protocol is sufficiently complex to require several remote procedures and data types, yet it is intuitive and conceptually simple enough to understand. The next section describes examples of the basic constant and type declarations used in the NFS protocol. Later sections show how the procedure declarations use the constants and types to specify arguments and results.

24.4 NFS Constant, Type, And Data Declarations

The NFS protocol standard defines constants, type names, and data structures that are used throughout the procedural declarations. All declarations are given using RPC declaration syntax.

24.4.1 NFS Constants

NFS defines six basic constants that specify the sizes of arrays used by the protocol. The declarations are given using the RPC language:

```
const MAXDATA    = 8192; /* Maximum bytes in a data transfer   */
const MAXPATHLEN = 1024; /* Maximum characters in a path name  */
const MAXNAMLEN  =  255; /* Maximum characters in a name       */
const COOKIESIZE =    4; /* Octets in a NFS magic cookie       */
const FHSIZE     =   32; /* Octets in an NFS file handle       */
```

In addition to the basic constants, the protocol also defines an enumerated set of constants used to report error status. Each remote procedure call returns one of these status values. The set is named *stat*, and is declared as:

```
enum stat {
        NFS_OK            = 0   /* Successful call                       */
        NFSERR_PERM       = 1,  /* Ownership mismatch or error           */
        NFSERR_NOENT      = 2,  /* File does not exist                   */
        NFSERR_IO         = 5,  /* I/O device error occurred             */
        NFSERR_NXIO       = 6,  /* Device or address does not exist.     */
        NFSERR_ACCES      = 13, /* Permission to access was denied       */
        NFSERR_EXIST      = 17, /* Specified file already exists         */
        NFSERR_NODEV      = 19, /* Specified device does not exist       */
        NFSERR_NOTDIR     = 20, /* Specified item not a directory        */
        NFSERR_ISDIR      = 21, /* Specified item is a directory         */
        NFSERR_FBIG       = 27, /* File is too large for server          */
        NFSERR_NOSPC      = 28, /* No space left on device (disk)        */
        NFSERR_ROFS       = 30, /* Write to read-only file system        */
        NFSERR_NAMETOOLONG= 63, /* File name was too long                */
        NFSERR_NOTEMPTY   = 66, /* Directory not empty                   */
        NFSERR_DQUOT      = 69, /* Disk quota exceeded                   */
        NFSERR_STALE      = 70, /* File handle is stale                  */
        NFSERR_WFLUSH     = 99  /* Write cache was flushed to disk       */
};
```

Each of these error values makes sense in the context of some call. For example, if a client attempts to perform a directory operation on a regular file, the server returns error code *NFSERR_NOTDIR*. If the client attempts to perform a regular file operation on a directory, the server returns error code *NFSERR_ISDIR*.

24.4.2 NFS Typedef Declarations

To make its structure declarations clearer, the NFS protocol standard defines names for types used in multiple structures. For example, the type *filename* is defined to be an array of characters large enough to contain a component name. In RPC syntax, the keyword *string* must be used to declare an array of characters. Thus, the declaration is:

```
typedef string filename<MAXNAMLEN>;
```

Similarly, the standard defines *fhandle* to be the type of a *32*-byte array that contains a file handle. The type is declared to be *opaque* because the client does not know the internal structure:

```
typedef opaque fhandle[FHSIZE];
```

24.4.3 NFS Data Structures

With constant and type definitions in place, a protocol designer can specify the types of all data structures used. NFS follows the convention of combining all the arguments for a remote procedure call into a single structure. Thus, the standard defines an argument structure for each remote procedure and a separate structure for each procedure result. In addition, the standard defines a few structures shared by several procedures. For example, Chapter *22* describes the *fattr* structure that NFS uses to specify file attributes. *Fattr* was derived from the data returned by the UNIX *stat* structure.

Some fields in the *fattr* structure record the time at which a file was last modified or accessed. Such fields are declared to be of type *timeval*, a structure:

```
struct timeval {                /* date and time used by NFS    */
    unsigned int seconds;   /* seconds past epoch (1/1/70)   */
    unsigned int useconds; /* additional microseconds       */
};
```

The declaration specifies that NFS stores a time value in two *32*-bit integers. The first integer records the number of seconds past an epoch date, and the second integer records additional microseconds (allowing for more precision). NFS uses the epoch date of January 1, 1970† to measure time values.

Most of the remaining declarations define the type of arguments passed to a remote procedure or the result the procedure returns. For example, when calling a procedure that performs an operation on a directory (e.g., *delete* a file), the client must pass the name of a file. NFS declares the argument type to be a structure, *diropargs* (*directory operation arguments*):

---

†The designers chose the NFS time epoch to be the same as that used by UNIX.

```
struct diropargs {        /* directory operation arguments    */
    fhandle  dir;         /* handle for directory file is in  */
    filename name;        /* name of file in that directory   */
};
```

The structure shows that the argument consists of a file handle for the directory and the name of a file in that directory. To understand why *diropargs* is needed, recall that the NFS client parses all path names. Thus, a client cannot use a full path name to identify a file. Instead, NFS requires all operations on files to be specified by giving the handle for the directory in which the file resides and the name of the file in that directory.

In addition to declarations for argument types, the standard defines the types returned by remote procedures. For example, a directory operation returns a union type named *diropres*:

```
union diropres switch (stat status) { /* result of dir. op  */
case NFS_OK:              /* If operation was successful    */
    struct {              /*    structure for success results */
        fhandle file;     /*    file handle for new file    */
        fattr   attributes;/* status of the file            */
    } diropok;            /* end of structure for success   */
default:                  /* If operation failed            */
    void;                 /*    get nothing back            */
};
```

The union allows two possible forms of a return value, with the choice depending on the status. If the operation succeeds, the status will have value *NFS_OK*, and the return value will consist of a file handle for the newly created file (or the file that changed) and a structure that contains the file's attributes. If the operation fails, the call will not return anything.

The arguments for other remote procedures sometimes include one or more file specifications. For example, the remote procedure used to rename a file requires two file names: the name of an existing file and the new name for that file. The arguments for the *rename* procedure are declared to be of type *renameargs*, a structure:

```
struct renameargs {       /* arguments to RENAME            */
    diropargs from;       /* an existing file               */
    diropargs to;         /* new location/name for file     */
};
```

Individual fields that give the old and new file names are declared to be of type *diropargs*.

Most other NFS argument types correspond to remote procedures. For example, NFS defines structure *writeargs* to specify arguments used in a call to *write* data to a file:

```
struct writeargs {              /* arguments to WRITE        */
        fhandle  file;          /* file to be written        */
        unsigned beginoffset;   /* obsolete (ignore)         */
        unsigned offset;        /* where to write data       */
        unsigned totalcount;    /* obsolete (ignore)         */
        nfsdata  data;          /* data to put into file     */
};
```

Similarly, structure *readargs* specifies the arguments for the *read* operation:

```
struct readargs {               /* arguments to READ         */
        fhandle  file;          /* file to be read           */
        unsigned offset;        /* where to read data        */
        unsigned count;         /* num. of bytes requested   */
        unsigned totalcount;    /* obsolete (ignore)         */
};
```

Procedure *readlink* allows the client to read the contents of a symbolic link. Its results are defined by the union *readlinkres*:

```
union readlinkres {     /* result of READLINK            */
case NFS_OK:            /* result if successful          */
case NFS_OK:            /* If operation was successful    */
    path data;         /*     path name found in link    */
default:                /* If operation failed            */
    void;              /*     nothing                    */
};
```

24.5 NFS Procedures

Once constants and data types have been declared, one only needs to specify the remote procedures that implement the protocol. An NFS server provides a remote program that implements *18* procedures. Using RPC language, the program can be declared:

```
program NFS_PROGRAM {
        version NFS_VERSION {
        void            NFSPROC_NULL(void)          = 0;

        attrstat        NFSPROC_GETATTR(fhandle)    = 1;

        attrstat        NFSPROC_SETATTR(sattrargs)  = 2;

        void            NFSPROC_ROOT(void)          = 3;

        diropres        NFSPROC_LOOKUP(diropargs)   = 4;

        readlinkres     NFSPROC_READLINK(fhandle)   = 5;

        readres         NFSPROC_READ(readargs)      = 6;

        void            NFSPROC_WRITECACHE(void)    = 7;

        attrstat        NFSPROC_WRITE(writeargs)    = 8;

        diropres        NFSPROC_CREATE(createargs)  = 9;

        stat            NFSPROC_REMOVE(diropargs)   = 10;

        stat            NFSPROC_RENAME(renameargs)  = 11;

        stat            NFSPROC_LINK(linkargs)      = 12;

        stat            NFSPROC_SYMLINK(symlinkargs)= 13;

        diropres        NFSPROC_MKDIR(createargs)   = 14;

        stat            NFSPROC_RMDIR(diropargs)    = 15;

        readdirres      NFSPROC_READDIR(readdirargs)= 16;

        statfsres       NFSPROC_STATFS(fhandle)     = 17;

        } = 2;          /* current version of NFS protocol    */
} = 100003;             /* RPC program number assigned to NFS */
```

24.6 Semantics Of NFS Operations

The semantics for most NFS operations follow the semantics of file operations in UNIX. The following sections each describe how one of the NFS remote procedures operates.

24.6.1 NFSPROC_NULL (Procedure 0)

By convention, procedure *0* in any RPC program is termed *null* because it does not perform any action. An application can call it to test whether a given server is responding.

24.6.2 NFSPROC_GETATTR (Procedure 1)

A client calls procedure *1* to obtain the attributes of a file, which include such items as the protection mode, owner, size, and time of last access.

24.6.3 NFSPROC_SETATTR (Procedure 2)

Procedure *2* permits a client to set some of the attributes of a file. The client cannot set all attributes (e.g., it cannot change the recorded file size except by adding bytes to the file or truncating it). If the call succeeds, the result returned contains the file's attributes after the changes have been applied.

24.6.4 NFSPROC_ROOT (Procedure 3)

Procedure *3* was defined for earlier versions of NFS, but is now obsolete. It has been replaced by the mount protocol.

24.6.5 NFSPROC_LOOKUP (Procedure 4)

Clients call procedure *4* to search for a file in a directory. If successful, the returned value consists of a file handle and the attributes for the specified file.

24.6.6 NFSPROC_READLINK (Procedure 5)

Procedure *5* permits the client to read the value from a symbolic link.

24.6.7 NFSPROC_READ (Procedure 6)

Procedure *6* provides one of the most important functions because it permits a client to read data from a file. The result returned by the server is a union, *readres*. If the operation succeeds, the result contains attributes for the file as well as the data requested. If the operation fails, the status value contains an error code.

24.6.8 NFSPROC_WRITECACHE (Procedure 7)

Procedure *7* is not used in the current protocol; it is intended for the next version of the protocol.

24.6.9 NFSPROC_WRITE (Procedure 8)

Procedure *8* provides another of the basic functions: it permits a client to write data into a remote file. The call returns a union, *attrstat*, that either contains an error code, if the operation fails, or the attributes of the file, if the operation succeeds.

24.6.10 NFSPROC_CREATE (Procedure 9)

A client calls procedure *9* to create a file in a specified directory. The file must not exist or the call will return an error. The call returns a union of type *diropres* that either contains an error status or a handle for the new file along with its attributes.

24.6.11 NFSPROC_REMOVE (Procedure 10)

A client invokes procedure *10* to delete an existing file. The call returns a status value. The status either indicates that the operation succeeded or provides an error code that tells why it failed.

24.6.12 NFSPROC_RENAME (Procedure 11)

Procedure *11* permits a client to rename a file. Because the arguments allow the client to specify a new directory for the file as well as a new name, the *rename* operation corresponds to the UNIX *mv* (*move*) command. NFS guarantees that *rename* will be atomic on the server (i.e., it cannot be interrupted). The guarantee of atomicity is important because it means the old name for the file will not be removed until the new name has been installed. Thus, the file will not appear to be missing during a *rename* operation.

24.6.13 NFSPROC_LINK (Procedure 12)

Clients call procedure *12* to form a hard link to an existing file. NFS guarantees that if a file has multiple hard links, the attributes visible for the file will be identical no matter which link is used to access it.

24.6.14 NFSPROC_SYMLINK (Procedure 13)

Procedure *13* creates a symbolic link. The arguments specify a directory handle and the name of a file to be created as well as a string that will become the contents of the symbolic link. The server creates the symbolic link, and then returns a status value that either indicates success or gives a reason for the failure.

24.6.15 NFSPROC_MKDIR (Procedure 14)

A client calls procedure *14* to create a directory. If the call succeeds, the server returns a handle for the new directory along with a list of its attributes. If the call fails, the returned status value indicates the reason for the failure.

24.6.16 NFSPROC_RMDIR (Procedure 15)

A client can use procedure *15* to remove a directory. As in UNIX, a directory must be empty before it can be removed. Thus, to remove an entire subtree, a client must traverse the subtree removing all files, and then remove the empty directories that remain. Usually, the removal of files and empty directories is accomplished in a single pass by using a post-order traversal of the directory tree.

24.6.17 NFSPROC_READDIR (Procedure 16)

A client calls procedure *16* to read entries from a directory. The argument structure, *readdirargs*, specifies a handle for the directory to be read, a magic cookie, and a maximum count of characters to read. On the initial call, the client specifies a magic cookie containing zero, which causes the server to read entries from the beginning of the directory. The value returned, of type *readdirres*, contains a linked list of zero or more directory entries and a Boolean value to indicate whether the last entry returned lies at the end of the directory.

After a successful return, each directory entry on the linked list contains the name of a file, a unique identifier for the file, a magic cookie that gives the file's position in the directory, and a pointer to the next entry on the list.

To read the sequence of entries in a directory, the client begins by calling *NFSPROC_READDIR* with a magic cookie value of zero and a character count equal to its internal buffer size. The server returns as many directory entries as fit into the buffer. The client iterates through the list of entries and processes each file name. If the returned value shows that the client has reached the end of the directory, it stops processing. Otherwise, the client uses the magic cookie in the last entry to make another call to the server and obtain more entries. The client continues reading groups of entries until it reaches the end of the directory.

24.6.18 NFSPROC_STATFS (Procedure 17)

Procedure *17* permits a client to obtain information about the remote file system on which a file resides. The returned result, a structure of type *statfsres*, contains fields that specify the optimum transfer size (i.e., the size of data in *read* or *write* requests that produces optimal transfer rates), the size of data blocks on the storage device, the number of blocks on the device, the number of blocks currently unused, and the number of unused blocks available to nonprivileged users.

A sophisticated client program can use *NFSPROC_STATFS* to optimize transfers or to estimate whether sufficient space remains on a disk to accommodate a *write* request.

24.7 The Mount Protocol

The mount protocol described in Chapter *22* is also defined using RPC. Although an NFS server must have a companion mount server, the two have been defined as separate remote programs. Thus, the protocol standard for mount specifies constants, types, and a set of remote procedures that comprise the server.

24.7.1 Mount Constant Definitions

Although the two protocols are defined separately, the values for many of the constants and types defined for the mount protocol have been derived from corresponding constants used in the NFS protocol. Indeed, the two protocols could not work together well unless they both used a common representation for objects like file handles. For example, mount defines the sizes of a file name, a path name, and a file handle as follows:

```
const MNTNAMLEN = 255;

const MNTPATHLEN = 1024;

const FHSIZE = 32;
```

The declarations use RPC syntax; they each express the lengths as a number of bytes.

24.7.2 Mount Type Definitions

The mount protocol also specifies type definitions that agree with their counterparts found in the NFS protocol. For example, mount specifies the type of a file handle:

```
typedef opaque fhandle[FHSIZE];
```

Similarly, the mount protocol specifies that a path name consists of an array of characters:

```
typedef string dirpath<MNTPATHLEN>;
```

24.7.3 Mount Data Structures

Because the mount protocol has been defined using RPC, it follows the convention of declaring a structure for the argument and result of each remote procedure. For example, one of the basic procedures in the protocol returns a file handle for the root directory in a named hierarchy. The value returned consists of a union, *fhstatus*, declared to be:

```
union fhstatus switch (unsigned status) {
case 0:                    /* If successful                  */
    fhandle directory;     /*    handle for specified root   */
default:                   /* Otherwise                      */
    void;                  /*    nothing                     */
};
```

As in the NFS protocol, each remote procedure in the mount protocol returns a status value along with other information. If the operation fails, the status value indicates the reason.

In addition to a procedure that returns a file handle, the mount protocol provides a procedure that allows a client to determine which file systems are available for access. The procedure returns the results in a linked list called an *export list*†. The type of a node on the export list is declared with structure *exportlist*:

```
struct *exportlist {       /* list of available hierarchies  */
    dirpath filesys;       /* path name for this hierarchy    */
    groups groups;         /* groups allowed to access it     */
    exportlist next;       /* pointer to next item in list    */
};
```

Field *groups* in an *exportlist* node contains a pointer to a linked list that specifies which protection groups are allowed to access the named hierarchy. Nodes on the list are defined to be a structure of type *groups*:

```
struct *groups {           /* list of group names             */
    name grname;           /* name of one group               */
    groups grnext;         /* pointer to next item on list    */
};
```

The mount protocol also allows a client to determine which remote file systems a given machine is accessing. Thus, it is possible to construct an NFS cross-reference list for a set of machines. To do so, one asks each of the machines in the set for a list of the remote file systems that the machine is accessing. Note that the set of remote file systems a given machine is accessing will be disjoint from the set of local file systems that the machine has exported for others to access.

---

†The term *export* refers to the idea that a server *exports* some of its files to other machines.

A reply from the mount protocol that lists remote accesses is a linked list where each node has type *mountlist*:

```
struct *mountlist {             /* list of remote mounts            */
        name      hostname; /* machine on which files resides */
        dirpath   directory;/* path name of hierarchy          */
        mountlist nextentry;/* pointer to next item on the list*/
};
```

24.8 Procedures In The Mount Protocol

Like NFS, the mount protocol defines all operations as procedures in a remote program. The RPC declaration of the mount program is:

```
program MOUNTPROG {
        version MOUNTVERS {

        void        MOUNTPROC_NULL(void)        = 0;

        fhstatus    MOUNTPROC_MNT(dirpath)      = 1;

        mountlist   MOUNTPROC_DUMP(void)        = 2;

        void        MOUNTPROC_UMNT(dirpath)     = 3;

        void        MOUNTPROC_UMNTALL(void)     = 4;

        exportlist  MOUNTPROC_EXPORT(void)      = 5;
        } = 1;          /* mount version 1 matches NFS vers. 2 */
    } = 100005;         /* RPC program number assigned to mount*/
```

24.9 Semantics of Mount Operations

The mount protocol defines the semantics of each of the operations listed above. The following sections give a brief summary of each.

24.9.1 MNTPROC_NULL (Procedure 0)

Following the RPC convention, procedure *0* does not perform any action.

24.9.2 MNTPROC_MNT (Procedure 1)

A client calls procedure *1* to obtain the handle for a particular hierarchy. The argument contains a path name that the server uses to distinguish among the hierarchies it exports for access; the result has type *fhstatus*. Names for the hierarchies available on a given server can be obtained by calling *MNTPROC_EXPORT* (see below).

24.9.3 MNTPROC_DUMP (Procedure 2)

Procedure *2* permits a client to obtain a list of the remote file systems that a particular machine is using. The information provided by *MNTPROC_DUMP* has little value to conventional applications; it is intended for system administrators.

24.9.4 MNTPROC_UMNT (Procedure 3)

A client can use procedure *3* to inform another machine that it will be out of service. For example, if machine *A* has mounted one or more file systems from the server on machine *B*, machine *B* can use *MNTPROC_UMNT* to inform *A* that a particular file system will be out of service (e.g., for disk maintenance). Doing so keeps *A* from sending additional requests to *B* while the files are offline.

24.9.5 MNTPROC_UMNTALL (Procedure 4)

Procedure *4* allows one machine to tell another that all of its NFS file systems will be unavailable. For example, a server can tell clients to unmount all its file systems before it reboots.

24.9.6 MNTPROC_EXPORT (Procedure 5)

Procedure *5* provides an important service: it allows a client to obtain the names of all the hierarchies accessible on a given server. The call returns a linked list that contains a single node of type *exportlist* for each available file system. The client must use one of the directory path names found in the export list when calling *MNTPROC_MNT* (procedure *1*).

24.10 NFS And Mount Authentication

NFS relies on the mount protocol to provide authentication. The mount protocol authenticates a client's request for the handle of a root directory, but NFS does not authenticate each individual client request.

Surprisingly, the mount protocol does not offer much protection. It uses RPC's *AUTH_UNIX* or *AUTH_NONE* to authenticate the client. Once a client has obtained a handle for a root directory, protections on individual files mean little. For example, if programmers obtain privilege on their private workstations, they may be able to access arbitrary files on NFS servers as well as on their local machines. Furthermore, if a programmer can guess the contents of an opaque file handle, the programmer can manufacture handles for arbitrary directories.

Early versions of NFS created handles by combining information about a file or directory in fixed ways. For example, Figure 24.1 shows how one UNIX implementation divides the *32*-byte handle into ten fields:

Field	Size	Contents
Fileid	4	UNIX's major and minor device numbers for the file
one	1	Always *1*
length$_1$	2	Total length of next three fields
zero$_1$	2	Always *0*
inode	4	UNIX's inode number for the file
igener	4	Generation number for file inode (randomized for security)
length$_2$	2	Total length of next three fields
zero$_2$	2	Always *0*
rinode	4	Unix's inode number for root of file system
rigener	4	Generation number for root inode (randomized for security)

Figure 24.1 The contents of the fields in an NFS file handle. This particular format comes from an NFS server that runs under the UNIX operating system; not all servers construct file handles the same way.

The chief danger in using a fixed format for file handles arises because NFS offers little protection against unauthorized access. A client wishing to access files can circumvent the mount protocol by manufacturing a handle for an arbitrary UNIX file. It can then obtain attribute information for the file, including the file ownership and protection bits. Thus, it will be able to access world-readable files even if the mount protocol does not authorize access. Furthermore, if the client has root privilege on the local machine, it will be able to send requests to a server that contain arbitrary user identifiers. Thus, a client that has root privilege can first find out who owns a particular file, and then send a request claiming to be that user.

To make it more difficult to guess file handles, many UNIX administrators use a utility that randomizes inode generation numbers. The utility goes through all the inodes on a disk and stores a random number in the inode's generation field. The mount protocol uses the generation number when passing out a file handle, and NFS checks that the value in the handle matches the generation number found in the inode.

Randomizing generation numbers increases security, but it does not increase the computational overhead required to form a handle because randomization is performed before the mount protocol runs. However, randomization makes file handles difficult to guess. A client attempting to obtain unauthorized access must choose among 2^{32} possible values for the generation number. Because the probability of guessing a valid handle is low, the probability of obtaining unauthorized access to a file is also low.

24.11 Summary

When using RPC to define a protocol, one must provide definitions for the constants and data types used in the specification, the definitions of the procedures that a server offers, the types of all procedure arguments and results, and the semantics of each procedure. Protocol definition differs from the use of RPC to form a distributed version of a program because it requires the designer to deal with abstract concepts instead of an existing program.

NFS has been defined using RPC. The protocol standard specifies *18* procedures that comprise a server. In addition to operations that allow a client to *read* or *write* a file, the protocol defines data structures and operations that permit a client to read entries from a directory, create a file, remove a file, rename a file, or obtain information about a file.

A companion to NFS, the mount protocol provides client authentication and allows a client to find the handle for the root of a hierarchy. The mount protocol permits a given server to export multiple hierarchies, and allows the client to specify a particular hierarchy using a full path name.

NFS relies on the mount protocol for security. It assumes that any client can send access requests once the client obtains the handle for a root directory. Most NFS implementations construct a handle for a file by encoding information about the file. Among other items, NFS servers running on a UNIX system often encode the file's inode generation number in the handle. To prevent clients from guessing a file handle and then using it to obtain unauthorized access, many UNIX administrators use a tool that randomizes inode generation numbers. The randomization makes it difficult for clients to guess a valid file handle.

FOR FURTHER STUDY

Sun Microsystems, Incorporated [RFC 1094] defines both the NFS and mount protocols using RPC. It provides declarations for the constants, types, and procedures that comprise each protocol as well as a description of the intended semantics and implementation hints. Another version of the document can be found in the *Network Programmer's Guide* that accompanies the SunOS operating system.

EXERCISES

24.1   Write a program that uses the mount protocol to obtain file handles. Does your system use UNIX authentication?

24.2   Using the program described in the previous exercise, check several files on a given UNIX server to see if the administrator has randomized inode generation numbers on that server's file systems.

24.3   Consult the protocol standard to find out about the *NFSPROC_WRITECACHE* operation that will become part of later versions of NFS. What is its purpose?

24.4   NFS uses UDP for transport. Several companies now market software that uses TCP instead. How can the protocol be optimized to take advantage of a reliable stream transport?

24.5   The NFS protocol specification mentions that several operations are potentially not idempotent. Find the operations and explain how each could be non-idempotent.

24.6   NFS semantics guarantee that a *write* request will not complete until the data has been stored on a stable storage device (e.g., a disk). Estimate how much faster a *write* operation would execute on your local server if the protocol permitted the server to copy the data into an output buffer and allowed the procedure call to return without waiting for the buffer to be written to the disk.

24.7   NFS is designed to permit clients and servers to operate in a heterogeneous environment. Explain how symbolic links cause problems. (Hint: consider the protocol carefully to determine whether the client or server interprets a symbolic link).

24.8   Read the protocol specification and find out which file attributes can be set by a client.

24.9   Because RPC uses UDP, a remote procedure call can be duplicated, delayed, and delivered out of order. Explain how a valid set of NFS calls can appear from the client's perspective to create a file and write data into it, and yet result in a zero-length file.

24.10   Suppose a client calls *NFSPROC_STATFS* to find the preferred data transfer size. What constraints may make transfers of that size suboptimal?

24.11   Read the protocol specification to find out about stale file handles. Why might a server declare that a handle has become stale? How can making a handle stale improve security?

24.12   Write a program that calls *MOUNTPROC_UMNTALL* on some server, *S*. Does the call have any effect on subsequent calls to *S*? Why or why not?

24.13   Write a program that calls *MOUNTPROC_EXPORT*. Run the program and print the list of exported file system names.

25

A TELNET Client (Program Structure)

25.1 Introduction

Previous chapters use simple examples to illustrate the concepts and techniques used in client-server software. This chapter and the next explore how the client-server paradigm applies to a complex application protocol. The example protocol is *TELNET*, one of the most widely used application protocols in the TCP/IP suite.

This chapter focuses on the overall program structure. It assumes the reader is familiar with the basics of the TELNET protocol, and concentrates on explaining an implementation. It discusses the design of the client software, the process structure, and the use of finite state machines to control processing. It also reviews UNIX terminal I/O and shows how a client maps TELNET communication to a UNIX terminal.

The next chapter completes the description. It focuses on the details of routines invoked to perform semantic actions associated with transitions of the finite state machines. The example code throughout both chapters illustrates clearly how the programming details dominate the code and how they complicate the implementation.

25.2 Overview

25.2.1 The User's Terminal

The TELNET protocol defines an interactive communication facility that permits users to communicate with a service on a remote machine. In most cases, users use TELNET to communicate with a remote login service. As the example in Chapter *1* shows, a well-designed TELNET client also permits a user to contact other services.

The TELNET protocol defines interactive, character-oriented communication. It specifies a *network virtual terminal (NVT)* that consists of a keyboard and display screen. The protocol defines the character set for the virtual terminal. Several of the keys correspond to conceptual operations instead of data values. For example, one key causes an *interrupt* or *abort*. The chief advantage of using a network virtual terminal is that it permits clients from a variety of computers to connect to a service. Like the XDR standard described in Chapter *19*, TELNET uses a symmetric data representation. Each client maps from its local terminal's character representation to the NVT character representation when it sends data, and from the NVT representation to the local character set when it receives data. To summarize:

> *TELNET is a character-oriented protocol that uses a standard encoding when it transfers data.*

25.2.2 Command And Control Information

In addition to character data, TELNET permits the client and server to exchange *command* or *control* information. Because all communication between the client and server passes across a single TCP connection, the protocol arranges to encode command or control information so the receiver can distinguish it from normal data. Thus, much of the protocol focuses on the definition of how the sender encodes a command and how the receiver recognizes it.

25.2.3 Terminals, Windows, and Files

TELNET defines communication between a user's *terminal* and a remote service. The protocol specification assumes that the terminal consists of a keyboard on which the user can enter characters and a display screen that can display multiple lines of text.

In practice, a user can decide to invoke a client with an input file in place of a keyboard or an output file in place of a display. Alternatively, the user can invoke the client from within a window on a bitmapped display. Although such alternatives introduce small additions to the code, it will be easiest to understand both the protocol and the implementation if we imagine that users who invoke the client each have a conventional terminal. To summarize:

> *TELNET client software is designed to handle interactive communication with a user's terminal.*

25.2.4 The Need For Concurrency

Conceptually, a TELNET client transfers characters between the user's terminal and a remote service. On one side, it uses the local operating system functions when it interacts with the user's terminal. On the other side, it uses a TCP connection when it communicates with the remote service. Figure 25.1 illustrates the concept:

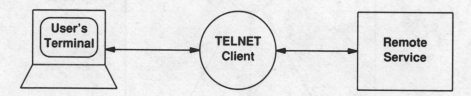

Figure 25.1 Conceptual role of a TELNET client. The client must transfer characters from the user's keyboard to a remote service, and it must transfer characters from the remote service to the user's display.

To provide a full-duplex connection between the user's terminal and a remote service, a TELNET client must perform two tasks simultaneously:

* The client must read characters that the user types on the keyboard and send them across a TCP connection to the remote service.
* The client must read characters that arrive from the TCP connection and display them on the user's terminal screen.

Because the remote service can emit output at any time or the user can type at any time, the client cannot know which source of data will become available first. Thus, it cannot block indefinitely waiting for input from one of the two sources without also checking for input from the other. In short, the client must transfer data in both directions concurrently.

25.2.5 A Process Model For A TELNET Client

To accommodate concurrent data transfer, a client must either consist of multiple processes that execute concurrently or it must implement concurrent I/O in a single process. Our example code uses the latter strategy: the client consists of a single process that blocks until one of the sources is ready. Figure 25.2 illustrates the process structure we have chosen:

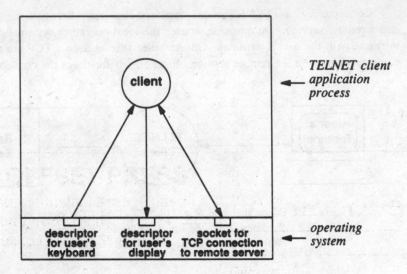

Figure 25.2 The process structure of the example TELNET client. A single process reads characters from the user's keyboard and sends them to the remote service across a TCP connection. The process also reads characters from the remote service and sends them to the user's display.

25.3 A TELNET Client Algorithm

Algorithm 25.1 specifies how a single-process TELNET client operates. Like the single-process, concurrent server design described in Chapter *12*, a UNIX implementation of a single-process, concurrent client uses the *select* system function to implement Step *3* of Algorithm *25.1*. When the client calls *select*, it specifies that the process should block until input arrives on the descriptor that corresponds to the user's keyboard or on the socket descriptor that corresponds to the TCP connection. When either descriptor becomes ready, the call to *select* returns and the client reads from whichever descriptor became ready.

Algorithm 25.1

1. Parse arguments and initialize data structures.
2. Open a TCP connection to the specified port on the specified remote host.
3. Block until the user types input or data arrives over the TCP connection.
4. If data arrived from the keyboard, read it, process it, translate it to NVT representation, and send it over the TCP connection. Otherwise, read data from the TCP connection, process it, translate it to the local character representation, and send it to the user's display.
5. Return to step *3* above.

Algorithm 25.1 A TELNET client. The single process relays characters in both directions; it blocks until data is available from the keyboard or socket.

25.4 Terminal I/O In UNIX

Algorithm 25.1 may seem extremely simple. However, the details of the TELNET protocol and the terminal I/O complicate the code. To understand how TELNET client software interacts with a user's terminal, one must understand in detail how the client operating system handles terminal I/O. This section describes how UNIX handles terminal I/O, and shows examples of code that controls the user's terminal.

In UNIX, I/O to a terminal device follows the same *open-read-write-close* paradigm used for I/O to files or sockets. An application program calls *open* to obtain an *I/O descriptor* for a terminal's keyboard or screen, *read* to receive data that the user types on the keyboard, and *write* to transfer data to the terminal's screen.

In practice, most applications do not call *open* to create a descriptor for the user's terminal because the command interpreter provides open descriptors automatically. The command interpreter usually leaves the keyboard connected to descriptor *0* (standard input) and the terminal screen connected to descriptor *1* (standard output).

Although terminal I/O follows the same basic paradigm as file I/O, a myriad of details complicate it. Many of the details arise because terminal hardware is primitive. For example, although most users think of the keyboard and display as a single unit, the hardware separates keyboard input from display output and treats them as two separate devices. Thus, the hardware does not automatically display each character that the user types. Instead, the hardware merely delivers characters as keyboard input and requires the computer to write a copy of each character to the display.

Most applications expect that users will see a copy of each character on the display as they type, but some applications need to suppress printing of input. In particular, to keep passwords from being observed, an application that requests a password usually stops displaying input characters while the user types the password.

Rather than have each application handle all the details associated with terminal I/O and character display, the UNIX operating system provides software to handle them automatically. Known as a *terminal device driver*, the software resides in the operating system kernel as Figure 25.3 illustrates.

The device driver associates keyboard input with the corresponding terminal display. It can be instructed to *echo* input characters (i.e., display each character the user types) or to suppress the echo (i.e., turn off display of input characters). It can allow the user to edit mistakes using a *backspace* or *delete* key, or it can pass all characters, including *backspace* and *delete*, directly to the application. The driver can also generate the special sequence of characters that position the cursor at the beginning of a new line when the application sends an end-of-line character†. Finally, the device driver can recognize a special character (or characters) that causes the system to *interrupt* or *abort* the current process. When the user types the special character, the device driver translates it into a UNIX *signal* that aborts the application program.

25.4.1 Controlling A Device Driver

Application programs use the system function *ioctl* (*I/O control*) to control the device driver. *Ioctl* permits the application to obtain or set parameter values that control the operation of the driver. Most important, a TELNET client can use *ioctl* to obtain a copy of all device driver parameters when it begins, then to change the parameters to make the terminal behave differently, and finally to restore the original parameter values before it exits. Thus, from the user's point of view, although terminal parameters change while the client operates, they return to their original value when the client exits or suspends.

---

†Most terminals require the operating system to send a *linefeed* character as well as a *carriage return* character to move the cursor to the beginning of the next line. The *linefeed* moves down the screen vertically, and the *carriage return* moves to the beginning of the current line.

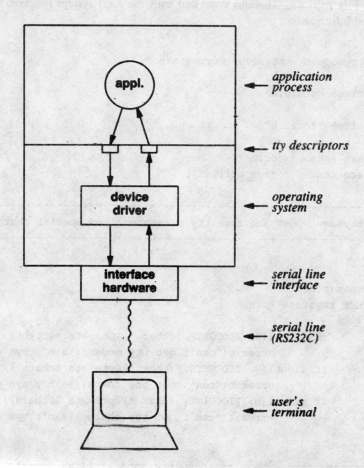

Figure 25.3 A terminal device driver in UNIX and the paths data follows when it flows into the system from a keyboard or out of the system to a terminal display. All terminal I/O passes through the device driver.

File *ttymode.c* contains code that uses the *ioctl* system function to manipulate terminal information.

```
/* ttymode.c - ttysave, ttyrestore */

#include <stdio.h>

#include "local.h"

extern int      errno;
extern char     *sys_errlist[];

/*-------------------------------------------------------------------------
 * ttysave - get and save tty parameters and special characters
 *-------------------------------------------------------------------------
 */
int
ttysave(pts)
struct ttystate *pts;
{
        if (ioctl(0, TIOCGETP, (char *)&pts->ts_sgttyb))
                errexit("can't get tty modes: %s\n", sys_errlist[errno]);
        if (ioctl(0, TIOCGETC, (char *)&pts->ts_tchars))
                errexit("can't get tty chars: %s\n", sys_errlist[errno]);
        if (ioctl(0, TIOCGLTC, (char *)&pts->ts_ltchars))
                errexit("can't get tty chars: %s\n", sys_errlist[errno]);
}


/*-------------------------------------------------------------------------
 * ttyrestore - set tty characters and special characters
 *-------------------------------------------------------------------------
 */
int
ttyrestore(pts)
struct ttystate *pts;
{
        if (ioctl(0, TIOCSETP, (char *)&pts->ts_sgttyb))
                errexit("can't set tty modes: %s\n", sys_errlist[errno]);
        if (ioctl(0, TIOCSETC, (char *)&pts->ts_tchars))
                errexit("can't set tty chars: %s\n", sys_errlist[errno]);
        if (ioctl(0, TIOCSLTC, (char *)&pts->ts_ltchars))
                errexit("can't set tty chars: %s\n", sys_errlist[errno]);
}
```

Procedure *ttysave* extracts the current parameters from the device driver associated with the keyboard (device *0*) and saves them in a structure of type *ttystate*. Procedure *ttyrestore* takes parameters previously saved in a *ttystate* structure and passes them to the device driver. Each procedure takes a single argument that gives the address of the structure to use.

25.5 Establishing Terminal Modes

When the client begins, it calls procedure *ttysetup* to establish parameters for the terminal device driver. File *ttysetup.c* contains the code.

```
/* ttysetup.c - ttysetup */

#include <stdio.h>

#include "local.h"

/*------------------------------------------------------------
 * ttysetup - set up tty
 *------------------------------------------------------------
 */
int
ttysetup()
{
        extern struct ttystate  tntty;

        ttysave(&oldtty);          /* save original tty state       */

        sg_erase = oldtty.ts_sgttyb.sg_erase;
        sg_kill = oldtty.ts_sgttyb.sg_kill;
        t_intrc = oldtty.ts_tchars.t_intrc;
        t_quitc = oldtty.ts_tchars.t_quitc;
        t_flushc = oldtty.ts_ltchars.t_flushc;

        tntty = oldtty;

        /* disable some special characters */
        tntty.ts_tchars.t_intrc = -1;
        tntty.ts_tchars.t_quitc = -1;
        tntty.ts_ltchars.t_suspc = -1;
        tntty.ts_ltchars.t_dsuspc = -1;

        ttyrestore(&tntty);
```

Ttysetup calls *ttysave* to record the initial terminal modes in global variable *oldtty*. Because *ioctl* only permits a program to extract or load all parameters at once, the client cannot set each parameter separately. To change one or more parameters, the client must make a copy of the initial parameters in local variable *tntty*, modify the copy to change one or more parameters, and then call *ttyrestore* to store the new parameters in the terminal device driver. The changes in *ttysetup* disable characters that cause *interrupt*, *quit*, *suspend*, and *delayed suspend*. In essence, setting the specified values to *-1* prevents the local device driver from interrupting or suspending the client program. Because *ttysetup* applies the changes to a copy of the initial terminal parameters, it leaves other terminal characteristics unchanged. For example, if the user has defined *control-C* to mean *abort the running program*, disabling it in the device driver means the client will be able to read *control-C* just like any other character. However, because *ttysetup* begins with a copy of the parameters, disabling interpretation of *control-C* does not affect other terminal characteristics (e.g., *echo*). We will see that the client uses the saved terminal mode to determine which character the user has defined for the interrupt signal. It sends the server side an interrupt command when the user types that character.

25.6 Global Variable Used For Stored State

File *local.h* contains the declaration of global variable *oldtty* along with other global variables that refer to the local terminal. It also defines structure *ttystate*, which contains all the important terminal characteristics.

```
/* local.h */

#include <sys/ioctl.h>

struct ttystate {
        struct sgttyb    ts_sgttyb;
        struct tchars    ts_tchars;
        struct ltchars   ts_ltchars;
};

extern FILE        *scrfp;
extern char        scrname[];
extern struct ttystate  oldtty;

extern char        t_flushc, t_intrc, t_quitc, sg_erase, sg_kill;
```

25.7 Restoring Terminal Modes Before Exit

When the client begins, it saves the original terminal modes in variable *oldtty*. When it exits, the client process calls *ttyrestore* to restore the saved terminal modes. For example, procedure *dcon* disconnects the TCP connection to a server; the client calls *dcon* when the user requests connection termination. *Dcon* prints a message, restores the terminal modes, and exits normally (i.e., it uses exit code *0*). File *dcon.c* contains the code:

```
/* dcon.c - dcon */

#include <sys/ioctl.h>

#include <stdio.h>

#include "local.h"

/*------------------------------------------------------------------------
 * dcon - disconnect from remote
 *------------------------------------------------------------------------
 */
/*ARGSUSED*/
int
dcon(sfp, tfp, c)
FILE    *sfp, *tfp;
int     c;
{
        fprintf(tfp, "disconnecting.\n");
        ttyrestore(&oldtty);
        exit(0);
}
```

If an error occurs, the client calls procedure *cerrexit* found in file *cerrexit.c*:

```
/* cerrexit.c - cerrexit */

#include <stdio.h>
#include <varargs.h>

#include "local.h"

/*------------------------------------------------------------------------
 * cerrexit - cleanup and exit with an error message
 *------------------------------------------------------------------------
 */
/*VARARGS1*/
int
cerrexit(format, va_alist)
char    *format;
va_dcl
{
        va_list args;

        va_start(args);
        _doprnt(format, args, stderr);
        ttyrestore(&oldtty);
        va_end(args);
        exit(1);
}
```

Like procedure *dcon*, *cerrexit* prints a message and restores the terminal modes before it exits. Unlike *dcon*, however, *cerrexit* uses exit code *1* to indicate an abnormal exit.

25.8 Client Suspension And Resumption

UNIX allows the user to suspend a running program temporarily. During suspension, control of the user's terminal reverts to another process, usually a command interpreter. When a TELNET client receives a signal that causes process suspension, it must restore the original terminal parameters before suspending and must reset the parameters to the values the client uses when the process resumes. File *suspend.c* contains the code for function *suspend* that restores the original terminal modes before it suspends the client process. When the client resumes execution, *suspend* regains control, resets the terminal modes, and returns to its caller.

```
/* suspend.c - */

#include <sys/types.h>
#include <sys/signal.h>

#include <stdio.h>

#include "local.h"

extern struct ttystate  tntty;

/*-------------\-----------------------------------------------------------
 * suspend - suspend execution temporarily
 *-------------------------------------------------------------------------
 */
/*ARGSUSED*/
int
suspend(sfp, tfp, c)
FILE    *sfp, *tfp;
int     c;
{
        ttysave(&tntty);        /* save current tty state       */
        ttyrestore(&oldtty);    /* restore old tty state        */

        (void) kill(0, SIGTSTP);

        ttysave(&oldtty);       /* may have changed             */
        ttyrestore(&tntty);     /* restore telnet modes         */
        return 0;
}
```

25.9 Finite State Machine Specification

The TELNET protocol specifies how a client passes characters to a remote service and how the client displays data that the remote service returns. Most of the traffic that passes across the connection consists of individual data characters. Data characters originate at the client when the user types on the keyboard; they originate from the server when the remote session generates output. In addition to data characters, TELNET also permits the client and server to exchange control information. In particular, the client can send a sequence of characters that comprise a *command* to the server that controls execution of the remote service. For example, a client can send a command sequence that *interrupts* the remote application program.

Most implementations of TELNET use a *finite state machine* (*FSM*) to specify the exact syntax and interpretation of command sequences. As a specification tool, a finite state machine provides a precise description of the protocol. It shows exactly how the sender embeds command sequences in the stream of data, and specifies exactly how the receiver interprets such sequences. More important, the finite state machine can be converted directly into a program that follows the protocol. Thus, it is possible to verify that the resulting program obeys the protocol specification. To summarize:

> Because TELNET is a character-oriented protocol that embeds command sequences in the data stream between the client and server, most implementations use a finite state machine to define the correct behavior.

25.10 Embedding Commands In A TELNET Data Stream

The idea underlying TELNET is simple: whenever a client or server wants to send a command sequence instead of normal data, it inserts a special, reserved character in the data stream. The reserved character is called an *Interpret As Command* character (*IAC*). When the receiver finds an IAC character in its incoming data stream, it processes succeeding octets as a command sequence. To send an IAC as data, the sender *character stuff*s an extra IAC in front of it.

An individual command sequence can contain an *option request* or an *option reply*. A request asks the receiving side to honor (or not honor) a particular *TELNET option*; a reply acknowledges the request and specifies whether the receiver will honor it.

The protocol defines two verbs that a sender can use to form a request: *DO* and *DONT*. Like most items that TELNET defines, the protocol standard specifies that each verb and each option must be encoded in a single character. Thus, a request usually consists of three characters when it appears in the data:

IAC verb option

where *verb* denotes an encoded character for either a *DO* or *DONT*, and *option* denotes an encoded character for one of the TELNET options.

The *TELNET echo option* provides a good example. Normally, the server echoes each character it receives (i.e., sends a copy back to the user's display). To turn off remote character echo, the client sends three encoded characters that correspond to:

IAC DONT ECHO

25.11 Option Negotiation

In general, the receiving side responds to a request using the verbs *WILL* or *WONT*. The receiver sends *WILL* to specify that it will honor the requested option and *WONT* to specify that it will not.

A response to a request provides an acknowledgement to the sender and tells the sender whether the receiver agrees to honor the request. For example, at startup, the client and server negotiate to decide which side will echo characters that the user types. Usually, the client sends characters to the server and the server echoes them to the user's terminal. However, if network delays become troublesome, a user may prefer to have the local system echo characters. Before a client enables character echo in the local system, it sends the server the sequence:

IAC DONT ECHO

When the server receives the request, it sends the 3-character response:

IAC WONT ECHO

Note that the verb *WONT* refers to the option; it does not necessarily mean that the server rejected the request. In this case, for example, the server has agreed to turn off echo as requested.

25.12 Request/Offer Symmetry

Interestingly, TELNET permits one side of a connection to offer a particular option before the other side requests it. To do so, the side offering to perform (or not perform) an option sends a message containing the verb *WILL* (or *WONT*). Thus, a *WILL* or *WONT* either acknowledges a previous request or offers to perform an option. For example, UNIX applications like text editors often send special control sequences to position the cursor. They cannot use the network virtual terminal encoding because it does not support all possible 8-bit characters. Thus, the TELNET server from BSD UNIX automatically sends *WILL* for the *transmit binary* option whenever a client connects to it, offering to use 8-bit binary (unencoded) character transmission instead of NVT encoding. A client must respond by sending a command sequence that specifies *DO transmit binary* or *DONT transmit binary*.

25.13 TELNET Character Definitions

File *telnet.h* contains the definitions of constants used in the protocol:

```
/* telnet.h */

/* TELNET Command Codes: */
#define TCSB              (u_char)250      /* Start Subnegotiation          */
#define TCSE              (u_char)240      /* End Of Subnegotiation         */
#define TCNOP             (u_char)241      /* No Operation                  */
#define TCDM              (u_char)242      /* Data Mark (for Sync)          */
#define TCBRK             (u_char)243      /* NVT Character BRK             */
#define TCIP              (u_char)244      /* Interrupt Process             */
#define TCAO              (u_char)245      /* Abort Output                  */
#define TCAYT             (u_char)246      /* "Are You There?" Function     */
#define TCEC              (u_char)247      /* Erase Character               */
#define TCEL              (u_char)248      /* Erase Line                    */
#define TCGA              (u_char)249      /* "Go Ahead" Function           */
#define TCWILL            (u_char)251      /* Desire/Confirm Will Do Option*/
#define TCWONT            (u_char)252      /* Refusal To Do Option          */
#define TCDO              (u_char)253      /* Request To Do Option          */
#define TCDONT            (u_char)254      /* Request NOT To Do Option      */
#define TCIAC             (u_char)255      /* Interpret As Command Escape   */

/* Telnet Option Codes: */
#define TOTXBINARY        (u_char)  0      /* TRANSMIT-BINARY option        */
#define TOECHO            (u_char)  1      /* ECHO Option                   */
#define TONOGA            (u_char)  3      /* Suppress Go-Ahead Option      */
#define TOTERMTYPE        (u_char) 24      /* Terminal-Type Option          */

/* Network Virtual Printer Special Characters: */
#define VPLF              '\n'     /* Line Feed                    */
#define VPCR              '\r'     /* Carriage Return              */
#define VPBEL             '\a'     /* Bell (attention signal)      */
#define VPBS              '\b'     /* Back Space                   */
#define VPHT              '\t'     /* Horizontal Tab               */
#define VPVT              '\v'     /* Vertical Tab                 */
#define VPFF              '\f'     /* Form Feed                    */

/* Keyboard Command Characters: */
#define KCESCAPE          035      /* Local escape character ('^]')    */
#define KCDCON            '.'      /* Disconnect escape command        */
#define KCSUSP            032      /* Suspend session escape command ('^Z')*/
#define KCSCRIPT          's'      /* Begin scripting escape command   */
#define KCUNSCRIPT        'u'      /* End scripting escape command     */
#define KCSTATUS          024      /* Print status escape command ('^T')   */
#define KCNL              '\n'     /* Newline character                */


#define KCANY             (NCHRS+1)
```

```
/* Option Subnegotiation Constants: */
#define TT_IS            0         /* TERMINAL_TYPE option "IS" command    */
#define TT_SEND          1         /* TERMINAL_TYPE option "SEND" command */


/* Boolean Option and State variables */
extern char      synching, doecho, sndbinary, rcvbinary;
```

Note that the file defines symbolic names for each of the characters TELNET uses, including verbs like *WILL* and *WONT* as well as option codes.

25.14 A Finite State Machine For Data From The Server

Figure 25.4 shows the principle finite state machine that specifies the TELNET protocol, including states that correspond to the option negotiation described above. Think of the machine as specifying how a client handles the sequence of characters it receives from the server.

The FSM diagram uses conventional notation. Each transition from one state to another has a label of the form α/β, where α denotes a specific input character that causes the transition and β denotes an action to be taken when following the transition. A label α/β on a transition from state X to state Y means: *if character α arrives while in state* X, *execute action β and then change to state* Y. The names of states and characters in the figure have been taken from the software. For example, file *telnet.h* defines constant *TCIAC* to correspond to TELNET's IAC character. As shorthand, the name *TCANY* denotes any character other than the transitions listed explicitly.

To understand how the FSM works, imagine that the client uses it whenever data arrives over the TCP connection from the server. When a character arrives from the server, the client follows a transition in the finite state machine. Some of the transitions keep the machine in the same state, but others transfer to a new state.

25.15 Transitions Among States

The client starts its state machine in the state labeled *TSDATA* when it begins execution. State *TSDATA* corresponds to a situation where the client expects to receive normal characters and send them to the user's display (i.e., the client has not begun reading a command sequence). For example, if character *q* arrives, the client remains in state *TSDATA* and executes the action labeled *K* (i.e., the client calls procedure *ttputc* to display the character on the user's terminal screen, and then follows the loop back to the same state).

If character *TCIAC* arrives when the FSM is in state *TSDATA*, the client follows the transition to state *TSIAC* and executes action labeled *E* in the diagram. The legend specifies that action *E* corresponds to "no operation." Once it moves to state *TSIAC*, the client has begun interpreting a command sequence. If the character following the *TCIAC* is a verb (e.g., *TCDO*), the client will follow a transition to one of the option processing states.

The finite state machine for TELNET only needs six states because interpretation of the protocol only depends on a short history of the characters that have arrived. For example, following a *TCIAC* character, the server could send one of the option requests or responses: *TCDO*, *TCDONT*, *TCWILL*, or *TCWONT*, or it could send an *option subnegotiation request*. Option subnegotiation permits the sender to include a variable-length string in the option (e.g., the option a client uses to pass a terminal type to a server uses subnegotiation so it can send a string that encodes the name of the terminal). Although subnegotiation permits variable-length command sequences, the FSM needs only two states to handle it because a 2-character sequence terminates subnegotiation. The client enters state *TSSUBNEG* when it first encounters a subnegotiation request. It moves to state *TSSUBIAC* when it receives character *TCIAC*, and moves out of subnegotiation altogether if character *TCSE* follows immediately. If any other 2-character sequence occurs, the FSM remains in state *TSSUBNEG*.

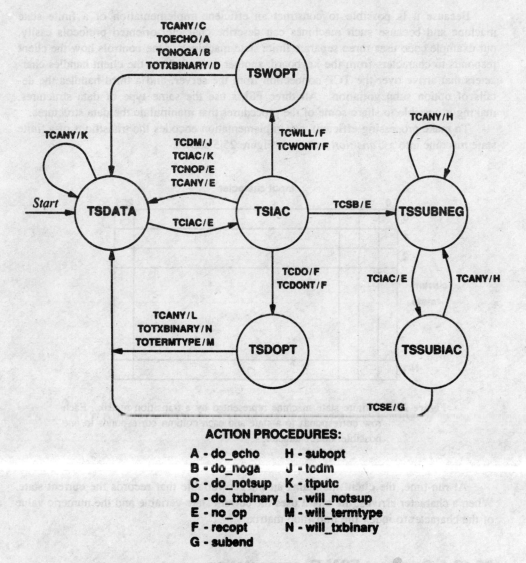

ACTION PROCEDURES:

A - do_echo   H - subopt
B - do_noga   J - tcdm
C - do_notsup   K - ttputc
D - do_txbinary   L - will_notsup
E - no_op   M - will_termtype
F - recopt   N - will_txbinary
G - subend

Figure 25.4 The finite state machine that describes how TELNET encodes
command sequences along with data. State and character names
have been taken directly from the software. *TCANY* stands for
"any character other than those shown explicitly."

25.16 A Finite State Machine Implementation

Because it is possible to construct an efficient implementation of a finite state machine and because such machines can describe character-oriented protocols easily, our example code uses three separate finite state machines. One controls how the client responds to characters from the keyboard, another controls how the client handles characters that arrive over the TCP connection from the server, and a third handles the details of option subnegotiation. All three FSMs use the same type of data structures, making it possible to share some of the procedures that manipulate the data structures.

To make processing efficient, our implementation encodes the transitions of a finite state machine into a *transition matrix* as Figure 25.5 shows.

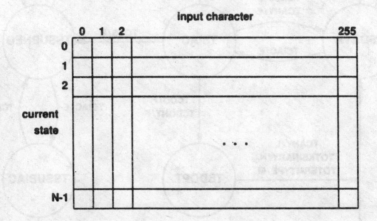

Figure 25.5 A finite state machine represented by a transition matrix. Each row corresponds to a state and each column corresponds to one possible input character.

At run-time, the client maintains an integer variable that records the current state. When a character arrives, the client uses the current state variable and the numeric value of the character to index the transition matrix.

25.17 A Compact FSM Representation

Writing C code to initialize a large matrix can be tedious. Furthermore, if each element of the transition matrix contains complete information about the action to take and the next state, the matrix can consume a large amount of memory. To keep the transition matrix small and to make initialization easy, our code uses a compact representation of a finite state machine.

In essence, the data structures chosen permit a programmer to create a compact data structure that represents a finite state machine and then arrange for the program to construct an associated transition matrix at run-time. File *tnfsm.h* contains the declaration of structure *fsm_trans* used in the compact representation:

```c
/* tnfsm.h */

/* Telnet Socket-Input FSM States: */
#define TSDATA          0       /* normal data processing             */
#define TSIAC           1       /* have seen IAC                      */
#define TSWOPT          2       /* have seen IAC-{WILL/WONT}           */
#define TSDOPT          3       /* have seen IAC-{DO/DONT}             */
#define TSSUBNEG        4       /* have seen IAC-SB                    */
#define TSSUBIAC        5       /* have seen IAC-SB-...-IAC            */

#define NTSTATES        6       /* # of TS* states                    */


/* Telnet Keyboard-Input FSM States: */
#define KSREMOTE        0       /* input goes to the socket           */
#define KSLOCAL         1       /* input goes to a local func.        */
#define KSCOLLECT       2       /* input is scripting-file name        */

#define NKSTATES        3       /* # of KS* states                    */


/* Telnet Option Subnegotiation FSM States: */
#define SS_START        0       /* initial state                      */
#define SS_TERMTYPE     1       /* TERMINAL_TYPE option subnegotiation */
#define SS_END          2       /* state after all legal input        */

#define NSSTATES        3       /* # of SS_* states                   */


#define FSINVALID       0xff    /* an invalid state number            */


#define NCHRS           256                 /* number of valid characters */
#define TCANY           (NCHRS+1)           /* match any character         */

struct fsm_trans {
        u_char  ft_state;               /* current state              */
        short   ft_char;                /* input character            */
        u_char  ft_next;                /* next state                 */
        int     (*ft_action)();         /* action to take             */
};
```

A compact FSM representation consists of a 1-dimensional array of *fsm_trans* structures. Each element specifies one transition. Field *ft_state* specifies the FSM state from which the transition begins. Field *ft_char* specifies the character that causes the transition (or *TC_ANY* to denote all characters other than those with explicit transitions). Field *ft_next* specifies the state in which the transition terminates, and field *ft_action* gives the address of the procedure to call that performs the action associated with the transition.

25.18 Keeping The Compact Representation At Run-Time

The example client does not copy all the information from the compact representation into the transition matrix. Instead, it leaves the compact representation unchanged and uses it to hold transition information. To do so, the software stores an integer in each element of the transition matrix. The integer gives the index of an entry in the compact representation that corresponds to the transition. Figure 25.6 illustrates the data structures:

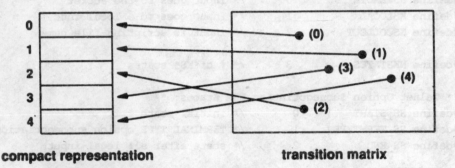

compact representation   **transition matrix**

Figure 25.6 The FSM data structures at run-time. Entries in the transition matrix contain an index that refers to an element of the compact representation.

25.19 Implementation Of A Compact Representation

File *ttfsm.c* contains an example compact FSM representation for the principle FSM shown in Figure 25.4:

```c
/* ttfsm.c */

#include <sys/types.h>
#include <stdio.h>
#include "telnet.h"
#include "tnfsm.h"
#include "local.h"

extern int do_echo(), do_noga(), do_notsup(), do_status(), no_op(),
        recopt(), subend(), subopt(), tcdm(), ttputc(), will_notsup(),
        will_termtype(), will_txbinary(), abort();

struct fsm_trans ttstab[] = {
        /* State          Input              Next State        Action  */
        /* ------         ------             -----------       -------  */
        { TSDATA,         TCIAC,             TSIAC,            no_op         },
        { TSDATA,         TCANY,             TSDATA,           ttputc        },
        { TSIAC,          TCIAC,             TSDATA,           ttputc        },
        { TSIAC,          TCSB,              TSSUBNEG,         no_op         },
/* Telnet Commands */
        { TSIAC,          TCNOP,             TSDATA,           no_op         },
        { TSIAC,          TCDM,              TSDATA,           tcdm          },
/* Option Negotiation */
        { TSIAC,          TCWILL,            TSWOPT,           recopt        },
        { TSIAC,          TCWONT,            TSWOPT,           recopt        },
        { TSIAC,          TCDO,              TSDOPT,           recopt        },
        { TSIAC,          TCDONT,            TSDOPT,           recopt        },
        { TSIAC,          TCANY,             TSDATA,           no_op         },
/* Option Subnegotion */
        { TSSUBNEG,       TCIAC,             TSSUBIAC,         no_op         },
        { TSSUBNEG,       TCANY,             TSSUBNEG,         subopt        },
        { TSSUBIAC,       TCSE,              TSDATA,           subend        },
        { TSSUBIAC,       TCANY,             TSSUBNEG,         subopt        },

        { TSWOPT,         TOECHO,            TSDATA,           do_echo       },
        { TSWOPT,         TONOGA,            TSDATA,           do_noga       },
        { TSWOPT,         TOTXBINARY,        TSDATA,           do_txbinary   },
        { TSWOPT,         TCANY,             TSDATA,           do_notsup     },

        { TSDOPT,         TOTERMTYPE,        TSDATA,           will_termtype },
        { TSDOPT,         TOTXBINARY,        TSDATA,           will_txbinary },
        { TSDOPT,         TCANY,             TSDATA,           will_notsup   },

        { FSINVALID,      TCANY,             FSINVALID,        abort         },
};
```

```
#define NTRANS (sizeof(ttstab)/sizeof(ttstab[0]))

int     ttstate;
u_char  ttfsm[NTSTATES][NCHRS];
```

Array *ttstab* contains 22 valid entries that each correspond to one of the transitions shown in Figure 25.4 (plus an extra entry to mark the end of the array). Each entry in the array consists of an *fsm_trans* structure that specifies a single transition. Note that *ttstab* is both compact and easy to define. It is compact because it does not contain any empty entries; it is easy to define because each entry corresponds directly to one of the transitions in the FSM.

25.20 Building An FSM Transition Matrix

The utility of the compact representation will become clear once we see how it can be used to generate a transition matrix. File *fsminit.c* contains the code:

```
/* fsminit.c - fsminit */

#include <sys/types.h>

#include "tnfsm.h"

#define TINVALID       0xff    /* an invalid transition index           */

/*------------------------------------------------------------------------
 * fsminit - Finite State Machine initializer
 *------------------------------------------------------------------------
 */
int
fsminit(fsm, ttab, nstates)
u_char              fsm[][NCHRS];
struct fsm_trans    ttab[];
int                 nstates;
{
        struct fsm_trans    *pt;
        int                 sn, ti, cn;

        for (cn=0; cn<NCHRS; ++cn)
                for (ti=0; ti<nstates; ++ti)
                        fsm[ti][cn] = TINVALID;
```

```
for (ti=0; ttab[ti].ft_state != FSINVALID; ++ti) {
        pt = &ttab[ti];
        sn = pt->ft_state;
        if (pt->ft_char == TCANY) {
                for (cn=0; cn<NCHRS; ++cn)
                        if (fsm[sn][cn] == TINVALID)
                                fsm[sn][cn] = ti;
        } else
                fsm[sn][pt->ft_char] = ti;
}
/* set all uninitialized indices to an invalid transition          */
for (cn=0; cn<NCHRS; ++cn)
        for (ti=0; ti<nstates; ++ti)
                if (fsm[ti][cn] == TINVALID)
                        fsm[ti][cn] = ti;
}
```

Procedure *fsminit* requires three arguments. Argument *fsm* specifies a transition matrix that must be initialized. Argument *ttab* gives the address of a compact FSM representation, and argument *nstates* specifies the number of states in the resulting FSM.

Fsminit first initializes the entire transition matrix to *TINVALID*. It then iterates through each element of the compact representation and adds the state transition specified by that element to the transition matrix. Finally, it iterates through the transition matrix again and changes any transitions that have not been filled in so they point to the invalid transition at the end of the compact representation.

Most of the code in *fsminit* is straightforward. When adding transitions, however, *fsminit* must distinguish between an explicit transition and an abbreviation. To understand the code, recall that the compact representation uses character *TCANY* to denote all characters that have not been specified explicitly. Thus, when *fsminit* examines an individual transition, it checks the character that causes the transition. If the entry specifies character *TCANY*, *fsminit* iterates through all possible characters and adds the transition to any character that has not been initialized. If the entry specifies any character other than *TCANY*, *fsminit* fills in the transition array for that single character.

25.21 The Socket Output Finite State Machine

The finite state machine shown in Figure 25.4 defines the actions the client takes for each character that arrives from the server. A separate, and simpler, finite state machine describes how the client handles characters that arrive from the keyboard. We call the FSM associated with keyboard input the *socket output FSM*. The name may seem unusual. Figure 25.7 shows how the client software organization supports such a name.

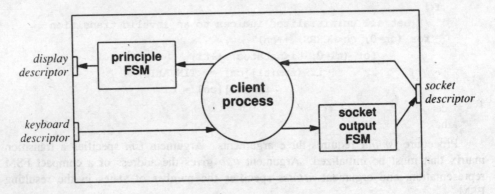

Figure 25.7 The client software organization. The central process reads data from either the socket or the keyboard and calls an FSM procedure to process it. The FSM that processes keyboard data is associated with socket output.

Figure 25.8 shows the socket output finite state machine:

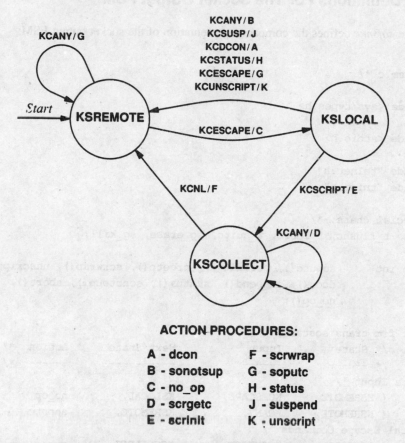

Figure 25.8 The socket output FSM used to define actions taken for each character the user types. The client sends most data characters to the remote server. However, the design permits the user to *escape* from the data connection and communicate with the local client program.

The socket output FSM begins in state *KSREMOTE*, which causes the client to send each character from the keyboard to the remote server. When the user types the *keyboard escape* key, the client enters state *KSLOCAL* where it waits for a keystroke. Most keystrokes that can follow the escape have no meaning, but a few cause the client to take action and return to state *KSREMOTE*. Only one, *KCSCRIPT*, causes the client to enter state *KSCOLLECT*, where it collects a file name to use for scripting.

25.22 Definitions For The Socket Output FSM

File *sofsm.c* defines the compact representation of the socket output FSM:

```
/* sofsm.c */

#include <sys/types.h>

#include <stdio.h>

#include "telnet.h"
#include "tnfsm.h"

/* Special chars: */
char     t_flushc, t_intrc, t_quitc, sg_erase, sg_kill;

extern int      soputc(), scrinit(), scrgetc(), scrwrap(), unscript(),
                dcon(), suspend(), status(), sonotsup(), abort(),
                no_op();

struct fsm_trans sostab[] = {
        /* State          Input            Next State        Action */·
        /* ------          ------            -----------        ------- */
/* Data Input */
        { KSREMOTE,      KCESCAPE,        KSLOCAL,          no_op          },
        { KSREMOTE,      KCANY,           KSREMOTE,         soputc         },
/* Local Escape Commands */
        { KSLOCAL,       KCSCRIPT,        KSCOLLECT,        scrinit        },
        { KSLOCAL,       KCUNSCRIPT,      KSREMOTE,         unscript       },
        { KSLOCAL,       KCESCAPE,        KSREMOTE,         soputc         },
        { KSLOCAL,       KCDCON,          KSREMOTE,         dcon           },
        { KSLOCAL,       KCSUSP,          KSREMOTE,         suspend        },
        { KSLOCAL,       KCSTATUS,        KSREMOTE,         status         },
        { KSLOCAL,       KCANY,           KSREMOTE,         sonotsup       },
/* Script Filename Gathering */
        { KSCOLLECT,     KCNL,            KSREMOTE,         scrwrap        },
        { KSCOLLECT,     KCANY,           KSCOLLECT,        scrgetc        },

        { FSINVALID,     KCANY,           FSINVALID,        abort          },
};

#define NTRANS   (sizeof(sostab)/sizeof(sostab[0]))

int      sostate;
u_char   sofsm[NKSTATES][NCHRS];
```

Array *sostab* contains the compact representation, and variable *sostate* contains an integer that gives the current state of the socket output FSM.

25.23 The Option Subnegotiation Finite State Machine

Figure 25.9 illustrates the third FSM used in the client. It handles the sequence of characters that arrive during *option subnegotiation*. Because it only recognizes one possible option subnegotiation (terminal type), the FSM only needs three states.

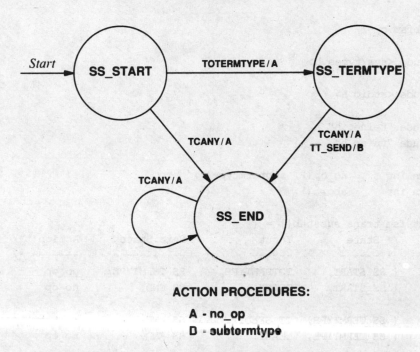

ACTION PROCEDURES:

A - no_op

D - subtermtype

Figure 25.9 The simple FSM used for option subnegotiation. The client reinitializes this machine each time it finishes an option subnegotiation.

The easiest way to think about subnegotiation is to imagine that it describes the interior structure of state *TSSUBNEG* in the principle FSM. While the main FSM operates in state *TSSUBNEG*, it calls procedure *subopt* to handle each incoming character. *Subopt* operates the subnegotiation FSM. As Figure 25.9 shows, the subnegotiation FSM makes an immediate decision that depends on the option. If it finds a terminal type subnegotiation, the machine moves to state *SS_TERMTYPE*. Otherwise, it moves directly to state *SS_END* and ignores the remainder of the subnegotiation string.

Once in state *SS_TERMTYPE*, the FSM checks the subnegotiation verb. It calls *subtermtype* if the verb is *TT_SEND*, and ignores the subnegotiation otherwise. The purpose and operation of the subnegotiation FSM will become clearer when we see how a client responds to the terminal type option.

25.24 Definitions For The Option Subnegotiation FSM

File *subfsm.c* contains the C declarations for the subnegotiation FSM:

```
/* subfsm.c */

#include <sys/types.h>

#include <stdio.h>

#include "telnet.h"
#include "tnfsm.h"

extern int      no_op(), subtermtype();
extern int      abort();

struct fsm_trans substab[] = {
        /* State         Input           Next State        Action */
        /* ------        ------          -----------       ------- */
        { SS_START,      TOTERMTYPE,     SS_TERMTYPE,      no_op        },
        { SS_START,      TCANY,          SS_END,           no_op        },

        { SS_TERMTYPE,   TT_SEND,        SS_END,           subtermtype  },
        { SS_TERMTYPE,   TCANY,          SS_END,           no_op        },

        { SS_END,        TCANY,          SS_END,           no_op        },
        { FSINVALID,     TCANY,          FSINVALID,        abort        },
};

int     substate;
u_char  subfsm[NSSTATES][NCHRS];
```

25.25 FSM Initialization

At startup, the client calls procedure *fsmbuild* to initialize all finite state machines. As the code in file *ttinit.c* shows, *fsmbuild* calls *fsminit* to build the required data structure for each machine, and assigns each machine's state variable an initial state.

```
/* ttinit.c - ttinit */


#include <sys/types.h>

#include <stdio.h>

#include "tnfsm.h"

extern struct fsm_trans ttstab[], sostab[], substab[];
extern u_char           ttfsm[][NCHRS], sofsm[][NCHRS], subfsm[][NCHRS];
extern int              ttstate, sostate, substate;

/*------------------------------------------------------------------------
 * fsmbuild - build the Finite State Machine data structures
 *------------------------------------------------------------------------
 */
int
fsmbuild()
{
        fsminit(ttfsm, ttstab, NTSTATES);
        ttstate = TSDATA;

        fsminit(sofsm, sostab, NKSTATES);
        sostate = KSREMOTE;

        fsminit(subfsm, substab, NSSTATES);
        substate = SS_START;
}
```

25.26 Arguments For The TELNET Client

File *tclient.c* contains the code for the main program that executes when a user invokes the client:

```
/* tclient.c - main */

char    *host = "localhost";    /* host to use if none supplied        */

/*------------------------------------------------------------------------
 * main - TCP client for TELNET service
 *------------------------------------------------------------------------
 */
int
main(argc, argv)
int     argc;
char    *argv[];
{
        char    *service = "telnet";    /* default service name        */

        switch (argc) {
        case 1: break;
        case 3:
                service = argv[2];
                /* FALL THROUGH */
        case 2:
                host = argv[1];
                break;
        default:
                errexit("usage: telnet [host [port]]\n");
        }
        telnet(host, service);
        exit(0);
}
```

The user can supply zero, one, or two command-line arguments that the program parses. With no arguments, ($argc = 1$), the client contacts a server on the local host and uses the *telnet* service. If one argument appears ($argc = 2$), the client takes the argument as the name of the remote host on which the server executes. Finally, if two arguments appear, the client takes the second to be the name of a service on the remote machine and takes the first to be the name of a remote host. After it has parsed its arguments, the main program calls function *telnet*.

25.27 The Heart Of The TELNET Client

File *telnet.c* contains the code that implements Algorithm *8.1*†:

```
/* telnet.c - telnet */

#include <sys/types.h>
#include <sys/socket.h>
#include <sys/time.h>
#include <sys/signal.h>
#include <sys/errno.h>

#include <stdio.h>

#include "local.h"

int     rcvurg();

extern int      errno;
extern char     *sys_errlist[];

#define BUFSIZE         2048    /* read buffer size      */

struct ttystate oldtty;

/*------------------------------------------------------------------------
 * telnet - do the TELNET protocol to the given host and port
 *------------------------------------------------------------------------
 */
int
telnet(host, service)
char    *host;
char    *service;
{
        int     s, nfds;        /* socket and # file descriptors */
        u_char  buf[BUFSIZE];
        int     cc;
        int     on = 1;
        fd_set  arfds, awfds, rfds, wfds;
        FILE    *sfp;

        s = connectTCP(host, service);

        ttysetup();
```

---

†See page 103 for a description of Algorithm 8.1.

```
fsmbuild();        /* set up FSM's */

(void) signal(SIGURG, rcvurg);
(void) setsockopt(s, SOL_SOCKET, SO_OOBINLINE, (char *)&on,
                sizeof(on));

nfds = getdtablesize();
FD_ZERO(&arfds);
FD_ZERO(&awfds);
FD_SET(s, &arfds);        /* the socket                    */
FD_SET(0, &arfds);        /* standard input                */

sfp = fdopen(s, "w");    /* to get buffered output        */

while (1) {
        bcopy((char *)&arfds, (char *)&rfds, sizeof(rfds));
        bcopy((char *)&awfds, (char *)&wfds, sizeof(rfds));

        if (select(nfds, &rfds, &wfds, (fd_set *)0,
                        (struct timeval *)0) < 0) {
                if (errno == EINTR)
                        continue;        /* just a signal
                cerrexit("select: %s\n", sys_errlist[errno]);
        }
        if (FD_ISSET(s, &rfds)) {
                cc = read(s, (char *)buf, sizeof(buf));
                if (cc < 0)
                        cerrexit("socket read: %s\n",
                                        sys_errlist[errno]);
                else if (cc == 0) {
                        printf("\nconnection closed.\n");
                        ttyrestore(&oldtty);
                        exit(0);
                } else
                        ttwrite(sfp, stdout, buf, cc);
        }
        if (FD_ISSET(0, &rfds)) {
                cc = read(0, (char *)buf, sizeof(buf));
                if (cc < 0)
                        cerrexit("tty read: %s\n",
                                        sys_errlist[errno]);
                else if (cc == 0) {
```

```
                                  (void) shutdown(s, 1);
                        } else
                                  sowrite(sfp, stdout, buf, cc);
                }
                (void) fflush(sfp);
                (void) fflush(stdout);
        }
}
```

Procedure *telnet* requires two arguments that specify the name of a remote machine and a service on that machine. The code begins by calling *connectTCP* to allocate a socket and form a TCP connection to the server. It calls *ttysetup* to initialize the local terminal parameters and *fsmbuild* to initialize the three finite state machines. It then calls the system function *signal* to establish a handler for urgent data. If TCP receives urgent data from the server after the call to *signal*, the system will invoke procedure *rcvurg* to handle it.

File *sync.c* contains the code for procedures *tcdm* and *rcvurg*:

```
/* sync.c - tcdm, rcvurg */

#include <stdio.h>

char     synching;            /* non-zero, if we are doing telnet SYNCH      */

/*------------------------------------------------------------------------
 * tcdm - handle the telnet "DATA MARK" command (marks end of SYNCH)
 *------------------------------------------------------------------------
 */
/*ARGSUSED*/
int
tcdm(sfp, tfp, c)
FILE     *sfp, *tfp;
int      c;
{
        synching = 0;
        return 0;
}

/*------------------------------------------------------------------------
 * rcvurg - receive urgent data input (indicates a telnet SYNCH)
 *------------------------------------------------------------------------
 */
/*ARGSUSED*/
```

```
int
rcvurg()
{
        synching++;
}
```

The TELNET protocol specifies that when urgent data arrives, the client must *synchronize* with the server. To synchronize, the client skips forward in the stream of data arriving from the server until it encounters the *DATA MARK* character. Thus, when an urgent data signal occurs, *rcvurg* merely increments global variable *synching* to place the client in synchronizing mode. While *synching* is set, the FSM action procedures discard incoming data without displaying it on the user's terminal. Later, when a *DATA MARK* character arrives, the client calls procedure *tcdm*, to set global variable *synching* back to zero and return the client to normal processing.

Once it finishes initialization, the client enters an infinite loop. At each iteration of the loop, it uses *select* to wait for I/O from the socket or from the keyboard (i.e., standard input associated with descriptor *0*). The *select* call will return value *EINTR* if the program receives a UNIX signal while the process is blocked. If that happens, the client continues with the next iteration of the loop. If the *select* call returns any other error code, the client prints a message to the user and exits.

If *select* returns normally, data can be available at the keyboard, at the socket, or at both. *Telnet* first checks the socket to see if data has arrived from the server. If so, it calls *read* to extract the data and *ttwrite* to write the data to the user's display. We will see below that *ttwrite* implements the principle finite state machine that interprets the incoming data stream and handles escapes and embedded command sequences.

After *telnet* checks for incoming data at the socket, it examines the descriptor for the keyboard. If data has arrived from the keyboard, *telnet* calls *read* to extract the data and *sowrite* to write it to the socket. *Sowrite* contains the code that executes the finite state machine for local escape processing. As a special case, the client interprets *end-of-file* to be a request to terminate the connection. If it receives an end-of-file (i.e., *read* returns *0*), *telnet* calls *shutdown* to send an end-of-file condition to the server. In any case, *telnet* calls *fflush* at each iteration to ensure that the output routines do not buffer the data that has been written. *Fflush* forces a call to the *write* system procedure.

25.28 Implementation Of The Main FSM

Procedure *ttwrite* implements the FSM from Figure 25.4 that interprets data as it arrives from the server. The code appears in file *ttwrite.c*:

```
/* ttwrite.c - ttwrite */

#include <sys/types.h>

#include <stdio.h>

#include "tnfsm.h"

extern struct fsm_trans ttstab[];
extern u_char           ttfsm[][NCHRS];
extern int              ttstate;


/*-------------------------------------------------------------------------
 * ttwrite - do output processing for (local) network virtual printer
 *-------------------------------------------------------------------------
 */
int
ttwrite(sfp, tfp, buf, cc)
FILE    *sfp, *tfp;      /* socket and terminal FILE ptrs*/
u_char  *buf;           /* buffer of data to send       */
int     cc;             /* # characters in buf          */
{
        struct fsm_trans        *pt;
        int                     i, ti;

        for (i=0; i<cc; ++i) {
                int     c = buf[i];

                ti = ttfsm[ttstate][c];
                pt = &ttstab[ti];

                (pt->ft_action)(sfp, tfp, c);
                ttstate = pt->ft_next;
        }
}
```

Ttwrite extracts *cc* characters from buffer *buf* one at a time. Each time it extracts a character, *ttwrite* uses the character and the current state (variable *ttstate*) to index the transition matrix. The transition matrix returns *ti*, the index of a transition in the compact representation (*ttstab*). *Ttwrite* calls the procedure associated with the transition (field *ft_action*), and sets the current state variable to the appropriate next state (field *ft_next*).

25.29 Summary

TELNET ranks among the most popular application protocols in the TCP/IP suite. The protocol provides for interactive character transport between a client and server. Usually, the client connects a user's terminal to a server across a TCP connection. Our example client software consists of a single process that uses the UNIX system function *select* to achieve concurrent transfer.

TELNET uses escape sequences to embed commands and control information in the data stream. To simplify the code, our example client implementation uses three finite state machines to interpret character sequences. One handles data that arrives from the server, another handles data that arrives from the user's keyboard, and a third handles option subnegotiation.

The example code in this chapter illustrates the implementation of the central client process as well as the data structures used to implement the finite state machines. The next chapter considers the details of the procedures that perform actions associated with transitions in the finite state machines.

FOR FURTHER STUDY

Postel [RFC 854] contains the standard for the basic TELNET protocol, including the network virtual terminal encoding. Postel and Reynolds [RFC 855] specifies the details of option negotiation and option subnegotiation. Details on individual options can be found in other RFCs. VanBokkelen [RFC 1091] specifies the terminal-type option. Postel and Reynolds [RFC 857] describes the echo option, while Postel and Reynolds [RFC 856] describes the binary transmission option.

Stevens [1990] describes UNIX's *rlogin* protocol, an alternative to TELNET, and shows an example of a simple client and server. Leffler *et. al.* [1989] discusses more about the details of UNIX terminal I/O.

EXERCISES

25.1 Compare a multi-process TELNET client to the design presented in this chapter. What are the advantages and disadvantages of each?

25.2 Read the *UNIX Programmer's Manual* to find out about UNIX terminal devices and device drivers. What are *cooked mode*, *cbreak mode*, and *raw mode*?

25.3 Write a program that disables *character echo* on the user's terminal. What happens to the echo parameter after the program exits?

25.4 Read the system documentation to find out about the UNIX command *stty*. What happens if one redirects the output from *stty* to a file? Why?

25.5   How does the code in *suspend.c* suspend the client process?

25.6   Rewrite the principle FSM to include states for option subnegotiation.

25.7   The example FSM implementation uses a compact representation to save space. Estimate the space required for the principle FSM using a conventional representation, and compare the estimate to the space required for the compact representation.

25.8   Under what conditions will *read* from a terminal return the value *0*?

25.9   Read the TELNET protocol specification to find the exact rules for synchronization. When does the sender transmit *urgent data*? Why is *synching* necessary?

25.10   A server can choose to send more data after the client sends an end-of-file. How does the client know when to terminate the connection to the server?

25.11   Rewrite *ttwrite* so it does not use an FSM. What are the advantages and disadvantages of each implementation?

25.12   In the example client, what happens if a *SYNCH* signal occurs while processing another *SYNCH*? Does this agree with the protocol specification?

26

A TELNET Client
(Implementation Details)

26.1 Introduction

The previous chapter discusses the structure of a TELNET client and shows how it uses finite state machines to control processing. This chapter concludes the discussion by showing how semantic action procedures implement the details of character processing.

26.2 The FSM Action Procedures

Finite state machines implement most of the TELNET protocol details. They control processing, coordinate responses with requests, and map incoming command sequences to actions. Each time the client follows a transition in a finite state machine, it calls a procedure to perform the actions associated with the transition. Figure 25.4† shows the procedure names associated with transitions in the FSM that handles characters arriving from the server.

An action may be simple (e.g., discard the incoming character), or it may be complex (e.g., respond by sending a string that identifies the local terminal). Encapsulating each action in a procedure helps keep the machine specifications uniform and simplifies the code at the top level. However, dividing the software into a set of procedures for each action means that the relationship between procedures can only be understood by referring to the finite state machine that interconnects them.

---

†The figure appears on page 371.

The following sections each describe one of the action procedures associated with an FSM transition.

26.3 Recording The Type Of An Option Request

In state *TSIAC* (i.e., following the arrival of a *TCIAC* character), the arrival of *TCWILL* or *TCWONT* causes a transition to state *TSWOPT*. The FSM specifies that procedure *recopt* should be called. *Recopt* records the character that caused the transition so it can be used later. Similarly, the FSM uses *recopt* to record character *TCDO* or *TCDONT* during a transition to state *TSDOPT*. File *recopt.c* contains the code:

```
/* recopt.c - recopt, no_op */

#include <sys/types.h>

#include <stdio.h>

u_char  option_cmd;       /* has value WILL, WONT, DO, or DONT          */

/*------------------------------------------------------------------------
 * recopt - record option type
 *------------------------------------------------------------------------
 */
/*ARGSUSED*/
int
recopt(sfp, tfp, c)
FILE    *sfp, *tfp;
int     c;
{
        option_cmd = c;
        return 0;
}

/*------------------------------------------------------------------------
 * no_op - do nothing
 *------------------------------------------------------------------------
 */
/*ARGSUSED*/
int
no_op(sfp, tfp, c)
FILE    *sfp, *tfp;
        c;
```

```
                return 0;
}
```

26.4 Performing No Operation

File *recopt.c* also contains code for procedure *no_op*. Because the FSM must have an action for all possible combinations of a state and an input character, procedure *no_op* can be used for those transitions that do not require any action. For example, a transition from state *TSDATA* to *TSIAC* does not require any action. Therefore, the FSM specifies a call to *no_op*.

26.5 Responding To WILL/WONT For The Echo Option

The server sends *WILL* or *WONT* followed by the *ECHO* option to inform the client that it is willing to echo characters or is willing to stop echoing characters. The FSM specifies that procedure *do_echo* should be called when such a message arrives.

```
/* do_echo.c - do_echo */

#include <sys/types.h>
#include <sys/ioctl.h>

#include <stdio.h>

#include "telnet.h"

char            doecho;                 /* nonzero, if remote ECHO      */
extern u_char   option_cmd;

/*------------------------------------------------------------------
 * do_echo - handle telnet will/won't ECHO option
 *------------------------------------------------------------------
 */
int
do_echo(sfp, tfp, c)
FILE    *sfp, *tfp;
int     c;
{
        struct sgttyb   ttyb;
        int             ok, tfd = fileno(tfp);

        if (doecho) {
```

```
                    if (option_cmd == TCWILL)
                            return 0;           /* already doing ECHO           */
        } else if (option_cmd == TCWONT)
                    return 0;                   /* already NOT doing ECHO       */

        if (ok = ioctl(tfd, TIOCGETP, (char *)&ttyb) == 0) {
                if (option_cmd == TCWILL) {
                        ttyb.sg_flags &= ~ECHO;
                        ttyb.sg_flags |= CBREAK;
                } else {
                        ttyb.sg_flags |= ECHO;
                        ttyb.sg_flags &= ~CBREAK;
                }
                ok &= ioctl(tfd, TIOCSETP, (char *)&ttyb) == 0;
        }
        if (ok)
                doecho = !doecho;
        (void) putc(TCIAC, sfp);
        if (doecho)
                (void) putc(TCDO, sfp);
        else
                (void) putc(TCDONT, sfp);
        (void) putc((char)c, sfp);
        return 0;
}
```

The TELNET protocol specifies that the server can send a *WILL* or *WONT* to advertise its willingness to perform a given option or it can send such a message in response to a client request. Therefore, if the client has sent a request containing a *DO* or *DONT*, the message from the server constitutes a reply; otherwise, it constitutes an advertisement.

The client uses its current condition to decide how to respond. Global variable *doecho* contains a nonzero value if the client currently expects the server to perform character echo. If the server sends *WILL* and the client already has remote echo enabled, the client does not reply. Similarly if the server sends *WONT* and the client has remote echo disabled, the client does not reply. However, if the server sends *WILL* and the client currently has remote echoing turned off, the client uses *ioctl* to disable local character echoing. If the client has local echo disabled when a *WONT* arrives, the client assumes that the server has disabled the remote echo. Therefore, the client calls *ioctl* to enable local echoing. The client only sends a *DO* or *DONT* response if it changes the echo mode.

26.6 Responding To WILL/WONT For Unsupported Options

When the client receives a *WILL* or *WONT* request for an option that it does not understand, it calls procedure *do_notsup* to reply *DONT*.

```
/* do_notsup.c - do_notsup */

#include <sys/types.h>

#include <stdio.h>

#include "telnet.h"

extern u_char    option_cmd;

/*------------------------------------------------------------------
 * do_notsup - handle an unsupported telnet "will/won't" option
 *------------------------------------------------------------------
 */
/*ARGSUSED*/
int
do_notsup(sfp, tfp, c)
FILE    *sfp, *tfp;
int     c;
{
        (void) putc(TCIAC, sfp);
        (void) putc(TCDONT, sfp);
        (void) putc((char)c, sfp);
        return 0;
}
```

26.7 Responding To WILL/WONT For The No Go-Ahead Option

The client uses procedure *do_noga* to repond when the server sends *WILL* or *WONT* requests for the *no go-ahead option*.

```
/* do_noga.c - do_noga */

#include <sys/types.h>

#include <stdio.h>

#include "telnet.h"

extern u_char    option_cmd;

/*------------------------------------------------------------------
 * do_noga - don't do telnet Go-Ahead's
 *------------------------------------------------------------------
 */
/*ARGSUSED*/
int
do_noga(sfp, tfp, c)
FILE    *sfp, *tfp;
int     c;
{
        static  noga;

        if (noga) {
                if (option_cmd == TCWILL)
                        return 0;
        } else if (option_cmd == TCWONT)
                return 0;
        noga = !noga;
        (void) putc(TCIAC, sfp);
        if (noga)
                (void) putc(TCDO, sfp);
        else
                (void) putc(TCDONT, sfp);
        (void) putc((char)c, sfp);
        return 0;
}
```

As with other options, the client does not respond if the client's current setting for the option agrees with the server's request. If the server requests a change, the client reverses the current setting by negating global integer *noga* and sends either a *DO* or *DONT* response.

26.8 Generating DO/DONT For Binary Transmission

The server can send characters to the client either encoded, using the network virtual terminal encoding, or unencoded, using 8-bit binary values. Global variable *rcvbinary* controls whether the client expects to receive data as binary characters or NVT encodings. The client calls procedure *do_txbinary* to respond when the server sends a *WILL* or *WONT* for the binary option. Like the other procedures that handle options, *do_txbinary* has been designed so it can be called to request that the server send binary or to respond to an advertisement from the server. It uses the global variable *option_cmd* to decide how to proceed, and assumes that it contains an incoming request. Procedure *do_txbinary* tests to see whether the client expects the server to send binary, sets *rcvbinary* according to the incoming request, and responds to the server if *rcvbinary* changes.

```
/* do_txbinary.c - do_txbinary */

#include <sys/types.h>

#include <stdio.h>

#include "telnet.h"

char            rcvbinary;       /* non-zero if remote TRANSMIT-BINARY   */
extern u_char   option_cmd;

/*------------------------------------------------------------------------
 * do_txbinary - handle telnet "will/won't" TRANSMIT-BINARY option
 *------------------------------------------------------------------------
 */
/*ARGSUSED*/
int
do_txbinary(sfp, tfp, c)
FILE    *sfp, *tfp;
int     c;
{
        if (rcvbinary) {
                if (option_cmd == TCWILL)
                        return 0;
        } else if (option_cmd == TCWONT)
                return 0;
        rcvbinary = !rcvbinary;
        (void) putc(TCIAC, sfp);
        if (rcvbinary)
                (void) putc(TCDO, sfp);
```

```
                else
                        (void) putc(TCDONT, sfp);
        (void) putc((char)c, sfp);
        return 0;
}
```

26.9 Responding To DO/DONT For Unsupported Options

The server sends *DO* or *DONT* messages to tell the client that it should enable or
disable a specified option. The client responds by sending *WILL* if it agrees to honor
the option, or *WONT* if it does not honor the option. As the FSM in Figure 25.4 shows,
the client calls procedure *will_notsup* when it does not support a particular option.

```
/* will_notsup.c - will_notsup */

#include <sys/types.h>

#include <stdio.h>

#include "telnet.h"

/*------------------------------------------------------------------------
 * will_notsup - handle an unsupported telnet "do/don't" option
 *------------------------------------------------------------------------
 */
/*ARGSUSED*/
int
will_notsup(sfp, tfp, c)
FILE    *sfp, *tfp;
int     c;
{
        (void) putc(TCIAC, sfp);
        (void) putc(TCWONT, sfp);
        (void) putc((char)c, sfp);
        return 0;
}
```

Procedure *will_notsup* sends *WONT* to tell the server it does not support the option.

26.10 Responding To DO/DONT For Transmit Binary Option

When the client starts, it uses the network virtual terminal encoding for all data it sends to the server. Although NVT encoding includes most printable characters, it does not provide an encoding for all control characters. Servers operating on systems that support screen-oriented applications usually need the ability to transfer arbitrary character data. Therefore, such servers usually advertise their willingness to transmit binary data and request that the client also transmit binary data.

A server sends *DO* for the *transmit binary option* to request that the client begin using 8-bit, unencoded transmission. The client calls procedure *will_txbinary* when such a request arrives.

```
/* will_txbinary.c - will_txbinary */

#include <sys/types.h>

#include <stdio.h>

#include "telnet.h"

char            sndbinary;          /* non-zero if TRANSMIT-BINARY         */
extern u_char   option_cmd;

/*------------------------------------------------------------------------
 * will_txbinary - handle telnet "do/don't" TRANSMIT-BINARY option
 *------------------------------------------------------------------------
 */
/*ARGSUSED*/
int
will_txbinary(sfp, tfp, c)
FILE    *sfp, *tfp;
int     c;
{
        if (sndbinary) {
                if (option_cmd == TCDO)
                        return 0;
        } else if (option_cmd == TCDONT)
                return 0;
        sndbinary = !sndbinary;
        (void) putc(TCIAC, sfp);
        if (sndbinary)
                (void) putc(TCWILL, sfp);
        else
                (void) putc(TCWONT, sfp);
```

```
        (void) putc((char)c, sfp);
        return 0;
}
```

The client uses global variable *sndbinary* to control its transmission mode. If the request forces a change in the status, the client acknowledges the request by sending a *WILL* or *WONT*.

26.11 Responding To DO/DONT For The Terminal Type Option

Communicating the terminal type from client to server requires two steps. First, the server asks the client whether it honors the *termtype option*. Second, if the client agrees that it will honor the terminal type option, the server uses option subnegotiation to request a string that identifies the user's terminal type.

In UNIX, the client finds the user's terminal type by examining variable *TERM* in the process' *environment*. To do so, it calls the library function *getenv*, which finds the specified variable and returns a pointer to its string value.

When a request arrives for the terminal type option, the client calls procedure *will_termtype*. File *will_termtype.c* contains the code:

```
/* will_termtype.c - will_termtype */

#include <sys/types.h>

#include <stdio.h>

#include "telnet.h"

char    *getenv();

char            termtype;       /* non-zero if received "DO TERMTYPE"   */
char            *term;          /* terminal name                        */
extern u_char   option_cmd;

/*------------------------------------------------------------------------
 * will_termtype - handle telnet "do/don't" TERMINAL-TYPE option
 *------------------------------------------------------------------------
 */
int
will_termtype(sfp, tfp, c)
FILE    *sfp, *tfp;
int     c;
```

```
{
        if (termtype) {
                if (option_cmd == TCDO)
                        return 0;
        } else if (option_cmd == TCDONT)
                return 0;
        termtype = !termtype;
        if (termtype)
                if (!term && !(term = getenv("TERM")))
                        termtype = !termtype;   /* can't do it... */
        (void) putc(TCIAC, sfp);
        if (termtype)
                (void) putc(TCWILL, sfp);
        else
                (void) putc(TCWONT, sfp);
        (void) putc((char)c, sfp);
        if (termtype) { /* set up binary data path; send WILL, DO */
                option_cmd = TCWILL;
                (void) do_txbinary(sfp, tfp, TOTXBINARY);
                option_cmd = TCDO;
                (void) will_txbinary(sfp, tfp, TOTXBINARY);
        }
        return 0;
}
```

Procedure *will_termtype* behaves much like other option handlers. It uses global variable *termtype* to record whether the server has requested the terminal type option previously, and checks to see if the current request changes the status. If so, it calls *getenv* to obtain the value associated with environment variable *TERM*. If no such variable exists, the client responds that it will not honor the request.

A server requests terminal type information so applications can prepare output specifically for the user's terminal. For example, a text editor uses the terminal type when it generates the sequence of characters that clears the screen, moves the cursor, or highlights text. Thus, the client expects that once the remote application receives terminal type information it will send control sequences for the terminal. Because such sequences cannot be sent using the NVT encoding, *will_termtype* sends a *WILL* message that advertises the client's willingness to use binary transmission and a *DO* message that requests the server use binary transmission. Because functions *do_txbinary* and *will_txbinary* can be called from the FSM option processing code, they use global variable *option_cmd* to control processing. When calling the functions directly, other procedures must initialize *option_cmd* explicitly as if the client had received the appropriate *WILL* or *DO* message from the server before the call.

26.12 Option Subnegotiation

Once a client agrees to handle the terminal type option, a server uses option subnegotiation to request the terminal name. Unlike normal options which all have a fixed length, subnegotiation permits the sender to insert an arbitrary-length string in the data stream. To do so, the sender brackets the string by sending a subnegotiation header, the data for that particular option subnegotiation, and a trailer that identifies the end of the subnegotiation.

When the main FSM (Figure 25.4) encounters a subnegotiation command sequence, it enters state *TSSUBNEG*. Once in state *TSSUBNEG*, the client calls procedure *subopt* each time it receives a character. As the code in file *subopt.c* shows, *subopt* runs the option subnegotiation FSM to handle subnegotiation.

```
/* subopt.c - subopt */

#include <sys/types.h>

#include <stdio.h>

#include "telnet.h"
#include "tnfsm.h"

extern struct fsm_trans    substab[];
extern int                 substate;
extern u_char              subfsm[][NCHRS];

/*------------------------------------------------------------------------
 * subopt - do option subnegotiation FSM transitions
 *------------------------------------------------------------------------
 */
int
subopt(sfp, tfp, c)
FILE    *sfp, *tfp;
int     c;
{
        struct  fsm_trans       *pt;
        int                     ti;

        ti = subfsm[substate][c];
        pt = &substab[ti];
        (pt->ft_action)(sfp, tfp, c);
        substate = pt->ft_next;
        return 0;
}
```

26.13 Sending Terminal Type Information

The option subnegotiation FSM† calls procedure *subtermtype* to reply to a request for a terminal type. The server sends the sequence:

IAC SUBNEG TERMTYPE SEND IAC SUBEND

to request a terminal type. The client replies by sending:

IAC SUBNEG TERMTYPE IS term_type_string IAC SUBEND

File *subtermtype.c* contains the code:

```
/* subtermtype.c - subtermtype */

#include <sys/types.h>

#include <stdio.h>

#include "telnet.h"

extern char     *term;              /* terminal name, from initialization   */

/*------------------------------------------------------------------------
 * subtermtype - do terminal type option subnegotation
 *------------------------------------------------------------------------
 */
/*ARGSUSED*/
int
subtermtype(sfp, tfp, c)
FILE    *sfp, *tfp;
int     c;
{
        /* have received IAC.SB.TERMTYPE.SEND */

        (void) putc(TCIAC, sfp);
        (void) putc(TCSB, sfp);
        (void) putc(TOTERMTYPE, sfp);
        (void) putc(TT_IS, sfp);
        fputs(term, sfp);
        (void) putc(TCIAC, sfp);
        (void) putc(TCSE, sfp);
        return 0;
}
```

---

†See page 381 for a description of the option subnegotiation finite state machine.

The option subnegotiation FSM calls *subtermtype* after receiving the *SEND* request. Previously, the client must have replied positively to a request to honor the terminal type option, so global variable *term* must already point to a string that contains the terminal type. *Subtermtype* sends the reply by calling *putc* to send the individual control characters and *fputs* to send the string that contains the terminal type information.

26.14 Terminating Subnegotiation

When the principle FSM shown in Figure 25.4 encounters the end of option subnegotiation, it moves back to state *TSDATA*. Whenever it does so, it calls procedure *subend*. *Subend* simply resets the option subnegotiation FSM to its start state so it is ready to handle the next subnegotiation. File *subend.c* contains the code:

```
/* subend.c - subend */

#include <sys/types.h>

#include <stdio.h>

#include "tnfsm.h"

extern int              substate;

/*------------------------------------------------------------------------
 * subend - end of an option subnegotiation; reset FSM
 *------------------------------------------------------------------------
 */
/*ARGSUSED*/
int
subend(sfp, tfp, c)
FILE    *sfp, *tfp;
int     c;
{
        substate = SS_START;
        return 0;
}
```

26.15 Sending A Character To The Server

The client calls procedure *soputc* to convert an output character into the network virtual terminal encoding and send it through the TCP socket to the server. File *soputc.c* contains the code:

```
/* soputc.c - soputc */

#include <sys/types.h>

#include <stdio.h>

#include "telnet.h"
#include "local.h"


/*------------------------------------------------------------------
 * soputc - move a character from the keyboard to the socket
 *------------------------------------------------------------------
 */
/*ARGSUSED*/
int
soputc(sfp, tfp, c)
FILE    *sfp, *tfp;
int     c;
{
        if (sndbinary) {
                if (c == TCIAC)
                        (void) putc(TCIAC, sfp); /* byte-stuff IAC     */
                (void) putc(c, sfp);
                return 0;
        }
        c &= 0x7f;      /* 7-bit ASCII only */
        if (c == t_intrc || c == t_quitc) {       /* Interrupt         */
                (void) putc(TCIAC, sfp);
                (void) putc(TCIP, sfp);
        } else if (c == sg_erase) {               /* Erase Char        */
                (void) putc(TCIAC, sfp);
                (void) putc(TCEC, sfp);
        } else if (c == sg_kill) {                /* Erase Line        */
                (void) putc(TCIAC, sfp);
                (void) putc(TCEL, sfp);
        } else if (c == t_flushc) {               /* Abort Output      */
                (void) putc(TCIAC, sfp);
                (void) putc(TCAO, sfp);
```

```
        } else if (c >= ' ' && c < TCIAC)         /* printable ASCII only */
                (void) putc(c, sfp);
    else
                switch (c) {
                case VPLF:
                case VPCR:
                case VPBEL:
                case VPBS:
                case VPHT:
                case VPFF:
                        (void) putc(c, sfp);
                default:
                        break;   /* invalid character */
                }
        return 0;
}
```

When transmitting in binary mode, only the *IAC* character needs to be character stuffed. That is, *soputc* must replace each *IAC* character with two *IAC* characters. For any other character, *soputc* merely calls *putc* to send it.

When transmitting in normal mode, *soputc* must convert from the local character set to the network virtual terminal character set. For example, if the character that arrives corresponds to either the UNIX *interrupt* character or the UNIX *quit* character, *soputc* sends a 2-character sequence:

IAC IP

It checks explicitly for each of the special characters that NVT defines as well as for printable ASCII. *Soputc* must also handle characters for which no NVT encoding exists. Following the protocol specification, the code ignores such characters. The consequence should be clear: if the server does not request that the client use binary transmission, the client will discard most control characters that the user types.

26.16 Displaying Incoming Data On The User's Terminal

Data that arrives over the TCP connection from the server can either be unencoded (if the server has agreed to transmit binary) or it can consist of characters encoded according to the rules for an NVT. The client calls procedure *ttputc* to display an incoming character on the user's terminal.

```
/* ttputc.c - ttputc */

#include <sys/types.h>

#include <stdio.h>

#include "telnet.h"

/*------------------------------------------------------------------
 * ttputc - print a single character on a Network Virtual Terminal
 *------------------------------------------------------------------
 */
/*ARGSUSED*/
int
ttputc(sfp, tfp, c)
FILE    *sfp, *tfp;
int     c;
{
        static  last_char;
        int     tc;

        if (rcvbinary) {
                (void) xputc(c, tfp);   /* print uninterpretted */
                return;
        }
        if (synching)                   /* no data, if in SYNCH */
                return;

        if ((last_char == VPCR && c == VPLF) ||
            (last_char == VPLF && c == VPCR)) {
                (void) xputc(VPLF, tfp);
                last_char = 0;
                return;
        }
        if (last_char == VPCR)
                (void) tcout("cr", tfp);
        else if (last_char == VPLF)
                (void) tcout("do", tfp);
        if (c >= ' ' && c < TCIAC)      /* printable ASCII     */
                (void) xputc(c, tfp);
        else {                          /* NVT special         */
                switch (c) {
                case VPLF:              /* see if CR follows    */
                case VPCR:      tc = 1; /* see if LF follows    */
```

```
                                        break;
                case VPBEL:     tc = tcout("bl", tfp);
                                        break;
                case VPBS:      tc = tcout("bc", tfp);
                                        break;
                case VPHT:      tc = tcout("ta", tfp);
                                        break;
                case VPVT:      tc = tcout("do", tfp);
                                        break;
                case VPFF:      tc = tcout("cl", tfp);
                                        break;
                default:
                        tc = 1;
                        break;   /* no action */
                }
                if (!tc)                        /* if no termcap, assume ASCII */
                        (void) xputc(c, tfp);
        }
        last_char = c;
}
```

If the server has agreed to send binary data, *ttputc* calls *xputc* to display it. File *xput.c* contains the code:

```
/* xput.c - xputc, xfputs */

#include <stdio.h>

extern FILE     *scrfp;

/*------------------------------------------------------------------------
 * xputc - putc with optional file scripting
 *------------------------------------------------------------------------
 */
int
xputc(ch, fp)
char    ch;
FILE    *fp;
{
        if (scrfp)
                (void) putc(ch, scrfp);
        return putc(ch, fp);
}
```

```
/*------------------------------------------------------------------
 * xfputs - fputs with optional file scripting
 *------------------------------------------------------------------
 */
int
xfputs(str, fp)
char    *str;
FILE    *fp;
{
        if (scrfp)
                fputs(str, scrfp);
        fputs(str, fp);
}
```

Xputc differs from the conventional UNIX *putc* because the client provides a *scripting* facility. If scripting has been enabled, *xputc* writes a copy of the output character to both the terminal and to the script file. Otherwise, it only writes a copy to the terminal.

If the server is not sending binary data, *ttputc* must translate from the NVT encoding into an appropriate character sequence for the user's terminal. Two cases arise: the client can be in normal mode or in *synchronize mode*. The client enters synchronize mode when it receives a TELNET *SYNCH* command. While in synchronize mode, the client reads and discards all data. The client returns to normal mode when it encounters a TELNET *DATA MARK*.

The server sends the SYNCH command as *urgent data*. When urgent data arrives at the client, UNIX sends signal *SIGURG* to the client, causing the client to execute the signal handler, *rcvurg*. *Rcvurg* sets global variable *synching* to cause the client to enter synchronize mode and seek to the next *DATA MARK* character in the data stream. The client discards all input in synchronize mode and does not display it. Thus, *ttputc* checks variable *synching* and drops the output character if *synching* is nonzero.

Once it has checked for synchronize mode, *ttputc* must interpret the remaining characters using the NVT encoding. Because some NVT encodings consist of a 2-character sequence, *ttputc* keeps a copy of the previous character in global variable *last_char*.

First, *ttputc* handles *carriage return* (CR) and *linefeed* (LF). It recognizes either of the 2-character sequences CR-LF or LF-CR as an end-of-line, and translates them to the single character *LF* that UNIX uses. Of course, if either a carriage return or line feed character occurs alone, *ttputc* performs the action associated with that character. To do so, it invokes procedure *tcout*, specifying a cursor movement operation as the first argument. For example, if it encounters a linefeed, *ttputc* calls *tcout* with the string argument *do*, which stands for *down*.

Ttputc calls *xputc* to print any of the printable ASCII characters directly. Otherwise, it handles the special characters. For example, if the character to be displayed is an NVT *BEL* character (*VPBEL* in the code), *ttputc* calls *tcout* with the code *bl*.

26.17 Using Curses To Control The User's Terminal

Procedure *tcout* takes a standard *curses* terminal capability name and a terminal's output file pointer as arguments. It uses function *getenv* to extract the terminal type from environment variable *TERM*, and then calls procedure *tgetstr* to look up the needed sequence of characters that will achieve the specified effect on the user's terminal. Finally it calls *xfputs* to write the resulting character sequence to the terminal.

```
/* tcout.c - tcout */

#include <stdio.h>

char    *getenv(), *tgetstr();

#define TBUFSIZE        2048

/*------------------------------------------------------------------------
 * tcout - print the indicated terminal capability on the given stream
 *------------------------------------------------------------------------
 */
int
tcout(cap, tfp)
char    *cap;
FILE    *tfp;
{
        static init;
        static char     *term;
        static char     tbuf[TBUFSIZE], buf[TBUFSIZE], *bp = buf;
        char            *sv;

        if (!init) {
                init = 1;
                term = getenv("TERM");
        }
        if (term == 0 || tgetent(&tbuf[0], term) != 1)
                return 0;
        if (sv = tgetstr(cap, &bp)) {
                xfputs(sv, tfp);
                return 1;
        }
        return 0;
}
```

26.18 Writing A Block Of Data To The Server

Telnet calls procedure *sowrite* to write a block of data to the server.

```
/* sowrite.c - sowrite */

#include <sys/types.h>

#include <stdio.h>

#include "tnfsm.h"

extern struct fsm_trans sostab[];
extern int                   sostate;
extern u_char                sofsm[][NCHRS];

/*------------------------------------------------------------------
 * sowrite - do output processing to the socket
 *------------------------------------------------------------------
 */
int
sowrite(sfp, tfp, buf, cc)
FILE    *sfp, *tfp;      /* socket and terminal FILE ptrs*/
u_char  *buf;           /* buffer of data to send        */
int     cc;             /* # characters in buf           */
{
        struct fsm_trans        *pt;
        int                     i, ki;

        for (i=0; i<cc; ++i) {
                int     c = buf[i];

                ki = sofsm[sostate][c];
                pt = &sostab[ki];

                if ((pt->ft_action)(sfp, tfp, c) < 0)
                        sostate = KSREMOTE;      /* an error occurred     */
                else
                        sostate = pt->ft_next;
        }
```

Sowrite iterates through each character in the specified block and runs finite state machine *sofsm* to process each character.

26.19 Interacting With The Client Process

Like most TELNET client programs, our implementation permits the user to interact with the client process. To do so, a user types the *keyboard escape character* followed by a *command*. The table in Figure 26.1 lists the possible commands that can follow an escape character along with their meanings:

Symbolic Name	Character Typed	Meaning
KCSUSP	↑Z	Suspend the client process temporarily.
KCDCON		Terminate the TCP connection to the server.
KCSTSTUS	↑T	Print status information about the current connection.
KCESCAPE	↑]	Send the escape character to the server as data.
KCSCRIPT	s	Begin scripting to a specified file.
KCUNSCRIPT	u	Terminate scripting.

Figure 26.1 Keyboard input characters that the TELNET client interprets as commands when they follow *KCESCAPE*. The notation ↑X refers to the character generated by holding *CONTROL* and typing *X*.

File *telnet.h*† contains symbolic definitions for each of the keyboard command characters. For example, it defines the keyboard escape character, *KCESCAPE*, to be ↑] (i.e., the character with octal value 035).

When the client encounters the keyboard escape character, it changes the state of the socket output FSM from *KSREMOTE* to *KSLOCAL* and interprets the succeeding character as a command. Because most commands consist of a single character, the socket output FSM usually moves back to state *KSREMOTE* and executes an action procedure associated with the command. For example, if the FSM encounters character *KCDCON* following *KCESCAPE*, it calls procedure *dcon*.

---

†File *telnet.h* appears on page 368.

26.20 Responding To Illegal Commands

If the user types an unrecognized character following a keyboard escape, the socket output FSM calls action procedure *sonotsup* which prints an error message. File *sonotsup.c* contains the code:

```
/* sonotsup.c - sonotsup */

#include <stdio.h>

/*------------------------------------------------------------------------
 * sonotsup - an unsupported escape command
 *------------------------------------------------------------------------
 */
/*ARGSUSED*/
int
sonotsup(sfp, tfp, c)
FILE    *sfp, *tfp;
int     c;
{
        fprintf(tfp, "\nunsupported escape: %c.\n", c);
        fprintf(tfp, "s  - turn on scripting\t\t");
        fprintf(tfp, "u  - turn off scripting\n");
        fprintf(tfp, ".  - disconnect\t\t\t");
        fprintf(tfp, "^Z - suspend\n");
        fprintf(tfp, "^T - print status\n");
        return 0;
}
```

26.21 Scripting To A File

Our example TELNET client has one novel feature not found in most other clients: it permits the user to dynamically create a script file that contains a copy of all data being sent to the user's display. The idea underlying scripting is that a user may need to keep a record of all or part of a TELNET session.

Scripting is *dynamic* because the user can start or stop it at any time. Furthermore, the user can change the file into which the client writes the script. Thus, to capture the output of a single remote command, the user can log into the remote system with scripting disabled, then enable scripting and issue the command or commands for which the output must be kept, and finally, disable scripting. The script file will contain a copy of everything that the client displayed on the user's terminal while scripting was enabled.

26.22 Implementation Of Scripting

The socket output finite state machine illustrated in Figure 25.8 defines how the client handles scripting. If the user types ↑]s (i.e. character *KCESCAPE* followed by character *KCSCRIPT*), the socket output FSM calls action procedure *scrinit* and enters state *KSCOLLECT*. Until the user types an end-of-line character (i.e., *KCNL*), the FSM stays in state *KSCOLLECT* and calls procedure *scrgetc* to collect a string of characters that form the name of the script file. Once the user terminates the line of input, the FSM calls *scrwrap* to open the script file and move back to state *KSREMOTE*. The following sections each discuss one of the action procedures associated with scripting.

26.23 Initialization Of Scripting

When the socket output FSM first encounters a request to begin scripting, it calls action procedure *scrinit*.

```
/* scrinit.c - scrinit */

#include <stdio.h>

#include "telnet.h"
#include "local.h"


extern int              scrindex;
extern struct ttystate  tntty;

/*------------------------------------------------------------------------
 * scrinit - initialize tty modes for script file collection
 *------------------------------------------------------------------------
 */
/*ARGSUSED*/
int
scrinit(sfp, tfp, c)
FILE    *sfp, *tfp;
int     c;
{
        struct ttystate newtty;

        if (!doecho) {
                fprintf(tfp, "\nscripting requires remote ECHO.\n");
                return -1;
        }
        if (scrfp) {
```

```
                    fprintf(tfp,"\nalready scripting to \"%s\".\n", scrname);
                    return -1;
            }
            scrindex = 0;
            ttysave(&tntty);                        /* save current tty settings     */

            newtty = oldtty;
            newtty.ts_tchars.t_intrc = -1;          /* disable interrupt     */
            newtty.ts_tchars.t_quitc = -1;          /* disable interrupt     */
            newtty.ts_ltchars.t_suspc = -1;         /* disable suspend     */
            newtty.ts_ltchars.t_dsuspc = -1;        /* disable suspend     */
            ttyrestore(&newtty);

            fprintf(tfp, "\nscript file: ");
            (void) fflush(tfp);
            return 0;
    }
```

Scrinit first verifies that the client is using remote echo (i.e., that all characters being displayed are coming from the server and not from the UNIX device driver). It also
verifies that the user does not already have scripting enabled. *Scrinit* sets global variable *scrindex* to zero. Another procedure will use *scrindex* to count characters as it
reads the name of the script file. Finally, before it prints a prompt, *scrinit* changes the
mode of the user's terminal so the local terminal driver will print the characters of the
file name as the user types them.

26.24 Collecting Characters Of The Script File Name

The socket output FSM uses action procedure *scrgetc* to read a sequence of characters that will be used as the name of a script file. File *scrgetc.c* contains the code:

```
/* scrgetc.c - scrgetc */

#include <stdio.h>

#include "local.h"

#define SFBUFSZ          2048     /* script filename buffer size  */

struct ttystate tntty;
FILE            *scrfp;
char            scrname[SFBUFSZ];
int             scrindex;


/*------------------------------------------------------------------------
 * scrgetc - begin session scripting
 *------------------------------------------------------------------------
 */
/*ARGSUSED*/
int
scrgetc(sfp, tfp, c)
FILE    *sfp, *tfp;
int     c;
{
        scrname[scrindex++] = c;
        if (scrindex >= SFBUFSZ) {        /* too far */
                fprintf(tfp, "\nname too long\n");
                ttyrestore(&oldtty);
                return -1;
        }
        return 0;
}
```

Each time a character arrives, the client calls *scrgetc*, which appends the character to
string *scrname*.

26.25 Opening A Script File

When the client encounters an end-of-line, it calls procedure *scrwrap* to open the
script file.

```
/* scrwrap.c = scrwrap */

#include <sys/file.h>

#include <stdio.h>

#include "local.h"

extern struct ttystate   tntty;
extern char              scrname[], *sys_errlist[];
extern int               scrindex, errno;

/*------------------------------------------------------------------------
 * scrwrap - wrap-up script filename collection
 *------------------------------------------------------------------------
 */
/*ARGSUSED*/
int
scrwrap(sfp, tfp, c)
FILE    *sfp, *tfp;
int     c;
{
        int     fd;

        if (scrindex) {
                scrname[scrindex] = '\0';
                scrindex = 0;
                fd = open(scrname, O_WRONLY|O_CREAT|O_TRUNC, 0644);
                if (fd < 0)
                        fprintf(tfp, "\ncan't write \"%s\": %s\n",
                                scrname, sys_errlist[errno]);
                else
                        scrfp = fdopen(fd, "w");
        }
        ttyrestore(&tntty);
        return 0;
}
```

Scrwrap adds a null terminator to the string that has been collected, resets global variable *scrindex* so it can be used again, and calls *open* to open the script file. If it successfully obtains a new descriptor for the script file, *scrwrap* calls *fdopen* to create a standard I/O file pointer for the script file and places the pointer in global variable *scrfp*. Before it returns, *scrwrap* calls *ttyrestore* to reset the terminal modes to the value they had before *scrinit* changed them.

26.26 Terminating Scripting

When the user decides to disable scripting, the socket output FSM calls action procedure *unscript*.

```
/* unscript.c - unscript */

#include <sys/types.h>
#include <sys/stat.h>

#include <stdio.h>

#include "local.h"

/*------------------------------------------------------------------
 * unscript - end session scripting
 *------------------------------------------------------------------
 */
/*ARGSUSED*/
int
unscript(sfp, tfp, c)
FILE    *sfp, *tfp;
int     c;
{
        struct stat     statb;

        if (scrfp == 0) {
                fprintf(tfp, "\nNot scripting.\n");
                return 0;
        }
        (void) fflush(scrfp);
        if (fstat(fileno(scrfp), &statb) == 0)
                fprintf(tfp, "\n\"%s\": %d bytes.\n", scrname,
                                statb.st_size);
        (void) fclose(scrfp);
        scrfp = 0;
        return 0;
}
```

Unscript prints an informational message to tell the user that the client has stopped scripting, uses the UNIX system function *fstat* to obtain information about the resulting script file, and prints a message that gives the size of the script file. Finally, *unscript* closes the script file and clears the global file pointer, *scrfp*.

26.27 Printing Status Information

The user can obtain status information about the current connection by using the
KCSTATUS command following a keyboard escape. The socket output FSM calls action procedure status to print the connection status.

```
/* status.c - status */

#include <sys/types.h>
#include <sys/socket.h>
#include <netinet/in.h>

#include <stdio.h>

extern  char    doecho, sndbinary, rcvbinary;   /* telnet options */
extern  char    *host, scrname[];
extern  FILE    *scrfp;

u_short ntohs();

/*------------------------------------------------------------------------
 * status - print connection status information
 *------------------------------------------------------------------------
 */
/*ARGSUSED*/
int
status(sfp, tfp, c)
FILE    *sfp, *tfp;
int     c;
{
        struct  sockaddr_in     sin;
        int                     sinlen;

        fprintf(tfp, "\nconnected to \"%s\" ", host);

        sinlen = sizeof(sin);
        if (getsockname(fileno(sfp), (struct sockaddr *)&sin,
                        &sinlen) == 0)
                fprintf(tfp, "local port %d ", ntohs(sin.sin_port));
        sinlen = sizeof(sin);
        if (getpeername(fileno(sfp), (struct sockaddr *)&sin,
                        &sinlen) == 0)
                fprintf(tfp, "remote port %d ", ntohs(sin.sin_port));
        (void) putc('\n', tfp);
```

```
        if (doecho || sndbinary || rcvbinary) {
                printf("options in effect: ");
                if (doecho)
                        fprintf(tfp, "remote_echo ");
                if (sndbinary)
                        fprintf(tfp, "send_binary ");
                if (rcvbinary)
                        fprintf(tfp, "receive_binary ");
                (void) putc('\n', tfp);
        }
        if (scrfp)
                fprintf(tfp, "scripting to file \"%s\"\n", scrname);
        return 0;
}
```

Procedure *status* prints information such as the name of the remote host, the local and remote TCP protocol ports used for the connection, and a list of the options in effect.

26.28 Summary

Our example TELNET client uses three finite state machines to interpret sequences of characters that arrive from the server or from the user's keyboard. Each incoming character causes a transition in a finite state machine. When the client performs a transition, it calls a procedure that implements the action associated with the transition.

This chapter describes action procedures for the three finite state machines that comprise the example client. Some actions are trivial while others are complex. The chief disadvantage of organizing the client software as action procedures for the finite state machine lies in readability. The resulting code can be difficult to understand because one cannot ascertain the relationships among the procedures without referring to the finite state machines.

FOR FURTHER STUDY

A series of RFCs document the details of TELNET options and contain protocol standards for each of the options handled by the example code. Postel and Reynolds [RFC 858] discusses the go-ahead option, while Postel and Reynolds [RFC 857] discusses character echo. Postel and Reynolds [RFC 856] describes the option that controls 8-bit binary transmission. Finally, VanBokkelen [RFC 1091] discusses the terminal-type option and the associated option subnegotiation.

EXERCISES

26.1   Some terminal types support multiple emulation modes, making it possible to have a set of terminal type names for a single terminal. Read RFC 1091. How can a client use a list of terminal names when it negotiates the terminal type with a server?

26.2   Read the protocol standard to find out exactly when a server must switch from sending data encoded using the network virtual terminal encoding to sending 8-bit binary data. In particular, how does the server handle transmission after it volunteers to transmit binary data but has not received an acknowledgement?

26.3   Does a client send *WILL* or *DO* when it requests the server to perform a given option? What does the server send when it requests the client to perform an option?

26.4   What does the mode argument *O_WRONLY/O_CREAT/O_TRUNC* mean in the call to *open* found in procedure *scrwrap*?

26.5   Instrument the client to print a message when it receives an option request. Use the modified client to contact a variety of servers. What option requests do they send automatically?

26.6   What happens if the client sends *DO ECHO* and the server sends *WILL ECHO* simultaneously?

26.7   What happens if a client sends *DO ECHO* to a server that already has *ECHO* enabled?

27.1 Introduction

The example server code throughout this text has been written to provide a clear, tutorial illustration of the concepts that will help the reader understand the fundamental design principles. Thus, the code omits many of the details needed in production software.

This chapter describes some of the techniques and conventional practices that professional UNIX programmers follow when building production server programs. The techniques presented make the code more robust and easier to debug. They also isolate the server from the process that starts it, and permit the server to follow conventions for safe operation in a UNIX environment. While none of these techniques is required to make a server correct, professional programmers recognize them as highly desirable.

27.2 Operating In Background

UNIX allows a process to execute in *foreground* or in *background*. The easiest way to understand the difference is to imagine a user typing commands to a command interpreter. Normally, each command executes in foreground, meaning that the command interpreter creates a process to execute the command, and then waits for the command process to complete before issuing a prompt and reading another command.

However, if the user specifies that a command should execute in background, the command interpreter creates a process to execute the command, and allows the new process to continue concurrently while it prompts for another command. To find out whether a background process has completed, the user must check its status. Background execution is convenient for tasks like printing because it permits the user to continue interactive execution of other commands at the same time.

Most servers operate in the background because they run forever. A server begins execution when the operating system starts, and executes in background waiting for requests to arrive. Usually, the initial process in a UNIX system starts each server when it runs the system startup script (*/etc/rc* on many systems). The startup script consists of commands that the system interprets exactly as if they had been typed at the console.

Although it is possible to program the startup script to place each server process in background, most production servers put themselves in background quickly and automatically. To understand why speed is important, consider the execution sequence. Imagine the startup script executing a sequence of steps that each start one server. If a server moves to the background quickly, the startup script can continue to execute and start more servers. If a server delays before moving to background (e.g., does not move to background until it finishes executing initialization code), the process running the startup script must wait for the server, so subsequent servers will be delayed.

Building a server that automatically moves to background also helps make system startup less prone to error. Consider what happens if a particular server, *S*, does not move to background automatically and the system manager accidentally fails to specify background execution for *S* in the startup script. The bootstrap process executes the sequence of startup commands until it reaches the command to start *S*. The startup process runs the server in foreground, waiting for it to complete before going on. Unfortunately, because a server runs forever, the entire bootstrap process will block waiting for a command that will never complete.

27.3 Programming A Server To Operate In Background

UNIX programmers uses the term *daemon* for any process that performs a service in background. Transforming a server into a daemon is straightforward. The technique consists of having the server call *fork* to create a new process, and then arranging for the parent process to exit. To do so, the server executes the following code almost immediately after it starts execution:

```
i = fork();
if (i < 0) {          /* less than zero means error occurred*/
        fprintf(stderr, "error when forking: %s\n",
                sys_errlist[errno]);
        exit(1);
}
if (i) {                      /* nonzero is parent                    */
```

```
            exit(0);     /* normal process exit              */
    }
    /* child continues execution here and becomes the server  */
```

The call to *fork* can produce three possible results: a negative value that means an error occurred (e.g., the system had insufficient memory to create a new process), a positive result that means the call succeeded and the process is the parent, and a zero result that means the call succeeded and the process is the newly created child.

In the example code, if an error occurs, the server prints a message on the *standard error* output stream and calls *exit* to terminate with an exit code of *1*. By convention, a nonzero exit code indicates an *abnormal process termination*.

If the call to *fork* succeeds, the *if* statement uses the return value to distinguish between the parent and child processes. The original parent process exits normally, while the child continues execution and becomes the server. It is easiest to visualize what happens from a user's point of view. Imagine that some server, *Q*, contains the above code. To run the server, a user types the server's file name as a command. When the user enters the command, it appears to complete almost instantly, and the user receives the prompt for another command. However, if the user requests a list of processes, it will show that the server has created a copy of itself and that the copy continues to execute in background.

The above code also handles a minor detail: it completely detaches the daemon from its parent. At any given time, each UNIX process has a *parent*, and the action taken by some UNIX system functions depends on the parent–child relationship. After the call to *fork*, the server's parent exits, leaving the newly created child temporarily *orphaned*. Whenever a process becomes orphaned, UNIX designates that the *initial system process* (*init*) becomes the parent. We say that the orphaned child has been inherited by *init*†. Although such inheritance is a minor detail, it means that the server can exit cleanly because *init* calls the UNIX system call *wait* to terminate each of its children.

27.4 Open Descriptors And Inheritance

A UNIX process inherits copies of descriptors for files or sockets that the parent had opened at the time the process was created. Thus, the set of descriptors that a server process inherits depends on how it was started.

Because UNIX uses a reference count mechanism for files and other objects, keeping descriptors open can use resources unnecessarily. For example, suppose a parent process opens a file, and then executes a server that forks and moves to background. Even if the parent closes its copy of the file descriptor, the server will still have a copy open and the file will not be closed. As a result, the file cannot be removed from the disk until the server exits.

---

†See section *8* of the *UNIX Programmer's Manual* for a description of the *init* process.

To summarize:

A server must close all file descriptors it inherits to prevent it from consuming resources unnecessarily.

27.5 Programming A Server To Close Inherited Descriptors

To close all inherited file descriptors, a server executes the following code after it starts:

```
for (i=getdtablesize()-1; i>= 0; --i)
        (void) close(i);
```

Because the number of descriptors available to a process varies among UNIX systems, the code does not contain a fixed constant. Instead, it calls function *getdtablesize* to find the size of the process descriptor table. The descriptor table is indexed starting at zero. After it finds the maximum number of descriptors, the code iterates from the descriptor table size minus one down through zero, calling *close* on each descriptor. Once it finishes, the server will have closed all the open descriptors it inherited; calling *close* on a unopened descriptor has no effect.

27.6 Signals From The Controlling TTY

Each process in UNIX inherits a connection to a terminal that has been designated as its *control terminal*. UNIX calls the control terminal a *controlling tty*. UNIX makes the association with a controlling tty to permit the user who started a process to control it (e.g., to send the process a *hangup signal* when a user who is logged in over a dialup line hangs up the phone).

Unlike most processes, a server should not receive signals generated from the process that started it. In fact:

To ensure that signals from a user's terminal do not affect a server running in background, the server must detach itself from its controlling terminal.

27.7 Programming A Server To Change Its Controlling TTY

The code required to detach a process from its controlling terminal consists of only three lines:

```
fd = open("/dev/tty", O_RDWR);
(void) ioctl(fd, TIOCNOTTY, 0);
(void) close(fd);
```

The call to *open* returns the descriptor for the controlling terminal, and the call to *ioctl* specifies that the process should be detached from that controlling terminal. Finally, the call to *close* releases the file descriptor, making it possible for the server to reuse the descriptor for other I/O (e.g., for an incoming connection).

27.8 Moving To A Safe And Known Directory

A server process should always execute in a known directory. Among other things, doing so guarantees that if the server aborts for any reason (or if the system manager decides to terminate a server that misbehaves), the manager will know the location of the resulting *core* file. Furthermore, all servers should execute in standard system directories, not the directory in which they are started. To understand why, consider what happens if a system manager notices that a server has failed and restarts it. If the manager is running a command interpreter in his or her home directory and forgets to change to a system directory before starting the server, it will execute in the manager's home directory. Having a process executing in a directory prevents any system management activities that require the file system to be unmounted. For example, it may be impossible to perform a routine file system dump. To summarize:

A server must move to a known directory where it can operate indefinitely without interfering with normal system management.

27.9 Programming A Server To Change Directories

To change into a known directory, a server calls system function *chdir*. For example, a server that needs to execute in the root directory makes the following call:

```
(void) chdir("/");
```

Choosing an appropriate directory can. be difficult because no single directory works best for all servers. For example a server that sends electronic mail might change to the directory where the system stores outgoing e-mail (*/usr/spool/mqueue* on many UNIX systems). However, a server that monitors idle terminal lines might change to the directory where all the terminal devices can be found (usually */dev*).

27.10 The UNIX Umask

Each executing process has a UNIX *umask* that specifies the protection mode for the files the process creates. The umask is an integer in which the low-order *9* bits provide a mask for the *9*-bit file protection mode. Whenever UNIX creates a file, it computes a protection mode for the file by performing a bit-wise *and* operation of the mode specified in the *open* call and the bit-wise complement of the process' umask. For example, suppose a process has umask *027* (octal). If the process tries to create a file with mode *0777* (readable, writable, and executable by everyone), the system arrives at the correct file mode by computing the bit-wise *and* of *0750* (the complement of umask *027*) and *0777* (the requested mode). As a result, the file mode will be *0750* (readable and executable by the owner and the file's group, writable only by the owner, and not accessible by others).

Think of a process' umask as a safety net that prevents accidental creation of files with too many read, write, or execute privileges. Such protection is important because servers often execute as super user, so files they create are owned by the super user. The point is:

> *No matter what protection modes are specified in a call to* open, *the system will not provide more access privilege to a file the process creates than the creating process' umask specifies. Thus, restricting the umask at the beginning of a server prevents problems that might arise from incorrect mode specifications.*

27.11 Programming A Server To Set Its Umask

The server code required to restrict file creation modes is trivial:

```
(void) umask(027);
```

The call sets the server's umask to the value specified. The umask remains in effect unless the process makes another call to *umask*.

27.12 Process Groups

UNIX places each process in a *process group*. The notion of process group allows UNIX to treat a set of related processes as a single entity. Often, users think of a process group as a single *job*. In particular, if a user creates three processes interconnected by pipes, the command interpreter places them in a process group so that a termination signal sent to them will reach all three.

Usually, each server operates independently from other processes. Thus, it should not be a part of any group and should not receive signals sent to its parent's group. In summary:

> *Every process inherits membership in a process group. To avoid receiving signals meant for its parent, a server must leave its parent's process group.*

27.13 Programming A Server To Set Its Process Group

The code required to place a server process in its own, private process group is trivial:

```
(void) setpgrp(0, getpid());
```

The call to *getpid* returns the process id of the currently executing process (i.e. of the server), and the call to *setpgrp* requests the system to place the specified process in a new, private process group.

27.14 Descriptors For Standard I/O

Many library routines expect three standard file descriptors to be open and available for I/O: *standard input (0)*, *standard output (1)*, and *standard error (2)*. In particular, standard library routines like *perror* (which prints error messages) write to the standard error descriptor without checking it. If any of these descriptors is open and the server calls a library routine to read or write on it, I/O may occur to a terminal or file. To be safe, programmers usually open the standard descriptors and connect them to a harmless I/O device. Then, if any routine in the server attempts I/O using a standard descriptor, the server will not perform unintended I/O. In summary:

> *Because many library routines assume the three standard I/O descriptors are open, a production server usually opens all three descriptors and connects them to a harmless I/O device.*

27.15 Programming A Server To Open Standard Descriptors

The code required to open standard I/O descriptors after they have been closed consists of three system calls:

```
fd = open("/dev/null", O_RDWR);   /* stdin */
(void) dup(fd);                   /* stdout */
(void) dup(fd);                   /* stderr */
```

The call to *open* specifies the special UNIX file name */dev/null*, which corresponds to a device. The device associated with */dev/null* always returns an end-of-file condition on input and discards all output. Thus, reading or writing to */dev/null* has no effect; no data accumulates on any storage device.

The calls to system function *dup* duplicate an existing file descriptor. By convention, UNIX assigns file descriptors sequentially, starting at *0*. Once the server has opened */dev/null* and obtained a descriptor for it, the calls to *dup* provide a copy for standard output (descriptor *1*) and standard error (descriptor *2*).

27.16 Mutual Exclusion For The Server

For most services, only one copy of the master server should exist at any time. If concurrent execution is needed, the master server should handle all concurrency. Restricting server execution can be especially important if multiple individuals have privilege. For example, suppose two system programmers both notice that a given server has failed, and they both restart it simultaneously. Unless the managers coordinate their activities, both copies of the server could attempt to execute, and the results may be unpredictable. As a rule:

> *Only one copy of a server program should start execution at a time;*
> *all concurrency should be handled by the server.*

27.17 Programming A Server To Avoid Multiple Copies

We say that multiple copies of a server are *mutually exclusive* and that the server must invoke a mechanism that guarantees *mutual exclusion* when it begins execution. In UNIX, most processes use a *lock file* to achieve mutually exclusive execution. Each server uses a separate lock file. For example, a server that provides line printer service might use the file */usr/spool/lpd.lock*, while a white pages server might use the file */usr/spool/wp.lock*. When a copy of the server begins execution, it attempts to establish its designated lock file. If no other process is holding the lock, the attempt succeeds; if another copy of the server has already locked the file, the attempt fails.

The code required to implement mutual exclusion consists of a few system calls:

```
/* Acquire an exclusive lock, or exit.  Assumes      */
/* symbolic constant LOCKF has been defined to be    */
/* the name of the server's lock file.  For example, */
/*          #define LOCKF /usr/spool/lpd.lock        */
/*                                                   */
lf = open(LOCKF, O_RDWR|O_CREAT, 0640);
if (lf < 0)              /* error occurred opening file */
    exit(1);
```

```
if (flock(lf, LOCK_EX|LOCK_NB))
        exit(0);          /* could not obtain a lock        */
```

As the comment suggests, the example code assumes symbolic constant *LOCKF* has been defined to be the name of the server's lock file. The call to *open* obtains a descriptor for the lock file, creating the file if necessary. Note that the file does not contain any data: it merely needs to exist so the server can hold the lock. The call to *flock* requests exclusive use of the lock file. *Flock* returns zero if successful and nonzero if the attempt fails. If the server cannot obtain an exclusive lock, it simply exits because another copy of the server must already be running. Although it is possible to use other mechanisms to obtain mutually exclusive execution (e.g., creating a lock file that has mode *000*), the chief advantage of using *flock* arises because it automatically releases the lock after a system crash. In fact, a process only holds a lock established by *flock* while it executes. If the server crashes or the system reboots, the lock will be released. Servers that use file creation to guarantee mutual exclusion require the system to remove the file before restarting the server after a system reboot (or no copies of the server can execute).

27.18 Recording A Server's Process ID

In most production environments, system managers need a quick way to find a server in case it misbehaves or crashes. Although it is possible to list all processes in the system, doing so on a heavily loaded machine can take considerable time. To avoid having the system manager search for a server process, most production servers record their process identifier in a well-known file. When managers need to find a server process, they look in the file for the server's process identifier.

Which file should a server use to hold its process identifier? The most obvious choice is the server's lock file. There must be one lock file for each service, and the lock file normally has no other useful contents.

27.19 Programming A Server To Record Its Process ID

Once the server opens a lock file and obtains a descriptor, using the lock file to record the server's process identifier is trivial. The code consists of:

```
char    pbuf[10];  /* an array to hold ASCII pid */

/* Assume the lock file has been opened and its  */
/* descriptor has been stored in variable lf as  */
/* the code in the previous section shows        */
```

```
(void) sprintf(pbuf, "%6d\n", getpid());
(void) write(lf, pbuf, strlen(pbuf));
```

To make the file easy to read, the code calls *sprintf* to convert the process id from
a binary integer to a printable string that contains the equivalent decimal value. It then
calls *write* to write the string into the lock file. Because the file consists of readable
text, the manager can find the process id by displaying the file; no special tools are required to read or format it.

27.20 Waiting For A Child Process To Exit

When a UNIX process exits, the system cannot complete the process termination
until it informs the parent process. The parent must call the system function *wait* before
termination can complete. Meanwhile, the terminating process exists in a *zombie state*
and is sometimes called a *defunct process*.

27.21 Programming A Server To Wait For Each Child To Exit

We said earlier that when the server forks and the parent exits, the child process
will become a child of *init*. Because *init* calls *wait* repeatedly, its children all terminate
cleanly. Thus, if the main server process ever exits, no problems will arise.

Processes the main server creates become its children, not children of *init*. Thus,
any server that creates processes must call *wait* when the processes terminate. The code
in Chapter *11* illustrates how a concurrent server can arrange to wait for children that
terminate. It shows that the server receives a signal for each terminating child and can
arrange code in the signal handler to call *wait*.

27.22 Extraneous Signals

Even if a server detaches itself from its controlling terminal, it may receive signals.
In particular, any system manager or privileged process can send a signal to the server.
Often, a manager sends signal *SIGKILL* (9) to terminate the server. A programmer may
decide to use one or more signals to control the operation of the server. For example,
the programmer could arrange for the server to reinitialize itself upon receipt of a
HANGUP signal (1).

27.23 Programming A Server To Ignore Extraneous Signals

Most production servers arrange to ignore all signals except for the few signals used to control them. To do so, the server either executes calls to the system function *signal* or to the system function *sigvec*. For example, to ignore the *HANGUP* signal, a server calls:

$$(void) \; signal(SIG\_IGN, \; SIGHUP);$$

27.24 Using A System Log Facility

27.24.1 Generating Log Messages

Servers, and to a lesser extent clients, generate output intended for system programmers or system administrators. During construction, of course, most of the output consists of messages intended to help the programmer debug the code. Once the server begins production service, output is usually restricted to error messages generated when the server finds unusual circumstances or unexpected events. However, even production software may emit output regularly. For example, a server can be programmed to keep a log of each connection request or each transaction. To help maintain system security a server can be programmed to record information each time it rejects a connection request from an unauthorized client.

Many early servers recorded all their output on a console log. The idea arose from early computer systems on which the console terminal printed its output on paper. If a program wrote information on the console, it became part of the permanent system log that could be reviewed later if needed. On such systems, when a server began operation, it opened an output descriptor for the system's console terminal and used that descriptor when writing log messages.

27.24.2 The Advantage Of Indirection And Standard Error

The chief disadvantage of arranging for servers to write log messages to the console terminal is inflexibility. While the programmer constructs and tests server code, the programmer must walk to the system console to see the log. Furthermore, system administrators frequently move copies of client and server software to new machines. Because some machines do not use a hard-copy device as a console, server software must be changed to write log messages to a file before it can be moved to such machines. Usually, changing the destination of log messages means recompiling the source code.

UNIX introduced an interesting convention by providing each process with a file descriptor for *standard error* output (descriptor *3*). When a UNIX programmer writes server software, the programmer does not need to know whether the server will send error messages to the console printer or to a file. Instead, the programmer writes all error messages to the standard error descriptor, and relies on whoever starts the server to attach its standard error descriptor to a file or the system console. In essence, the notion of standard error provides a level of *indirection* that isolates the source program from the run-time environment: the source program references the standard error descriptor without knowing whether it will be bound to a file or to a terminal.

The flexibility gained through the use of the standard error descriptor becomes evident when one considers a site that has multiple copies of a given brand of machine, with each running a copy of a given server. One machine may use a console printer to log error messages, while another uses a file. A system administrator can run the same server code on both machines without recompiling because UNIX permits I/O redirection when starting the server.

27.24.3 Limitations Of I/O Redirection

While the use of a standard error descriptor makes server code more flexible than code that writes messages to a specific device or file, it does not solve all problems. A programmer, or the system administrator, may decide to have a server send some (or all) of the error messages to a user's terminal. Or the programmer may arrange to forward error messages to a machine other than the one on which the server executes (i.e., to send messages to a computer that has a printer).

UNIX's standard error descriptor mechanism does not provide sufficient flexibility to handle all possible destinations because the system does not allow one to redirect output to an arbitrary program or to a network connection. Instead another, more powerful mechanism is needed.

27.24.4 A Client-Server Solution

Not surprisingly, system designers have found that they can use the client-server paradigm to build an error logging mechanism with more flexibility than I/O redirection offers. In essence, each participating computer operates a *log server* that accepts and handles messages intended for the system's log. The log server can be programmed to write the messages it receives on the computer's console terminal, write them to a file, send them to a system administrator's terminal, or even send them to the log server on another machine.

When a running program needs to write a message to the system's log, it becomes a client of the log server. The running program sends its message to the log server and then continues execution. The log server handles the message by writing it to the system's log.

If the system manager decides to change the way a system handles error messages, the manager only needs to change the log server. For example, the manager can configure a log server so it prints all log messages on the system console. Later, the manager can change the log server so it appends all log messages onto a file.

Notice that a log server provides indirection much like the standard error descriptor described above. A program only has information about the log server compiled into the code; it does not know how the log server will handle each message. Furthermore, the address of the log server can be represented using the special name *localhost*, allowing a compiled program to find the log server on its machine without knowing the machine's address.

27.24.5 The Syslog Mechanism

BSD UNIX includes a log mechanism that uses the client-server approach described above. Known as *syslog*, the mechanism includes code for a log server (*syslogd*) as well as library routines that programs use to contact the server and send it messages.

The syslog mechanism provides two important features: (1) it groups messages into classes and (2) it uses a configuration file to allow the system administrator to specify how the server should handle each message class. Because *syslog* separates the handling for each message class, the system offers considerable flexibility. For example, the system administrator on one system might choose to send a message to the system manager whenever a serious error occurs, but choose to place low priority (informational) messages in a file without informing anyone. The system administrator on another system can make a different choice.

Because *syslog* uses a configuration file to allow a system administrator to specify how to handle each message class, the system is convenient to use. To change how *syslog* handles error messages, an administrator only needs to change a configuration file; the client and server software remain unchanged.

27.24.6 Syslog Message Classes

Syslog divides message classes in two ways. First, it partitions programs into groups, with each group known as a *facility*. Second, it subdivides messages from each facility into eight priority levels.

27.24.7 Syslog Facilities

The table in Figure 27.1 lists the facilities that *syslog* defines and their meanings.

Facility Name	Subsystem that uses it
LOG_KERN	The operating system kernel
LOG_USER	Any user process (i.e., a normal application program)
LOG_MAIL	The electronic mail system
LOG_DAEMON	System daemons that operate in background
LOG_AUTH	The authorization and authentication system
LOG_LPR	The printer spooling system
LOG_RPC	The RPC and NFS subsystem
LOG_LOCAL0	Reserved for local use; names LOG_LOCAL1 through LOG_LOCAL7 are also reserved

Figure 27.1 The facility types defined by *syslog*. Each log message must originate from one of these facilities.

As the figure shows, *syslog* has a facility for each major subsystem. For example, programs associated with e-mail belong to the *LOG_MAIL* facility, while most servers that run in background belong to the *LOG_DAEMON* facility.

27.24.8 Syslog Priority Levels

Syslog defines eight priority levels as Figure 27.2 shows.

Priority	Description
LOG_EMERG	An extreme emergency; the message should be broadcast to all users
LOG_ALERT	A condition that should be corrected immediately (e.g., a corrupted system database)
LOG_CRIT	A critical condition like a hardware error (e.g. disk failure)
LOG_ERR	An error that requires attention but is not critical
LOG_WARNING	A warning that an error condition may exist
LOG_NOTICE	A condition that is not an error, but may need attention
LOG_INFO	An informational message (e.g., a message issued when a server starts execution)
LOG_DEBUG	A message used by a programmer for debugging

Figure 27.2 The eight priority levels defined by *syslog*. Each log message must have one of these priority levels specified.

Priority levels range from *LOG_EMERG*, which is intended for the most severe emergencies, to *LOG_DEBUG*, which programmers use when they need to log debugging information.

27.24.9 Using Syslog

Whenever a program uses *syslog* to handle a log message, the program must specify a facility and a priority level for the message. To make *syslog* easier to use, the library routines permit a programmer to specify a facility when the program begins and to have *syslog* use that facility for successive messages. To specify an initial facility, a program calls procedure *openlog*. *Openlog* takes three arguments that specify an identification string, a set of handling options, and a facility specification. *Syslog* prepends the identification to all successive messages that the program writes so they can be found in the log. Usually, a programmer chooses the name of the program as its identification string. *Openlog* initializes logging and stores the identification string and facility for later use. For example, a programmer who is testing a private program can call:

```
openlog("myprog", LOG_PID, LOG_USER);
```

to specify identification string *myprog*, logging option *LOG_PID*, and facility *LOG_USER*. Option *LOG_PID* requests that *syslog* record the program's process identifier with each log message.

When a program needs to send a log message, it calls procedure *syslog*. Syslog sends the message to the *syslogd* server on the local machine. Procedure *syslog* takes a variable number of arguments. The first specifies a priority for the message and the second specifies a *printf*-like format. As in *printf*, arguments following the format contain values referenced in the format. In the simplest case, a program can call *syslog* with a constant string as a message. For example, to record a debugging message on the system log, a program can call:

```
syslog(LOG_DEBUG, "my program opened its input file");
```

Once a program finishes using *syslog*, it can call procedure *closelog* to close the log file (i.e., terminate contact with the server). *Closelog* terminates the log file connection and releases the I/O descriptor allocated for it. Thus, it can be important to call *closelog* to deallocate the log file descriptor (e.g., before a call to *fork*).

27.24.10 An Example Syslog Configuration File

Much of the flexibility in the *syslog* mechanism arises because it uses a configuration file to control the server. The configuration file uses patterns to allow the system administrator to specify how to handle each combination of facility and priority.

The *syslog* configuration file, */etc/syslog.conf* on most systems, is a text file that contains specifications, one per line. A specification consists of a pair of strings separated by white space. The left string specifies a *pattern* that matches some combination of facility and priority. The right string specifies a *disposition* for messages that match the pattern. For example, the specification:

lpr.debug   /usr/adm/printer-errs

contains a pattern that matches all messages with facility *lpr* and priority *debug*. Because the disposition string begins with a slash, *syslogd* interprets it as a file name. Thus, if it encounters the above specification, *syslogd* will send debug messages from the *lpr* facility to file */usr/adm/printer-errs*. *Syslogd* interprets an asterisk as a disposition string to mean "broadcast the message to all users." It interprets other disposition strings that do not begin with a slash as the login name of users who should receive the message.

An example configuration file will clarify the concept and show how system administrators can specify logging behavior. The following is a sample configuration file used on one system:

```
*.err;kern.debug;auth.notice                          /dev/console
kern.debug;daemon,auth.notice;auth.info;*.err;mail.crit /usr/adm/messages
lpr.debug                                             /usr/adm/printer-errs
mail.debug                                            /usr/spool/mqueue/syslog
*.alert;kern.err;daemon.err                           operator
*.alert                                               root
*.emerg                                               *
```

Pattern matching is a powerful mechanism because it permits a system administrator to represent specifications without writing down individual combinations of facility and priority. For example, the configuration file above uses the pattern *.*err* to mean, "messages at the error priority of any facility."

27.25 Summary

Production servers employ a set of techniques that make them easier to manage and debug, more robust, and less susceptible to errors. This chapter discusses the motivation for such techniques, and shows the code required for each. The particular techniques discussed include the following conceptual operations:

- Operate the server as a background process (daemon).
- Close inherited file descriptors.
- Detach the server from its controlling TTY.
- Move the server to a safe, known directory.
- Set the UNIX umask.
- Place the server in a private process group.
- Open the three standard I/O descriptors.
- Guarantee mutually exclusive execution.
- Record the server's process identifier.
- Wait for child processes that terminate.
- Ignore extraneous signals.
- Use *syslog* to handle error messages.

FOR FURTHER STUDY

Many of the rules UNIX programmers follow when implementing servers come from unwritten conventions and heuristics; often programmers learn techniques by reading existing programs. Stevens [1990] discusses how to write daemon programs and describes some of the techniques outlined in this chapter.

EXERCISES

27.1   Build a procedure, *daemonize*, that includes the code from this chapter.

27.2   Read about signals in the *UNIX Programmer's Manual*. Which signals cannot be ig-
nored? What happens if a server receives one of them?

27.3   Some programmers arrange for a server to terminate gracefully if it receives a special
signal (e.g., *SIGHUP*). Doing so allows the system manager to terminate a server by
sending the designated signal. How can the manager send such a signal if the server has
detached itself from the controlling terminal?

27.4   In the previous question, is it possible for an unprivileged user to terminate a server by
sending it the designated signal?

27.5   Our example code closes all file descriptors and then opens standard input, output, and
error again. Some servers leave these three descriptors with the values inherited from
their parents. What are the advantages and disadvantages of doing so? (Hint: think
about logging error messages).

27.6   Most servers execute with root privilege (in UNIX, root privilege means absolute
privilege). Why might a server choose to run with less privilege? How can it do so?

27.7   Write a server that uses the UNIX system function *creat* to provide mutual exclusion.
(Hint: the technique is well-known and widely-used, especially in older UNIX programs).

27.8   Compare mutual exclusion using *creat* (see the previous exercise) to mutual exclusion
using *O_EXCL* in a call to *open* and to mutual exclusion using *rename*. Which of the
three techniques is preferable? Why?

27.9   Examine the source code for a production server. What techniques from this chapter
does it use? Does it use other techniques?

27.10 Read the UNIX manual pages for *syslogd*. How can a system administrator change the
configuration after the server has begun? Can you suggest an alternative?

Appendix 1

System Calls And Library Routines Used With Sockets

Introduction

In BSD UNIX, communication centers around the socket abstraction. Applications use a set of socket system calls to communicate with TCP/IP software in the operating system. A client application creates a socket, connects it to a server on a remote machine, and uses it to transfer data and to receive data from the remote machine. Finally, when the client application finishes using the socket, it closes it. A server creates a socket, binds it to a well-known protocol port on the local machine, and waits for clients to contact it.

Each page of this appendix describes one of the system calls or library functions that programmers use when writing client or server applications. The functions are arranged in alphabetic order, with one page devoted to a given function. The functions listed include: *accept, bind, close, connect, fork, gethostbyaddr, gethostbyname, gethostid, gethostname, getpeername, getprotobyname, getservbyname, getsockname, getsockopt, gettimeofday, listen, read, recv, recvfrom, recvmsg, select, send, sendmsg, sendto, sethostid, setsockopt, shutdown, socket,* and *write*.

The Accept System Call

Use

retcode = accept (socket, addr, addrlen);

Description

Servers use the *accept* function to accept the next incoming connection on a passive socket after they have called *socket* to create a socket, *bind* to specify a local IP address and protocol port number, and *listen* to make the socket passive and to set the length of the connection request queue. *Accept* removes the next connection request from the queue (or waits until a connection request arrives), creates a new socket for the request, and returns the descriptor for the new socket. *Accept* only applies to stream sockets (e.g., those used with TCP).

Arguments

Arg	Type	Meaning
socket	int	A socket descriptor created by the *socket* function.
addr	&sockaddr	A pointer to an address structure. *Accept* fills in the structure with the IP address and protocol port number of the remote machine.
addrlen	&int	A pointer to an integer that initially specifies the size of the *sockaddr* argument and, when the call returns, specifies the number of bytes stored in argument *addr*.

Return Code

Accept returns a nonnegative socket descriptor if successful and −*1* to indicate that an error has occurred. When an error occurs, the global variable *errno* contains one of the following values:

Value in errno	Cause of the Error
EBADF	The first argument does not specify a valid descriptor.
ENOTSOCK	The first argument does not specify a socket descriptor.
EOPNOTSUPP	The socket is not of type SOCK_STREAM.
EFAULT	The pointer in argument 2 is invalid.
EWOULDBLOCK	The socket is marked nonblocking and no connections are waiting to be accepted (i.e. the call would block).

The Bind System Call

Use

retcode = bind (socket, localaddr, addrlen);

Description

Bind specifies a local IP address and protocol port number for a socket. *Bind* is primarily used by servers, which need to specify a well-known protocol port.

Arguments

Arg	Type	Meaning
socket	int	A socket descriptor created by the *socket* call.
localaddr	&sockaddr	The address of a structure that specifies an IP address and protocol port number.
addrlen	int	The size of the address structure in bytes.

Chapter 5 contains a description of the *sockaddr* structure.

Return Code

Bind returns 0 if successful and −*1* to indicate that an error has occurred. When an error occurs, the global variable *errno* contains a code that specifies the cause of the error. The possible errors are:

Value in errno	Cause of the Error
EBADF	Argument *socket* does not specify a valid descriptor.
ENOTSOCK	Argument *socket* does not specify a socket descriptor.
EADDRNOTAVAIL	The specified address is unavailable (e.g., an IP address does not match a local interface).
EADDRINUSE	The specified address is in use (e.g., another process has allocated the protocol port).
EINVAL	The socket already has an address bound to it.
EACCES	The application program does not have permission to use the address specified.
EFAULT	The *localaddr* argument pointer is invalid.

The Close System Call

Use

retcode = close (socket);

Description

An application calls *close* after it finishes using a socket. *Close* terminates communication gracefully and removes the socket. Any unread data waiting at the socket will be discarded.

In practice, UNIX implements a reference count mechanism to allow multiple processes to share a socket. If *n* processes share a socket, the reference count will be *n*. *Close* decrements the reference count each time a process calls it. Once the reference count reaches zero (i.e. all processes have called *close*), the socket will be deallocated.

Arguments

Arg	Type	Meaning
socket	int	The descriptor of a socket to be closed.

Return Code

Close returns 0 if successful and −*1* to indicate that an error has occurred. When an error occurs, the global variable *errno* contains the following value:

Value in errno	Cause of the Error
EBADF	The argument does not specify a valid descriptor.

The Connect System Call

Use

retcode = connect (socket, addr, addrlen);

Description

Connect allows the caller to specify the remote endpoint address for a previously created socket. If the socket uses TCP, connect uses the 3-way handshake to establish a connection; if the socket uses UDP, connect specifies the remote endpoint but does not transfer any datagrams to it.

Arguments

Arg	Type	Meaning
socket	int	The descriptor of a socket.
addr	&sockaddr_in	The remote machine endpoint.
addrlen	int	The length of the second argument.

Chapter 5 contains a description of the *sockaddr* structure.

Return Code

Connect returns zero if successful and –1 to indicate that an error has occurred. When an error occurs, the global variable *errno* contains one of the following values:

Value in errno	Cause of the Error
EBADF	The first argument does not specify a valid descriptor.
ENOTSOCK	The first argument does not specify a socket descriptor.
EAFNOSUPPORT	The address family specified in the remote endpoint cannot be used with this type of socket.
EADDRNOTAVAIL	The specified endpoint address is not available.
EISCONN	The socket is already connected.
ETIMEDOUT	(TCP only) The protocol reached timeout without successfully establishing a connection.
ECONNREFUSED	(TCP only) Connection refused by remote machine.
ENETUNREACH	(TCP only) The network is not currently reachable.
EADDRINUSE	The specified address is already in use.
EINPROGRESS	(TCP only) The socket is nonblocking and a connection attempt would block.
EALREADY	(TCP only) The socket is nonblocking and the call would wait for a previous connection attempt to complete.

The Fork System Call

Use

retcode = fork ( );

Description

   Although not directly related to communication sockets, *fork* is essential because servers use it to create concurrent processes. *Fork* creates a new process executing the same code as the original. The two processes share all socket and file descriptors that are open when the call to *fork* occurs. The two processes have different process identifiers and different parent process identifiers.

Arguments

   Fork does not take any arguments.

Return Code

   If successful, *fork* returns 0 to the child process and the (nonzero) process identifier of the newly created process to the original process. It returns *–1* to indicate that an error has occurred. When an error occurs, the global variable *errno* contains one of the following values:

Value in errno	Cause of the Error
EAGAIN	The system limit on total processes has been reached, or the per-user limit on processes has been reached.
ENOMEM	The system has insufficient memory for a new process.

The Gethostbyaddr Library Function

Use

retcode = gethostbyaddr (addr, alen, atype);

Description

Gethostbyqddr searches for information about a host given its IP address.

Arguments

Arg	Type	Meaning
addr	&char	A pointer to an array that contains a host address (e.g., an IP address).
alen	int	An integer that gives the address length (*4* for IP).
atype	int	An integer that gives the address type (AF_INET for an IP address).

Return Code

Gethostbyaddr returns a pointer to a *hostent* structure if successful and *0* to indicate that an error has occurred. The *hostent* structure is declared to be:

```
struct hostent {            /* entry for a host         */
     char  *h_name;         /* official host name       */
     char  *h_aliases[];    /* list of other aliases    */
     int    h_addrtype;     /* host address type        */
     int    h_length;       /* length of host address   */
     char **h_addr_list;    /* list of addresses for host */
};
```

When an error occurs, the global variable *h_errno* contains one of the following values:

Value in h_errno	Cause of the Error
HOST_NOT_FOUND	The name specified is unknown.
TRY_AGAIN	Temporary error: local server could not contact the authority at present.
NO_RECOVERY	Irrecoverable error occurred.
NO_ADDRESS	The specified name is valid, but it does not correspond to an IP address.

The Gethostbyname Library Call

Use

retcode = gethostbyname (name);

Description

Gethostbyname maps a host name to an IP address.

Arguments

Arg	Type	Meaning
name	&char	The address of a character string that contains a host name.

Return Code

Gethostbyname returns a pointer to a *hostent* structure if successful and *0* to indicate that an error has occurred. The *hostent* structure is declared to be:

```
struct hostent {          /* entry for a host           */
      char  *h_name;      /* official host name         */
      char  *h_aliases[]; /* list of other aliases      */
      int    h_addrtype;  /* host address type          */
      int    h_length;    /* length of host address     */
      char **h_addr_list; /* list of addresses for host */
};
```

When an error occurs, the global variable *h_errno* contains one of the following values:

Value in h_errno	Cause of the Error
HOST_NOT_FOUND	The name specified is unknown.
TRY_AGAIN	Temporary error: local server could not contact the authority at present.
NO_RECOVERY	Irrecoverable error occurred.
NO_ADDRESS	The specified name is valid, but it does not correspond to an IP address.

The Gethostid System Call

Use

$$hostid = gethostid();$$

Description

Applications call *gethostid* to determine the unique *32*-bit host identifier assigned to the local machine. Usually, the host identifier is the machine's primary IP address.

Arguments

Gethostid does not take any arguments.

Return Value

Gethostid returns a long integer containing the host identifier.

The Gethostname System Call

Use

retcode = gethostname (name, namelen);

Description

Gethostname returns the primary name of the local machine in the form of a text string.

Arguments

Arg	Type	Meaning
name	&char	The address of the character array into which the name should be placed.
namelen	int	The length of the *name* array (should be at least 65).

Return Code

Gethostname returns *0* if successful and *−1* to indicate that an error has occurred. When an error occurs, the global variable *errno* contains the following value:

Value in errno	Cause of the Error
EFAULT	The *name* or *namelen* arguments were incorrect.

The Getpeername System Call

Use

retcode = getpeername (socket, remaddr, addrlen);

Description

An application uses *getpeername* to obtain the remote endpoint address for a connected socket. Usually, a client knows the remote endpoint address because it calls *connect* to set it. However, a server that uses *accept* to obtain a connection may need to interrogate the socket to find out the remote address.

Arguments

Arg	Type	Meaning
socket	int	A socket descriptor created by the *socket* function.
remaddr	&sockaddr	A pointer to a *sockaddr* structure that will contain the endpoint address.
addrlen	&int	A pointer to an integer that contains the length of the second argument initially, and the actual length of the endpoint address upon return.

Chapter 5 contains a description of the *sockaddr* structure.

Return Code

Getpeername returns 0 if successful and −1 to indicate that an error has occurred. When an error occurs, the global variable *errno* contains one of the following values:

Value in errno	Cause of the Error
EBADF	The first argument does not specify a valid descriptor.
ENOTSOCK	The first argument does not specify a socket descriptor.
ENOTCONN	The socket is not a connected socket.
ENOBUFS	The system had insufficient resources to perform the operation.
EFAULT	The *remaddr* argument pointer is invalid.

The Getprotobyname Function Call

Use

retcode = getprotobyname (name);

Description

Applications call *getprotobyname* to find a protocol's official integer value from its name alone.

Arguments

Arg	Type	Meaning
name	&char	The address of a string that contains the protocol name.

Return Code

Getprotobyname returns a pointer to a structure of type *protoent* if successful and *0* to indicate that an error has occurred. Structure *protoent* is declared to be:

```
struct protoent {           /* entry that describes a protocol  */
    char  *p_name;          /* official name of protocol        */
    char  **p_aliases;      /* list of aliases for the protocol */
    int   p_proto;          /* official protocol number         */
};
```

The Getservbyname Library Call

Use

retcode = getservbyname (name, proto);

Description

Getservbyname obtains an entry from the network services database given a service name. Clients and servers both call *getservbyname* to map a service name to a protocol port number.

Arguments

Arg	Type	Meaning
name	&char	A pointer to a string of characters that contains a service name.
proto	&char	A pointer to a string of characters that contains the name of the protocol to be used (e.g., *tcp*).

Return Code

Getservbyname returns a pointer to a *servent* structure if successful and a null pointer (0) to indicate that an error has occurred. The *servent* structure is declared to be:

```
struct servent {              /* one service entry          */
        char  *s_name ;       /* official service name      */
        char  **s_aliases;    /* list of other aliases      */
        int    s_port;        /* port used for this service */
        char  *s_proto;       /* protocol used for service  */
};
```

The Getsockname System Call

Use

retcode = getsockname (socket, name, namelen);

Description

Getsockname obtains the name for the specified socket.

Arguments

Arg	Type	Meaning
socket	int	A socket descriptor created by the *socket* function.
name	&char	A pointer to an array of characters.
namelen	&int	The number of positions in the *name* array; returned as the length of the name.

Return Code

Getsockname returns *0* if successful and *−1* to indicate that an error has occurred. When an error occurs, the global variable *errno* contains one of the following values:

Value in errno	Cause of the Error
EBADF	The first argument does not specify a valid descriptor.
ENOTSOCK	The first argument does not specify a socket descriptor.
EBOBUFS	Insufficient buffer space was available in the system.
EFAULT	The address of *name* or *namelen* is incorrect.

The Getsockopt System Call

Use

retcode = getsockopt (socket, level, opt, optval, optlen);

Description

Getsockopt permits an application to obtain the value of a parameter (option) for a socket or a protocol the socket uses.

Arguments

Arg	Type	Meaning
socket	int	The descriptor of a socket.
level	int	An integer that identifies a protocol level.
opt	int	An integer that identifies an option.
optval	&char	The address of a buffer in which the value is returned.
optlen	&int	Size of buffer; returned as length of the value found.

The socket-level options that apply to all sockets include:

SO_DEBUG	Status of debugging information
SO_REUSEADDR	Allow local address reuse?
SO_KEEPALIVE	Status of connection keep-alive
SO_DONTROUTE	Bypass Routing for outgoing messages?
SO_LINGER	Linger on close if data present?
SO_BROADCAST	Permission to transmit broadcast messages?
SO_OOBINLINE	Receive out-of-band data in band?
SO_SNDBUF	Buffer size for output
SO_RCVBUF	Buffer size for input
SO_TYPE	Type of the socket
SO_ERROR	Get and clear the last error for the socket

Return Code

Getsockopt returns *0* if successful and *−1* to indicate that an error has occurred. When an error occurs, the global variable *errno* contains one of the following values:

Value in errno	Cause of the Error
EBADF	The first argument does not specify a valid descriptor.
ENOTSOCK	The first argument does not specify a socket descriptor.
ENOPROTOOPT	The *opt* is incorrect.
EFAULT	The address of *optval* or *optlen* is incorrect.

The Gettimeofday System Call

Use

retcode = gettimeofday (tm, tmzone);

Description

Gettimeofday extracts the current time and date from the system along with information about the local time zone.

Arguments

Arg	Type	Meaning
tm	&struct timeval	The address of a timeval structure.
tmzone	&struct timezone	The address of a timezone structure.

The structures that *gettimeofday* assigns are declared:

```
struct timeval {             /* structure for storing time    */
     long tv_sec;            /* seconds since epoch (1/1/70) */
     long tv_usec;           /* microseconds beyond tv_sec    */
};

struct timezone {            /* structure for timezone info   */
     int  tz_minuteswest;/* minutes west of Greenwich     */
     int  tz_dsttime;        /* type of correction to apply   */
};
```

Return Code

Gettimeofday returns *0* if successful and *-1* to indicate that an error has occurred. When an error occurs, the global variable *errno* contains the following value:

Value in errno	Cause of the Error
EFAULT	The *tm* or *tmzone* arguments contained an incorrect address.

The Listen System Call

Use

retcode = listen (socket, queuelen);

Description

Servers use *listen* to make a socket passive (i.e., ready to accept incoming requests). *Listen* also sets the number of incoming connection requests that the protocol software should enqueue for a given socket while the server handles another request. *Listen* only applies to sockets used with TCP.

Arguments

Arg	Type	Meaning
socket	int	A socket descriptor created by the *socket* call.
queuelen	int	The size of the incoming connection request queue (usually up to a maximum of 5).

Return Code

Listen returns 0 if successful and –1 to indicate that an error has occurred. When an error occurs, the global variable *errno* contains one of the following values:

Value in errno	Cause of the Error
EBADF	The first argument does not specify a valid descriptor.
ENOTSOCK	The first argument does not specify a socket descriptor.
EOPNOTSUPP	The socket type does not support *listen*.

The Read System Call

Use

retcode = read (socket, buff, buflen);

Description

Clients or servers use *read* to obtain input from a socket.

Arguments

Arg	Type	Meaning
socket	int	A socket descriptor created by the *socket* function.
buff	&char	A pointer to an array of characters to hold the input.
buflen	int	An integer that specifies the number of bytes in the the *buff* array.

Return Code

Read returns zero if it detects an end-of-file condition on the socket, the number of bytes read if it obtains input, and –1 to indicate that an error has occurred. When an error occurs, the global variable *errno* contains one of the following values:

Value in errno	Cause of the Error
EBADF	The first argument does not specify a valid descriptor.
EFAULT	Address *buff* is illegal.
EIO	An I/O error occurred while reading data.
EINTR	A signal interrupted the operation.
EWOULDBLOCK	Nonblocking I/O is specified, but the socket has no data.

The Recv System Call

Use

retcode = recv (socket, buffer, length, flags);

Description

Recv obtains the next incoming message from a UDP socket.

Arguments

Arg	Type	Meaning
socket	int	A socket descriptor created by the *socket* function.
buffer	&char	The address of a buffer to hold the message.
length	int	The length of the buffer.
flags	int	Control bits that specify whether to receive out-of-band data and whether to look ahead for messages.

Return Code

Recv returns the number of bytes in the message if successful and *–1* to indicate that an error has occurred. When an error occurs, the global variable *errno* contains one of the following values:

Value in errno	Cause of the Error
EBADF	The first argument does not specify a valid descriptor.
ENOTSOCK	The first argument does not specify a socket descriptor.
EWOULDBLOCK	The socket has no data, but nonblocking I/O has been specified.
EINTR	A signal arrived before the read operation could deliver data.
EFAULT	Argument *buffer* is incorrect.

The Recvfrom System Call

Use

retcode = recvfrom (socket, buffer, buflen, flags, from, fromlen);

Description

Recvfrom extracts the next message that arrives at a socket and records the sender's address (enabling the caller to send a reply).

Arguments

Arg	Type	Meaning
socket	int	A socket descriptor created by the *socket* function.
buffer	&char	The address of a buffer to hold the message.
buflen	int	The length of the buffer.
flags	int	Control bits that specify out-of-band data or message look-ahead.
from	&sockaddr	The address of a structure to hold the sender's address.
fromlen	&int	The length of the *from* buffer, returned as the size of the sender's address.

Chapter 5 contains a description of the *sockaddr* structure.

Return Code

Recvfrom returns the number of bytes in the message if successful and *–1* to indicate that an error has occurred. When an error occurs, the global variable *errno* contains one of the following values:

Value in errno	Cause of the Error
EBADF	The first argument does not specify a valid descriptor.
ENOTSOCK	The first argument does not specify a socket descriptor.
EWOULDBLOCK	The socket has no data, but nonblocking I/O has been specified.
EINTR	A signal arrived before the read operation could deliver data.
EFAULT	Argument *buffer* is incorrect.

The Recvmsg System Call

Use

retcode = recvmsg (socket, msg, flags);

Description

Recvmsg returns the next message that arrives on a UDP socket. It places the message in a structure that includes a header along with the data.

Arguments

Arg	Type	Meaning
socket	int	Socket descriptor created by the *socket* function.
msg	&struct msghdr	Address of a message structure.
flags	int	Control bits that specify out-of-band data or message look-ahead.

The message is delivered in a *msghdr* structure with format:

```
struct msghdr   {
        caddr_t   msg_name;       /* optional address        */
        int       msg_namelen;    /* size of address         */
        struct iovec *msg_iov;    /* scatter/gather array     */
        int       msg_iovlen;     /* # elements in msg_iov */
        caddr_t   msg_accrights;  /* rights sent/received */
        int       msg_accrghtslen;/* length of prev. field */
};
```

Return Code

Recvmsg returns the number of bytes in the message if successful and *–1* to indicate that an error has occurred. When an error occurs, the global variable *errno* contains one of the following values:

Value in errno	Cause of the Error
EBADF	The first argument does not specify a valid descriptor.
ENOTSOCK	The first argument does not specify a socket descriptor.
EWOULDBLOCK	The socket has no data, but nonblocking I/O has been specified.
EINTR	A signal arrived before the read operation could deliver data.
EFAULT	Argument *buffer* is incorrect.

The Select System Call

Use

retcode = select (numfds, refds, wrfds, exfds, time);

Description

Select provides asynchronous I/O by permitting a single process to wait for the first of any file descriptors in a specified set to become ready. The caller can also specify a maximum timeout for the wait.

Arguments

Arg	Type	Meaning
numfds	int	Number of file descriptors in the set.
refds	&fd_set	Address of file descriptors for input.
wrfds	&fd_set	Address of file descriptors for output.
exfds	&fd_set	Address of file descriptors for exceptions.
time	&struct timeval	Maximum time to wait or zero.

Arguments that refer to descriptors consist of integers in which the ith bit corresponds to descriptor i. Macros *FD_CLR* and *FD_SET* clear or set individual bits. The UNIX manual page that describes *gettimeofday* contains a description of the *timeval* structure.

Return Code

Select returns the number of ready file descriptors if successful, 0 if the time limit was reached, and -1 to indicate that an error has occurred. When an error occurs, the global variable *errno* contains one of the following values:

Value in errno	Cause of the Error
EBADF	One of the descriptor sets specifies an invalid descriptor.
EINTR	A signal arrived before the time limit or any of the selected descriptors became ready.
EINVAL	The time limit value is incorrect.

The Send System Call

Use

retcode = send (socket, msg, msglen, flags);

Description

Applications call *send* to transfer a message to another machine.

Arguments

Arg	Type	Meaning
socket	int	Socket descriptor created by the *socket* function.
msg	&char	A pointer to the message.
msglen	int	The length of the message in bytes.
flags	int	Control bits that specify out-of-band data or message look-ahead.

Return Code

Send returns the number of characters sent if successful and *–1* to indicate that an error has occurred. When an error occurs, the global variable *errno* contains one of the following values:

Value in errno	Cause of the Error
EBADF	The first argument does not specify a valid descriptor.
ENOTSOCK	The first argument does not specify a socket descriptor.
EFAULT	Argument *buffer* is incorrect.
EMSGSIZE	The message is too large for the socket.
EWOULDBLOCK	The socket has no data, but nonblocking I/O has been specified.
ENOBUFS	The system had insufficient resources to perform the operation.

The Sendmsg System Call

Use

retcode = sendmsg (socket, msg, flags);

Description

Sendmsg sends a message, extracting it from a *msghdr* structure.

Arguments

Arg	Type	Meaning
socket	int	Socket descriptor created by the *socket* function.
msg	&struct msghdr	A pointer to the message structure.
flags	int	Control bits that specify out-of-band data or message look-ahead.

The page that describes *recvmsg* contains a definition of structure *msghdr*.

Return Code

Sendmsg returns the number of bytes sent if successful and *−1* to indicate that an error has occurred. When an error occurs, the global variable *errno* contains one of the following values:

Value in errno	Cause of the Error
EBADF	The first argument does not specify a valid descriptor.
ENOTSOCK	The first argument does not specify a socket descriptor.
EFAULT	Argument *buffer* is incorrect.
EMSGSIZE	The message is too large for the socket.
EWOULDBLOCK	The socket has no data, but nonblocking I/O has been specified.
ENOBUFS	The system had insufficient resources to perform the operation.

The Sendto System Call

Use

retcode = sendto (socket, msg, msglen, flags, to, tolen);

Description

Sendto sends a message by taking the destination address from a structure.

Arguments

Arg	Type	Meaning
socket	int	Socket descriptor created by the *socket* function.
msg	&char	A pointer to the message.
msglen	int	The length of the message in bytes.
flags	int	Control bits that specify out-of-band data or message look-ahead.
to	&sockaddr	A pointer to the address structure.
tolen	int	The length of the address in bytes.

Chapter 5 contains a description of the *sockaddr* structure.

Return Code

Sendto returns the number of bytes sent if successful and −*1* to indicate that an error has occurred. When an error occurs, the global variable *errno* contains one of the following values:

Value in errno	Cause of the Error
EBADF	The first argument does not specify a valid descriptor.
ENOTSOCK	The first argument does not specify a socket descriptor.
EFAULT	Argument *buffer* is incorrect.
EMSGSIZE	The message is too large for the socket.
EWOULDBLOCK	The socket has no data, but nonblocking I/O has been specified.
ENOBUFS	The system had insufficient resources to perform the operation.

The Sethostid System Call

Use

(void) sethostid (hostid);

Description

The system manager runs a privileged program at system startup that calls *sethostid* to assign the local machine a unique *32*-bit host identifier. Usually, the host identifier is the machine's primary IP address.

Arguments

Arg	Type	Meaning
hostid	int	A value to be stored as the host's identifier.

Errors

An application must have root privilege, or *sethosid* will not change the host identifier.

The Setsockopt System Call

Use

retcode = setsockopt (socket, level, opt, optval, optlen);

Description

Setsockopt permits an application to change an option associated with a socket or the protocols it uses.

Arguments

Arg	Type	Meaning
socket	int	The descriptor of a socket.
level	int	An integer that identifies a protocol (e.g., TCP).
opt	int	An integer that identifies an option.
optval	&char	The address of a buffer that contains a value (usually *1* to enable an option or *0* to disable it).
optlen	int	The length of *optval*.

The socket-level options that apply to all sockets include:

SO_DEBUG	Toggle status of debugging information
SO_REUSEADDR	Toggle local address reuse
SO_KEEPALIVE	Toggle status of connection keep-alive
SO_DONTROUTE	Toggle bypass routing for outgoing messages
SO_LINGER	Linger on close if data present
SO_BROADCAST	Toggle permission to broadcast messages
SO_OOBINLINE	Toggle reception of out-of-band data in band
SO_SNDBUF	Set buffer size for output
SO_RCVBUF	Set buffer size for input

Return Code

Setsockopt returns *0* if successful and *–1* to indicate that an error has occurred. When an error occurs, the global variable *errno* contains one of the following values:

Value in errno	Cause of the Error
EBADF	The first argument does not specify a valid descriptor.
ENOTSOCK	The first argument does not specify a socket descriptor.
ENOPROTOOPT	The option integer, *opt*, is incorrect.
EFAULT	The address of *optval* or *optlen* is incorrect.

The Shutdown System Call

Use

retcode = shutdown (socket, direction);

Description

The *shutdown* function applies to full-duplex sockets (i.e., a connected TCP socket), and is used to partially close the connection.

Arguments

Arg	Type	Meaning
socket	int	A socket descriptor created by the *socket* call.
direction	int	The direction in which shutdown is desired: *0* means terminate further input, *1* means terminate further output, and *2* means terminate both input and output.

Return Code

The *shutdown* call returns *0* if the operation succeeds or *-1* to indicate that an error has occurred. When an error occurs, the global variable *errno* contains a code that specifies the cause of the error. The possible errors are:

Value in errno	Cause of the Error
EBADF	The first argument does not specify a valid descriptor.
ENOTSOCK	The first argument does not specify a socket descriptor.
ENOTCONN	The specified socket is not currently connected.

The Socket System Call

Use

retcode = socket (family, type, protocol);

Description

The *socket* function creates a socket used for network communication, and returns an integer descriptor for that socket.

Arguments

Arg	Type	Meaning
family	int	Protocol or address family (PF_INET for TCP/IP, AF_INET can also be used).
type	int	Type of service (SOCK_STREAM for TCP or SOCK_DGRAM for UDP).
protocol	int	Protocol number to use or 0 to request the default for a given family and type.

Return Code

The *socket* call either returns a descriptor or −1 to indicate that an error has occurred. When an error occurs, the global variable *errno* contains a code that specifies the cause of the error. The possible errors are:

Value in errno	Cause of the Error
EPROTONOSUPPORT	Error in arguments: the requested service or the specified protocol is invalid.
EMFILE	The application's descriptor table is full.
ENFILE	The internal system file table is full.
EACCESS	Permission to create the socket is denied.
ENOBUFS	The system has no buffer space available.

The Write System Call

Use

retcode = write (socket, buf, buflen);

Description

Write permits an application to transfer data to a remote machine.

Arguments

Arg	Type	Meaning
socket	int	A socket descriptor created by the *socket* call.
buf	&char	The address of a buffer containing data.
buflen	int	The number of bytes in *buf*.

Return Code

Write returns the number of bytes transferred if successful and −*1* to indicate that, an error has occurred. When an error occurs, the global variable *errno* contains one of the following values:

Value in errno	Cause of the Error
EBADF	The first argument does not specify a valid descriptor.
EPIPE	Attempt to *write* on an unconnected stream socket.
EFBIG	Data written exceeds system capacity.
EFAULT	Address in *buf* is incorrect.
EINVAL	Socket pointer is invalid.
EIO	An I/O error occurred.
EWOULDBLOCK	The socket cannot accept all data that was written without blocking, but nonblocking I/O has been specified.

Appendix 2

Manipulation Of UNIX File And Socket Descriptors

Introduction

In UNIX, all input and output operations use an abstraction known as the *file descriptor*. A program calls the *open* system call to obtain access to a file or the *socket* system call to obtain a descriptor used for network communication. Chapters 4 and 5 describe the socket interface; Chapter 23 describes UNIX descriptors and I/O in more detail. It points out that a newly created process inherits copies of all file descriptors that the parent process had open at the time of creation. Finally, Chapter 27 discusses how production servers close extra file descriptors and open standard I/O descriptors.

This appendix describes how programs can use standard I/O descriptors as arguments, and illustrates how a parent rearranges existing descriptors to make them correspond to the standard I/O descriptors before invoking a child. The technique is especially useful in multiservice servers that invoke separate programs to handle each service.

Descriptors As Implicit Arguments

When the UNIX *fork* function creates a new process, the newly created child inherits a copy of all file descriptors that the parent had open at the time of the call. Furthermore, the child's descriptor for a given file or socket appears in exactly the same position as the parent's. Thus, if descriptor 5 in the parent corresponds to a TCP socket, descriptor 5 in the newly created child will correspond to exactly the same socket.

473

Descriptors also remain open across a call to *execve*. To create a new process that executes the code in a file, *F*, a process calls *fork* and arranges for the child to call *execve* with file name *F* as an argument.

Conceptually, file descriptors form implicit arguments to newly created processes and to processes that overlay the running program with code from a file. The parent can choose which descriptors to leave open and which to close before a call to *fork*, and can choose exactly which descriptors will remain open across a call to *execve*.

UNIX programs often use descriptors to control processing instead of explicit arguments. In particular, a UNIX program expects three standard I/O descriptors to be open when the program begins: *standard input* (descriptor *0*), *standard output* (descriptor *1*), and *standard error* (descriptor *2*). The program reads input from descriptor *0*, writes output to descriptor *1*, and sends error messages to descriptor *2*.

Choosing To Use A Fixed Descriptor

A server can also use descriptors as implicit arguments if it invokes a separate program to handle a given request. For example, a slave program that is part of a connection-oriented server can be written to expect descriptor *0* to correspond to a TCP connection. The master server establishes a connection on descriptor *0*, and then uses *execve* to execute the slave. The master could also be programmed to use an arbitrary descriptor and to pass an argument to the slave that specifies which descriptor corresponds to the connection. However, using a fixed descriptor simplifies the code without sacrificing any functionality. In summary:

> *Processes use descriptors as implicit arguments in calls to* execve.
> *Master servers are often programmed to use a single descriptor as an*
> *implicit argument for the slave programs they invoke.*

The Need To Rearrange Descriptors

If a master server calls the system function *socket* to create a socket for connectionless communication or calls *accept* to obtain a socket for connection-oriented communication, the server cannot specify which descriptor the call will return because the operating system chooses a descriptor. If the slave expects descriptor *0* to correspond to the socket used for communication, the master cannot merely create a socket on a random descriptor and then execute the slave. Instead, it must rearrange its descriptors before making the call.

Rearranging Descriptors

A process uses the UNIX system calls *close* and *dup2* to rearrange its descriptors. Closing a descriptor detaches it from the file or socket to which it corresponds, deallocates any resources associated with it, and makes it available for reuse. For example, if a process needs to use descriptor *0*, but it is already in use, the process calls *close* to make it free. Appendix *1* describes how a server can close unnecessary file descriptors when it begins.

A process calls function *dup2* to create a duplicate copy of one file descriptor in another. The call has two arguments:

```
(void) dup2(olddesc, newdesc);
```

where *olddesc* is an integer that identifies an existing descriptor and *newdesc* is an integer that identifies the descriptor where the copy should appear. If *newdesc* is currently in use, the system deallocates it as if the user had called *close* before duplicating *olddesc*. After *dup2* finishes, both *olddesc* and *newdesc* refer to the same object (e.g., the same TCP connection).

To "move" a socket from one descriptor to another, the program first calls *dup2* and then calls *close* to deallocate the original. For example, suppose a master server calls *accept* to obtain an incoming connection, and suppose *accept* chooses to use descriptor *5* for the new connection. The master server can issue the following two calls to move the socket to descriptor *0*:

```
(void) dup2(5, 0);
(void) close(5);
```

Close-On-Exec

A server can choose to close unneeded file descriptors before executing another program. One approach requires the server to explicitly call *close* for each unneeded file descriptor. Another approach uses a system facility to close descriptors automatically.

To use the automatic facility, a server must set the *close-on-exec* flag in each descriptor that it wants the system to close. When the server calls *execve*, the system checks each descriptor to see if the flag has been set and calls *close* automatically if it has. While it may seem that automatic closing does not make programming easier, one must remember that in a large, complex program the purpose of each descriptor may not be apparent at the point of the call to *execve*. Using *close-on-exec* permits the programmer to decide whether a descriptor should remain open at the point in the program where the descriptor is created. Thus, it can be quite useful.

Summary

Processes use descriptors as implicit arguments when creating a new process or when overlaying the running program with code from a file. Often, servers that execute separately compiled programs rely on a descriptor to pass a TCP connection or a UDP socket.

To make programs easier to write and maintain, programmers usually choose a fixed descriptor for each implicit argument. The caller must rearrange its descriptors before invoking *execve* so that the socket used for I/O corresponds to the descriptor chosen as an implicit argument.

A process uses the *dup2* and *close* system calls to rearrange its descriptors. *Dup2* copies an existing descriptor into a specified location, and *close* deallocates a specified descriptor. To move descriptor A to descriptor B, a process first calls *dup2(A,B)* and then calls *close(A)*.

FOR FURTHER STUDY

The *UNIX Programmer's Manual* contains further information on the *dup2* and *close* system calls.

EXERCISES

A2.1 Read about the UNIX command interpreter and find out which descriptors it assigns before executing a command.

A2.2 Sketch the algorithm a command interpreter uses to handle file redirection. Show how it moves file descriptors before calling *execve*.

A2.3 Modify the multiservice server from Chapter *14* so it uses descriptor *0* as an implicit argument and calls *execve* to execute a slave program.

A2.4 Read about the 4.3BSD program *inetd*. How does it use descriptors as implicit arguments?

A2.5 What does the call *dup2(n, m)* do if *n* already equals *m*? Write a version of *dup* that works for arbitrary values of *n* and *m*.

Bibliography

ABRAMSON, N. [1970], The ALOHA System – Another Alternative for Computer Communications, *Proceedings of the Fall Joint Computer Conference*.

ABRAMSON, N. and F. KUO (EDS.) [1973], *Computer Communication Networks*, Prentice Hall, Englewood Cliffs, New Jersey.

AHO, A., B. W. KERNIGHAN, and P. J. WEINBERGER [1988], *The AWK Programming Language*, Addison-Wesley, Reading, Massachusetts.

ANDREWS, D. W., and G. D. SHULTZ [1982], A Token-Ring Architecture for Local Area Networks: An Update, *Proceedings of Fall 82 COMPCON*, IEEE.

AT&T [1989], *UNIX System V Release 3.2 – Programmer's Reference Manual*, Prentice Hall, Englewood Cliffs, New Jersey.

BACH, M. [1986], *The Design Of The UNIX Operating System*, Prentice Hall, Englewood Cliffs, New Jersey.

BALL, J. E., E. J. BURKE, I. GERTNER, K. A. LANTZ, and R. F. RASHID [1979], Perspectives on Message-Based Distributed Computing, *IEEE Computing Networking Symposium*, 46-51.

BBN [1981], A History of the ARPANET: The First Decade, *Technical Report*, Bolt, Beranek, and Newman, Inc.

BBN [December 1981], Specification for the Interconnection of a Host and an IMP (revised), *Technical Report 1822*, Bolt, Beranek, and Newman, Inc.

BERTSEKAS D. and R. GALLAGER [1987], *Data Networks*, Prentice-Hall, Englewood Cliffs, New Jersey.

BIRRELL, A. and B. NELSON [February 1984], Implementing Remote Procedure Calls, *ACM Transactions on Computer Systems*, 2(1), 39-59.

BOGGS, D., J. SHOCH, E. TAFT, and R. METCALFE [April 1980], Pup: An Internetwork Architecture, *IEEE Transactions on Communications*.

BOLSKY, M. I. and D. G. KORN [1989], *The Kornshell Command And Programming Language*, Prentice-Hall, Englewood Cliffs, New Jersey.

BORMAN, D. [April 1989], Implementing TCP/IP on a Cray Computer, *Computer Communication Review*, 19(2), 11-15.

BROWN, M., N. KOLLING, and E. TAFT [November 1985], The Alpine File System, *Transactions on Computer Systems*, 3(4), 261-293.

BROWNBRIDGE, D., L. MARSHALL, and B. RANDELL [December 1982], The Newcastle Connections or UNIXes of the World Unite!, *Software – Practice and Experience*, 12(12), 1147-1162.

CERF, V. and E. CAIN [October 1983], The DOD Internet Architecture Model, *Computer Networks*.

CERF, V. and R. KAHN [May 1974], A Protocol for Packet Network Interconnection, *IEEE Transactions of Communications*, Com-22(5).

CERF, V. [October 1989], A History of the ARPANET, *ConneXions, The Interoperability Report*, Mountain View, California.

CHERITON, D. R. [1983], Local Networking and Internetworking in the V-System, *Proceedings of the Eighth Data Communications Symposium*.

CHERITON, D. R. [April 1984], The V Kernel: A Software Base for Distributed Systems, *IEEE Software*, 1(2), 19-42.

CHERITON, D. [August 1986], VMTP: A Transport Protocol for the Next Generation of Communication Systems, *Proceedings of ACM SIGCOMM '86*, 406-415.

CHERITON, D. and T. MANN [May 1984], Uniform Access to Distributed Name Interpretation in the V-System, *Proceedings IEEE Fourth International Conference on Distributed Computing Systems*, 290-297.

CHESSON, G. [June 1987], Protocol Engine Design, *Proceedings of the 1987 Summer USENIX Conference*, Phoenix, Arizona.

CLARK, D. [December 1985], The Structure of Systems Using Upcalls, *Proceedings of the Tenth ACM Symposium on Operating Systems Principles*, 171-180.

CLARK, D., M. LAMBERT, and L. ZHANG [August 1987], NETBLT: A High Throughput Transport Protocol, *Proceedings of ACM SIGCOMM '87*.

COHEN, D. [1981], On Holy Wars and a Plea for Peace, *IEEE Computer*, 48-54.

COMER, D. E. and J. T. KORB [1983], CSNET Protocol Software: The IP-to-X25 Interface, *Computer Communications Review*, 13(2).

COMER, D. E. [1984], *Operating System Design – The XINU Approach*, Prentice-Hall, Englewood Cliffs, New Jersey.

COMER, D. E. [1987], *Operating System Design Vol II. – Internetworking With XINU*, Prentice-Hall, Englewood Cliffs, New Jersey.

COMER, D. E., T. NARTEN, and R. YAVATKAR [April 1987], The Cypress Network: A Low-Cost Internet Connection Technology, *Technical Report TR-653*, Purdue University, West Lafayette, Indiana.

COMER, D. E. [1991], *Internetworking With TCP/IP Vol 1: Principles, Protocols, and Architecture*, 2nd edition, Prentice-Hall, Englewood Cliffs, New Jersey.

COMER, D. E. and D. L. STEVENS [1991], *Internetworking With TCP/IP Vol 2: Design, Implementation, and Internals*, Prentice-Hall, Englewood Cliffs, New Jersey.

COTTON, I. [1979], Technologies for Local Area Computer Networks, *Proceedings of the Local Area Communications Network Symposium.*

CROWLEY, T., H. FORSDICK, M. LANDAU, and V. TRAVERS [June 1987], The Diamond Multimedia Editor, *Proceedings of the 1987 Summer USENIX Conference,* Phoenix, Arizona.

DALAL, Y. K. and R. S. PRINTIS [1981], 48-Bit Absolute Internet and Ethernet Host Numbers, *Proceedings of the Seventh Data Communications Symposium.*

DEERING, S. E. and D. R. CHERITON [May 1990], Multicast Routing in Datagram Internetworks and Extended LANs, *ACM Transactions on Computer Systems,* 8(2), 85-110.

DENNING, P. J. [September-October 1989], The Science of Computing: Worldnet, *American Scientist,* 432-434.

DENNING, P. J. [November-December 1989], The Science of Computing: The ARPANET After Twenty Years, *American Scientist,* 530-534.

DIGITAL EQUIPMENT CORPORATION., INTEL CORPORATION, and XEROX CORPORATION [September 1980], *The Ethernet: A Local Area Network Data Link Layer and Physical Layer Specification.*

DION, J. [Oct. 1980], The Cambridge File Server, *Operating Systems Review,* 14(4), 26-35.

DRIVER, H., H. HOPEWELL, and J. IAQUINTO [September 1979], How the Gateway Regulates Information Control, *Data Communications.*

EDGE, S. W. [1979], Comparison of the Hop-by-Hop and Endpoint Approaches to Network Interconnection, in *Flow Control in Computer Networks,* J. L. GRANGE and M. GIEN (EDS.), North-Holland, Amsterdam, 359-373.

EDGE, S. [1983], An Adaptive Timeout Algorithm for Retransmission Across a Packet Switching Network, *Proceedings of ACM SIGCOMM '83.*

ENSLOW, P. [January 1978], What is a 'Distributed' Data Processing System? *Computer,* 13-21.

FALK, G. [1983], The Structure and Function of Network Protocols, in *Computer Communications, Volume I: Principles,* W. CHOU (ED.), Prentice-Hall, Englewood Cliffs, New Jersey.

FARMER, W. D. and E. E. NEWHALL [1969], An Experimental Distributed Switching System to Handle Bursty Computer Traffic, *Proceedings of the ACM Symposium on Probabilistic Optimization of Data Communication Systems,* 1-33.

FCCSET [November 1987], A Research and Development Strategy for High Performance Computing, *Report from the Executive Office of the President and Office of Science and Technology Policy.*

FEDOR, M. [June 1988], GATED: A Multi-Routing Protocol Daemon for UNIX, *Proceedings of the 1988 Summer USENIX Conference,* San Francisco, California.

FEINLER, J., O. J. JACOBSEN, and M. STAHL [December 1985], *DDN Protocol Handbook Volume Two, DARPA Internet Protocols,* DDN Network Information Center, SRI International, Menlo Park, California.

FRANK, H. and W. CHOU [1971], Routing in Computer Networks, *Networks,* 1(1), 99-112.

FRANK, H. and J. FRISCH [1971], *Communication, Transmission, and Transportation Networks,* Addison-Wesley, Reading, Massachusetts.

FRANTA, W. R. and I. CHLAMTAC [1981], *Local Networks*, Lexington Books, Lexington, Massachusetts.

FRICC [May 1989], *Program Plan for the National Research and Education Network*, Federal Research Internet Coordinating Committee, US Department of Energy, Office of Scientific Computing Report ER-7.

FRIDRICH, M. and W. OLDER [December 1981], The Felix File Server, *Proceedings of the Eighth Symposium on Operating Systems Principles*, 37-46.

FULTZ, G. L. and L. KLEINROCK, [June 14-16, 1971], Adaptive Routing Techniques for Store-and-Forward Computer Communication Networks, presented at *IEEE International Conference on Communications*, Montreal, Canada.

GERLA, M. and L. KLEINROCK [April 1980], Flow Control: A Comparative Survey, *IEEE Transactions on Communications*.

GOSIP [April 1989], *U.S. Government Open Systems Interconnection Profile (GOSIP) Version 2.0*, GOSIP Advanced Requirements Group, National Institute of Standards and Technology (NIST).

GRANGE, J. L. and M. GIEN (EDS.) [1979], *Flow Control in Computer Networks*, North-Holland, Amsterdam.

GREEN, P. E. (ED.) [1982], *Computer Network Architectures and Protocols*, Plenum Press, New York, New York.

HINDEN, R., J. HAVERTY, and A. SHELTZER [September 1983], The DARPA Internet: Interconnecting Heterogeneous Computer Networks with Gateways, *Computer*.

INTERNATIONAL ORGANIZATION FOR STANDARDIZATION [June 1986a], Information processing systems — Open Systems Interconnection — *Transport Service Definition*, International Standard 8072, ISO, Switzerland.

INTERNATIONAL ORGANIZATION FOR STANDARDIZATION [July 1986b], Information processing systems — Open Systems Interconnection — *Connection Oriented Transport Protocol Specification*, International Standard 8073, ISO, Switzerland.

INTERNATIONAL ORGANIZATION FOR STANDARDIZATION [May 1987a], Information processing systems — Open Systems Interconnection — *Specification of Basic Specification of Abstract Syntax Notation One (ASN.1)*, International Standard 8824, ISO, Switzerland.

INTERNATIONAL ORGANIZATION FOR STANDARDIZATION [May 1987b], Information processing systems — Open Systems Interconnection — *Specification of Basic Encoding Rules for Abstract Syntax Notation One (ASN.1)*, International Standard 8825, ISO, Switzerland.

INTERNATIONAL ORGANIZATION FOR STANDARDIZATION [May 1988a], Information processing systems — Open Systems Interconnection — *Management Information Service Definition, Part 2: Common Management Information Service*, Draft International Standard 9595-2, ISO, Switzerland.

INTERNATIONAL ORGANIZATION FOR STANDARDIZATION [May 1988a], Information processing systems — Open Systems Interconnection — *Management Information Protocol Definition, Part 2: Common Management Information Protocol*, Draft International Standard 9596-2, ISO, Switzerland.

JACOBSON, V. [August 1988], Congestion Avoidance and Control, *Proceedings ACM SIGCOMM '88.*

JAIN, R. [January 1985], On Caching Out-of-Order Packets in Window Flow Controlled Networks, *Technical Report*, DEC-TR-342, Digital Equipment Corporation.

JAIN, R. [March 1986], Divergence of Timeout Algorithms for Packet Retransmissions, *Proceedings Fifth Annual International Phoenix Conference on Computers and Communications*, Scottsdale, Arizona.

JAIN, R. [October 1986], A Timeout-Based Congestion Control Scheme for Window Flow-Controlled Networks, *IEEE Journal on Selected Areas in Communications*, Vol. SAC-4, no. 7.

JAIN, R., K. RAMAKRISHNAN, and D. M. CHIU [August 1987], Congestion Avoidance in Computer Networks With a Connectionless Network Layer. *Technical Report*, DEC-TR-506, Digital Equipment Corporation.

JENNINGS, D. M., L. H. LANDWEBER, and I. H. FUCHS [February 28, 1986], Computer Networking for Scientists and Engineers, *Science* vol 231, 941-950.

JUBIN, J. and J. TORNOW [January 1987], The DARPA Packet Radio Network Protocols, *IEEE Proceedings.*

KAHN, R. [November 1972], Resource-Sharing Computer Communications Networks, *Proceedings of the IEEE*, 60(11), 1397-1407.

KARN, P., H. PRICE, and R. DIERSING [May 1985], Packet Radio in the Amateur Service, *IEEE Journal on Selected Areas in Communications*,

KARN, P. and C. PARTRIDGE [August 1987], Improving Round-Trip Time Estimates in Reliable Transport Protocols, *Proceedings of ACM SIGCOMM '87.*

KENT, C. and J. MOGUL [August 1987], Fragmentation Considered Harmful, *Proceedings of ACM SIGCOMM '87.*

KLINE, C. [August 1987], Supercomputers on the Internet: A Case Study, *Proceedings of ACM SIGCOMM '87.*

KOCHAN, S. G. and P. H. WOODS [1989], *UNIX Networking*, Hayden Books, Indianapolis, Indiana.

LAMPSON, B. W., M. PAUL, and H. J. SIEGERT (EDS.) [1981], *Distributed Systems - Architecture and Implementation (An Advanced Course)*, Springer-Verlag, Berlin.

LANZILLO, A. L. and C. PARTRIDGE [January 1989], Implementation of Dial-up IP for UNIX Systems, *Proceedings 1989 Winter USENIX Technical Conference*, San Diego, California.

LAQUEY, T. L. [July 1989], *User's Directory of Computer Networks*, Digital Press, Bedford, Massachusetts.

LAZAR, A. [November 1983], Optimal Flow Control of a Class of Queuing Networks in Equilibrium, *IEEE Transactions on Automatic Control*, Vol. AC-28:11.

LEFFLER, S., M. MCKUSICK, M. KARELS, and J. QUARTERMAN [1989], *The Design and Implementation of the 4.3BSD UNIX Operating System*, Addison-Wesley, Reading, Massachusetts.

LYNCH, D. C. and O. J. JACOBSEN (PUBLISHER and EDITOR) [1987-], *ConneXions, the Interoperability Report*, Interop Company, Mountain View, California.

LYNCH, D. C. (PRESIDENT) [1987-], *The Interop Conference*, Interop Company, Mountain View, California.

MARZULLO, K. and S. OWICKI [July 1985], Maintaining The Time In A Distributed System, *Operating Systems Review*, 19(3), 44-54.

MCKUSICK, M., W. JOY, S. LEFFLER, and R. FABRY [August 1984], A Fast File System For UNIX, *ACM Transactions On Computer Systems*, 2, 181-197.

MCNAMARA, J. [1982], *Technical Aspects of Data Communications*, Digital Press, Digital Equipment Corporation, Bedford, Massachusetts.

MCQUILLAN, J. M., I. RICHER, and E. ROSEN [May 1980], The New Routing Algorithm for the ARPANET, *IEEE Transactions on Communications*, (COM-28), 711-719.

MERIT [November 1987], *Management and Operation of the NSFNET Backbone Network: A Proposal Funded by the National Science Foundation and the State of Michigan*, MERIT Incorporated, Ann Arbor, Michigan.

METCALFE, R. M. and D. R. BOGGS [July 1976], Ethernet: Distributed Packet Switching for Local Computer Networks, *Communications of the ACM*, 19(7), 395-404.

MILLER, C. K. and D. M. THOMPSON [March 1982], Making a Case for Token Passing in Local Networks, *Data Communications*.

MILLS, D. [September 1991], On the Chronometry and Metrology of Computer Network Timescales and Their Application to the Network Time Protocol, *Proceedings of ACM SIGCOMM '91*, 8-17.

MILLS, D. and H. W. BRAUN [August 1987], The NSFNET Backbone Network, *Proceedings of ACM SIGCOMM '87*.

MITCHELL, J. and J. DION [April 1982], A Comparison of Two Network-Based File Servers, *Communications of the ACM*, 25(4), 233-245.

MORRIS, R. [1979], Fixing Timeout Intervals for Lost Packet Detection in Computer Communication Networks, *Proceedings AFIPS National Computer Conference*, AFIPS Press, Montvale, New Jersey.

NAGLE, J. [April 1987], On Packet Switches With Infinite Storage, *IEEE Transactions on Communications*, (COM-35:4).

NARTEN, T. [Sept. 1989], Internet Routing, *Proceedings ACM SIGCOMM '89*.

NEEDHAM, R. M. [1979], System Aspects of the Cambridge Ring, *Proceedings of the ACM Seventh Symposium on Operating System Principles*, 82-85.

NELSON, J. [September 1983], 802: A Progress Report, *Datamation*.

OPPEN, D. and Y. DALAL [October 1981], The Clearinghouse: A Decentralized Agent for Locating Named Objects, Office Products Division, XEROX Corporation.

PADLIPSKY, M. [1983], A Perspective On The ARPANET Reference Model, *Proceedings of the IEEE INFOCOM Conference*, San Diego, California.

PARTRIDGE, C. [June 1986], Mail Routing Using Domain Names: An Informal Tour, *Proceedings of the 1986 Summer USENIX Conference*, Atlanta, Georgia.

PARTRIDGE, C. [June 1987], Implementing the Reliable Data Protocol (RDP), *Proceedings of the 1987 Summer USENIX Conference*, Phoenix, Arizona.

PARTRIDGE, C. and M. ROSE [June 1989], A Comparison of External Data Formats, in *Message Handling Systems and Distributed Applications*, E. STEFFERUD and O. JACOBSEN (EDS.) Elsevier-North Holland.

PETERSON, L. [1985], *Defining and Naming the Fundamental Objects in a Distributed Message System*, Ph.D. Dissertation, Purdue University, West Lafayette, Indiana.

PETERSON, J. and A. SILBERSCHATZ [1985], *Operating System Concepts*, 2nd edition, Addison-Wesley, Reading, Massachusetts.

PIERCE, J. R. [1972], Networks for Block-Switching of Data, *Bell System Technical Journal*, 51.

POSTEL, J. B. [April 1980], Internetwork Protocol Approaches, *IEEE Transactions on Communications*, (COM-28), 604-611.

POSTEL, J. B., C. A. SUNSHINE, and D. CHEN [1981], The ARPA Internet Protocol, *Computer Networks*.

PRESOTTO, D. L. and D. M. RITCHIE [June 1990], Interprocess Communication in the Ninth Edition Unix System, *Software – Practice And Experience*, 20(S1), S1/3-S1/17.

QUARTERMAN, J. S. [1990], *The Matrix: Computer Networks and Conferencing Systems Worldwide*, Digital Press, Digital Equipment Corporation, Maynard, Massachusetts.

QUARTERMAN, J. S. and J. C. HOSKINS [October 1986], Notable Computer Networks, *Communications of the ACM*, 29(10).

REYNOLDS, J., J. POSTEL, A. R. KATZ, G. G. FINN, and A. L. DESCHON [October 1985], The DARPA Experimental Multimedia Mail System, *IEEE Computer*.

RITCHIE, D. M. and K. THOMPSON [July 1974], The UNIX Time-Sharing System, *Communications of the ACM*, 17(7), 365-375; revised and reprinted in *Bell System Technical Journal*, 57(6), [July-August 1978], 1905-1929.

ROSENTHAL, R. (ED.) [November 1982], *The Selection of Local Area Computer Networks*, National Bureau of Standards Special Publication 500-96.

SALTZER, J. [1978], Naming and Binding of Objects, *Operating Systems, An Advanced Course*, Springer-Verlag 99-208.

SALTZER, J. [April 1982], Naming and Binding of Network Destinations, *International Symposium on Local Computer Networks*, IFIP/T.C.6, 311-317.

SALTZER, J., D. REED, and D. CLARK [November 1984], End-to-End Arguments in System Design, *ACM Transactions on Computer Systems*, 2(4), 277-288.

SCHWARTZ, M. and T. STERN [April 1980], *IEEE Transactions on Communications*, COM-28(4), 539-552.

SHOCH, J. F. [1978], Internetwork Naming, Addressing, and Routing, *Proceedings of COMPCON*.

SHOCH, J. F., Y. DALAL, and D. REDELL [August 1982], Evolution of the Ethernet Local Computer Network, *Computer*.

SNA [1975], *IBM System Network Architecture – General Information*, IBM System Development Division, Publications Center, Department E01, Research Triangle Park, North Carolina.

SOLOMON, M., L. LANDWEBER, and D. NEUHEGEN [1982], The CSNET Name Server, *Computer Networks* (6), 161-172.

STALLINGS, W. [1984], *Local Networks: An Introduction*, Macmillan Publishing Company, New York.

STALLINGS, W. [1985], *Data and Computer Communications*, Macmillan Publishing Company, New York.

STEVENS, W. R. [1990], *UNIX Network Programming*, Prentice-Hall, Englewood Cliffs, New Jersey.

SWINEHART, D., G. MCDANIEL, and D. R. BOGGS [December 1979], WFS: A Simple Shared File System for a Distributed Environment, *Proceedings of the Seventh Symposium on Operating System Principles*, 9-17.

TANENBAUM, A. [1981], *Computer Networks: Toward Distributed Processing Systems*, Prentice-Hall, Englewood Cliffs, New Jersey.

TICHY, W. and Z. RUAN [June 1984], Towards a Distributed File System, *Proceedings of Summer 84 USENIX Conference*, Salt Lake City, Utah, 87-97.

TOMLINSON. R. S. [1975], Selecting Sequence Numbers, *Proceedings ACM SIGOPS/SIGCOMM Interprocess Communication Workshop*, 11-23.

WARD, A. A. [1980], TRIX: A Network-Oriented Operating System, *Proceedings of COMPCON*, 344-349.

WATSON, R. [1981], Timer-Based Mechanisms in Reliable Transport Protocol Connection Management, *Computer Networks*, North-Holland Publishing Company.

WEINBERGER, P. J. [1985], The UNIX Eighth Edition Network File System, *Proceedings 1985 ACM Computer Science Conference*, 299-301.

WELCH, B. and J. OSTERHAUT [May 1986], Prefix Tables: A Simple Mechanism for Locating Files in a Distributed System, *Proceedings IEEE Sixth International Conference on Distributed Computing Systems*, 184-189.

WILKES, M. V. and D. J. WHEELER [May 1979], The Cambridge Digital Communication Ring, *Proceedings Local Area Computer Network Symposium*.

XEROX [1981], Internet Transport Protocols, *Report XSIS 028112*, Xerox Corporation, Office Products Division, Palo Alto, California.

ZHANG, L. [August 1986], Why TCP Timers Don't Work Well, *Proceedings of ACM SIGCOMM '86*.

Index

/

/ (UNIX root directory) 315, 429
/dev/null 432
/dev/tcp 41
/dev/tty 429
/etc/inetd.conf 168
/etc/syslog.conf 439
/usr/adm/printer-errs 439
/usr/local/bin/rfc 217
/usr/spool/lpd.lock 432
/usr/tmp/RFC 216
/usr/ucb/mail 216, 217, 218

A

abnormal process termination 427
abort 354, 358
Abstract Syntax Notation One 232
accept 104, 161, 444, 474
accept system call 51, 54, 127
active socket 47
address family 44, 47
address parsing 60
AF_INET 47
AF_UNIX 48
Aho 219
algorithm
    RPC port mapper 248
    TELNET client 357
    connection-oriented client 64
    connection-oriented server 103, 108, 110

connectionless client 69
connectionless server 105, 107
apparent concurrency 109, 139
application gateway 205
application interface 35
application services
    customized 11
    locally-defined 11
    standard 11
application-level gateway 214, 218
application-level tunneling 200
application-oriented design 234
argument marshaling 250
argument serializing 250
ASN.1 232
asymmetric data conversion 222
asymmetric data representation 231
asynchronous I/O 109
at least once semantics 244
attrstat 343
authentication 11, 252
authorization 11
authunix_create 258
AUTH_NONE 348
auth_type 251
AUTH_UNIX 348
auth_unix structure 251
awk 217

B

background execution 425

backslash 324
backspace 358
bcopy 80
BEL 411
Berkeley socket interface 43, 443
Berkeley UNIX 43
best effort delivery 13
big-endian 251
bind 445
bind system call 51
block-oriented 67
block-special 322
Bolsky 219
BSD UNIX 43
buffer paradigm 226
bursty traffic 178
byte order 62, 87
byte stuff
    see character stuff
bzero 80

C

C include statement 54
CALL 249
callrpc 257
call_body 249, 250
carriage return 358, 411
cbreak mode 390
cerrexit in *cerrexit.c* 364
character stuff 366, 408
character-special 322
CHARGEN service 165
chdir 429
Clark, David D. 5
client 9, 10
client
    deadlock 184
    observed response 102
    single-process 187
    standard 11
client-server and RPC 238
client-server paradigm 9
clnt_create 257
close 40, 43, 306, 428, 429, 446, 475

close system call 50, 54
close-on-exec 475
closelog 439
CNRI 4
command 354, 365, 414
communication endpoint 47
communication procedure 263
communication-oriented design 234
compact FSM 372
conceptual interface 37
concurrency 21
    cost 173
    demand-driven 173
    level 172
    management 171
concurrency example 27
concurrency in clients 23, 183, 185
concurrency in servers 23
concurrent execution 25
concurrent file access 313, 314
concurrent processing 6
concurrent server 96, 106
conditional compilation 223
configuration file 439
connect 447
connect system call 50, 54, 66, 70
connected mode 69
connection-oriented 13, 96
connectionless 13, 96
connectionless server 99
connections 97
connectsock in *connectsock.c* 78
connectTCP in *connectTCP.c* 77
connectUDP in *connectUDP.c* 78
console terminal 435
context switch 31
control 354
control process 186
control terminal 428
control-C 362
controlling tty 428
cooked mode 390
core file 429
Corporation For National Research
    Initiatives 4

CR-LF 411
creat 441
ctime 87
current position 313
curses 412

D

daemon 299, 426
Data Encryption Standard 250
DATA MARK 388, 411
data representation 221
data security 11
data-driven processing 139
date 124
    epoch 84, 87
DAYTIME service 81, 124, 149, 165
DAYTIME service in *TCPdaytime.c* 82
daytimed.c 150
dcon in *dcon.c* 363
deadlock 112
    client 184
DECNET 195, 197
defunct process 434
delay 174
delayed allocation 180
delayed suspend 362
delete 358
DELETEW in *rdict.x* 281
deletew in *dict.c* 270
deletew in *dict2.c* 278
deletew in *rdict_cif.c* 290
deletew in *rdict_srp.c* 297
deletew_1 in *rdict_clnt.c* 285
deletew_1 in *rdict_sif.c* 292
demand-driven concurrency 173
descriptor 427
dict.c 270
dict1.c 276
dict2.c 278
dictionary example 268
directory 311
    NFS 322
    position 307
diropargs 338, 339

diropres 339, 343
dispatch 260
display buffer 109
distributed program creation 269
DO 366, 396, 398, 400, 401, 403
doecho 396
domain name 61
DONT 366, 396, 397, 398, 400
do_echo.c 395
do_noga.c 398
do_notsup.c 397
do_txbinary.c 399
dup 432
dup2 475

E

ECHO option 395
ECHO service 87, 103, 131, 142, 165,
    185, 188
EINTR 388
electronic mail 2
electronic mail client 12
electronic mail service 2
encapsulation 199
end of string 80
end-of-file 68, 83, 132, 137, 144, 311,
    388
end-to-end delay 98
endpoint address 47
environment 31, 402
epoch date 84, 121, 338
errexit in *errexit.c* 80
escape character 414
example client 353
exec 31
execute 308
execve 33, 109, 160, 474
exit 427
export list 346
exportlist structure 346
eXternal Data Representation 224
external data representation 224
extra hop problem 211

F

facility 437
family of protocols 44
fattr 323
fd2sv 161
FD_CLR 144, 464
FD_ISSET 152, 161
FD_SET 144, 464
FD_ZERO 144
fhandle 338
fhstatus 346
file 307, 322, 323
    NFS 322
    block-special 322
    byte numbering 308
    character-special 322
    concurrent access 313
    inode 315
    link 315
    name resolution 320
    position 307
    stat 322
file access 305
file access mode 309
file attributes 323
file descriptor 39, 473
file group 308
file handle 328
file mode 309
file naming 317
file offset 314
file ownership 308
file protection 308, 316
file server 11
file size 308
file system 307, 318
    UNIX 307
file transfer 305
file transfer client 12
file transfer service 2
filename 338
FINGER service 169
finite state machine 366
flock 314, 433

flow of control 237
folder 311
foreground execution 425
fork 27, 30, 32, 108, 109, 313, 427, 448,
    473
forward 218
FSM implementation 388
FSM initialization 383
fsmbuild in *fsmbuild.c* 383
fsminit in *fsminit.c* 376
fsm_trans in *tnfsm.h* 373
fstat 420
FTP 12
ftype 322
ft_action 374
ft_char 374
ft_next 374, 389
ft_state 374
full path name 314
fully parameterized client 12

G

gateway machine 205
getdtablesize 428
getenv 402, 403, 412
gethostbyaddr 449
gethostbyname 61, 450
gethostid 451
gethostname 452
getpeername 453
getpid 431
getportbyname 103
getprotobyname 63, 454
getservbyname 455
getsockname 456
getsockopt 457
gettimeofday 458
Greenwich Mean Time 84
group identifier 308
groups 346
groups structure 346

H

handle 15, 257
HANGUP 434, 435
hangup signal 428
hard link 315
hard mount 327
Harrenstien 92, 122
hierarchy 311
hostent in *netdb.h* 489
htonl 53
htons 53

I

I/O 307
I/O descriptor 357
IAC 366
idempotent 17, 245
ifdef 223
INADDR_ANY 104
include statement 54
index node 315
indexed files 308
indirection 436
inetd 168
inet_addr 61
inheritance 427
init 177, 427, 434
init process 177, 427
initial system process 427
INITW in *rdict.x* 281
initw in *dict.c* 270
initw in *dict2.c* 278
initw in *rdict_cif.c* 290
initw in *rdict_srp.c* 297
initw_1 in *rdict_clnt.c* 285
initw_1 in *rdict_sif.c* 292
inode 315
input process 186
INSERTW in *rdict.x* 281
insertw in *dict.c* 270
insertw in *dict2.c* 278
insertw in *rdict_cif.c* 290
insertw in *rdict_srp.c* 297

insertw_1 in *rdict_clnt.c* 285
insertw_1 in *rdict_sif.c* 292
instruction pointer 25
int 222
integer representation 222
interface 35
interface procedure 263
internetwork
    see internet
Interpret As Command 366
interrupt 354, 358, 362, 365, 408
ioctl 39, 43, 358, 429
iterative 171
iterative server 96

J

January 1, 1900 87
January 1, 1970 87
job 25, 430

K

KCDCON 414
KCESCAPE 414
Kernighan 219
keyboard escape 379, 414
Knowbot Information Service 4
Korb 202
Korn 219

L

last_char 411
least recently used 101, 199
least significant byte 221
Leffler 33, 55, 390
level of concurrency 172
LF-CR 411
linearize arguments 250
linefeed 358, 411
link 315
lint program 49
listen 104, 459
listen system call 51
local.h 362

localhost 436
locally-defined application services 11
locally-defined services 11
locating a server 58
lock file 432
lockf 314
log server 436
LOG_DAEMON 438
LOG_DEBUG 438
LOG_EMERG 438
LOG_MAIL 438
LOOKUPW in *rdict.x* 281
lookupw in *dict.c* 270
lookupw in *dict2.c* 278
lookupw in *rdict_cif.c* 290
lookupw in *rdict_srp.c* 297
lookupw_1 in *rdict_clnt.c* 285
lookupw_1 in *rdict_sif.c* 292
loosely specified 35
LRU 199
lseek 43, 312
L_SET 312

M

machine name 61
magic cookie 331
mail forwarding 218
mail gateway 205
mailbox files 210
mailboxes 210
main in *TCPtecho.c* 188
main in *rdict.c* 294
main in *rdict_svc.c* 287
main in *superd.c* 162
main in *tclient.c* 384
Makefile 300
marshal arguments 250
Marzullo 122
master server process 106
Mills 92, 122
MNTPROC_DUMP 348
MNTPROC_EXPORT 348
MNTPROC_MNT 347
MNTPROC_NULL 347

MNTPROC_UMNT 348
MNTPROC_UMNTALL 348
mode 322, 323
    NFS 322
most significant byte 221, 224
mount 318, 320, 326, 327
mount authentication 348
mount constants 345
mount data structures 346
mount procedures 347
mount protocol 332, 335, 345
mount types 345
mounted file system 319
mountlist 347
mountlist structure 347
MS-DOS 324
msg_type 249
mstime in *TCPtecho.c* 188
multiprocessing 21
multiprotocol environments 195
multiprotocol server 147
multiservice server 155
mutual exclusion 432
mv 343

N

n-squared conversion problem 223
name
    machine 61
    server 61
name resolution 61
names
native data representation 222
network byte order 52, 62, 87, 223
Network File System 306
network virtual terminal 354, 401
next-hop 65
next-hop address 198
nextin in *dict.c* 270
nextin in *dict1.c* 276
nextin in *rdict.c* 294
NFS 306, 335, 338
    client 324, 325
    constant declarations 337

directory 322
directory access 331
diropargs 339
diropres 339
fattr 323
file 322
file attributes 323
file handle 328
file mode 322, 323
file semantics 321
file types 322
handle 349
magic cookie 331
mode 322
mount 327
mount protocol 332
multiple hierarchies 332
procedures 341
readargs 340
readlinkres 340
renameargs 339
server 324
stat declaration 337
type declarations 338
writeargs 340
NFS semantics
    307
NFSPROC_CREATE 343
NFSPROC_GETATTR 342
NFSPROC_LINK 343
NFSPROC_LOOKUP 342
NFSPROC_MKDIR 344
NFSPROC_NULL 342
NFSPROC_READ 342
NFSPROC_READDIR 344
NFSPROC_READLINK 342
NFSPROC_REMOVE 343
NFSPROC_RENAME 343
NFSPROC_RMDIR 344
NFSPROC_ROOT 332, 342
NFSPROC_SETATTR 342
NFSPROC_STATFS 344
NFSPROC_SYMLINK 343
NFSPROC_WRITE 343

NFSPROC_WRITECACHE 342
NFS_OK 339
nic.ddn.mil 3
NIST 250
no go-ahead option 397
noga 398
non-selfreferential 491
nonstandard application services 11
nonstandard protocols 2
no_op in *recopt.c* 394
NREN 1
nri.reston.va.us 3, 4
ntohl 53, 87
ntohs 53
NTP 92, 122
null 342
numeric group id 308
numeric user id 308
NVT 354

O

observed response time 102
oldtty 362
on demand 173
opaque 251, 328, 338
opaque_auth 251
open 39, 43, 306, 310, 313, 324, 357,
    429, 430, 433
open-read-write-close 310, 321, 357
openlog 438
option subnegotiation 381
option subnegotiation request 370
orphaned 427
output process 186
Owicki 122
owner 308
O_CREAT 310
O_EXCL 314, 441
O_RDWR 310

P

Padlipsky 232
parent 427

parsing addresses 60
partial close 68
Partridge 232
passive mode 51
passive socket 47
passivesock in *passivesock.c* 117
passiveTCP in *passiveTCP.c* 124
passiveUDP in *passiveUDP.c* 116
path name 314
pattern 439
peer-to-peer 9
permission bits 309
perror 431
Peterson 33
PF_INET 46, 47, 49
pid 30
pipe 48
port
    well-known 11, 62
port mapper 246
port number choice 65
portbase 116
portbase in *passivesock.c* 117
position
    file 307
position identifier 331
Postel 92, 129, 138, 145, 154, 390, 422
preallocation of processes 175
preallocation on multiprocessor 179
presentation level 221
Presotto 55
printf 81, 439
privacy 11
procedure 282
procedure activation record 26
procedure call 236
procedure execution 236
process 25
process group 430
process id 30
process identifier 30
process preallocation 175
process resumption 364
process suspension 364

program versions 242
protection 11
protection bits 308
protocol
    block-oriented 67
    connection-oriented 96
    connectionless 96
    standard 2
    stream-oriented 67
protocol family 44
protoent in *netdb.h* 492
protoent structure 63

Q

queue overflow 102
quit 362, 408

R

random file access 308
raw mode 390
rcvbinary 399
rcvurg 411
rcvurg in *sync.c* 387
rdict.c 294
rdict.h 283
rdict.x 281
rdictprog_1 in *rdict_svc.c* 287
rdict_cif.c 290
rdict_clnt.c 285
rdict_sif.c 292
rdict_srp.c 297
rdict_svc.c 287
rdict_xdr.c 284
read 39, 43, 140, 306, 308, 311, 357,
    460
read system call 50, 54
readargs 340
readdirargs 344
readdirres 344
reader in *TCPtecho.c* 188
readlink 340
readlinkres 340
readres 342

real concurrency 109
reaper 137
rearranging descriptors 474
recopt in *recopt.c* 394
record blocking 308
record boundaries 308
record-oriented interface 231
recv 461
recvfrom 105, 121, 462
recvmsg 463
remote file access 305
remote file operations 306
remote login service 2, 12
remote procedure call model 234
remote program 240
remote program number 241, 242
remote program versions 242
remote terminal client 12
rename 441
renameargs 339
rendezvous 10
REPLY 249
reply_body 249
representation of data 221
Request For Comments 213
request processing time 102
request queue overflow 102
request-response interaction 66, 68
resolution 320
resolve a name 320
response 66
retransmission 245
return 236
Reynolds 154, 390, 422
rfc 214
rfc-in *rfc* 214
rfcd 216
rfcd in *rfcd* 216
Ritchie 55
root 315
Rose 232
RPC 240, 257, 335
RPC at-least-once-execution 244
RPC authentication 253

RPC dynamic port assignment 246
RPC example 268
RPC message dispatch 260
RPC model 234
RPC opaque data 251
RPC port mapper 246
RPC program mapping 245
RPC retransmission 245
RPC semantics 244
RPC specification file 280
RPC stub names 261
RPC stub procedures 259
RPC zero or more semantics 244
rpcgen 262
rpcgen .x file 280
rpcgen client interface 289
rpcgen example 268
rpcgen execution 282
rpcgen input files 265
rpcgen output 284
rpcgen procedures 262
rpcgen server interface 291
rpcgen specification file 263
rpcgen strings 280
rpc_msg 249

S

sa_data 48
sa_family 48
scrfp 419
scrgetc in *scrgetc.c* 418
scrinit in *scrinit.c* 416
scripting 411, 415
scrwrap in *scrwrap.c* 419
search permission 311
secure partition 204
security 204
seek 306
select 32, 109, 158, 356, 390, 464
SEND 406
send 465
sendmail 219
sendmsg 466

sendto 105, 467
serialize arguments 250
servent in *netdb.h* 494
server 9, 11
    ECHO 133, 142
    algorithms 95
    comparison of types 110
    concurrency 23
    concurrent 106, 108, 131, 158
    connection-oriented 96, 103, 108,
       110, 124, 131, 157, 158, 176
    connectionless 96, 97, 99, 104, 107,
       115, 118, 156, 177
    data-driven 139
    deadlock 112
    delay 175
    design 95
    four basic types 101
    identifying location 58
    iterative 118, 124, 157
    iterative algorithm 104
    level of concurrency 172
    master 159, 177
    master process 106
    multiprotocol 147
    multiservice 155, 157
    multiservice multiprotocol 160
    preallocation 176, 177
    request processing 102
    single-process 142, 158
    slave 177
    slave process 106
    state 14, 98
    stateful 14, 95, 98, 307
    stateless 14, 95, 98, 307, 330
    summary of types 111
    throughput 175
service 11
    CHARGEN 165
    DAYTIME 81, 124, 149, 165
    ECHO 87, 165
    TIME 84, 85, 119, 165
service structure 161
sethostid 468

setpgrp 431
setsockopt 469
shutdown 470
shutdown system call 68
SIGCHLD 137
SIGKILL 434
signal 137, 358, 387, 435
SIGURG 411
sigvec 435
Silberschatz 33
simple services 156
sin_addr 49
sin_family 49
sin_port 49
sin_zero 49
size 308
slash 315
slave server process 106
SMTP 12
SNA 195
sndbinary 402
sockaddr structure 48
sockaddr_in 48, 52, 61
socket 46, 49, 471, 474
    active 51
    connected 69
    passive 51
    unconnected 69
socket descriptor 46
socket interface 36, 43
socket output FSM 378
socket system call 46, 49
sockets 36
SOCK_DGRAM 54, 70
SOCK_STREAM 46, 54
sofsm 414
sofsm.c 380
soft mount 327
sonotsup.c 415
soputc.c 407
sostab 381
sowrite.c 413
special file 322
sprintf 434

SS_END 381
standard
    client 11
standard error 427, 431, 435, 474
standard I/O stream 230
standard input 357, 431, 474
standard output 357, 431, 474
standard protocols 2
standard services 11
stat 316, 337
stat function 316
stat operation 322
stat structure 317
state information 14, 98
stateful server 14, 15, 98
stateless server 14, 98
statfsres 344
status in *status.c* 421
Stevens 18, 72, 113, 390
strcpy 80
stream transfer 44
stream-oriented 67
string 338
stty 390
stub generator 257
stub procedure
    see RPC stub
stub procedures 259
subend 406
subend.c 406
subfsm in *subfsm.c* 382
subnegotiation 404, 406
subopt 381
subopt.c 404
substab in *subfsm.c* 382
subtermtype.c 405
Sun RPC 240
super server 161
superd.c 162
suspend 362
suspend in *suspend.c* 365
svent 161
sv_func 161
sv_funcs.c 166

symbolic link 321
symmetric data conversion 223
symmetric data representation 231
sync.c 387
SYNCH 411
synching 388, 391, 411
synchronize 388
synchronize mode 411
syslog 437, 439
syslog pattern 439
syslogd 437, 441
system call 37
    accept 51, 444
    bind 51, 445
    close 40, 50, 446
    connect 50, 447
    execve 31, 109
    fork 27, 109, 448
    gethostbyaddr 449
    gethostbyname 450
    gethostid 451
    gethostname 452
    getpeername 453
    getprotobyname 454
    getservbyname 455
    getsockname 456
    getsockopt 457
    gettimeofday 458
    listen 51, 459
    open 39
    read 39, 50, 460
    recv 461
    recvfrom 462
    recvmsg 463
    select 464
    send 465
    sendmsg 466
    sendto 467
    sethostid 468
    setsockopt 469
    shutdown 470
    socket 46, 49, 471
    write 40, 50, 472

T

task 25
TCANY 371
tcdm 388
tcdm in *sync.c* 387
TCDO 394
TCDONT 394
tclient.c 384
tcout in *tcout.c* 412
TCP 13
TCPdaytime in *TCPdaytime.c* 82
TCPdaytimed in *TCPdaytimed.c* 126
TCPecho in *TCPecho.c* 88
TCPechod in *TCPechod.c* 134
TCPmechod in *TCPmechod.c* 142
TCPtecho in *TCPtecho.c* 188
TCSE 370
TCWILL 394
TCWONT 394
TELNET 3, 12, 353
    DO 366, 394
    DONT 366, 394
    ECHO 395
    Go-Ahead 397
    IAC 366, 408
    IP 408
    NVT 354
    WILL 367, 394
    WONT 367, 394
    arguments 383
    binary option 399
    client 353
    keyboard escape 379
    option 394
    options 367
    subnegotiation 404
    terminal type 402, 405
telnet 3
telnet in *telnet.c* 385
TELNET echo option 366
TELNET option 366
TELNET service 12
telnet.c 385
telnet.h 368

TERM 402, 412
term 406
terminal 354
terminal device driver 358
terminal type 381, 402
termtype 403
termtype option 402
tgetstr 412
thrashing 101
thread 25
thread of control 236
thread of execution 236
three-way handshake 72
time
    epoch 84, 87
    representation 84
time epoch 121, 128, 338
time of day 124
TIME service 84, 85, 119, 165
time-of-day clock 84
time-sharing 21
timeslicing 29
timestamp 328
timeval 338
TLI 36, 41
tnfsm.h 373
transition matrix 372
transmit binary 367
transmit binary option 401
Transport Layer Interface 36
TSSUBIAC 370
TSSUBNEG 370
ttfsm in *ttfsm.c* 375
ttputc 370
ttputc in *ttputc.c* 409
ttstab 376, 389
ttstab in
ttstate 389
ttwrite in *ttwrite.c* 389
ttymode.c 360
ttyrestore in *ttymode.c* 360
ttysave in *ttymode.c* 360
ttysetup in *ttysetup.c* 361
ttystate 361

TT_SEND 382
tunneling 199, 207
type of service 44
typed files 308

U

UCT 84
UDP 13, 115
UDPecho in *UDPecho.c* 90
UDPtime in *UDPtime.c* 86
UDPtimed in *UDPtimed.c* 120
umask 430
unconnected mode 69
Universal Coordinated Time 84
UNIX
   .forward 218
   /dev/null 432
   /dev/tty 429
   C compilation 274
   I/O 307
   access mode 309
   awk program 217
   background execution 299, 425
   cbreak mode 390
   command interpreter 218
   concurrent access 313
   concurrent file access 314
   control-C 362
   controlling tty 428
   cooked mode 390
   core file 429
   creat 441
   ctime 128
   curses 412
   daemon 426
   delayed allocation 180
   descriptor 427
   directory 311
   directory search 311
   dup2 475
   end of file 311
   exit code 427
   file group 308
   file mode 309

file naming 317
file offset 314
file ownership 308
file permissions 309
file protection 308
file semantics 307
file system 318
foreground execution 425
getdtablesize 428
hints for servers 425
init process 177, 427
inode 315
interrupt 408
ioctl 358
link 315
linker invocation 296
lock file 432
lseek 312
mail forwarding 218
make 299
mount 327
mount call 318
mount command 320
move 343
mv 343
name resolution 320
object file names 289
open 310
orphan process 427
path name 314
preallocation of processes 176
process group 430
protection bits 308
quit 408
random file access 311
raw mode 390
read 311
resumption 364
root directory 315
root directory (slash) 315
rpcgen execution 282
special file 322
standard error 431
standard input 357, 431

standard output 357, 431
stat 322
stat operation 316
stty 390
suspension 364
syslog 437
telnet command 3
terminal I/O 357
terminal device 358
time 128
umask 430
write 311
zombie process 177
UNIX daemon 299
UNIX File System 320
UNIX file system 307
UNIXEPOCH 121
unscript in *unscript.c* 420
unsecure partition 204
urgent data 391, 411
UT 84

V

VanBokkelen 390, 422
version number 242
virtual circuit 198
VPBEL 411

W

wait 434
wait3 137, 177
Weinberger 219
well-known port 11, 62, 95
wildcard address 104
WILL 367, 395, 396, 397, 399, 400, 402,
    403
will_notsup in *will_notsup.c* 400
will_termtype.c 402
will_txbinary.c 401
WNOHANG 137
WONT 367, 395, 396, 397, 399, 400,
    402
write 40, 43, 306, 308, 311, 357, 472

write system call 50, 54
writeargs 339
writer in *TCPtecho.c* 188

X

X.25 195, 196, 198
X.25 virtual circuit 198
XDR 224
XDR Language 249
XDR stream 227
xdrmem_create 227
xdrrec_create 231
xput.c 410
xputc in *xput.c* 410
xputs in *xput.c* 410

Z

zero or more semantics 244
zombie 137
zombie process 177
zombie state 434